D1562096

Morality and the Meaning of Life

An Introduction to Ethical Theory

Joseph Ellin
Western Michigan University

Harcourt Brace College Publishers

Fort Worth   Philadelphia   San Diego   New York   Orlando   Austin   San Antonio
Toronto   Montreal   London   Sydney   Tokyo

Publisher	Ted Buchholz
Senior Acquisitions Editor	David Tatom
Project Editor	Christopher Nelson
Editorial Assistant	Leanne Winkler
Production Manager	Serena Manning
Art Directors	Garry Harman and Jim Taylor

Cover Caspar David Friedrich, *The Wanderer.* Hamburger Kunsthalle, photographed by Elke Walford, Fotowerkstatt.

ISBN: 0-15-501308-4

Library of Congress Catalog Card Number: 94-076131

Address for Editorial Correspondence: Harcourt Brace College Publishers, 301 Commerce Street, Suite 3700, Fort Worth, TX 76102.

Address for Orders: Harcourt Brace & Company, 6277 Sea Harbor Drive, Orlando, FL 32887-6777. 1-800-782-4479, or 1-800-433-0001 (in Florida).

Printed in the United States of America

4 5 6 7 8 9 0 1 2 3 066 10 9 8 7 6 5 4 3 2 1

Preface

Most people prefer theory to practice, under the impression that arguing about morals proves them to be philosophers, and that in this way they will turn out to be fine characters.
Aristotle, *Ethics*

For the point of the book [is] not to enable a student to go through the hoops, but to enable him to understand why the hoops are placed where they are.
Simon Blackburn, *Spreading the Word*

Many students of philosophy as well as much of the general public think that the goal of an ethics course should be to help students become more ethical by improving their moral perceptions and attitudes, or to teach them to think intelligently about contemporary moral problems, such as drug abuse and sexual promiscuity. Important as these concerns are, they are not the primary goal of this book, which is not to make students moral but to teach them moral theory. This is a philosophical investigation whose aim is to discover the truth about morality. In the belief that the search for truth about an important and complex subject such as morality is intrinsically interesting, I address this book to students who wish to pursue moral theory in the spirit of disinterested inquiry. However, as I explain in Chapter One, moral theory is an important part of moral education, the development of the perceptions, attitudes, and emotions that constitute morality. To the extent that no one can lead an ethical life without reflecting on what such a life might be, this book will help students see how they can lead more ethical lives. To paraphrase Kant, moral perceptions, emotions, and attitudes without moral theory are blind; moral theory without moral perceptions, emotions, and attitudes is empty.

Morality and the Meaning of Life covers the standard topics of an introductory ethics course, including relativism, egoism, naturalism, natural law and the naturalistic fallacy, social contract, utilitarianism, Kantian ethics, and deontology. Some topics inevitably appear under more than one heading; for example, "Why be moral?" is discussed in two contexts in which the question naturally arises: egoism, and contemporary statements of the attitude theory. Classical thinkers from Plato and Aristotle to G. E. Moore and John Dewey are discussed, as are such contemporary philosophers as R. M. Hare, Alasdair MacIntyre, Simon Blackburn, and Bernard Williams. The book also covers certain frontier issues and other topics often omitted from standard texts. These include moral realism, projectivism and quasirealism, virtue ethics, supererogation and sainthood, feminist ethics, and communitarianism. One chapter is devoted to lying, a chronic moral problem that everyone faces. The final chapter discusses the meaning of life, which, arguably, is what all education, and certainly philosophy, is ultimately about.

Morality and the Meaning of Life follows the standard division of the subject into conceptual and normative questions. Part One addresses questions about the nature of morality, such as how subjectivism and egoism challenge ethics, whether there are universal moral truths, and whether morality needs or can have foundations. Part Two raises normative questions: What is good moral character? What is lying and why is it wrong? What is the connection between right and wrong and good consequences? How is happiness connected with morality? But this division, as Plato was aware, is a bit artificial, so the two parts of the book are entitled "substantially conceptual" and "substantially normative" issues.

A premise of *Morality and the Meaning of Life* is that philosophical views respond to real questions that puzzle thoughtful people, so that the larger issues must be seen to grow from the moral choices we confront daily. Artificiality of examples is avoided throughout. Another premise is that all standard views deserve to be presented fairly, clearly, and cogently, so that the student can make up his or her own mind about what is true. Not all theories are equally valid, however, and I do not hesitate to make clear which theories I find implausible.

A constant concern has been clarity in exposition without sacrifice of logical rigor. In some places the argument may seem rather advanced; these sections may be assigned as optional reading. This is especially true in Chapter 5, "Moral Facts," in which discussions of supervenience, internalism and externalism, and logical transformations might be too challenging for some students. Those with a facility for philosophy, however, will gain from these sections a strong foundation in certain contemporary discussions.

Every discipline has its unique vocabulary, and mastering the discipline necessarily requires mastering these terms. All technical terms, including names of theories, are defined in the text when first presented, as well as in the glossary at the back of the book. To save space and facilitate reading, abbreviations are used for key terms and theories after they are introduced; for example, psychological egoism and ethical egoism are referred to as PE and EE, respectively. A listing of all such abbreviations follows the glossary.

ACKNOWLEDGMENTS

Earlier drafts of *Morality and the Meaning of Life* were "class-tested" at Western Michigan University and at California State Polytechnic University, where I had the pleasure of teaching for a semester. My thanks to the many students who gave me their opinions. I have been fortunate to receive much detailed criticism from students and colleagues, among whom I must mention Angie Yesh, John Dilworth, Helen Wenck, Jean Patt, Quentin Smith, David Paul, and Sharen Campbell. I also thank Pat Nelson, who did some of the typing and production work and graciously helped me through frequent self-inflicted computer crises.

Several readers for Harcourt Brace gave me the benefit of their candid opinions: Marcia Baron, University of Illinois at Urbana-Champaign; Donna Bestock, Skyline College; Karen Hanson, Indiana University—Bloomington; Joel Lidz, Bentley College; John Serembus, Widener University; and Bill Wilcox, California State Polytechnic University. They will be gratified to see how much I have profited from their advice. Karen Hanson read the entire manuscript and offered unfailing support and innumerable helpful ideas, for which I am more than grateful.

I want to specially thank Lynn Osborn, who toiled on the index; Craig Gallup, my teaching assistant for four semesters; my colleague Harvey Williams, who honored me by choosing the penultimate draft as a class text; Leanne Winkler, my editor at Harcourt Brace, for her encouragement and wise counsel; and Michael Pritchard, the chair of my department and my long-time colleague and friend, whose support has been all that anyone could hope for and far more than anyone has a right to expect.

Contents

Preface *iii*

Chapter One: AN INTRODUCTION TO
MORAL THEORY.. *1*

Ethics, Morality, and Moral Theory *1*

Morality *3*

Moral Theory and Science *7*

Empirical Versus Conceptual *7*
Descriptive Versus Normative *8*

**Moral Education: Becoming Moral and
Studying Moral Theory** *10*

Moral Sensitivity and Perception *12*
Moral Emotions *12*

Part One: *Substantially Conceptual Issues*........ *17*

Chapter Two: CHALLENGES TO ETHICS:
RELATIVISM *18*

Three Ways to Challenge Ethics *18*

Challenges from Above *19*
Challenges to Ethics as Such *20*
Challenges from Below *23*

The Idea of Universal Moral Truths *24*

Subjectivism *27*

Opinions and Attitudes *27*
Sophisticated Subjectivism *29*
Two Problems with Sophisticated Subjectivism *33*

Cultural Relativism *35*

What Is Cultural Relativism? *35*
Problems with Cultural Relativism *37*
The Argument from Respect *41*
What Is True in Cultural Relativism? *44*

Chapter Three: CHALLENGES TO
ETHICS: EGOISM................................. 48

Psychological Egoism *48*

Theories of Ethical Egoism *52*

How Ethical Egoism Differs from Conventional Morality *52*
Theories and Strategies *52*

Arguments for Ethical Egoism *55*

Can Ethical Egoism Support Social Morality? *57*

Arguments Against Ethical Egoism *60*

An Assessment of Ethical Egoism *65*

A Note on Determinism *68*

Chapter Four: THE FOUNDATIONS OF ETHICS   75

Why Ethics Is Said to Need a Foundation *75*

Religion *78*

Justifying One's Moral Beliefs by Appealing to Religion *78*
Basing Morality on the Word of God *80*

Nature *85*

Senses of the Term "Nature" *86*
General Problems with Naturalism *90*
Two Kinds of Naturalism *92*
Three Naturalistic Theories *93*
The Naturalistic Fallacy *103*

The Self *106*

Plato: The Healthy Soul *106*
Self-Realization *109*

Chapter Five: MORAL FACTS.................................. *115*

History or Literature? *116*

Arguments Against Moral Facts *120*

Is There Knowledge of Moral Facts? *120*
Supervenience *123*
Does Morality Motivate? *127*

Three Points That Support Moral Realism *134*

Error Theory *134*
Logical Configurations *137*
The Possibility of Morality *139*

A Middle Ground? Quasirealism *140*

Three Advantages of Projectivism *144*

Hume's Theory *144*
Moral Disagreement *146*
Why Be Moral? *149*

Part Two: Substantially Normative Issues........... *157*

Chapter Six: LYING.. *158*

A Definition of Lying *159*

Is It Always Wrong to Lie? *164*

Two Types of Absolutists *167*

Lying and Deception *171*

What Is Wrong with Lying? *173*

Social Contract *173*
Respect *175*
Bad Consequences *177*

The Connection Between Lying and Deception *178*

**Why Lying Is So Easy: Self-Serving and
Other Harmless Lies** *179*

Summary *181*

Chapter Seven: GOOD CHARACTER............................ *184*

Virtue Ethics *184*

The Importance of the Virtues *185*

The Priority of the Virtues   *186*
What Good Are the Virtues? The Flourishing View   *190*

What Are the Virtues?   *197*

Which Traits Are Virtues?   *197*
Is There Any Principle by Which a List of Virtues
Can Be Generated?   *200*
Moral and Nonmoral Virtues   *201*
Self-Control and Motivation   *202*
The Golden Mean   *204*
Vices   *205*

Saints, Heroes, and Supererogation   *207*

What Is a Saint?   *207*
Supererogation   *209*

The Moral Character of Men and Women   *212*

Men: Morality of Principle   *213*
Women: Morality Based on Relationships   *213*

Community and Autonomy   *217*

Chapter Eight: UTILITARIANISM *226*

Two Kinds of Moral Theory   *227*

Consequentialism and Nonconsequentialism   *227*
Five Notes on Terminology   *230*

Utilitarianism   *232*

Maximizing and Minimizing   *234*
Actual or Expected Consequences   *235*

Objections to Utilitarianism, and Replies   *236*

Act and Rule Utilitarianism   *241*

Counterexamples to Act Utilitarianism   *243*
How Rule Utilitarianism Answers the Criticisms   *246*
Two Questions for Rule Utilitarianism   *248*

Hedonism and Alternatives   *250*

Is the Good Pleasure?   *250*
Quantity and Quality of Pleasure   *252*
Evaluation of Hedonism   *254*
"Dolorism"   *256*
Ideal Utilitarianism   *256*

Summary   *258*

Chapter Nine: KANT: EVIL AS IRRATIONALITY   *260*

Kant's Presuppositions   *261*

The Supreme Principle of Morality   *265*

One Supreme Principle?   *265*
Kant's Supreme Principle   *266*
Hypothetical and Categorical Imperatives   *267*
The Categorical Imperative   *268*

Universalization   *269*

Why Universalize?   *269*
Formalism   *271*

Maxims and the Rational Will   *273*

Maxims   *273*
Will   *275*
Rational and Reasonable Wills   *276*

Kant's Four Examples   *277*

How Kant Organizes the Examples   *277*
Kant's Examples   *281*

The Problem of Universalization Once Again   *285*

The Test of Sufficient and Necessary Condition   *285*
What Good Is Universalization?   *289*
The Cyrano Problem   *290*
Conclusion: Is Morality Based on Logic?   *291*

Other Aspects of Kant's Moral Philosophy   *292*

Autonomy   *292*
Dignity and Respect   *295*
Ends and Means   *297*

Summary   *298*

Chapter Ten: THE MEANING OF LIFE........................ *300*

How the Question of the Meaning of Life Arises   *300*

Is the Meaning of Life a Kind of Knowledge?   *302*

Is the Meaning of Life Happiness?   *306*

The Death Argument   *309*

**Repetitive Pointlessness, Ultimate Insignificance,
and Absurdity**   *313*

"Big Picture" Meaning and Faith   *318*

Is the Question of Meaning Meaningful?   *322*

If Life Has No Meaning, What Then? *325*
Meaning and Morality *327*

GLOSSARY *329*
LIST OF ABBREVIATIONS *334*
INDEX *335*

Chapter One

An Introduction to Moral Theory

Morality: Ethical wisdom, knowledge of moral science. . . . Moral truth or significance. The doctrine or system concerned with conduct and duty. Points of ethics, moral principles or rules. . . .

Oxford English Dictionary

ETHICS, MORALITY, AND MORAL THEORY

"Can virtue be taught?" Meno asks Socrates at the beginning of one of Plato's best-known dialogues. Nearly 2400 years later, Meno's question is as urgent as it must have seemed to Plato's Athenian audience around 390 B.C. Greece was in a turmoil of cultural, social, and political changes; the old traditions were under attack, long-standing loyalties had been abandoned, and traditional values had come to seem stuffy and ridiculous to many people. Moral values were subject to extensive and angry debate. Skepticism, moral relativism, cynicism about civic virtues, and a spirit of success at any price seemed to have taken hold among significant numbers of the population. Philosophers called *Sophists* travelled from city to city preaching a gospel of relativism, self-interest, and power. They regarded the old-fashioned Greek virtues—justice, courage, self-control, wisdom—as so much convenient fiction invented by the powerful to control the gullible masses. Although these teachings scandalized many respectable citizens, audiences paid good money to listen to the Sophists lecture, and rich fathers paid more for private lessons for their ambitious sons.

In his series of dialogues illustrating how his mentor Socrates (470–399 B.C.) debated philosophical questions with anyone who would talk with him, Plato (c. 428–348 B.C.) sets himself the task of opposing such dangerous doctrines. Virtue, Plato believed, is real and not just a social convention. It is not only real

1

but the most important object of our investigation, for virtue is the foundation of the good life and the just society. In the dialogues, Plato shows Socrates arguing that the cultivation of the virtues is vastly more important than the pursuit of wealth, power, and social status. A person who is truly virtuous has the most important of all good things, compared to which other goods are of little account.

Is it too much to think that there are parallels between our own situation and that of Plato's time? As in ancient Greece, "good" people are shocked by the decay of morality. If virtue can be taught, many today would say, the lesson is clearly not being learned by everyone. People no longer seem to know what is good and what is evil. Violence, drug use, and casual sex are at unprecedented levels. Lying, corruption, cynicism about public figures and national leaders, self-indulgence, and lack of commitment seem to pervade public and even private life. Public discussion is dominated by cultivated grievances and "in your face" provocativeness. Music glorifying hatred, violence, drugs, and sex is given star billing. Court dockets are overcrowded by lawsuits seeking to shift blame and make someone pay for bad luck and misadventure. Puritans wage campaigns of fear against even moderate pleasures. Professors teach that there is no truth, and squabble over ideological orthodoxies, while universities inhibit inquiry into taboo subjects, encourage racial isolation, and pretend to teach norms of civility by coercion.

Little wonder that Ann Landers, doubtless America's most popular moral philosopher, says, "American society seems to be falling apart. One out of every two marriages ends in divorce. The drug problem is horrendous and getting worse. Let's face it. America is sick."

This situation is not made any less confusing by rapidly changing moral opinions and a lack of consensus on points once thought fundamental. Is every point of view equally legitimate? Should society promote social unity, or ethnic diversity and divisiveness? Is every self-defined victim group entitled to restitution? Must all sensitivities be respected? Does religion have a place in public life? Should public schools distribute condoms, teach abstinence, or leave sex education to parents? Must sex and violence in popular culture be tolerated by a free society? Do terminally ill people have a right to end their own lives? Is it wrong to hunt animals and eat meat?

This can become very confusing. Who's right in all this? And how do you know? It seems that what is badly needed is a good dose of philosophy. For as Plato was well aware, it's the deep philosophical questions that are put into play by all this confusion. Where do values come from? Who decides what's right and wrong? What do we mean by "right" and "wrong" anyway? When Meno asks Socrates if virtue can be taught, Socrates' initial response is to say that he can't answer, since he doesn't even know what virtue is. He tells Meno to define virtue, and he will then consider whether it can be taught. Socrates is not putting his cards on the table at this point. Saying he does not know what virtue is, is very likely his way of teaching Meno virtue. Meno will learn virtue by figuring out for himself what virtue is. So Meno and Socrates begin to investigate the question, "What is virtue?"

And so the dialogue, to the disappointment of Meno and the confusion of many a subsequent philosophy student, turns away from the initial question of how people can learn to be morally good into the apparently endless bypaths of moral theory. But how can it be otherwise? The object is to become virtuous, and how can we be virtuous if we can't explain what virtue is?

One of the motives people have in studying ethics—and in recommending it to others, especially to students—is precisely what troubled Meno. They think people aren't sufficiently moral, and hope that the study of ethics will make them more so. Moral theory is part of philosophy, they argue; philosophy is taught at universities; and, *ergo* (it is natural to conclude), virtue can, should, and must be taught by college professors in philosophy courses. So if you want to be virtuous, enroll in an ethics course, read the text, and there you are. Too simple? Of course. We shall explain why in this introductory chapter.

First we should clarify some terms. The book you are reading is an introduction to moral theory. Moral theory studies morality. Virtue is part of morality, so the study of virtue is part of moral theory. If you are reading the book as part of a college course, the title of the course probably contains the word "ethics"—perhaps the title of the course *is* the word "Ethics." Ethics is one of the major branches of philosophy. But what you will learn in your ethics course is moral theory. This terminology can be confusing.

In English we have two words, *ethics* and *morality,* which refer to the same thing but in different contexts. "Morality" refers to ethical standards in the personal or social context, and "ethics" refers to ethical standards in the professional or commercial context: thus, a liar is called immoral, but a lying lawyer is called unethical. This book is not about professional or business ethics, so we make nothing of this distinction: we shall use the two words interchangeably.

We must distinguish between ethics, or morality, and the subject that studies it. Ethics, or morality, is a reality that can therefore be studied. The subject that studies it is called *moral theory,* or ethical theory. Unfortunately, this investigation is often also called "ethics," especially in university curricula, where "ethics" is the name of a course, just as "biology" or "physics" are names of courses. Calling courses "ethics" implies that there exists some kind of organized field of study, also called "ethics." Biology and physics, which are fields of study or sciences, do not study themselves, but something else—namely, living things, and matter and energy; these are not sciences but realities. In the same way, ethics, the field of study, does not study itself either; it studies a reality, also called "ethics." To avoid using the same word for both the study and what is studied, in this book we call the field of study "moral theory" and confine the terms "ethics" and "morality" to the reality being investigated. When you study biology, what you learn is biology but what you learn about is living things; when you study this book, what you learn is moral theory but what you learn about is ethics or morality.

MORALITY

Moral theory studies morality, but what is morality? Many people are skeptical about morality. They are even uncertain whether or not there is such a thing.

There is a point to this uncertainty, but there is also an important confusion. Morality is real. It is not made up, nor is it some kind of theoretical construction or pie-in-the-sky ideal. Morality is practical; it is possibly the most practical thing there is. It is as much a part of life as religion, law, sports, education, or any other similar institution. Morality in fact is a more important part of life, since we can imagine life without any of these other things, but it is scarcely possible to imagine life without morality.

Consider what we all do. We use rules, principles, or standards to guide our behavior, and to appraise and influence the behavior of others. This is the predominant activity of morality. For example, you notice people cheating on a test. You could cheat too. But you invoke the rule, "Do not cheat," and decide not to cheat. You use this rule to guide your behavior. At the same time, you apply the rule to the cheaters: "They shouldn't cheat." You use the rule to appraise their conduct. Later, your friend asks you if you noticed the people cheating. You reply, "I hope they got caught." You are using your principle to influence your friend against cheating. In doing these things, you are engaging in the enterprise of morality. Since everybody does this, morality is certainly real.

But the fact that something may be real does not mean that it can easily be defined. Love is real, but can you give a good definition? How about religion or poetry? For that matter, it's not so easy to define philosophy. The first task of a theory of something, as Socrates understood, is to try to figure out a good definition for it.

This book does not offer a general definition of morality. This may seem like a deficiency, but defining morality, or ethics, is an exercise in futility, since such definitions tend to be essentially circular or merely verbal, (as the epigraph at the beginning of this chapter illustrates). They do not give the student any more information about what ethics is than he or she already knows. The reader is encouraged to try to formulate a definition and see what results. Or look up "morality" and "ethics" in a good dictionary and see if you learn anything you didn't already know. You already know that morality has to do with what is right and what is wrong—morally right and wrong, not right and wrong in arithmetic or grammar; with good and bad (but not good or bad in the sense of being good for your health or bad for your golf swing); with what is permissible and not permissible (morally, not legally, nor in terms of religious or other requirements). Morality has to do with what your obligations are: your moral obligations. But if morality consists of moral obligations, what is a moral obligation? The answer is: a moral obligation is an obligation imposed by morality!

This circularity of definition should not hinder anyone from understanding what this book is about. Unless you have just arrived from some very strange intergalactic civilization, you have been familiar with morality all of your thinking life, and know enough about it to understand what it is in an informal, but essentially adequate, sense. Chances are, you also know many of the questions studied by moral theory, because intelligent people ask these questions when they think about right and wrong. What you do not know are the answers, which is why you are reading this book!

Though we offer no definition of morality, we shall identify some of its main features. Part of any theory, whether about morality or something else, is to describe its subject matter by listing characteristics of the subject that are interesting and distinctive. Here are eight.

1.   Morality is binding on those to whom it applies. This means that if some principle is part of morality, then the people to whom the morality applies ought to obey that principle. For example, Christians ought to love their neighbors and turn the other cheek, since these principles are part of Christian morality. This feature follows simply from the fact that morality consists of rules, for being binding is part of what it means for something to be a rule. It would be incoherent or "logically odd" (as philosophers say) to hold that some rule applies to some group of people, and yet to say that these people are not obligated to follow the rule. This is true of rules of etiquette and politeness as well as moral rules.

2.   Morality in an important sense is *not voluntary*. You can't just choose your moral principles. Suppose a person were to argue that she is free to hold any morality she wants. "I want to tell lies, therefore I hold a morality in which 'Do not lie' is not a moral principle. Therefore, I shall lie whenever I feel like it." What would we say about such a person? We'd regard her as rotten. We'd think her morality is wrong. We don't think she's free to adopt just any morality. But this is not to deny that some parts of morality might be optional; some individuals have personal moral codes that impose strong moral obligations they voluntarily undertake, such as a commitment to community service, but which are applicable only to people who choose to accept them.

3.   Morality consists of rules, but unlike law or sports, there is *no rule book.* No one makes the rules, no one has the authority to change them, no one is officially entitled to interpret or apply them, no one can add to the rules or subtract from them. This does not mean that morality does not change; in some sense, morality may change, as many people think. But it does mean that change in morality does not occur by explicit human decision. No person or group of people can change morality just by deciding to do so.

4.   Morality *does not depend on what people think*. If it did, which people would it depend on? Not the majority, because we all recognize that the majority can be as wrong about morality as they can about anything else. Not the powerful people or the opinion makers; we reserve the right to question their morality as well as anyone's. And not any other subgroup of people either, for no matter what subgroup you mention—such as the clergy, oppressed minorities, or philosophy professors—even if as a group they are more moral than other people, they will not have any special authority to decide what is moral and what is not. Nor can morality depend on unanimity, because there is no

moral principle that is endorsed by absolutely everyone, and no single person in the whole world has the right to veto a moral principle.

5.   There are often *correct answers* to moral questions. Most people have no trouble distinguishing good moral actions from bad ones. What would you think of someone who liked to torture animals? Or of a person who refused to help someone in trouble, simply because it was too much trouble and he couldn't be bothered? There is very little room for ambiguity or debate here; everyone thinks these things are wrong, just as everyone thinks certain other actions are right.

6.   Moral deliberation consists in finding *good reasons* for one's decisions, and moral debate consists in presenting good arguments for one's moral views. No one would say, "I hate abortion, therefore it is wrong and people should not do it": personal likes and dislikes are not good arguments. (Pounding your fist on the table and shouting is not a good argument either). Hence, intelligent discussion of moral questions is possible, and it is possible for someone to develop well-considered, intelligent moral opinions.

If you do not have good reasons for your moral opinions, why should anyone pay attention to them? More important, why should you yourself pay attention to them, if you do not have good reasons for holding them? Here is a kind of theorem: two competing moral principles for which the reasons are equal are equally good. (Let us say, "You may tell a lie to avoid a small unpleasantness" and "You may not." If the reasons for each position are equally good, then the positions themselves are equally good—that is, it is a standoff between them.) From this it follows that a moral opinion for which you have no reason at all can be no better than any other moral opinion whatever, so that logically it is a matter of indifference whether you hold it or not.

7.   Despite this, morality is sometimes *unclear or ambiguous*. The rules of morality are not always as clear or obvious as we might like, which is why people debate and argue moral questions without reaching agreement, and which is also why you sometimes have to make a moral decision without being confident that you have made the right decision. For example, everyone agrees that it is wrong to cheat, but must you always correct errors in your favor? (Suppose your professor gives you an A when you know your grade should have been a B. Is it wrong not to tell her? Does it depend on the circumstances?) When people debate, sometimes the best they can do is agree about what the wrong answers are, clarify the points where they don't see eye to eye, and agree to disagree.

8.   Morality is *an end in itself*. If you ask, what is the purpose of being moral?, the correct answer is, there is no purpose other than morality itself. We ought to be moral, just because to be moral is what we ought to be. If you seek some other end that being moral serves (be moral so that you can succeed in

life; be moral so that God, or your parents, will love you), then you haven't understood the point of morality. Being moral may, and usually does, serve some other end (people generally don't like immoral people, so if you want people to like you you'd be well-advised to be moral), but these other ends are not the justification for being moral. So if someone were to ask, "What good is morality? What's it for?" the answer would have to be that morality is not *for* anything. It exists so that people can lead the most moral lives they are capable of.

MORAL THEORY AND SCIENCE

Morality is studied by moral theory. Like all forms of investigation, moral theory has one primary goal: the truth. Its aim is to discover the truth about its subject, which is morality. But moral theory is not the only area of investigation that studies morality. Sociology, anthropology, and psychology have important things to tell us about morality, as do history, literature, and religion. This should not be surprising, since morality is obviously an important and complex phenomenon. In the same way, religion and law are studied by sociology, history, anthropology, and psychology, as well as by religion, law, and philosophy. These other investigations—the social sciences—also aim at the truth about morality, so it may be interesting to point out how they differ from moral theory.

The difference is twofold: sciences are essentially empirical, whereas philosophy is essentially conceptual; and sciences are entirely descriptive and explanatory, whereas moral theory is partly normative.

Empirical Versus Conceptual

Scientific method is *empirical*. In the sciences, the methods employed involve the analysis of data gathered by laboratory experiments, by techniques using special instruments, and by field observations. Gathering of data must be done under controlled conditions so that meaningful conclusions may be drawn from the data collected. Contaminated tissue cultures or unrepresentative opinion samples contain no useful information about the organism's biology or the public's opinions. This clever construction of controlled methods of collecting data has provided the so-called "scientific method" with its proven record of reaching generally true and reliable conclusions.

But moral theory, like philosophy generally, makes no experiments and gathers no data, controlled or otherwise. Although moral theory may use data that it borrows from the sciences, and theorists must always be careful to take account of the established facts about society and human nature, the job of moral theory is *conceptual;* its work is done with concepts, hypotheses and theories, and logic. The method used is the classical method of philosophy: analyzing, explaining, clarifying, and defining ideas and principles; proposing and examining theories;

and working out logical arguments to support conclusions. Philosophers search for truth by such conceptual methods because the questions they try to answer are conceptual and not empirical questions.

Let us illustrate this by considering a point just noted. People wonder whether morality is real. They may well have in mind questions about moral rules. Where do the rules come from? Who makes the rules? Who decides what is right and what is wrong? You cannot solve this by collecting data in a scientific controlled experiment, because these questions require us to investigate our concept of morality. What is it that we are thinking about when we think about morality? Is morality the kind of thing whose rules are made by someone? If you are unsure of the answer, what you need is not some new information, but more reflection on your concept of morality.

Here is a theory that is evidently fairly popular: moral rules are made by society. Moral theory investigates whether this theory is true by raising questions that the theory might have trouble answering. If moral rules are made by society, what about someone who disagrees with one of the rules, such as, "Sex outside of marriage is wrong." Is it wrong to disobey this rule? Are you a bad person if you disobey? Since there is no Official Rule Book, how do you even know that this is one of the rules in the first place? This and other problems make the theory seem not so plausible; they suggest reasons for thinking that the theory is not true.

So one way to conduct investigations in moral theory is by learning to ask good questions. If moral rules are not made by society, who does make them? Religion? Someone else? How do they do it, by vote? These questions show that the idea behind the original question is itself mistaken: morality has rules, but the rules are not made in any normal sense of the word "made." So we will have to think harder if we are going to figure out where the moral rules come from.

Descriptive Versus Normative

Norms are standards; an investigation is said to be *normative* if it investigates which ideas ought to be norms, values, or standards. Normative inquiry is an attempt to discover standards of good and bad. When the social sciences investigate morality, the investigation is not normative but *descriptive*. Sciences investigate morality as it actually is (or was, in the case of history), which is to say, the moral ideas that are accepted by somebody somewhere. Social sciences might describe a given morality and try to determine how it functions in a society (or in a person's life), or explain why the society has the morality it does. Being descriptive, explanatory, and causal, the sciences investigate what *is;* they have no special method for investigating what *ought to be.* Because sciences cannot validate any moral idea, it is not within the competence of sociology, anthropology, history, or the rest to determine what morality ought to require. Try to imagine what anthropological observations, sociological data collection, or historical documentation could be devised to discover whether, for example, it is more moral to love your enemy or to hate your enemy. You will not be able to think of any, because moral conclusions are not supported by documentation and data collection. Of course, empirical information and scientific understanding of social, psychological, and biological phenomena may prove important if we are to arrive at good moral values; but the role of scientific knowledge is to provide the facts without which ethical thinking might be irrelevant to real life. Scientific understanding is not itself a special kind of moral thinking.

It is easy to fall into confusion about this point. People often claim that science really is normative because it is not value-free. That science is not value-free is certainly correct, since science values honesty and truth, assumes that knowledge is better than ignorance, and requires moral qualities such as hard work, diligence, and imagination for success. But what this shows is that science has norms and values, not that science discovers or validates norms and values. An investigation is not normative because it has and uses norms. Science can never find out that one thing is bad and some other thing good, and hence can never tell you what it is right or wrong for you to do. Science values truthfulness over dishonesty, and knowledge over ignorance, but no laboratory experiment or field observation will ever show that lying is morally wrong and telling the truth morally good, or that knowing something is better than not knowing it.

Among the questions people ask about morality are these: What makes some actions right and other wrong? How can I know which rules are good rules? What does it even mean that some rules are better than other rules? Take lying; we all think it is wrong, but do we know why is it wrong? And are we clear whether it is always wrong, in all circumstances? Is it also wrong to mislead, evade, and deceive? These are among the normative questions that moral theory examines. How do you answer such questions? You have to work out the best set of moral beliefs you can. You do this by using logic and by carefully considering your moral opinions.

This introduces an element that is important in philosophy but of no account in science: opinion. In science, opinions that are unsupported by data prove nothing. Science rests on facts and data. But in philosophy, and especially in moral theory, opinions play a role, because ultimately there is no way of establishing which moral principles are the best other than by appealing to the considered, thoughtful, consistent conclusions of thinking people. This does not mean that morality consists of nothing but opinions (we shall discuss the view that it does in Chapter Two), since some opinions are better than others. Many people hold opinions outside of morality that are false, and this might well be the case about moral opinions too; and if some moral opinions are false, then others (the denials of the false ones) are true.

But even if some moral opinions are true, it is not obvious how moral opinions can be proved; unlike scientific facts, moral principles cannot be proved in any obvious way by experiments or laboratory studies. (For example, try an informal experiment: you don't think the ice on the pond is thin, so you walk out on it and see what happens. Now try an informal experiment in morality: you don't believe lying is wrong. . . . What? Do you try lying and see what happens? What might happen that would prove that lying is wrong? Do you think your nose will grow when you tell a lie? Why would *that* prove that lying is wrong?) Whether moral opinions are true, and how good moral opinions can be distinguished from bad ones, are topics that concern us a great deal in moral theory. But even if we do not arrive at very satisfactory answers, it does not follow that all opinions are correct, or that everybody's opinions are as good as anyone else's. Many people hold opinions that are quite shaky, and crumble when they are examined.

So one goal of normative moral theory is to help us reach the best moral beliefs. Until we have begun to do this, your moral opinions are merely *conventional,* which means not that your beliefs are necessarily bad but that you haven't thought them out for yourself, and so you hold them because they have been taught to you, or because everyone else does. As you begin to consider them critically and philosophically, they become more and more *reflective.* This change from conventional opinions to reflective opinions is what happens as you study moral theory. So if in the last resort we fall back on opinions, the opinions we fall back on are not just any old opinions, but those that have withstood philosophical analysis and criticism.

Hence, moral theory has two parts, the conceptual and the normative. We have made it clear what these parts investigate, and what their goals are. The conceptual part investigates fundamental questions about the nature of morality; its goal is truth. The normative part investigates what the best moral beliefs are; its goal is to figure out the best set of moral beliefs.

MORAL EDUCATION: BECOMING MORAL AND STUDYING MORAL THEORY

We now come to the questions that often motivate the study of moral theory: How can people learn to be moral? Must you study moral theory to become moral, as Socrates seemed to think? If you do study it, will learning it make you moral, as Socrates also assumed? There is good reason to think that Socrates was wrong on both points. Moral theory is a body of knowledge that has to be studied and learned. When you learn the subject, you know it, but even if you become an expert in moral theory, you have not necessarily become a moral person. And there certainly are many moral people who have not studied moral theory, and who may not have even heard of it.

The reason is that being moral requires something that is not knowledge, namely, a desire. You can have this desire to be moral without knowing anything about moral theory, and, if you do not have the desire, you can learn all about moral theory without acquiring it. This is why a student who is a brute and a barbarian can get an A in this subject as easily as can an angel (more easily if the barbarian studies more), and remain as much a barbarian as ever. How then to account for the fact that many people think that the point of ethics courses is to teach people to be moral?

Socrates was the first person to think that you become moral by learning something about morality. Socrates had a theory: he held that virtue is really a kind of knowledge. From this, he was quick to point out, it follows that morality certainly can be taught. If virtue (morality) is knowledge, the problem is to discover the knowledge, and teach it to students. Hence, Socrates went about looking for definitions: what is virtue, anyway? According to his view, the relation between moral theory and morality is not in the least like that between science and nature; protons and electrons are not the same thing as nuclear physics, and a person who studies physics becomes a physicist, not a subatomic particle. The study of moral theory is more like the study of carpentry, or raising horses, analogies that Socrates employs to make his point. You will not become a geranium by studying biology, but the good student does become a carpenter by studying carpentry: you cannot get an A in your carpentry class unless you are well on your way to being a carpenter. And so, Socrates thought, you cannot learn the subject of morality without becoming, or being on the way to becoming, a moral person.

Socrates never explains very clearly his claim that morality is a kind of knowledge, at least not in Plato's dialogues. His problem is that he does not distinguish well enough between the kind of knowledge you acquire by looking for definitions and logical arguments, and the kind you need to become good at some craft or skill. He does not think you become a carpenter by learning how to define "hammer" and "nail," but he does seem to think that you become a moral person by learning how to define "virtue" and "justice." (Hence, in Plato's *Republic*, Socrates hints that only philosophers can be truly moral.) It was left to Plato's great student Aristotle (384–322 B.C.) to make clear what both Socrates and Plato had noticed but insufficiently understood, that morality is not a kind of theoretical knowledge but a kind of practical knowledge, a skill employing knowledge of facts and principles. This distinction makes more sense of the analogy with carpentry, which is the skill of knowing how to work with wood, based on factual knowledge about tools and materials. A student acquires this skill from someone who already knows it, partly by instruction and study, and partly by imitation and practice. Virtue, according to Aristotle (answering Socrates' challenge to Meno), is the skill of knowing how to live well, based on knowledge of the material of human nature. You acquire this skill from someone who knows it, again partly by instruction, partly by imitation and practice.

But even this improvement on the theory that virtue is knowledge overlooks the fact that the carpenter may exercise his skill when and for what purposes he chooses; having the skill and using it are quite distinct. No special desires are part of the carpenter's skills. When and what the carpenter builds depends on what the carpenter wants to do: the world's best carpenter may be utterly lazy and never have the desire to work. Aristotle knows that to be virtuous you have to desire (or "be disposed") to do the right thing, for he says that the virtuous person "must will his action, and will it for its own sake" (*Nicomachean Ethics*, II, 4). But he fails to notice how this shows that being virtuous is not a skill, but a question of right desires. The virtuous person wants to help other people in need, wants to be honest and truthful, wants to be kind rather than cruel, and so on. One can make the argument (as Aristotle does) that unless you know how to do these things, you will not succeed in being virtuous no matter how much you may want to. But unless you want to be these things, you certainly will not be a virtuous person, no matter what kind of skills you have. And it would seem that no instruction can teach a person to want to be good.

So it does not look as if mastering any form of knowledge is going to make a person moral. But the Greeks were not wrong in suggesting that morality can be learned, and that there is such a thing as moral education. We can say that this consists of three parts, of which moral theory is but one. The others are moral sensitivity and perception, and moral emotions. These three parts mutually support each other without being linked necessarily, which is why a person ignorant of moral theory might be morally sensitive and have good emotions, while an expert on moral theory might have neither.

Moral Sensitivity and Perception

A person who is morally sensitive *understands or appreciates the moral aspects of things,* and recognizes the elements in a situation that give it its moral nature. A sensitive person knows how to apply moral ideas and wants to act in a morally sensitive way. For example, everybody knows that people resent insults and no one would want to insult someone they are fond of. But not everybody understands what behavior is offensive. It doesn't occur to some people that addressing a woman as "babe" is insulting, as are some ways of expressing friendly feelings physically (for example, for a male to pat a female friend on the rear). The same applies to cruelty. A good person does not want to be cruel, but might not always realize how cruel certain words and actions are. Knowing what to do is what Aristotle calls "perception." You do not learn it by studying theory, but from experience, and by observing the behavior of people who are already sensitive.

You have to want to do the right thing. If you are morally sensitive you try to be fair, you recognize the importance of principle, you seek to understand people's feelings, you try to be kind and considerate, and generally you strive to act in a way that takes into account other people's interests, goals, and points of view. You will not do any of this unless you have, not just a generalized desire to do the right thing, but specific desires to do specific kinds of right things. Cultivating these desires is what is meant by good character, and learning how to do it is part of the sensitivity training of moral education.

Moral Emotions

Moral emotions are those emotions that enter into moral reactions. Because people are not robots, they not only take in data and emit behavioral responses, but also react emotionally, both to what they observe and to what they themselves do. These emotions have a moral dimension, in that some emotions are morally appropriate to certain kinds of situations, and others are inappropriate, just as not having any feeling at all about something would be inappropriate. What would you think of a person who witnessed a terrible accident and didn't feel bad about it, not even the least sorrowful? We would regard such lack of feeling as morally, and say humanly, inappropriate. A good person ought to feel bad about a tragedy. So we think it is important to develop suitable feelings about many things. For example, a person who has well-developed moral emotions is indignant at injustice, cruelty, and lies; is contemptuous toward cheats and bullies; and feels compassion toward the suffering of others. (Compassion is not exactly sadness, but a kind of sympathy we feel for those who suffer or are oppressed.)

This is a large topic, but as an illustration, consider the very important moral emotions that cluster around one's own faults and failures. We feel regret, guilt, shame, embarrassment, or humiliation at our own shortcomings, and think it is important that we do feel these unpleasant emotions. If you do something bad, we expect you to feel guilty about it later; when you realize you have done something foolish, you ought to be embarrassed. You ought to feel sorry if you hurt someone's feelings, even if inadvertently, and regretful if you do not have an opportunity to apologize. If you do less than you are capable of, especially if your failure lets down other people who rely on you, you ought to feel ashamed of yourself. Not to feel these reproachful emotions shows a lack of something important in your moral character.

So a morally good person has well-developed sensitivity and moral emotions. These you do not learn by studying theory in a philosophy class. Nevertheless, sensitivity and proper emotions are learned forms of behavior. We learn them through experience, by reading, listening, and discussion, by meeting good role models, from our inner character and reflection, and maybe through a certain amount of good "moral luck." It may even be the case that someone can learn to want to be good, though it is quite unclear how this can happen. Perhaps it is best to say that though you can want to be good, no one can teach you to want to be good. It is something you have to teach yourself.

Moral education should not be confused with indoctrination and exhortations to virtue. Some people seem to think that moral education succeeds only if students leave the ethics course filled with good moral opinions. Of course, we want students to have good moral opinions, but, like Socrates, we recognize that the process by which these opinions are formed is at least as important as the opinions themselves. Cheering for unquestioned values such as integrity, honesty, fairness, not cheating your customers, and being a good neighbor and citizen creates moral parrots, not moral people. To indoctrinate is to try to build into someone "right thinking" without giving them a chance to figure out for themselves what thinking is right. This is why what passes for "sensitivity training" today in large corporations and even in universities is a counterfeit based on coercion—be sensitive or lose your job!—that has the effect not that its victims want to be sensitive, but are afraid not to be, and resent getting pushed around. No one becomes virtuous through fear and resentment.

What then is the role of moral theory in moral education?

We return to the two parts of moral theory, conceptual and normative. It is easy to see how the normative part figures in moral education, since a person whose beliefs are merely conventional, even if the beliefs are themselves morally unimpeachable, is without reflection and understanding; his morality is due to luck, not judgment. Without reflection, a person is not prepared to face and resolve moral problems, or even to adapt to new situations. It is difficult to imagine anyone being satisfied holding moral principles which he has not seriously thought about.

The conceptual part may seem less important. When we said that you can be moral without even knowing about moral theory, perhaps we should have said, the conceptual part of moral theory. Nevertheless, as Socrates demonstrates in Plato's dialogues, if you begin with normative questions you get into conceptual ones soon enough, and the two kinds of inquiries cannot be kept separate except artificially (which is why the two parts of this book are titled, "substantially" conceptual and "substantially" normative issues). Unless you are prepared to cut yourself off when conceptual questions arise, you will find that your moral education raises conceptual questions in moral theory. To remain with our very basic example: can you even hope to decide what you think is morally right, unless you have some theory about where the rules come from?

So, in the end, can this book teach virtue? The answer is not an unqualified yes, but it is not an unqualified no either. An ethics text is similar to the many books that come out about playing the stock market; if any of them really contained a method for beating the market, everyone would already have read the book and become rich. If there were an ethics text that taught virtue, virtue would be far more common than it is. We have already explained that virtue, though it cannot be taught, can certainly be learned. An ethics text can help you learn what virtue is, and why. But just as no book can make you learn if you do not want to learn, so no book can make you virtuous. This book can teach you moral theory. Only you can make yourself virtuous.

REFERENCES AND FURTHER READING

There are many translations of Plato's "Meno." A useful edition is *Five Dialogues of Plato,* trans. by G. W. A. Grube (Indianapolis, IN: Hackett, 1981). These short works, all basic documents of Western civilization, are also delightful introductions to ethical theory and to philosophy generally.

G. Wallace and A. D. M. Walker, eds., *The Definition of Morality* (London: Methuen, 1970), is a collection of interesting essays.

Many standard books in ethical theory contain views of what ethics is. Among the more readable are G. J. Warnock, *The Object of Morality* (London: Methuen, 1971), and Bernard Gert, *Morality* (New York: Oxford University Press, 1991).

An excellent general introduction to the subject is William Frankena, 2nd ed., *Ethics* (Englewood Cliffs, NJ: Prentice Hall, 1973). Another is Bernard Williams, *Morality* (New York: Harper & Row, 1972).

For a relatively short (250 pages), if idiosyncratic, history of the subject, see Alasdair MacIntyre, *A Short History of Ethics* (New York: Macmillan, 1966).

An even shorter (147 pages), but nonetheless excellent, book is Mary Warnock, *Ethics Since 1900* (New York: Oxford University Press, 1966), which adds Jean-Paul Sartre to the British figures covered.

The idea that morality is binding is discussed by Bernard Williams, *Ethics and the Limits of Philosophy* (London: Fontana, 1985), who thinks the idea is "intimidating." This entire book is a sensitive discussion of what philosophy can and cannot accomplish in ethics.

Plato argues that virtue is knowledge in his dialogue "Protagoras," which, like many of Plato's major dialogues, is available in several translations and editions.

Moral sentiments and attitudes are discussed in the context of moral development by Michael Pritchard, *On Becoming Responsible* (Lawrence, KS: University Press of Kansas, 1991).

Part One

Substantially Conceptual Issues

Chapter Two

Challenges to Ethics: Relativism

There is nothing either good or bad, but thinking makes it so.

***Hamlet*, II, ii, 227**

THREE WAYS TO CHALLENGE ETHICS

Ethics is a subject with which we are never satisfied; it always has to justify itself. This is to say that ethics can be challenged. There are three distinct ways in which something can be challenged, and ethics can be challenged in all three ways. First, something can be challenged by being provoked to *become better than it is*, to improve or elevate itself. Thus athletes often challenge themselves to do better: to run faster, jump higher or further, and so on. When something is challenged to be better than it is, we will say that it is **challenged from above.**

Second, to challenge something is to regard it with skepticism and to require that it *explain, defend, or justify itself.* It is to ask what good something is, what purpose it serves, and why is it needed. Religion, as an example, is frequently challenged on these grounds. In this sense, you might challenge your philosophy professor to explain what good studying philosophy does for anyone. Since the challenge here is to the value of the enterprise, we call this **challenging** something **as such.** Third, something is *unmasked or exposed,* as when the defense attorney challenges the testimony of the prosecution witness. Here, what is being said is that the person or thing being challenged is less good than it takes itself to be, so that we call this a **challenge from below.**

We will discuss briefly the first and second of these challenges to ethics. But it is the third challenge, "from below," that shall largely concern us. Is ethics not quite as good as it claims to be? We discuss two different critiques that make this claim: relativism, which denies that there are any moral truths binding on everyone, and egoism, which denies that we have any moral obligation to look out for the well-being of other people. Many people do think that at least some moral

18

obligations are true for everyone; we call these universal moral truths—for example, "Do not murder" or "Be kind to animals." And, clearly, many people do think that ethics requires us to take into account the well-being of other people. So these two challenges amount to rather far-reaching criticisms of ethics as conventionally understood. Relativism is the topic of the second half of this chapter, and egoism is the subject of Chapter Three.

Challenges from Above

It might seem odd to challenge ethics to be better than it is, since it is ethics that sets the standards of good and bad; by what standard can something be better than the standard of what is good? But there is no doubt that conventional or ordinary ethics can be so challenged. This is the job of moral criticism and moral reform, and it has occupied philosophers at least since the time of Socrates (who died in 399 B.C.). Socrates tried to convince his followers that acting unjustly was the greatest evil, so that given the choice it was preferable to be the victim of an injustice than to commit an injustice against someone else. This teaching contradicted common-sense Greek morality, which held that the greatest evil was suffering injustice, not doing it. Socrates refused to act unjustly, as he considered it, even when he might have done so to escape an unjust legal prosecution: after being tried and convicted on various trumped-up charges, he told his friends that it would be wrong of him to escape from prison—his friends had bribed the jailer—although his conviction was unjust. He had no right to repudiate the laws of Athens, even when they had been used unjustly against him. His friends, who thought that since he should not have been in prison in the first place he had every right to escape if he could, were forced to admit that Socrates' moral position was more admirable than their own.

Moral reform is often advocated by religious thinkers. Here is perhaps the most famous example of moral reform in Western history:

> You have heard that it was said, "Love your neighbors and hate your enemies." But now I tell you: love your enemies. Bless those that curse you, do good to those that hate you, and pray for those who persecute you, so that you may become the children of your Father in heaven. For He makes the sun to shine on good and bad alike, and gives rain to those who do good and to those who do evil. Why should God reward you if you love only the people who love you? Even the tax collectors do that! (Sermon on the Mount, Matt. 5:43–48).

Here Jesus criticizes the ordinary moral belief that we should love our friends but hate our enemies. He is speaking as a moral critic: he knows that conventional morality allows or encourages us to return hate for hate. Note that Jesus is not simply telling his followers what to do, and demanding that they accept it on faith; he gives reasons and arguments for his position. Even dubious characters like tax collectors love their friends, he says; God loves everyone equally, without regard for good or evil: we ought to be like Him. It is interesting to examine Jesus' arguments and see how convincingly they make his case. You may find that you are not quite clear about the key term, "love"; does Jesus mean that you should feel love for your enemies in your heart, or only that you should act towards them lovingly? Does Jesus forbid you to protect yourself against your enemies, or to seek redress for your grievances against them, perhaps by suing them in court? Or does Jesus allow such self-protection and retaliation, provided you harbor no evil thoughts toward them, such as hatred and the desire for revenge? All these questions have to be answered if Jesus is to explain why loving enemies is better than hating them.

A more contemporary example of moral reform is offered by the Australian philosopher Peter Singer, who, writing about a terrible famine in Asia, argues with considerable cogency that our conventional morality, while calling on us to help those in need, does not go anywhere near far enough. It is not enough for prosperous Westerners to give a tiny percentage of our national wealth to help starving multitudes, argues Singer; we ought to do everything we can to prevent famine and suffering, short of causing even greater hardship here or elsewhere. If we even came close to following this principle, he points out, our moral code would be very different from what it is, and our efforts to relieve suffering would be vastly greater than they are.

Challenges to Ethics as Such

Let us turn to the second sense of challenge. Here we are not challenging any given system of ethics or any particular ethical belief or principle, but ethics itself. Does it make sense to suppose that we can do without ethics, or that something better might be put in its place? One reason to think not is that, presumably, everybody has some sort of ethics, some sort of beliefs or guiding principles that they use to decide how to act. If people didn't have some sort of ethics, they couldn't do anything at all, not even stay in bed all day, since even doing that implies that you think it's better to stay in bed than to get up. So if everybody must have some sort of ethics, the only question would be, which code of ethics is best?, and not, should we have any ethical code at all? The difficulty with this argument is its overly broad definition of ethics. If what is meant by ethics is any belief or principle that guides our actions in some way, then it is true that everybody needs and has some ethics; but then the question we are examining has to be clarified. It is: do we need ethics in the narrower sense, in which ethics refers to a set of beliefs that is contrasted with other action-guiding sets of principles, such as religion, law or the maxims of prudence? (For example, one reason not to stay in bed all day is that it would be imprudent, as you might starve to death.)

Let us examine the question whether religion or law might take the place of ethics. This is in fact sometimes argued. People who are in business sometimes think that they are required to do everything the law requires, but nothing more. Obedience to law is their only moral obligation. They argue that if society wants them to act in a certain way, it can pass a law so stating. Society, they are quick to point out, has passed many such laws. It is the law that defines the limits of their obligations: what the law does not require need not be done, and business is free to act as it sees fit. We may call this **minimal ethics.**

Suppose you are a stockbroker and you heavily promote investments your firm is selling, even if these might not be best for your clients. This tactic is not illegal, and evidently not prohibited in any code of ethics, so you argue that nothing forbids it. Or your university has a code prohibiting insulting or disrespectful language. You want to insult someone so you make an obscene gesture, which is not prohibited by the code. Everything not explicitly prohibited is allowed: morality as such is irrelevant.

Certain religious people also take the view that morality is irrelevant. They think that everything a person needs to know to live a good and ethical life is to be found in religion. They think that religion provides all the answers to whatever perplexities and obstacles life may put in one's path. Morality as distinct from the teaching of religion is not needed, since morality could have nothing to add to what religion already provides. Only a person who does not believe in any religion might need morality, but such a person needs religion even more.

These views claim that the system they favor (such as the law, or religion) is both complete and correct as far as morality goes: there is nothing morally required that is not found in the system, and everything found in the system is morally correct. It is for this reason that ethics is unnecessary; if the competing system were either incomplete or in some way in error, it would be inadequate, and ethics would be required again to make the improvement. But there are problems with the claim that a system of rules other than ethics is either necessarily complete or necessarily correct.

First, consider *completeness*. Can the law be a complete guide to ethical conduct, as minimal ethics holds? The truth would seem to be just the opposite: that ethics is a guide to what the law should require. Society enacts certain requirements into law just because society thinks these obligations are ethically required, and finds that businesses and the professions are not adhering to them. But if certain activities were not ethically required before the laws were passed, what is the ground of the complaint that businesses are failing to do something that they ought to do? If the activities were ethically required even before the laws were passed, they would be ethically required even if the laws had not been passed, so that obedience to law cannot be all that is ethically required. Morality comes first, laws afterwards, from which it follows that the system of laws that happens to have been enacted at any given time cannot be regarded as necessarily containing all the obligations that anyone, in or out of business, has. Therefore, to obey the law cannot be our only obligation.

Can we say that to follow the teaching of your religion might be someone's only moral obligation? We obviously cannot consider all the religions or all their holy books, so let us consider only whether the Christian Bible gives us complete moral answers. If you studied the Bible, you would find that it has nothing to say about such questions as whether you may bite your fingernails, or whether it is wrong to floss your teeth in public, or whether you should chew gum in your philosophy class. This would not surprise you, since these matters are not usually considered points of morality. But now suppose you also discovered that the

Bible has nothing to say about abortion. If the Bible is a complete guide to morals, it should follow that abortion also is not a point of morality; but most people, especially people who think they base their morality on the Bible, disagree with this. So what happens is that those who are opposed to abortion and also think that all morality is found in the Bible, pick out certain passages that they then claim support their moral belief. Here is the most commonly cited such passage: "You put me together in my mother's womb. . . . When my bones were being formed, carefully put together in my mother's womb, you knew that I was there" (Psalm 139:13, 16). This passage neither mentions abortion nor says that it is wrong, so it may be unlikely that a person who had no prior opinion on the subject could learn that abortion is wrong from reading this passage.

What this indicates is that even Bible-believers seem to take some of their moral beliefs from outside of the Bible. When someone thinks that nail-biting is not a moral question, they do not think this because they have discovered that no commandment in the Bible prohibits nail-biting, but because they have already some conception of what is and is not immoral and expect the Bible to have a similar conception. When they find a passage in the Bible that could be interpreted to be against abortion, they so interpret it because they have, independently of the Bible, decided that abortion is wrong and expect to find their opinion confirmed somewhere in the Bible. They are not getting their moral belief from the Bible, but interpreting the Bible to agree with their moral belief. This is strong evidence that at least Christian religion is not a complete guide to morality.

Some people hold an oversimplified view about morality. They think that morality comes from a single source, when in fact it comes from many different sources, including perhaps some people's independent thinking. What they actually do is pick and choose from the moral ideas they find around them—a perfectly intelligent and legitimate method. But since they are so committed intellectually and emotionally to the idea that everything comes from their one favored source, they search the source trying to find something that supports their morality, and come up with all sorts of implausible interpretations.

It is not only Bible-believers who do this. In China, people used to comb through the *Sayings of Chairman Mao* expecting to find all wisdom contained therein. Communists everywhere used to search the works of Karl Marx and Friedreich Engels for answers to all of society's problems. Today, there are those who think that by "following nature" they will find solutions to life's problems or the cure to society's ills. But in fact, most people find in such sources only what they are looking for. They take what they like and ignore the rest. They are all pickers and choosers.

Let us turn to *correctness*. It is hard to imagine that anyone wants to defend the proposition that the law must necessarily be morally correct, since there always have been many laws that are far from moral. But what about religion? People do maintain that their religion could not be wrong in its moral teachings, and this is not illogical, since religious people believe that their religion comes from God, and God is infallible. But this argument might be somewhat circular, since if they had any question about the religion's moral teaching, they might doubt whether it did come from God, so a reason why they think that the religion comes from God might be that they think its moral teachings are correct. (There are many other such reasons—for example, miracles and prophecies.)

So if you have good grounds, independent of its moral teaching, for thinking that your religion is infallible, then it is not illogical to conclude that morality is unnecessary to determine whether the religion's ethical teachings are correct or not. Of course, once a person has such grounds, then in all consistency he or she will reject moral ideas that are incompatible with the religion and only follow what the religion says. Such a believer will be especially careful not to interpret ambiguous messages in terms of his or her own prior moral convictions, but to try to figure out the meaning of the message in its own terms. Hence, when the Old Testament warns us that adulterers must be put to death (Lev. 20:10), a believer will not attempt to rationalize away this rather stark commandment in the uneasy belief that God could not have meant it literally: the judgment that God could not have meant it literally is a reflection of one's own ethical standards, and shows that the believer, despite his or her religious convictions, wants the Bible's morality improved according to contemporary ethics. (Christian theologians point out that Jesus Christ taught his followers not to stone adulteresses [John 8:3–11], thus nullifying the Hebrew commandment. Since theologians hold both Old and New Testaments come from God, they evidently think the Unchanging God changed His mind, but why or even how He did so is obscure.)

What we conclude from this is that ethics can be made irrelevant only if one accepts the infallibility of religion. Apart from this, it cannot be maintained that either law or religion can substitute for ethics, because neither law nor religion are complete systems of right and wrong, and because unless they were infallible we would need morality to enable us to determine that they are correct. Any system, such as law or religion, that offers standards of right and wrong, must itself be judged by the standards of morality.

Challenges from Below

The third kind of challenge is the kind that unmasks morality, exposing it as being less important or less excellent than it seems. We call it "from below," as the challenge insists that the status of morality is too high, and ought to be reduced. The challenge from below alleges that there are certain erroneous assumptions made about morality, assumptions that make morality out to be better than it really is. Although these assumptions are widespread and comfortable, they are nonetheless illusions, it is said, and in the interest of truth and clear thinking should be identified and exposed, even at the cost of making morality seem less impressive than it is commonly thought to be.

In this book, we deal with two such assumptions from which, the proponents of the challenge from below claim, morality needs to be liberated. First, there is the assumption that *morality is universal.* This is the idea that there exist certain principles, call them universal moral truths, which are valid for everybody, regardless of culture, historical epoch, and so on. Everybody everywhere ought to live by these principles, it is thought; but the challenge denies that such principles exist.

The second common assumption is that morality includes, among its basic principles, or indeed as its most basic and fundamental principle, the idea of *altruism,* the duty to help your fellow humans. Looking out for other people, taking their interests into account, caring about what happens to them, wishing them well, even loving them as you would love yourself, are often regarded as not only essential to morality, but as what morality is all about; the whole point of morality, it can be said, is to call us away from concern with our own selves and toward concern with other people.

The theory that asserts that the first of these assumptions is an illusion is called **relativism.** This is the view that there are no universal moral truths, that all morality is relative to something. The theory that holds the second assumption to be an illusion is called **egoism.** This is the view that no one has any duty to care for or care about any other person, but that everyone is morally free (and in a stronger version, morally obligated) to put himself or herself ahead of everyone else. In the remainder of this chapter, we discuss relativism; we turn to egoism in Chapter Three.

THE IDEA OF UNIVERSAL MORAL TRUTHS

That there exist universal moral truths (UMTs) is to some people almost self-evident. Relativism, however, thinks it equally obvious that there are no UMTs. Those who hold that UMTs exist might admit that just what these truths are can be disputed, and that people disagree, sometimes strongly. "Do not commit adultery" and "Homosexuality is a sin" were once considered UMTs by practically everybody, but now perhaps are not by many people. It is the province of ethics to debate these matters. Such debate may or may not lead to universal agreement about the UMTs, but when people do disagree, what they disagree about, according to the defenders of UMTs, is not whether there are any UMTs, but what the UMTs are.

What is a **universal moral truth?** It is a moral principle that is true for everyone, regardless of epoch, culture, religion, stage of civilization, or personal creed. It may therefore be formulated in the form of a universal proposition or commandment: "Nobody should tell a lie," "Everyone must honor his or her father and mother," and "It is wrong for anyone to return evil with evil" are obvious examples of UMTs because of the way they are stated. But any moral principle might be a UMT, no matter how it is stated. If, let us say, "Do not lie" is a moral principle, then it might be a UMT, because it might mean that it is wrong for anyone to lie.

Some defenders of UMTs think that universality is built into the structure of morality. They hold that nothing can be thought of as a moral principle unless it is also thought of as true for everybody. Principles that are not universal are not moral principles at all; they should be regarded as matters of local custom, folkways, mores, and so on. Whether or not to eat snails and frogs, as the French do but the Americans typically do not, is not itself a moral question, but rather one of taste, habit, and acculturation, precisely because there is no universal rule. But on questions of morality, it cannot be permissible for certain men to beat their wives, but not permissible for certain other men to do so: either wife-beating is wrong, or it is not, for everyone.

To hold that all moral principles are UMTs is to hold a stronger position than the one we are examining, which is that at least some moral principles are UMTs. But even the weaker position can be attacked. It might be acknowledged that ethics as conventionally understood does put forward principles that are allegedly true for everyone; some of the principles just mentioned are examples. But how can these so-called UMTs be known? Who is to say whether a given principle is or is not a UMT? Given that for almost any moral principle you can imagine, there are all sorts of people, indeed entire cultures, who do not accept it and regard it as invalid, how can any principle be true for everyone? To say that everyone should hold the same morality is as if one should say that everyone should eat the same food or live in the same style of house. These must and will be adapted to local needs, tastes, and understanding of what is good and bad. Furthermore, if there are UMTs, and they apply strictly to everyone, they would also seem to be eternal; and how can we say that any moral principle is good or valid literally forever? Morality depends on human thinking, which changes: what we take to be moral truths one day, may not be moral truths the next. Is it not a kind of arrogance on the part of defenders of UMTs to claim that nonetheless certain principles apply to everyone?

Let us clarify two points.

1.   Some people perhaps oppose UMTs because they fail to distinguish between a principle *applying to* everyone, and a principle *being accepted by* everyone. A principle applies to you if it ought to control your behavior; it is accepted by you only if you acknowledge that it ought to control your behavior and act accordingly. This distinction is evident with regard to laws: the law that no one may sell, purchase, or consume certain well-known substances applies to everyone, although some people don't accept it. The same could be true of moral principles. Maybe some people treat animals too roughly. They do not accept the principle "Do not abuse animals." But this hardly proves that the principle does not apply to them: they ought to obey the principle even if they do not accept it. A defender of UMTs says that UMTs are principles that apply to everyone, whether everyone accepts them or not. From this it follows that it is not a good argument against UMTs that most, or indeed all, moral principles in actual fact are not accepted by everyone. A UMT does not have to be accepted by everyone to apply to everyone.

Unless we could make this distinction between morality being applied and morality being accepted, morality would be toothless; in a sense it would have no point. For if the only moral principles that applied to anyone were those the person already accepted, there would be no point in telling someone to improve his or her morality; none of the principles he does not accept even apply to him, so his morality is already as good as it should be. To say that morality would be toothless is just to say that if morality is to have any bite, that is, if it is to be used to criticize people's actual moral opinions, it must be possible to apply principles to them which they do not in fact accept.

2.   It is important to distinguish the idea of a universal moral truth from that of an **absolute moral truth.** Unfortunately, the word "absolute" is often used to refer to what we are calling UMTs. This is a terminological question only, provided the conceptual distinction is not neglected. An "absolute rule," as we use the term, has no exceptions: it must always be followed. If "Do not lie" is an absolute rule, then no one is allowed to lie, no matter what the circumstances. For example, it would be wrong to lie even to save a life. But something can be a UMT without being absolute in this sense: UMTs can have exceptions. Thus, it might be a UMT that it is wrong to tell a lie except to save a life. To hold that this principle, with the built-in exception, is a UMT is to hold that it is wrong for everybody to tell a lie, except. . . . So the fact that a principle is universal does not mean that it cannot allow exceptions. Furthermore, the fact that a principle is said to be absolute does not necessarily imply that it is universal: someone might hold that there are absolute moral rules, but that they only apply to certain people, for example, to members of certain religions, or to people from some cultures but not others. Thus, "Do not work on the Sabbath" is an absolute rule, but only for members of certain religions: other people can do what they please on the Sabbath. Thus, we must distinguish between a principle that applies *to everyone* and a principle that applies *in all circumstances*. A universal principle applies to everyone; an absolute rule applies in all circumstances. Hence, if you think that there might be exceptions to any moral rule, then by our terminology you think that no moral rules are absolute; this does not commit you to holding that there are no UMTs.

Whether there are any UMTs is a question that shall concern us for the rest of this chapter. The strategy of the argument is this. Rather than examining directly the question whether there are UMTs, we shall argue indirectly by asking what would be the case if there are no UMTs? If moral principles are not universal, they must be relative. But relative to what? It would seem that they can be relative either to the individual, or to the culture. For what else is there that would cause moral principles to vary from place to place, age to age, or person to person? The view that morality is relative to individuals is called **subjectivism;** the view that morality is relative to cultures is called **cultural relativism** (CR). We shall see that there are two versions of the view that morality is relative to individuals: we call these simple subjectivism and sophisticated subjectivism. This gives us three theories to examine. Our strategy then is to argue that none of these three theories is terribly attractive. What this means is that the person who does not accept UMTs is forced to adopt an unattractive theory. Of course, this does not show that universalism (acceptance of UMTs) is better than the three alternatives: it is very difficult to measure theories and say which has the fewest defects. But our conclusion should at least make the antiuniversalist wonder whether universalism might not be such a bad theory after all.

Possible Views

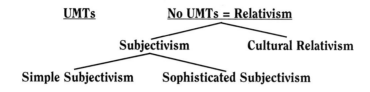

UMTs   No UMTs = Relativism

Subjectivism   Cultural Relativism

Simple Subjectivism   Sophisticated Subjectivism

Hence, the three relativistic views: simple subjectivism, sophisticated subjectivism, and cultural relativism.

SUBJECTIVISM

Opinions and Attitudes

There is a commonly held view that ethics is only "a matter of opinion." Ethics, it is said, is subjective; there is nothing else involved at all but what people happen to think. But what can this mean? An opinion is a belief you hold but can't prove. We contrast opinion with fact, which is something you know to be true. Although you can't prove your opinions, anyone holding one would want to support it with good reasons: no one would defend a mere opinion not based on some facts and data. When you have an opinion, you always suggest that there is more involved than mere opinion; there are facts as well. To say about some idea you have that "It's only my opinion" is a sort of lame concession that you don't really know much about the subject. To have an opinion about something implies that there is more to the question than what you think, and the view that ethics is "a matter of opinion" does not seem to support the view that there is nothing else to ethics but what people think.

So it is better to consider the view that there is nothing to ethics but what people think, understanding this by the word "opinion." We call this view **simple subjectivism** (SimpS). Despite its popularity, it is open to serious criticism.

1.   SimpS would seem to have a deleterious effect on morality. Ask someone who holds that ethics is only a matter of opinion whether murder, for example, is wrong. Presumably, he will tell you that he thinks so, but this is only his opinion; other people may have different opinions. So ask him what he thinks of the opinion of the murderer, who presumably does not think murder is wrong. If the subjectivist says that the murderer's opinion is wrong, then he evidently does not think ethics is only a matter of opinion, since some opinions can be wrong. But if he sticks to his philosophical guns and insists that the murderer's opinion is not

wrong, then ask him whether in his view there is some reason why the murderer should not murder. If there is no such reason, how can the subjectivist say to the murderer that he should not do so, or even complain against the murderer's murders? But if there is such a reason, then again ethics seems not to be a mere matter of opinion, but also to involve reasons why some things are wrong and others not wrong.

2.   SimpS cannot explain what is happening when two people disagree in their ethical opinions. Suppose Mary says, "In my opinion, casual sex is wrong," and suppose Harry replies, "Well, in my opinion, it isn't." What are they saying, if ethics is only a matter of opinion? Presumably, they are telling each other what their opinions are. But in that case, they have not stated a disagreement, for each has correctly reported what his and her opinion actually is. Neither Mary nor Harry disagrees with the other about what their opinions are: Harry accepts that Mary thinks that casual sex is wrong, and Mary accepts that Harry thinks it isn't. If you are a nonsubjectivist, you would want to say that they are disagreeing about something that is not an opinion, namely, whether casual sex is wrong or not. But this is exactly what the subjectivist cannot allow, since for subjectivism there isn't anything but opinions. So if they are not disagreeing about what their opinions are, and there is nothing else to disagree about, they are not disagreeing at all. But they are.

When Mary says something is wrong and Harry says it isn't, it seems that they are saying contradictory things, so that only one of their assertions can be true. If Harry is right, Mary is not, and vice versa. But if they are only telling each other what their opinions are, then assuming they are not lying, both of their assertions would be true. Harry is correct, since what he has said is in fact his opinion, and so is Mary for the same reason. But if both are correct, they cannot be disagreeing; when two people disagree, at least one must be incorrect. And further, suppose Harry should change his mind and on reflection he comes to decide that casual sex really is wrong. So can we now say, as one might expect, that Harry now thinks that he used to be mistaken? Not at all according to SimpS, because Harry knows that he really did formerly hold that opinion. Having changed his opinion, Harry cannot say now that what he used to say was wrong; he said it was his opinion and when he said it was, it was.

3.   SimpS cannot explain why people are interested in discussing morality. Normally, when we exchange opinions with someone we are talking about a subject that is interesting to both of us but which we may see from different points of view. In exchanging opinions, we hope to learn something about the subject. But if there is nothing but opinion, why bother exchanging opinions or discussing the subject at all? The only reason to do so would be if you are interested in the other person; otherwise, conversation in ethics would be totally pointless and would go like this:

Mary: In my opinion, casual sex is wrong.

Harry: Well, I hardly know you so I am not interested in your opinions.

End of conversation. And typically, of course, this is not the end of the conversation. Having stated their opinions, each person then goes on to argue by giving the reasons why they think their opinion is correct.

Most people, including many subjectivists, find these criticisms of SimpS fairly compelling. Therefore, they conclude that subjectivism either must be abandoned, or must be refined or improved in such a way that the criticisms can be met. However, neither of these alternatives is forced on us by logic: the SimpS-ist could stick to his guns and simply report all these conclusions as philosophical discoveries (philosophers who make "discoveries" typically are only announcing their willingness to believe the bizarre conclusions that follow from their premises). That is, if the SimpS-ist concluded that, as a matter of fact, people never do disagree about ethics but only think they do, then logic alone could not refute this position. Common sense tells us, however, that people do disagree about ethics, often vehemently. We would much prefer to find a theory that does not conclude that all that people are doing when they have a dispute about ethics is telling each other truly what their opinions are.

Antisubjectivists say that ethics is about fact or truth that people can disagree about; but subjectivists are not ready to abandon subjectivism quite so easily. Even if it is implausible to hold that ethics is merely opinion, it might still be the case that there is nothing else to ethics but subjective states of mind. These would not be opinions, however, but some other states of mind. Let us call them attitudes. Attitudes are postures of approval or disapproval. We then can have a revised version of subjectivism, which is going to hold that what there is at bottom in ethics is, not opinion, but *attitudes:* positive or negative stances that we take to various acts, ideas, and people. We are for some things, and against other things, in varying degrees of strength, and what we call ethics is simply a collection of these attitudes. An ethical utterance is not a statement of an opinion, but an expression of an attitude. We shall call this view **sophisticated subjectivism** (SophS), which we can define as the view that an ethical utterance is nothing but an expression of some attitude of the speaker.

Sophisticated Subjectivism

This theory, which is often called the "attitude theory of ethical language," was first stated forcefully in the late 1930s by the British philosopher A. J. Ayer, and developed into a fairly impressive view by several Americans, notably C. L. Stevenson and Paul Edwards.

The sophisticated version of subjectivism makes the following points.

1.   When people assert their ethical opinions, they are not really stating anything at all—in particular, they are not stating what their opinions are. Ethical utterances are not technically statements; there is no such thing (technically) as stating an ethical opinion, and ethical evaluations are not statements. When you

make an ethical judgment, you do not technically state anything. You are using language, but you are doing something else with it, something other than stating, saying, or telling people what your attitudes or opinions are.

2. If to utter an ethical opinion is not to state anything, what is it? To utter an ethical opinion is to express what your attitude is about something. It is to show your attitude, without saying that it is your attitude. The distinction between *stating* and *expressing* (or *showing)* is the heart of the difference between the two versions of subjectivism. With this distinction, the sophisticated subjectivist can argue that, though people do not disagree in their statements about ethics (since they do not make statements), they do disagree in their attitudes. Thus, Mary and Harry are not telling each other what their attitudes are about casual sex, and so are not each saying true things about themselves. Harry and Mary do disagree, but not in what they say; they disagree in their attitudes. Mary has a negative attitude toward casual sex, and Harry has a positive attitude. So the common-sense belief that people disagree about ethics is vindicated; people disagree in attitude.

The distinction between showing and stating may seem hard to grasp, but it is not in the least bit strange; we all recognize the difference between telling somebody what your attitude is, and showing that person what it is without actually telling. For example, suppose a student yawns in class, shuffles around a lot, and sneaks glances at her watch every few minutes. After class the professor says, "I'm afraid you're bored in this class." The student indignantly replies, "I never said I'm bored." And indeed, she did not: but she showed it by her actions. We may call attitude-revealing actions *gestures:* these may be involuntary or unconscious and include body language and facial expressions as well as certain intentional gestures, many not complimentary, which are too well-known to require description. Typically gestures are nonverbal, though we also have a repertoire of verbal and quasiverbal gestures. (A quasiverbal gesture is a noise we make that is not really a word: "Hooray" and "Ugh" are examples). Under verbal gestures, we include lots of celebrated expressions: "Go to hell," "O my god!" and "No kidding?" as well as others not mentionable in a philosophy text. None of these expressions actually states anything; they all express the speaker's state of mind ("Go to hell!" expresses anger, for instance; "O my god!" expresses dismay) without stating what that state of mind is.

The main claim of SophS is that our evaluative language (and this includes all other evaluations in addition to ethical ones, for example esthetic terms such as "beautiful" and "ugly") consists of verbal gestures that do not truly state anything. Whenever we make an evaluation, we are really showing what we feel without actually saying what that is. For example, if I say, "What a pig Sam is," do I mean Sam is literally a pig? No. Have I said anything about Sam's table manners, personal habits, or libidinous inclinations? No. Have I said anything about my own attitudes toward Sam? Again, no. What I said does not actually state anything, but it does show or express what I think about Sam, namely, that I disapprove rather intensely of certain of his habits and appetites that I find inappropriate, excessive, and unsuitable for display in front of civilized companions like myself.

We are used to thinking of ethical utterances as statements; our prephilosophical linguistic theorizing puts ethics on the side not of gestures but of typical factual statements such as "John is intelligent" or "John will get an A in philosophy." But SophS claims that ethical utterances are not statements at all, not even statements about the speaker's attitudes. If I say, "Murder is wrong," I am not telling you that I have a negative attitude toward murder, although I do; what I am doing is showing you what my attitude is. If I say, "Mother Teresa is a true saint," I am showing you what my attitude toward her is. My utterance is not a statement, even though it is a string of words that grammatically takes the form of a statement.

Once the distinction between stating and showing is understood, we can see how SophS copes with the problem of disagreement that overthrew SimpS. The simple theory had the consequence that people do not disagree when they engage in ethical debate; this seemed implausible. The sophisticated version avoids this by holding that people do not actually state anything, not even something about themselves, when they use ethical language; instead, they show what their attitudes are, and so they do disagree, but not in the sense of disagreement of which it must be the case that if two people disagree, one must be mistaken. Rather, they disagree in holding contrary attitudes. Their attitudes are inconsistent, yet neither is false because neither is stating anything, and only statements can be true or false.

3. Since people do disagree in attitude, there is something they can try to accomplish by expressing their attitudes. What you can try to accomplish is to change the attitude of the other person so that it becomes more like your attitude. By saying that casual sex is wrong, Mary is trying to change Harry's attitude to be something closer to her own. When people engage in disagreement about points in ethics, what each is trying to do is to change the other person's attitudes. The purpose of discussion in ethics is to bring the parties closer together, but not closer in belief, as common sense thinks, but closer in attitude.

4. Ethical terminology is designed to accomplish these attitude shifts by the emotive connotations attached to certain words. Ethical words like "good," "wicked," "fair," "unfair," "heroic," "kind," "sweet," "nasty," and so on carry strong emotive connotations, negative or positive. Nobody likes to be called by the negative labels, but we all want very much to be called by the positive ones. It is very wounding if someone calls us nasty, or a cheat, or unfair, and very rewarding if someone calls us trustworthy, or courageous, or honest. Thus, we will go to some lengths to avoid the first set, and attract the second, shaping our behavior and even changing our attitudes in accordance with the labels. The whole point of the use of ethical language is to get people to do this.

Because of its theory about the emotive connotations of ethical terms, SophS is sometimes called **emotivism** (as it was by Ayer himself). The theory, however, is not about emotions but about the emotive connotations of ethical words. No implication is suggested that in using ethical language people show or express their emotions; for instance, I can be very opposed to something, let us say, to racial prejudice, without getting emotional about it. I might become angry if I saw prejudice in operation, but my being opposed to it does not itself involve getting angry, only in holding a strong negative attitude. Hence, we avoid the term "emotivism" in favor of "sophisticated subjectivism."

A term coined by Stevenson to describe attitude shifters is "persuasive definition." A persuasive definition is a redefinition of a word so as to shift the attitude associated with it. An excellent example is the word "imperialism," which in the nineteenth century carried positive overtones to many Europeans because it had the connotation of bringing the advantages of advanced civilization to people in backward countries. Today, of course, the same word has a totally negative emotive force for practically everybody, since it has been "persuasively defined" to connote racial discrimination, suppression of liberty, interference with other cultures, and economic exploitation.

Someone once said that what matters is the name you succeed in imposing on the facts and not the facts themselves. The idea that language can be used to change attitudes is of the greatest interest, and the student ought to see how widespread the practice is. Seemingly innocent, neutral-sounding words can carry emotive charge and be used to produce changes in attitudes among the readers or listeners. Here is a quote from a letter to the editor in a local newspaper: "Recent revisions of the Clean Water Act will gut wetlands protection and put millions of acres up for grabs by private interests who will use these formerly protected lands for personal gain, as has been the usual procedure in the Reagan–Bush era." Note that this sentence contains no facts or pieces of information. If you think about it, it tells you nothing except perhaps (even this isn't stated) that, as a result of the revisions to the Act, some people will buy land and build things on it. But informing the reader is not the purpose of the sentence. The sentence uses emotionally charged words to convey the attitude of the writer and, more important, to make the reader feel that something terrible is about to happen: "gut," "millions of acres," "up for grabs," "private interests," "formerly protected," even "Reagan–Bush era," are all used (very successfully) to induce attitude changes in the reader: one can hardly go away from this sentence without feeling that something terrible is afoot.

Altering attitudes is what ethical language does. To call someone untrustworthy, dishonest, greedy, selfish, and so on is not only to express your own attitude but to try to produce a negative attitude on the part of other people, and indeed on the part of the person so characterized. Here are some examples of ethical language at work: "Clean your plate, it's a sin to waste food," says your mother; "Don't pick your nose in public, that's rude," says your father. What is going on here but the use of evaluative language to impose negative attitudes toward certain behavior? And, of course, positive words ("reliable," "hard-working," "conscientious," "fair" and "loving") do the same, in reverse: "You ate all your peas, you can be proud of yourself."

Unlike SimpS, SophS can explain why people bother to argue about ethics. People do so because it is important to them that other people share the same attitudes they have. For one thing, it makes it easier to live with people if you all share a lot of the same attitudes. But also, it seems to be a basic human trait to want people to hold the attitudes you hold. A person who feels strongly about something seems just naturally to want everyone else to have the same attitude. The fact that this is so important to each of us explains the intensity of many of our discussions about ethics. It is not that there is some great ethical truth that we want everyone to know and believe (as commonsense seems to imagine); SophS denies there is any ethical truth. What we want is that others share our attitudes.

And, therefore, the theory of SophS won't have a deleterious effect on morality (see the first criticism of SimpS). Why not? Because morality is about caring for things. So long as people care deeply about injustice, about the rights of other people, about honesty and decency and truthfulness, they will want other people to share these same attitudes and will have deep negative attitudes toward those who don't. We dislike murder and will continue to say, "Murderers are evil people and deserve severe punishment," so as to strengthen everybody's negative attitudes against murderers. We will not stop saying this just because of our philosophical theory that there is nothing to morality but our subjective states of mind. Or so the SophS argues.

Two Problems with Sophisticated Subjectivism

To criticize SophS, there is no need to deny that ethical beliefs express attitudes and ethical arguments are attempts to change people's attitudes. SophS holds that this is *all* that is involved in discussing morality or in holding moral beliefs. There are problems with this.

1.   Suppose I try to convince you that Jack, whom you rather admire, is someone you ought to dislike. Now suppose I happen to know that you do not particularly like Mexicans, and that Jack is in fact of Mexican descent. So I say to you, "You know, his name wasn't always Jack Richards; he used to be José Ricardo." Now suppose I thereby succeed in changing your attitude toward Jack from mildly positive to fairly negative. I have achieved my goal, but have I done so in a morally appropriate way? Not at all. But then there would seem to be more to moral discussion than simply changing attitudes; everything depends upon how the attitudes are changed. We can distinguish between appropriate and inappropriate ways of changing attitudes: we often use the terms "propaganda" or brainwashing" for those methods that are unacceptable, and "education" for the acceptable methods. Appeal to racial prejudice is an ethically improper method of changing attitudes. But SophS fails to make this most important distinction. It cannot make it, since according to its theory, to do so would be

only to express another attitude. But unless we could make this distinction, we could not have ethics at all, it would seem; all we would have is people trying to change each other's attitudes, by any means that worked. The most powerful or clever propagandist would win. Everyone would wind up adopting his attitudes, and there would be no way to say whether this is good or bad.

Today the public is deluged by attitude-changers. Corporations, government, politicians, sports teams, your own university, and just about everyone with enough money and something at stake employ large staffs of public relations people, image makers, "spin doctors," and others proficient in the art of creating favorable attitudes. We resent this just because what we want is to have favorable attitudes toward what is truly worthwhile, not toward just anything public relations experts massage us into liking. But if SophS is true this desire is misguided, since nothing is "truly worthwhile." To call something worthwhile is simply to express your attitude, perhaps built into you by attitude-changers. Propaganda would rule the world.

It may very well be the case that propaganda does rule the world. This is clearest during times of stress such as war, when just about everyone winds up hating the enemy because the state's propaganda is so powerful. Ethical theory cannot keep this from happening (would that philosophy were as powerful as the government!), but ethical theory ought to provide a way to say that this is not necessarily a good thing. Subjectivism does not provide any such way.

2.   If moral beliefs are nothing but attitudes, is the subjectivist really in a position to have any moral convictions? Is it not at best a little strange to hold a moral belief while thinking that moral beliefs are nothing but attitudes? The reason for this is that moral beliefs have to be justified, and justification implies going beyond attitudes to something else. Suppose, for example, I am strongly in favor of sending aid to the world's starving peoples. Then I ask myself, "What's so good about doing that, anyway?" Being a subjectivist, I respond to myself, "Well, there's no reason really, I just happen to have a strong attitude about it." But if I did think that, sooner or later I would have to ask myself why I should hold that attitude rather than its opposite; after all, a person who is opposed to helping anybody ("We didn't put them into the mess they're in, so we don't have to help them get out of it") has an attitude too; why do I regard mine as more valid or morally better? It seems to be totally arbitrary. If there is nothing to ethics but attitudes, then no attitude can be any better than any other, so there is no reason to have one attitude rather than another, and so no way to hold any ethical position about anything.

SophS-ists reject this criticism. They think that ethics is a question of caring about things, and that they have as good a right to care about things as anybody else. This is certainly true. If the subjectivist cares about starving people, he will have a positive attitude toward helping them, and if he does not, then he will not. In this regard, he is in no worse position than anybody else. A person who cares about nothing would be cold and unfeeling, and the subjectivist has a strong attitude against being like that.

But in making this reply, the subjectivist seems to forget that in his view, ethics is not about feelings; ethics is about nothing but feelings. Hence, it does not do to say that ethics is a question of caring. Of course ethics is a question of caring, one might reply, and if you did not care about anything, you would be a poor excuse for a human being. But the question is whether ethics is about caring about just anything, or about caring about the things that one ought to care about. To hold an ethical position is not only to care, but to claim that what you care about is something worth caring about. And since the subjectivist holds that this claim itself is reduced to an attitude, it is difficult to see how he can hold ethical positions.

Whatever the strength of these points, they do not really amount to a refutation. Perhaps there really is no ethical truth, and everything is propaganda after all. Perhaps there is nothing that is really valuable, so anyone's ethical views are arbitrary preference. If that is what you think, you will adopt SophS. But if you think that there might be moral truth as well as propaganda and that some attitudes are morally better than others, subjectivism is not going to be your preferred ethical theory because you will want an ethical theory that at least tries to explain how this can be. Since most people believe that there are morally appropriate and morally inappropriate ways of changing attitudes, most people are not subjectivists.

However, subjectivism is a very resilient theory and some of the best philosophers are subjectivists, so we are not finished with the theory. We shall discuss it again in Chapter Five.

CULTURAL RELATIVISM

What Is Cultural Relativism?

The second relativistic challenge to ethics is cultural relativism. Some people will be surprised to see CR described as a challenge to ethics. They might think that moral principles are obviously relative to culture; or they might think that CR supports something that is highly ethical, which is respect for all cultures. Both these reasons for adopting CR need to be examined carefully.

Before setting out to examine CR, we should define it. We define CR as the view that morality necessarily depends on culture. Because morality depends on culture, there can be no UMTs, since cultures adopt the moral rules they consider best. And for the same reason, moral standards apply only to those cultures in which they are found. Therefore, for CR, morality operates just like law. For what is certainly true is that laws apply only to the country or state in which they are in force. If you are in Indiana, the law that applies to you is the law of Indiana; you are not governed by the laws of Michigan, or of China, which may be different. Exactly the same point is true of moral rules, according to CR.

We should take care to avoid two common misunderstandings about CR.

Confusion Between UMTs and Universal Values   It is sometimes argued against CR that there may be **universal values.** For example, every society regulates sex in some way, prohibits violence and murder, at least by some people (Aztec priests sacrificed young women to the gods, but Aztec young women were not allowed to sacrifice priests), defines property and makes rules about its use, or makes rules about who should do the necessary work. These values are therefore universal. They are accepted by every culture.

But CR does not deny that there are universal values. To see this, perform the following thought experiment. Imagine that through some catastrophe, every culture but one was destroyed. This would have the result that there would be universal values, in that every culture in the whole world (there is only one) would hold the same values. But it is obvious that CR is not refuted just because large numbers of people suddenly die. So it cannot be the case that CR holds that there cannot be universal values; for in our thought experiment there are universal values, but CR is not refuted. Therefore, CR must be saying something else.

What CR says is that there are no UMTs. UMTs do not depend on culture; they apply whether or not any culture says they do. But universal values do depend on culture; they apply only to the cultures that accept them, even if this happens to be all the cultures there are. Suppose all the countries in the world adopted the same set of laws. Even though laws became universal, they would still not be like UMTs, because they would be valid in each country only because each country says they are. Similarly, if every culture adopted the same set of moral rules, CR would maintain that the rules only apply to any given culture because the culture says they do. And should a culture change its mind, the rules would no longer apply. Hence universal values are not UMTs, and the existence of universal values does not refute CR.

Confusion Between Cultural Relativism and Social Determinism   Very often when someone is asked to explain or defend a moral opinion, that person says something like, "That's what my culture has taught me," or, "In our culture, we consider such a thing (wife-beating, for example) wrong." Here are two distinct things that should not be confused. **Social determinism** is the view that no one can think beyond the limits of his or her culture. According to this view, for example, the reason why white Southerners of pre–Civil War times supported slavery is that slavery was part of the morality of their culture and they could not understand or accept moral ideas, such as racial equality, that were contrary to the ideas instilled in them by their culture. This view may or may not be true, but it is not a view about ethics or morality as such, rather a view about how people think and where their ideas come from. In particular, it is a view that asserts the essential lack of creativity in the human mind: people simply mirror the beliefs found in their cultures, and have no possibility of thinking original thoughts or breaking away from what their cultures have taught them.

Social determinism can be described as the view that values are relative to culture, but it is not the same thing as CR. Confusion arises because CR is also often described as the view that values are relative to culture, which shows how important it is to pay attention to the descriptions you use. CR says nothing about how people think, and is entirely consistent with the possibility of people thinking any thoughts they want, whether brand-new original thoughts or thoughts borrowed from cultures other than their own. CR holds the different theory that moral principles apply only to the members of the culture in which they are found. This could be true even if social determinism is not true; and furthermore, social determinism could be true even if CR is not true, though it might be a bit unfair for a social determinist to say that the white Southerners should not have supported slavery, even though they were incapable of understanding racial equality.

Let us now briefly turn to the arguments for CR; we recognize three.

Diversity   Because of cultural diversity, many people think it is just obvious that morality is relative to culture. Morality is a cultural product like the clothes we wear, the food we eat, and the language we speak. These are not universals; why should morality be universal? Virtually any moral principle you like has probably been rejected by some culture somewhere. Murder and cannibalism are considered wrong and indeed horrifying by us, but the pre-Columbian Americans not only practiced human sacrifice on an enormous scale (thousands were killed in a single ritual slaughter) but the priests ate the flesh of the victims, and did so thinking it was commanded by their gods. Given the wide disparities of practice and belief, how can there be any UMTs? CR seems consistent with the facts of cultural diversity, whereas "UMTs" seems an arbitrary hypothesis not supported by the evidence.

Respect   The CR-ist is anxious to combat twin moral evils, cultural chauvinism and cultural imperialism. These evils consist primarily in holding that one's own culture's values are superior to those of other cultures. What is lacking is respect for other people and their cultures. CR-ists think that what supports and fosters chauvinism and imperialism is the belief that there are UMTs. If UMTs are the philosophical evil that lie behind the moral evils, then it is better to adopt a philosophical theory in which there are no UMTs. Take away UMTs, and take away chauvinism and imperialism, CR-ists think.

A Sensible Middle Ground Between Subjectivism and UMTs   If you think that UMTs don't exist and that subjectivism, which seems to allow each person to adopt whatever morality he or she prefers, would be unworkably anarchistic, CR might seem to be right in the middle. It seems to allow for common rules or standards in a society, without going overboard and making these commonalities into universals.

Problems with Cultural Relativism

Although CR is often regarded as just about self-evident by those who hold it, it is not without its difficulties. It forces you to make uncomfortable moral choices, seems to support majority rule, and suffers from a logical problem as well.

Difficult Choices   Assume you are attracted to CR and try to test this attraction with a concrete example. There is a rather horrifying short story by Prosper

Merimée (the nineteenth-century French writer whose novel *Carmen* is the basis of the famous opera) about a peasant in the island of Corsica. In those days, the law of hospitality was strong; equally strong was distrust and dislike of governmental authority. Now this peasant, Mateo Falcone by name, is a man of some wealth and great repute in his neighborhood. One day when Falcone and his wife are both away, a bandit, Gianetto, comes running in, fleeing the militia. Gianetto asks Falcone's son, Fortunato, who is 11 years old, to help him; Fortunato hides him on the farm. Soon the squad of soldiers arrive. The wily lieutenant befriends Fortunato, plays with him, flatters him, and, noticing that Fortunato is admiring his gold watch, offers to give it to him if he will reveal Gianetto's hiding place. The temptation is too much for Fortunato, who betrays Gianetto. As the bandit is being led away, Falcone arrives; the bandit curses him: "Traitor!" No one has ever dared call Falcone such a name. He is shocked; he soon uncovers what has happened.

Falcone is stunned. "Is this truly my child?" he demands of his wife. "This child is the first of his family who has ever betrayed anyone." Falcone knows what he must do. The laws of hospitality cannot be denied; violators must be punished. He takes his son into the woods, tells him to say every prayer he knows, and kills him with a single shot.

This story ought to make the defender of CR just a bit uncomfortable. "Do not execute your child" would strike anyone as a pretty good candidate for a UMT. But in denying UMTs, CR seems to hold that there is nothing wrong with what Falcone did. He was following his culture's values, and if we, with our different values, find Falcone's act unacceptable, that is simply because our values are different from his. If, on the other hand, you are inclined to maintain that murder, and child murder at that, cannot be condoned because of cultural differences, then clearly you are not going to find CR a very attractive theory.

This story should demonstrate why many people are unhappy with CR, but it is far from a refutation. If you are an adherent of CR, you will not be convinced that what Falcone did was wrong. But what the story does demonstrate is that philosophical theories are not cost-free; the price you pay for adopting a theory is that you may have to abandon certain things you previously believed (unless you prefer to be illogical, but in that case you are abandoning logic). What must be given up if you adopt CR? Many people who are happy to give up both chauvinism and imperialism might find that CR forces them to abandon more than they expect. They will find that though they cannot say that Falcone was wrong to kill his child, they still must say that a twentieth-century nonpeasant in the same situation would be wrong to kill *his* child. They are thus abandoning the view that certain acts, such as child murder, are just wrong; what CR requires you to say instead is that whether an act is wrong depends on who is doing it. One right and wrong for Falcone, and another for François.

What would you want to say about the following little anecdote? In a certain city in Italy, let us suppose, there live many stray cats and numerous unemployed young men. The cats are hungry and the young men bored. For amusement, the young men sometimes take a little piece of food—hamburger meat, some bread—wrap in it a lighted firecracker, and toss it before a hungry cat. The cat swallows the firecracker in a single gulp, and the young men howl with gleeful laughter as the firecracker explodes in the cat's stomach, causing the animal to flee with pain down the street.

Readers of this book will doubtless find this story rather appalling, and will immediately want to make the universal judgment that nobody should do such a thing. "Do not torture animals" is another good candidate for a UMT. (Strangely, many people find the cat story more appalling than the Falcone story. Apparently, in our culture some people value animals more than children). But the CR-ist will realize that whatever other theories may say, CR is in no position to make such a judgment, for the young men have their own culture, and according to it, there is nothing wrong with this form of amusement. So CR forces a choice between itself, and at least some of the moral judgments we might be inclined to make.

But does it make sense to say that what someone did was wrong from our point of view, but not wrong from his own point of view? The CR-ist cannot give coherent moral advice to people from a different culture. Suppose Falcone comes to you for advice: "What should I do to this son of mine who has irredeemably stained my family's honor?"

You: Don't shoot him! That would be wrong!

F. *(who although a mere peasant has read philosophy):* Wrong for you, you mean. But is it wrong for me?

You *(remembering you're a CR-ist):* Oh right, not wrong for you. I guess you should shoot him then.

F. *(who's also very good at logic):* Hang on, you just told me that according to your way of thinking, it would be wrong. Now you're telling me I should do it. Can't you make up your mind?

You: I meant it would be wrong for me. It's not wrong for you.

F.: So you're advising me to do something you wouldn't do yourself?

You: Absolutely! I would never do such a thing. Shoot my own child? The very thought makes my skin crawl.

F.: I don't really understand how you can be so opposed to something and yet calmly tell me I ought to do it.

You: Well you see, I'm not opposed to doing it exactly. What I'm opposed to is my doing it, because of my culture.

F.: Now I'm even more confused. Doesn't your culture tell you that child killing is wrong?

You: Very definitely. Not only wrong, but horrifying.

F.: Well then how can you tell me to kill a child? Does your culture regard child killing as wrong or not?

You *(still gamely trying to both follow your culture and be a CR-ist):* Well, my culture tells me child-killing is wrong, but my philosophy tells me that what my culture says applies only to me, so I conclude that what my culture says doesn't apply to you.

F. *(who is really very good at logic, which probably explains both why he's rich and why he's respected):* So you admit that because you're a CR-ist, you're going against what your culture says! That doesn't make a lot of sense. I think maybe I'll go talk to the priest and see if he makes better sense than you do.

Notice that the problem here is not that the CR-ist can't advise Falcone, but that anything the CR-ist says is incoherent. If he tells Falcone to kill the child, he contradicts his morality; if he tells him not to kill the child, he contradicts CR.

Now consider what the CR-ist would say about the possibility of moral progress. Many Americans think that the United States is a less racist society than it was during the days when racial segregation was the norm in certain parts of the country: we think we have made some moral progress on the question of race. But CR cannot accept the idea of moral progress, since there are no standards by which to judge one stage or one era against another: there is change—the USA is less racist than it used to be—but not progress, for there is no way to say that the less racist stage is morally better than the more racist stage. This conclusion is a consequence of giving up the idea that cultures can be compared one against the other. But no one really wants to give up the idea that moral progress is possible.

Majority Rule   CR has some difficulties in explaining its key terms, for example, what is to count as a "culture" and what it means for a culture to "adopt" a set of rules or "determine" that the rules apply. In a culturally complex society such as the present-day United States, it is not clear what should be regarded as a single culture, or which culture is supposed to set the rules for anybody. Suppose someone grows up in a certain culture, but comes to reject its values (a Catholic who supports the right to abortion, for example). Does she have no right to reject some of the culture's values if she chooses? Does the legitimacy of her choice depend on whether she moves from a minority to a majority opinion? Or are we to say that this person is no longer a member of her original culture? None of these alternatives seems especially attractive. Here CR seems to deteriorate into the view that morality is decided by majority rule, and the minority must conform. Few CR-ists actually want to hold this, so you should not adopt CR until you can work out whether it can be avoided.

An Interesting Logical Problem   We have defined CR as the theory that moral standards necessarily depend on culture. Why include the word "necessarily" in the definition? This will make it clear that it isn't simply a matter of empirical fact that moral rules depend on culture. It doesn't just happen to be the case, given perhaps some interesting facts about human cultures, that moral rules depend on culture; for what facts, cultural or otherwise, could make this the case? Are there some facts that, if they were different, would have the effect that moral rules would not depend on culture? No; CR holds that there cannot be a moral rule that does not depend on culture, because of what moral rules are. A moral rule that does not depend on culture is impossible. (This is not to say that it is conceptually impossible, which is stronger. The expression "X is wrong" does not mean "X is wrong for some culture C," since the concept of UMTs does not seem unintelligible or self-contradictory: a person who knew that wife beating is the accepted norm in a certain culture, but who nonetheless held that husbands ought not to beat their wives, would not be contradicting himself.) This explains why, as noted above, CR would not be refuted even if there were only one culture with a single set of values. This would be an unprecedented fact in our world, but would not refute CR, because the presence or absence of any particular fact cannot refute a necessary truth.

But if the proposition that morality depends on culture is necessarily true, and thus not refutable by empirical evidence, it follows that it is not confirmable by empirical evidence either. Hence, one of the most persuasive arguments for CR immediately vanishes: the facts of cultural diversity cannot have the slightest tendency to confirm CR. Empirical facts are strictly irrelevant to necessary truths. And it ought to be obvious that if CR would not be refuted if there were only one culture and a single morality, then it cannot be confirmed by the fact that there is neither one culture nor a single morality.

In summary, there are difficulties with CR that are quite serious. If you adopt CR, you are going to be unable to make certain moral judgments you might otherwise want to make; you will at best be flirting with majority rules or social conformism ethics; and the best evidence for your theory will turn out to be worthless. These are not difficulties to be put aside lightly; yet they are not refutations either. Before coming to a full accounting of the theory, we must examine the claim that CR supports respect.

The Argument from Respect

Some people will think that the argument from respect is by itself important enough to merit adoption of CR. Let us examine this more carefully. We are urged to respect other peoples' cultures and to shun chauvinism and imperialism. **Cultural chauvinism** is the view, or perhaps the attitude, that my culture is superior to that of other peoples. Cultural chauvinists hold that in important matters, for example in social organization, or material wealth, their culture is better or best. They hold this about their culture's morality as well. They like to think that their own culture's ideas are more advanced and more civilized. But there are many people who feel uncomfortable with these attitudes of superiority, and to them, CR seems to offer a moral theory that rejects chauvinism. For CR seems to make out that all cultures are equal: the standards that a culture holds are its standards, and that is all there is to say about it.

Cultural imperialism is the next step after chauvinism. If our morality is superior, then we have the right, even the moral duty, to suppress the inferior morality of other people and impose our own: we do this to give to these inferiors the benefit of our greater moral wisdom. Thus, Christian missionaries attempted to suppress African customs that they found offensive: different sexual mores, little respect for personal privacy or property, a casual attitude toward time and work, and so on. Contemporary people are embarrassed with this form of imperialism, which they think is part and parcel of political and economic imperialism, and so look for a philosophical theory of morality that excludes it. CR seems to fill the bill.

We should make explicit exactly why CR seems to be the theory of choice for those who wish to reject both chauvinism and imperialism. The reason is that CR denies that there are UMTs. If there were UMTs, then it would be reasonable to suppose that some cultures had a better understanding than other cultures of what they were. Morality would be very much like science: some cultures (in fact, Western cultures) have a better grasp of scientific reasoning and scientific knowledge than other cultures. If there were such a superior understanding of morality, it would put a culture in a position to practice chauvinism and imperialism; it might even justify such practices. A culture that claimed to know such moral principles might even have a good reason for imposing the principles on other cultures, in order to bring them the benefit of superior morality. If all morality is relative to culture, however, then no culture can be in a position to say that it can benefit other cultures by bringing to them its superior knowledge of moral principles.

But is the attack CR launches against chauvinism and imperialism well-advised? It is not that the targets are ill-chosen—let us grant that we want an ethical theory that gives no comfort to these two evils—but that the means adopted may be unfit for the task at hand. Consider the following parable of the Vikings and the Farmers. The Farmers want nothing but to cultivate their fields, take in the harvest every fall, and live quietly all winter long enjoying the fruits of their labors. The Vikings, however, who live up the coast, spend all summer working on their ships; then in the fall after the Farmers have taken in their harvests, the Vikings sail down the coast, fall upon the farming villages, steal the food, rape the women, burn the houses, and kill all the men they can find. They then sail back up the coast to pass the winter eating the Farmers' stolen food and telling each other elaborate lies (called sagas) about what brave warriors they are.

If these two peoples were philosophically inclined, it ought to be clear who would be relativists and who universalists. For the Farmers believe in a UMT, namely, "Do not steal other people's property." What they want is that the Vikings adopt this moral principle. But the Vikings do not care a hoot whether the Farmers adopt the Vikings' principle (which, evidently, is something like, "Prey on those weaker than you"). As far as the Vikings are concerned, the Farmers can live by any principles they choose; all that the Vikings want (philosophically speaking) is that the Farmers do not impose their Farmers' principle on the Vikings. So in holding that there are no UMTs, CR seems to be stacking the deck against the Farmers. For if there are no UMTs, how can the Farmers complain if the Vikings violate the Farmers' moral principle?

It seems that CR, while purporting to be neutral among all moral views, actually stacks the deck in favor of some. Consider hunters and animal lovers. Which are CR-ists? Clearly, the animal lovers hold a UMT: "Nobody should kill animals for sport." And the hunters? They are perfectly content if the animal lovers read books and listen to music for enjoyment: the hunters are not pushing their moral principles on anyone. They would seem to be relativists: their thought is that if you think it's all right to hunt, you may do so; but if you don't think it's all right, why then, don't do it.

This is not merely a theoretical point. Listen to a representative of the Fur Council, an organization of fur coat manufacturers who, like the hunters, are under heavy fire from animal rights activists. "People who want to buy and wear fur are doing so. The protesters have made consumers aware of their point of view. It's a free society and the animal rights people and fur wearers have the right to do what they want." Notice how it is in the interests of furriers that the debate with animal lovers should be resolved on the level of philosophical theory, before any arguments are made specific to the moral issues. Is the CR-ist so certain that each side has the right to do what it wants? Though professing to be neutral, CR seems to give support to hunters, aggressors, and those who are indifferent to the rights of others; principles like "Don't kill" and "Respect other people's rights" seem to be UMTs. (Have you ever seen the button, "If you're opposed to abortion, don't have one!"? This button misses the point, which is that antiabortionists think "Don't have abortions" is a UMT. So CR is not even neutral on a moral question such as abortion.)

Hence, it is clear that CR cannot do the job it claims to do, averting both chauvinism and imperialism. The reason is that cultures in which chauvinism and imperialism are considered moral precepts (imagine a culture that says: "To spread our ideas all over the world is a great moral commandment") can only be countered by some principle that says this is wrong; and since this principle is not by definition going to be a principle accepted by that culture, it must be a principle that applies to that culture, even if the culture does not accept it. In other words, the principle, "Don't practice chauvinism and imperialism" must itself be a UMT that applies to all cultures.

This can be put as a neat little argument. Let us say that people in a culture have a moral reason not to do something, call it X, if there is a moral principle prohibiting X that applies to their culture. According to CR, a moral principle applies to a culture only if it is accepted by the people of that culture. So suppose culture A practices cultural imperialism; therefore, the people of A do not accept the principle "Do not practice cultural imperialism." Therefore the principle "Do not practice cultural imperialism" does not apply to them; and therefore, they have no moral reason why they should not practice cultural imperialism. So CR, which intends to combat imperialism and chauvinism, has the consequence that there is no moral reason why imperialistic and chauvinistic people should not be imperialistic and chauvinistic. Thus, CR turns startlingly into an argument supporting imperialism and chauvinism.

CR is mistaken in thinking that the way to combat such moral evils is to reject UMTs, for without UMTs there are no grounds for opposing the evils. But the CR-ist is in even worse difficulty than this. For CR is a terrible theory with which to oppose any cross-cultural evil. Suppose you know about a culture in which mutilation of children is the norm, or where children are sold as servants by their parents, or where women are routinely abused. CR prevents you from issuing any criticism of these practices. And notice how strong the CR prohibition is: it does not say that you should refrain from criticism of other peoples' business on grounds of humility and tolerance; this might be good moral advice. Instead, it says that you are philosophically incorrect in supposing that your moral values could apply to the other culture. So no matter how appalling these practices may seem to you, CR requires that you remember that your moral principles apply only to your own culture and bite your tongue. In other words, CR imposes moral paralysis; it renders us mute on all matters pertaining to other cultures.

Nowadays we believe in universal human rights. What are they? They are the values of Western culture applied to everybody: for Westerners think that everybody has the right to be free from oppression, discrimination, ethnic and religious intolerance, and so on. How can the CR-ist possibly accept such a notion? Women in some cultures are required to walk several steps behind their husbands; our idea of universal rights tells us that nobody should be subject to such demeaning treatment. Are we making a moral and philosophical mistake in taking this view? CR would seem to require us to think so. Try holding CR and meeting this challenge: how do you avoid concluding that universal human rights, like any other universal moral ideal, is just another cultural principle, and a Western one at that, imposed on cultures where it does not belong?

Finally, an ironic sidelight of CR is that, if it were logically consistent, CR would also prevent us from using the values of other cultures to criticize our own culture. We might point out, for example, that people in some other culture seem less intense, more relaxed, carefree, warmer, and friendlier than we are. Irrelevant, says the logical CR-ist, those are their values: we value success, competition, and ambition at all costs. Their values apply to them, not to us.

So what would one have to say to combat chauvinism? If you are going to reject certain chauvinistic practices, then what you have to do is argue that the principles behind these practices are not in fact UMTs. If you think, for example, it is wrong to suppress female seminudity in certain "primitive" cultures, then you should argue that "Women should not walk about bare-breasted" is not a UMT, although perhaps your culture thinks it is. In other words, it is necessary to ask substantive moral questions so as to arrive at the principles that might really be UMTs.

What Is True in Cultural Relativism?

Having said all this, what should be our final conclusion about CR? First, it must be emphasized that CR has not been refuted; all we have shown is that you cannot accept CR without paying the price of being unable to make judgments you would otherwise want to make. Some people conclude that CR is therefore morally crippling and leads to "moral quietism"; but even if this point is correct it does not show that CR is false. Second, nothing we have said shows that there are UMTs, still less which moral principles are UMTs. Third, we have not said that no moral principles are relative to culture, nor have we said that the principles held by our culture are the very ones that are the UMTs. Finally, despite its shortcomings, CR is a major theory that contains an important caution.

CR alerts us to the fact that people tend to regard their deepest feelings about conduct as UMTs. Take, for example, public modesty. How much flesh is it permissible to show in public? Consider this, written by a woman who grew up in late Victorian England: "One of our governesses, thinking to be very modern and dashing, once ordered a new skirt, which cleared the ground by quite two inches. But . . . she was too bashful to wear it . . . for ankles ought never to be seen and if they were, the lady they belonged to was not quite a nice lady." Now any European who went to sleep in the 1880s and did not awake for a hundred years would be morally shocked by contemporary standards of public decency. We, on the other hand, think we have liberated ourselves from Victorian repression and wonder how they survived all their clothes and all their decency. Is either principle a UMT? Probably not.

One harsh contemporary critic of CR, Bernard Williams, nonetheless holds that there is something true in CR, which he calls "the relativism of distance." It is simply the observation that some societies are so distant from us that the life of those societies is not a real option for anyone in our cultural situation. For example, no one today can truly expect, or even want, to live the life of a Teutonic Knight, or a Samurai warrior. There is simply no way of taking on the outlooks embodied in these societies. Some societies are so distant from ours that it is pointless to say that their moral rules apply to us, or that ours apply to them; to do otherwise is simply not to take these societies realistically. When there is distance, Williams says, we must adopt "the relativistic suspension of ethical judgment."

This view is allied with **moral isolationism,** which claims that we just cannot understand other cultures, especially distant ones (distance, of course, is defined neither spatially nor temporally—the ancient Greeks were very much like us in some ways—but culturally). We do not understand how other people thought, we do not understand their values, and we do not understand why they did the things they did. Therefore, we are in no position to judge them.

The claim that we cannot understand any culture that is different from ours is farfetched. We understand people from other cultures by reading about them, living among them, talking to them, and inviting them to live among us. But with cultures far distant and no longer extant, isolationism has a point. Even contemporary Japanese might have a hard time understanding their Samurai ancestors. However, the conclusion that we cannot judge them is exaggerated. Samurai warriors are said to have had the practice of testing their new swords on the heads of unfortunate non-Samurai passersby: that we are not in a position today to understand how this may have been accepted as their right does not prevent us from condemning the practice retroactively. To do so would be simply to affirm our own confidence in human rights.

Nonetheless, much of what we take to be UMTs may in fact be little more than our own local prejudices. Other peoples' social practices that do not accord with our own may simply be different practices, not violations of true UMTs. The relativist insists that defenders of UMTs have the burden of presenting some plausible theory of what counts as a UMT and what does not. In the absence of such a theory, the relativist is not going to be prevented from asserting that the belief in UMTs is nothing more than a cultural prejudice of our own.

REFERENCES AND FURTHER READING

Subjectivism

The classical statement of emotivism is by A. J. Ayer, *Language Truth and Logic* (New York: Dover, 1956; first published 1936), Ch. 6. Ayer's theory was developed into sophisticated subjectivism largely by C. L. Stevenson in *Ethics and Language* (New Haven, CT: Yale University Press, 1944). Stevenson's papers are collected in his book, *Facts and Values* (New Haven, CT: Yale University Press, 1963).

G. E. Moore gives the standard criticism of simple subjectivism in his *Ethics* (New York: Oxford University Press, 1912), Ch. 3.

A good introductory critical book is J. O. Urmson, *The Emotive Theory of Ethics* (London: Hutchinson, 1968). Brief but powerful criticisms are made by G. J. Warnock, *Contemporary Moral Philosophy* (New York: Macmillan, 1967), Ch. 3, and, more sympathetically and interestingly, by Mary Warnock, *Ethics Since 1900* (New York: Oxford University Press, 1966), Ch. 4.

A well-known critique is in Alasdair MacIntyre, *After Virtue,* 2nd ed. (South Bend, IN: University of Notre Dame Press, 1984), Chs. 2 and 3.

Cultural Relativism

Defenses of cultural relativism are found in Ruth Benedict, *Patterns of Culture* (Boston: Houghton Mifflin, 1934); William Graham Sumner, *Folkways* (New York: Dover, 1959; first published in 1906); and Melville Herskovits, *Cultural Anthropology* (New York: Knopf, 1955). Excerpts from Benedict are reprinted in Christina Sommers, *Right and Wrong* (San Diego: Harcourt Brace Jovanovich, 1986); and from Herskovits in Joel Feinberg, *Reason and Responsibility,* 7th ed. (Belmont, CA: Wadsworth, 1978).

Relativism is more often attacked than defended; a philosophical defense is found in an essay by Gilbert Harman originally published in the *Philosophical Review,* vol. 84 (1975), and reprinted in Michael Krausz and Jack W. Meiland, eds., *Relativism, Cognitive and Moral* (South Bend, IN: University of Notre Dame Press, 1982). Harman takes seriously the relativistic implications of social contract theory.

A partial and somewhat reluctant defense of relativism is found in Michael Walzer, *Spheres of Justice* (New York: Basic Books, 1983).

A standard though somewhat dated critique is in W. T. Stace, *The Concept of Morals* (New York: Macmillan, 1937).

Bernard Williams' chapters on the problem in his *Morality* (New York: Harper & Row, 1972), and especially in his *Ethics and the Limits of Philosophy* (London: Fontana, 1985), are superb.

There is an anthology, *Ethical Relativism,* edited by John Ladd (Belmont, CA: Wadsworth, 1973), which is actually about cultural relativism, not relativism generally.

The description of modesty in late Victorian England is from the delightful autobiography *Period Piece* (New York: Norton, 1952), p. 221, by Gwen Raverat, a granddaughter of Charles Darwin.

Chapter Three

Challenges to
Ethics: Egoism

I have no brother . . .
And this word "love," which greybeards call divine,
Be resident in men like one another,
And not in me! I am myself alone.

Henry VI, Part III, V, vi, 80

"What's in it for me?" Ask this question and you expose yourself as a paltry human being, someone who is not interested in anyone other than yourself. Its philosophical counterpart, however, "Why should anyone do something unless he gets some benefit in return?" poses a challenge to the conventional moral view, altruism, that people ought to concern themselves with the welfare of others. The view that says they should not is egoism, or selfishness theory.

It is important to distinguish two distinct theories: **psychological egoism** (PE) and **ethical egoism** (EE). PE holds that people *are* selfish; EE says it is *good* that people be selfish. Although it is perfectly possible (logically) to hold either theory without the other, it is natural for PE to be given as the basis of EE: if you are inclined to be selfish and want to give yourself permission to be so, you will naturally want to say that everyone is selfish anyway, so why not you? PE seems very much at odds with our ordinary experience of human motivation, as its proponents well know. They are taking what they themselves often perceive as a minority view of things, but not only does this not deter them, it confirms their view that they are, in the end, rather more clearheaded and honest than most people.

PSYCHOLOGICAL EGOISM

PE is the view that human motivation is essentially selfish. This means that people are basically self-interested, out for themselves, and never really concerned about the other fellow. "All society," asserted the greatest egoist philosopher,

Thomas Hobbes (1588–1679), "is either for gain, or for glory; that is, not so much for love of our fellow man, as for the love of ourselves." We do nothing for the other fellow, because we do not truly care for or about him; we only care about ourselves.

PE advances four arguments.

1. Apparently unselfish acts have selfish motivation. How can PE account for heroism, friendship, love, and even little things like going out of your way to assist a stranger? PE-ists such as Hobbes reply to these counterexamples that in such cases, the actor is really out for himself in some way: the hero expects glory, the person who does a small favor expects the reward of gratitude, and so on. No selfless act is really what it seems, since there is always a hidden motivation: what's in it for me? If you do someone a favor, you expect him to show gratitude; if he does not, you will regret having done the favor, and might be less willing to help the next person. Helping for helping's sake does not motivate anyone: what people want is some kind of reward or recognition.

2. People basically look out for themselves. Students try to get good grades, athletes to score the basket or the goal, lawyers to win cases, business people to make profits. We do not expect a student to help anyone to the extent that she sacrifices her own grades. Especially when the chips are down—when push comes to shove—people act in their own interest. They are basically selfish.

3. Any act is selfish if you get pleasure from it. Suppose a parent makes sacrifices to assure that his or her child receives a good education. When you love someone, you want to see that person prosper and flourish, and you want to do what you can to help him or her prosper and flourish, even at some expense to yourself. You get some pleasure from such sacrifices, and even more if your sacrifice succeeds and the loved one prospers as a result of your assistance. But the pleasure you get from helping other people is just as selfish as the pleasure you get from helping yourself. Pleasure is selfish no matter what causes you to enjoy it, just because pleasure is something you enjoy. Hence, even people who make sacrifices to help someone else are really selfish.

4. When people get pleasure from their apparently unselfish actions, it is this anticipated pleasure that is the reason why they do them: what the unselfish actor is really after is the pleasure that he gets from giving pleasure to another person. This is because no one ever does anything but for the pleasure expected from doing it (or to avoid the pain expected from not doing it). In modern jargon, we act to obtain rewards or positive reinforcement, or to avoid negative reinforcement. You learn which behavior brings you pleasure, and you repeat it; you learn which brings you pain, and you stop. Even when we do something disagreeable, like studying for a test, we do it because we anticipate that the pain of failing the test will be greater than the pain of studying for it. We are selfish just because we never really do anything other than to attain pleasure or avoid pain.

These arguments can be answered.

1.   PE seems to be wrong about the facts, in that everybody knows from experience that people sometimes, indeed often, do unselfish acts without expectation of reward. You see a homeless person so you give him the Big Mac you just bought. What's in it for you? You would like him to feel gratitude, but is his gratitude the reason you gave him the burger? No; the reason you did it is that you wanted to help, or you felt sorry for him. These are evidently not selfish reasons.

2.   Here PE seems to confuse being self-interested with being selfish. A self-interested person is not necessarily selfish; you are selfish only if you are indifferent to the well-being of other people. Suppose there are ten cookies and a child. If the child eats all the cookies, we might call her spoiled, but we would not call her selfish. But suppose there are ten cookies and three children. If Julia eats six of the cookies, she is selfish for not sharing. A student who studied a lot would be self-interested, but would not be selfish unless she did not care whether or not the other students succeeded and never helped anyone. Since a person who seeks to benefit herself is self-interested but not necessarily selfish, you cannot prove people are selfish by proving they are self-interested.

3.   This seems to be little more than a redefinition of the word "selfish." PE calls any act selfish provided the actor enjoys doing it. In ordinary thinking, however, an unselfish action is exactly an action in which someone gets pleasure from causing success, prosperity, or pleasure for another person. If I make you happy and so I am happy because you are, we would normally hold that my action is unselfish: that is what an unselfish action is. A person who enjoys getting lots of unselfish pleasure is an unselfish person. Now, PE does not deny that such actions, typically called unselfish, happen; it only denies they are unselfish. So PE and conventional thinking agree on all the facts, but only disagree on what to call them. They both agree that people do things without expecting any further benefit than the pleasure of helping people. Ordinary thinking calls these actions unselfish; PE calls them selfish.

Like any theory, PE is entitled to define its terms as it sees fit, but as a consequence of its unusual definition of selfish, the thought that underlies PE seems to have been sacrificed. For the thought behind PE was that people are pretty cold: self-serving, unfeeling, indifferent to others. With its new definition of selfish, PE has abandoned this underlying cynical point of view. Its thesis has become tame and not very interesting, for it now concedes that people do get pleasure from helping people and seeing others succeed, without any further self-interested motivation, but holds that for that very reason people may be said to be selfish. But there does not seem to be anything very shocking in selfishness that consists in getting pleasure from helping other people.

4. This argument is guilty of the fallacy known as putting the cart before the horse, a criticism made by the British cleric and philosopher Joseph Butler in the eighteenth century, who pointed out that if our goal were pleasure, we would

simply go out and get some pleasure; but this is impossible. Our goal has to be to perform some particular action that we want to do; only if we enjoy doing it will we get pleasure from it. In other words, if our goal is pleasure, we will not be able to get any; our goal must be some activity. When we do this activity, the pleasure will follow.

So if we didn't enjoy doing things for their own sake, we would not obtain any pleasure from them. Pleasure is the cart, interesting activity the horse. Since we must like the activity to get the pleasure, it can't be that we do the activity for the pleasure, and so it can't be our own pleasure that is the goal of our activities.

But isn't it true that we want to do only those activities we enjoy? People don't want to do things they find disagreeable. This is true, but this argument confuses a *necessary condition* of an action with *the end* of that action. Pleasure may be a necessary condition of action, in the sense that if we did not get pleasure from some activity we would soon stop doing it. But it does not follow that pleasure is our end in doing the activity, or that what we hope to get out of the activity is pleasure. What I hope to get out of studying for a test, for example, is a good grade. It is true that I like good grades, and no doubt if I did not, I would not study very much. But my goal in studying is the grade, not the pleasure it brings.

No doubt many of the things we do, we do for pleasure: when I am hiking in the woods, the pleasure of doing so is the goal of my activity, and the reason I do it is that I like it. But when I help a friend study, my goal is that he should pass the test, not that I should enjoy seeing him do so. The answer to the question, "Why did you help Freddy study math?" is so that he could pass the test. Even on the assumption that I would not have helped Freddy unless I enjoyed doing so, the reason I helped him was not to enjoy the pleasure of helping him, but so that he could pass.

But is the assumption correct that I would never do anything unless I anticipated pleasure (or avoidance of pain) from doing it? Experience seems to teach that expectation of pleasure is not a necessary condition of doing something, and neither is desire to avoid pain. Perhaps I did not in the least enjoy helping Freddy, and perhaps it would not have pained me all that much if he had failed the test. I just did it because he needed my help and I am basically a nice guy, with a few minutes of free time. So anticipation of pleasure does not seem to be even necessary. No doubt activities that do not please us are not those we would be likely to repeat too often; and of course activities we find positively painful we do not do unless we really have no choice. This is the most that has to be conceded to PE.

So PE's arguments turn out to be not very persuasive, and its cynical picture of human nature does not seem to be supported by facts or philosophical argument. But it is a useful theory to test a point about morality. For it is possible to argue hypothetically: suppose people were as selfish as PE says they are, what then? Could there be any hope for the possibility of ethics? Or does ethics have to postulate that people are not entirely selfish and go on from there? Hobbes argues that even selfish people would adopt ethics. Although he defends PE and thinks (incorrectly) that PE entails EE, his theory can be read as an attempt to develop an important thought: even if people were totally selfish, ethics would still be possible, for even totally selfish people have good reason to become ethical. Clearly, if ethics can be made secure even if people are selfish, think of how much more secure it would be if, in fact, they are not. How Hobbes and his contemporary followers try to demonstrate this move from selfishness to morality we shall examine later in this chapter.

THEORIES OF ETHICAL EGOISM

How Ethical Egoism Differs from Conventional Morality

We turn now to ethical egoism, the theory that holds that selfishness, and only selfishness, is morally good. So let us define EE as the view that says that the only morally good thing is to pursue your own interests. And to begin, EE may seem like a self-contradiction; how can something be ethical if it is also selfish? But to call the theory ethical is not to say that it is ethical in the sense of endorsing what is conventionally considered morally good, for clearly EE does not do this. Rather, EE is ethical in the sense of being a theory about what is ethical. EE holds that what is conventionally considered morally good, namely, to help other people, is not so; according to EE, the only thing that is really morally good is to help yourself.

Note that EE is not merely asserting that people have obligations to themselves. That people have such obligations is a part of many ethical theories. What EE is saying is that people do not have obligations to others. Their only obligations are to themselves. And this means that, from the moral point of view as EE sees it, you are free to be entirely indifferent to what happens to other people. Whatever you do should be entirely for yourself. You have no (moral) reason ever to help another person.

There are many EE theories, as we shall see, but each is quite different from conventional morality. To see this, we first note what conventional morality holds. Then we shall distinguish four EE theories and see how each differs from conventional morality.

Conventional morality holds:

CM 1: Altruism: Helping people is sometimes required.

CM 2 : Anti-immoralism: Harming people is prohibited.

CM 3: Altruism is allowed (this follows from CM 1).

Theories and Strategies

Actual EE-ists are fairly rare, at least among philosophers, so there are certain important distinctions that typically do not get made. These distinctions mark different possible versions of the theory. We shall explain two such distinctions;

combining these gives four distinct versions of EE. We shall also note two egoistic strategies. Anyone who is attracted to EE—and many people are, though not all of them are willing to admit it—has to decide which of the versions and strategies he or she prefers.

Strong or Weak Ethical Egoism?　　EE holds that because people have obligations only to themselves, there is nothing wrong with being selfish; but this can be taken in two ways. **Strong ethical egoism** says that is it positively wrong to be altruistic; **weak ethical egoism** does not go that far and says only that it is not required that we be altruistic. The difference is that the weak version says we do not have an obligation to help other people, while the strong version says that we do have an obligation not to help other people. In other words, the weak version makes helping people morally optional, whereas the strong version prohibits it. Most people who are EE-ists hold the weak version, since the strong version is pretty strong, at least compared to conventional morality, but it seems to have found its advocates—for example, Thrasymachus in Plato's *Republic* and the twentieth-century novelist-philosopher Ayn Rand.

Immoralism Versus Nonaltruism　　There is a distinction between harming people and not helping them. The **immoralist** is perfectly willing to harm people when it is in his interest to do so; the **nonaltruist** will not go that far, but will never help them unless it is in his interest to do so. For example, consider university students. Every student is to a certain extent in competition with every other student for the best grades. Now the nonaltruist opposes one student helping another student, for example by giving good advice or assisting in studying. But the immoralist goes further and argues that students may actually hinder each other, for example by giving deliberately bad advice, making studying difficult (perhaps by playing loud music in the dorms), deliberately hiding or mutilating library books, and so on.

Nonaltruistic EE is what is probably meant when people think about egoism. Its adherents believe that we need not go out of our way to help another person who might need our aid. They typically do not go so far as to hold also that we are free to do anything we consider in our own interest, even if it hinders the interests of others. (It should be pointed out that the distinction between harming and not-helping is a bit rough and in need of clarification, and is sometimes attacked.) The nonaltruist EE would not go out of his way to rescue a person who was in trouble; for example, who was drowning. But the nonaltruistic EE would not go so far as to put the person in trouble in the first place, by pushing him into the water. The immoralist EE, on the other hand, for whom the interests of another person are as nothing, would indeed commit murder, arson, or any other crime if he found it in his interest to do so. Though these examples are extreme, because most people have normal inhibitions that prevent them from even considering such crimes, in principle immoralism commits to such acts. In reality, immoralists of the more ordinary kind are willing to deceive, cheat, abuse confidences, and do whatever they think necessary to get ahead at the expense of the other person.

Now the combination of these two distinctions yields four possible EE theories: **strong nonaltruism** (SNa), **weak nonaltruism** (WNa) **strong immoralism** (SIm), and **weak immoralism** (WIm). Which of the four propositions of conventional morality are rejected by each of the four EE theories?

SNa rejects CM 1 and CM 3. It does not reject CM 2.

WNa rejects CM 1. It does not reject CM 2 or CM 3.

SIm rejects CM 1, CM 2, and CM 3.

WIm rejects CM 1 and 2. It does not reject CM 3.

The reader should work this out to be sure that it is correct. What it shows is that which EE theory you accept depends on exactly what part of conventional morality you reject. Of course, if you endorse all four propositions of conventional morality, you will not accept any version of EE, so you will not be an EE-ist.

Up to this point, we have distinguished four versions of EE. It is also worth noting that the EE-ist may adopt two distinct strategies, which we shall call intelligence and stupidity. The **stupid egoist** (SE) just refuses to help people; he thinks it is not worth his time and effort. He applies egoism directly to everything he does. But the **intelligent egoist** (IE) tries to develop a plan of action. The goal of the plan is to attain as much good for yourself as you can over a period of time, which may be your whole life if you think you can plan so much but might be only until the end of the year or until you graduate from college. Since the plan is aimed at producing as much good over a period of time, it permits us to do altruistic acts, for sometimes a little altruism in the short run can result in a big egoistic gain in the end. Hence, the IE cooperates with others and indeed sometimes acts just as if she were an altruist, and sacrifices some immediate, short-term interests to help someone else. (She misses her favorite TV program to help you study for your test next day.) But she always expects to get something back. However, this does not mean that she has extracted a promise from you to do something for her later. The IE treats her time as an investment that, if made wisely, will eventually bear fruit. Hers is the principle, you have to give something to get something.

Even when there is not much of a difference between how the IE acts and how the altruist acts, there is a great deal of difference in their motivation (and in their moral theories). The altruist wants other people to do well because she wants them to do well: presumably, this gives her pleasure. The IE is not interested in how well other people do, and does not care if they succeed or not. She helps them because it is in her interest to help them. The only person she wants to succeed is herself.

It may seem the IE must reject strong EE, since strong EE prohibits altruistic acts, and the IE is willing to do such acts if it suits her interests. To avoid this consequence, we should understand strong EE as prohibiting, not altruistic acts as such, but only altruistic acts done with altruistic motivation. Thus, strong EE says you may help someone, but only if you do so to help yourself. This is consistent with IE.

ARGUMENTS FOR ETHICAL EGOISM

As all forms of EE are quite inconsistent with conventional morality, one might expect that its proponents would offer pretty strong arguments in its defense. Unfortunately, they often do not make the distinctions we have drawn, so it is sometimes not clear what exactly is being defended (in fairness, the opponents of EE are often unclear about what they are attacking). Nevertheless, if we turn to the defense of EE, we are able to distinguish six arguments. We shall indicate (using the above system of abbreviations) which egoistic theories these arguments are most likely meant to support. The argument that appeals most to you will determine the egoistic theory you prefer. (If you do not like any egoistic theory, you should not like any of the following arguments.)

1. *Everyone would be better off.* Here the claim is that if everybody practiced egoism, we would all benefit in the end. How? Because people would be more self-reliant, more capable of thinking and acting for themselves, less willing to allow other people to solve their problems for them, and so on. An analogy is sometimes drawn between egoism and capitalism. Capitalism is the system embodying EE, it is said, because each person is expected to earn his or her own living, under penalty of being poor and having to do without things. Socialism, in contrast, embodies an ethic of altruism and reliance on others (the government) to provide the necessities of life. And it is clear, both from theory and experience, which is the better system, at least as far as economic growth and the overall standard of living is concerned. Some people may fall back and suffer under a self-reliance system, but most people wind up far better off than under socialism. Form of EE: SNa.

2. *Weak versus strong.* This argument is made by Thrasymachus in Book I of *The Republic* of Plato. He claims that there are weak people and strong ones; by nature, the strong wish to dominate the weak, and the weak must submit. However, the weak, being more numerous, conspire against the strong by inventing morality, which introduces notions such as justice and fairness, and which tells people not to try to dominate others. This morality is entirely constructed in the interests of the weak; it offers protection to them, but offers nothing to the strong except a mandate to suppress their natural superiority. Hence, those who wish to be strong will treat this morality with contempt. Although Thraysmachus does not actually say what the morality of the strong would be, presumably it is one of combat and conquest, that is, a morality that denies or is indifferent to the interests of anyone other than the strong themselves. Form of EE: SIm.

3. *Conventions of society.* This argument is also made in Plato's *Republic* (Book II), and has points in common with the second one. Glaucon and Adeimantus, two other characters in the dialogue (who were, in fact, brothers of Plato), put forth a view evidently well-known in the Athens of the time. This view holds that morality is a compromise invented by society. What each individual

wants, the view asserts, is to achieve his or her own good to the greatest extent possible. In effect, this means to triumph over those you oppose and to be able to defeat those who would triumph over you. To be in this position is the best one can want and have. However, if we all followed this principal desire, the consequence would be an unstable, even chaotic and warlike, society, in which each person advanced his or her own interests at the expense of everyone else. The consequence for any given individual might be that instead of achieving the best, he or she achieves the worst, which is just the opposite of the best, namely, not to be able to triumph over anyone but instead to be the victim of those who would defeat you. To avoid the worst, people invent a compromise in the form of a social contract: each of us agrees to renounce our desires for the best, and settle instead for a middle ground in which we live in a kind of rough concord with everyone else.

So the result is that if everyone followed his or her natural inclinations and aimed at the best, no one would ever help any one else (except as expediency dictated). This is what we much prefer. It is only out of fear of failure that anyone (reluctantly) adopts a morality that contains principles of altruism. Form of EE: WIm.

4.   *Resources for others.* This may be found in the writings of Ayn Rand (whose views also contain elements of the first argument). As she sees it, altruism requires that people turn themselves into resources for the well-being of other people; we must sacrifice our own interests to serve the interests of others. Rand finds this offensive: Why should *I* become a resource for *you?* Why can't I live my own life and be a resource only for myself? Although Rand seems to regard people who act as resources for others as contemptible weaklings, it is not clear whether she would prohibit such selflessness or merely hold that it is not required. What is clear is that she does not think selflessness is the least bit commendable. Form of EE: WNa or SNa.

5.   *Stand on your own two feet.* This argument is allied to the previous one: it holds that people ought to make their own way in life and not rely on the goodwill or services of others. The principle of life ought to be: sink or swim. People ought to be capable of achieving a good life by their own efforts; if they can't, if they fail or get into trouble, they cannot complain because they have only themselves to blame. Even a backup principle of altruism, according to this view, ought to be rejected. Suppose someone took the view that "sink or swim" is acceptable, but only to the point at which someone makes a good-faith effort to succeed; if he fails through no fault of his own, altruism can come into play. (This could be called the social safety net.) However, it might be countered, the existence of the backup altruistic principle would have the consequence that some people, knowing that real failure is precluded by the safety net, would not try as hard to succeed as they might otherwise: they would be subtly encouraged not to swim by the very fact that rescue is available. Therefore, if we are really serious that we want people to succeed by their own

efforts and not by the assistance of someone else, it is best not to accept the principle of backup altruism. Form of EE: SNa.

6. *The liberty argument.* Here the argument is that people should have as much freedom as possible. This means that they should be free of all moral obligations other than those that protect their freedom. Hence, we should be prohibited from physical violence, theft, deceit, and certain other actions that limit the freedom of others; but we should not be required to actively assist or help anyone else, because this restricts the freedom of the person on whom the obligation falls. But neither should morality forbid us from helping people, since that also limits our freedom: liberty means that I am free to adopt altruism as part of my moral code if I want to. Form of EE: WNa.

CAN ETHICAL EGOISM SUPPORT SOCIAL MORALITY?

EE is a personal morality, not a social morality; that is, it tells people how they should act, but does not tell society what rules it ought to have. Many EE-ists are not interested in this question; the EE-ists whose opinions were represented by Plato, for example (see the second and third arguments in the previous section), put forward a view explicitly in opposition to social rules. But some proponents of EE have argued that EE can provide a firm foundation for social morality. The leading philosopher of this group is Hobbes.

Social morality is the rules people require to live together in society; without such rules, in Hobbes' view, society would be impossible and human life barely tolerable. Hobbes imagines a condition, which he calls the State of Nature, in which there are no such rules, and everybody is forced to survive as best he or she can. Without rules, people would have no internal restraints, and everybody would simply take whatever they wanted, or do whatever they thought they could get away with. Everyone would in effect be at war against everyone else: "The war of everyone against everyone," Hobbes calls it, in which "force and fraud are . . . the two Cardinal virtues." But such a condition would be so grim that if people actually lived in it, they would soon enough be driven to construct a set of rules and agree to abide by them. Fear and necessity would persuade us to enter the social contract, that is, the rules of social morality by which we agree to live.

But what could motivate people to abide by the terms of the social contract? Altruistic theories rely on the higher motives, such as generosity, fellow feeling, a desire to see other people well off, or a wish that the world live in peace; but even if such sentiments exist (and Hobbes believes they do not exist), they may well be too weak and insufficiently widespread to support obedience to rules. Egoists think that it is self-interest, properly understood, that will provide the motivation where fellow feeling fails. To understand why, we must explain how the Hobbesean thinks the egoist should reason.

Earlier, in discussing the different kinds of EE, we introduced the character called the intelligent egoist, the person who looks out for long-range rather than short-range well-being. The Hobbesean egoist has a more advanced philosophy than does the IE. The IE has learned a basic rule: you have to give a little to get a little. Although she is indifferent to other people, since she has no fellow feelings whatever, she is not unwilling to help other people when she thinks there is something in it for her. She makes trade-offs, sacrificing a little present inconvenience in return for some payback that she hopes will come later.

The Hobbesean egoist is also indifferent to the interests of others, but her thinking and her actions are more altruistic than the IE's. This may seem paradoxical, but it is not. Consider an example: helping people in distress. Why should I go out of my way to help someone in trouble unless I stand to benefit in some way (maybe I will get a reward, or my picture will be in the papers)? The IE will help people in trouble, but only if she expects to get something out of it; either she will get a reward of some kind, or perhaps the person she helps will help her later, or perhaps other people might want to help her. She understands that by being altruistic, you cast your bread upon the waters; you never can tell what nice fish you might pull up.

But the IE has no conception of social rules, nor any idea of abiding by rules without the prospect of a reward. This is where the Hobbesean egoist is more advanced. This individual is so advanced in her thinking that she is often given the title, **enlightened egoist** (EnE). The EnE is the figure posited by Hobbeseans to explain how morality would be possible, even if people are as selfish as PE says they are. Unlike the IE, the EnE supports morality. For the IE has gotten only to the point of figuring out that in order to get, you must first give. But the EnE has decided that morality is so important to everyone, that she will support morality even when it is not in her direct interest to do so. The EnE argues as follows: we all benefit from social morality, myself equally with everyone else. But each person must do his or her part to make morality work. We might say that morality is like a wall; take away one brick and the wall will stand, but take away too many, and the whole structure collapses. Each person is only one of the bricks, but each person has an interest to ensure that the wall of morality does not collapse, and each person knows that if enough people act immorally, the wall will collapse. Now I am just one brick among many, so I cannot make the wall stand up all by myself, nor can I cause it to collapse; yet at the same time, I am one brick, and I have a part in maintaining that wall. Furthermore, it is impossible to know which one is the brick whose removal might be the one to cause the wall to fall; it might be me. Since it is not in my interest that the wall collapse, I must do my part and act morally, even when I might further my interest by acting immorally.

So the EnE helps people because she wants there to be a social rule, "Help people in distress." She wants people to follow this rule, whether or not they expect to benefit by doing so. Of course, her basic motivation is selfish: she wants this rule because she wants other people to be prepared to help her, not because she cares about helping them. She wants them to help her even if they might not anticipate getting a reward; she does not want to buy the help she needs, she wants it as a free gift. That people help each other only on condition that they anticipate getting something out of it is not really good enough to satisfy anyone. In other words, the EnE appreciates the virtue of generosity. And she knows that the best way to assure that people will be generous is to implant a rule in everybody's head: "Thou must willingly help those in need." She reasons that unless she obeys the rule herself and helps people even when she does not necessarily expect to gain by it, then it is that much less likely that the rule will ever be respected by others. Why should she expect them to follow the rule if she does not? She must do her part to support morality's wall.

The same kind of reasoning applies in situations of competition and conflict, such as Hobbes envisions. Why doesn't the egoist hide the books in the library after she has finished studying, so that other students will not do as well as she will on the test? Why doesn't she mutilate the books by slitting out the chapters she needs, since she doesn't care if anyone else studies them or not? The rule "Give in order to get," which defines the IE, might not take us very far here. "Once I am done studying, what good does it do me if the books remain available to everybody?" the IE might reason. "No one is going to reward me for not destroying them." Enlightenment is necessary to get to the next step. The EnE would realize that certain rules, which would be in everybody's interest, would be in her own interest as well. Here are some relevant rules: "Do not interfere with other people's work"; "Do not interfere with anyone's right to use and enjoy public property"; "Do not destroy property that does not belong to you." These are rules that might benefit the egoist herself someday; she would be better off living in a society in which these rules were respected rather than ignored. And so she will respect them herself.

So the EnE does not mutilate books because she knows that if too many people started mutilating books, she herself would not be able to study. She supports morality because it is in her own interest to do so. The EnE thus arrives at morality by a logical argument through consultation of her own interests alone. It is true that the egoist's motivation is not terribly commendable, from the point of view of conventional morality; according to our conventions, people ought to be moral because they are altruistic, or because they believe in morality for its own sake, or some such moral reason. Of course, PE holds that there are no such people, and certain EE-ists such as Hobbes himself start with PE, but that is not the point here. EE holds that it is better that we support morality for egoistic reasons than for altruistic ones. Because it is in the egoist's interest to support morality, her support is far stronger than that given by the mere altruist, who supports morality just because he is a nice person who does not want to hurt anyone and likes to play by the rules. This "nice guy" support for morality is unthinking, weak, and likely to collapse when something important is at stake. Or so the egoist argument goes.

This is not the whole story, at least as far as Hobbes is concerned. Hobbes worries that even the perception of self-interest will not be a strong enough motivator, because there are just too many temptations to violate the rules. The

EnE is, after all, an egoist, out for herself first and foremost; how can we be so sure that she will not hide those books after all? Fundamentally, people cannot be trusted to respond to any motivation, in Hobbes' view, other than fear. It is from fear that the rules are established in the first place, and only through fear that they will be obeyed. Hobbes does not trust people to act morally unless they are pretty sure they will be punished for acting immorally, and this means laws with teeth. Hence, strong government with strong power to enforce the law is an absolute prerequisite not only for social peace, but even for moral action, in his view.

ARGUMENTS AGAINST ETHICAL EGOISM

Many philosophers think that EE can be refuted, or at least shown to be a far from adequate moral theory. Since you cannot refute egoism simply by pointing out that it is immoral (since the theory admits it is immoral by conventional standards), philosophers like to claim either that it is illogical, that is, that it suffers from a self-contradiction, or that in some way it fails as a moral theory.

Let us now consider seven arguments against EE. Arguments 1–4 and 7 are directed against all versions of EE. Arguments 5 and 6 concern the Hobbesean attempt to derive morality from egoism.

1. *EE cannot be a kind of morality.* There are two reasons. One is that the whole point of morality is to provide rules by which we should restrain self-interest, whereas EE holds that self-interest should not be restrained. Therefore, EE is not a theory about morality. It does not matter that EE, at least in its intelligent and enlightened versions, does endorse restraints on self-interest; this does not meet the criticism because these restraints are only for strategic purposes, to augment ultimate or long-range self-interest. But morality, according to the criticism, is such that it might require sacrifice even of long-range self-interest. A person (the IE) whose life plan does not allow the possibility of sacrificing long-range self-interest is simply not moral, even if he does sacrifice immediate self-interest. But a person who does allow sacrifice of long-range self-interest cannot be an EE-ist.

The other reason is that morality is by definition based on nonselfish motivation: to act from selfish reasons is not to act morally, no matter how you act; therefore, even if EE might lead you to follow moral rules, it would not do so for moral reasons, and so is not a theory of morality. This criticism distinguishes motivation into selfish and nonselfish, and says that morality is about nonselfish motivation. Moralities may differ as to what conduct they impose, but any morality whatever must require that our motivation be nonselfish, at least sometimes. Since EE rejects nonselfish motivation, EE cannot be a kind of morality.

Both of these points rely on the ordinary conception of morality. But it is the ordinary conception of morality that egoism denies. Egoism holds that we should never sacrifice ultimate self-interest, and that our motivation should always be selfish. In holding these positions, egoism is aware that it goes against ordinary conceptions of morality; indeed, it regards this as a strength, since it thinks ordinary morality is false and insipid. Hence, it is not a criticism of EE to point out that it would not qualify as morality under our ordinary conceptions of morality. Egoism puts forward ideas about how we ought to think and act; whether you call this morality or not seems to be only a verbal question.

2. *EE cannot be publicly advocated.* It is said that a morality must be such that it must be capable of being publicly advocated, and who would advocate lying, cheating, or being indifferent to others? Someone might believe you and wind up cheating or being indifferent to you. So EE cannot be a morality. But this argument also seems verbal or conventional, and question-begging. If morality has to be something that can be publicly advocated, then EE is not a morality by that definition. But what difference does it make whether EE is called morality or not? This is hardly a reason not to hold EE.

3. *EE is self-contradictory.* The alleged contradiction is said to be this. What is the advice the egoist gives to two competitors? The EE-ist says to A, "You should defeat B." And he says to B, "You should defeat A." This seems to imply that the egoist wants A to defeat B, and wants B to defeat A, which is a contradiction (the contradiction is sometimes said to be that the egoist holds that A should win, and also that B should win).

This is also a poor criticism. The egoist gives exactly the same advice to both A and B. It is: do whatever you think necessary to win. Win, no matter what the (moral) price. The egoist is not saying that somebody in particular should win; he is just giving advice about how the game should be played. There is no contradiction in this, and there does not seem to be anything wrong with EE just from the point of view of logic.

4. Anyone who really acted according to EE principles *would not be very happy*, because no one would trust him, he would have no friends, and the price for whatever material success he may win would mean an impoverished personal life. All this is undoubtedly true, but it shows only that the EE-ist must be clever in applying his theory. In his own interest, he has to make an exception for the people he wants to befriend: they need to know that the EE will not apply his principles to them. If they are also EE-ists, and make the same exception, they can all get along quite well together, happily cheating everyone outside their circle. It may be said that this is implausible, because a person who is in the habit of dishonesty will be dishonest to everyone; but why should this be so? We all treat our friends differently from the way we treat strangers, and it is a kind of platitude that many a hard-driving businessman is a loving father and husband at home. "No honor among thieves" is simply not the case, at least if the thieves are philosophers who have thought out their situation carefully.

5. EE pretends to be an alternative to conventional morality, but is *only another route to conventional morality.* This criticism would be correct if it

were true that people who started out as EE-ists would support morality in the end, as the Hobbeseans argue. EE would then amount to a second motivation to be moral: if you are not motivated to be moral because you prefer morality, than you will be motivated to be moral because you prefer egoism. Moralists should welcome EE and not fear it, for it assures that morality will be supported by all thinking people: if they are altruists, they will support morality out of fellow feeling, and if they are egoists, they will support morality out of self-interest. So although EE presents itself as a daring and revolutionary alternative to morality, a thinking person's unmasking of moral pretenses as Thrasymachus and others see it, in the end the EE-ist comes weakly crawling back to morality by logical argument. Egoism itself proclaims that morality triumphs.

This criticism assumes that the argument about the EnE given in the last section is a good argument; hence it directly contradicts the following criticism.

6. *EE does not support morality.* This much more substantial criticism denies that EE really can support social morality. This is not a verbal question about whether we would call EE's principles morality, for EE itself admits, at least in its most philosophical formulations, that rules of social morality are good and necessary. The present criticism is that the argument presented in the last section about the EnE is unsound, because the EE would not, through logic, arrive at the position of the EnE. This creature is a logical myth, or at best an intermediate step toward a more permanent position, which would be not morality but immorality. Hence, if we are to have morality, we had better start with altruism.

Let us see this by an example. Suppose our EE owns a supermarket, a very competitive business with low profit margins in which survival depends on getting people into the store and turning over inventory. How would she compete? She would have low prices, put on specials, buy lots of advertising, keep her store neat and attractive, make sure the shelves were well-stocked, instruct her employees to be helpful and polite to the customers, and so on. So why would she not hire a bunch of tough guys to shop in the stores belonging to the competition and "accidentally" knock over the shelves, or stand around in the aisles and scowl at the customers and block the passages, or complain loudly at the checkout lines that the cashiers were overcharging them? We regard these methods as unfair; even in a competitive industry, we do not accept that anything goes, and society makes rules about what is permitted and what is not. Unfair tactics are those that do not benefit anybody but the perpetrators, and which would harm everybody, even those who practiced them, if they became widespread. But since our store owner is an EE, she is not concerned with fairness or harming anybody or even obeying the law (except that she doesn't want to get sued); if she is going to obey the rules, she will have to be convinced that otherwise she will be the one who suffers in the end.

This is what the EnE argument tries to do, but it does not succeed in doing it. The argument urges the EE-ist to take the point of view of society as a whole, but does not give her any sufficient reason why she should. It is quite true that, from the point of view of society as a whole, distinctions between what may and may not be done in pursuit of one's interests are necessary for the benefit of everyone. But this argument succeeds only if it makes no distinction between the point of view of society, and the point of view of any individual in society. Of course, any individual can take the social point of view and understand that a situation in which students mutilate books and supermarkets frighten away each other's customers would not benefit anyone. But if I have finished my studying and am after the best grade in the class, does not my individual point of view tell me that it is in my interest to hide the books? And if I am in the middle of a tough fight for customers, does not my interest tell me that I should do whatever it takes to triumph? What do I care for the point of view of society when I may be in danger of going out of business? Why should I take the social point of view if it is not in my interest to do so? So I will hire the toughs, and before my competitors realize what's happening I will have put them out of business.

We have attributed to the EnE the following reasoning: morality benefits everyone; therefore, immorality is not in anyone's interest; therefore, it is not in my interest; therefore, I will act morally. Unfortunately, this reasoning is not sound. It is not, strictly speaking, true that morality benefits everyone. What is true is that I benefit from the morality practiced by everyone else, just as they benefit from my morality. But (by definition of the problem) I do not benefit from my own morality, any more than anyone else benefits from his or her own morality. Hence, if everyone else practiced morality and I did not, I would benefit even more than if everyone, including me, practiced morality. Of course, everybody can say that, and if they did, there would be no morality; but why should the EE-ist care about that? Why should she not prefer that the rest of the world practice morality, leaving her free to be as immoral as she likes? This would be her first preference, just as the social contract argument (argument 3) for EE holds.

There are only two reasons one might have for practicing morality. Either you think it would not work to practice immorality, because you might get caught, or the rest of the world might follow your example into immorality; or you think it would be unfair not to do your part in upholding the system you rely on. But the second reason is not a self-interested reason, but a moral reason: it appeals to someone who wants to act fairly, and make the same sacrifices everyone else makes for the system that benefits everyone to succeed. Hence, it could not appeal to the EE-ist. The first reason does appeal to the EE-ist, but depends for its force on how likely the EnE-ist thinks these outcomes will be. In other words, the position of the EnE-ist degrades into that of a new character in our drama, the **superenlightened egoist** (SEE), who holds: act morally only if necessary to avoid getting caught, or to prevent others from following your example and abandoning morality. And this in turn depends on your immoral actions becoming known, for if no one knows that you are acting immorally, neither of the bad consequences feared will occur. So the EnE-ist, to whom we are attributing remarkable powers of logic, quickly becomes superenlightened, concluding: act immorally, but keep it secret (or, act immorally only when you can keep it secret).

This outcome of EE is often called the *free-rider problem.* Suppose several people keep house together. For the system to work, each must take turns at the housework; a fair person will not want to do less than his or her fair share of the work needed to keep the house running properly. But caring about fairness is a moral quality; a person who cared only about herself would prefer to be a parasite: "Let the rest of them do the work, I'll avoid as much of it as I can." To such a person there can be only two responses: either they will throw you out of the house, or if the others follow your example, no one will do any work and the place will be a slum. To which our superenlightened free-riding parasite answers, "Not if I can fool them into thinking I'm working."

The EnE's argument appealing to fairness will not work, but the EnE also has an argument appealing to logic. "You agree that 'Nobody gets a free ride' is a good rule," says the EnE to the SEE. "But you are no different from anyone else. If the rule applies to them, in all logical consistency it ought to apply to you." To this the SEE is going to reply, "You misunderstand why I think the rule is a good rule. I don't think it's good because it's good for society, although it may be good for society. Don't forget, I couldn't care less about other people. I think the rule is good because it's good for me. But it's only good for me if it applies to everybody else; the application of the rule to me is not good for me. So I am totally consistent."

We are likely to go round and round at this point, because the EnE wants to say that if you can try to free-ride, so can anybody else, and there goes the system. But either this is an argument based on fairness (if you have a right to free-ride, so does everyone else), and so not an appeal to self-interest; or it is an assessment of the likely outcomes. But the superenlightened egoist will not free-ride if she made that assessment; she only free-rides when she thinks no one will find out.

It is for precisely this reason that Hobbes says that strict enforcement of the rules is absolutely necessary if the system is to survive. But in this he is not quite correct. The system will survive provided most people obey the rules, even if they are not strictly enforced; most people do not commit murder even though we know that many murderers are not caught. But if the rules cannot be strictly enforced, an element of unfairness will creep in, in that some people will benefit from the restraints of others, without imposing comparable restraints on themselves. This is unfair, whether or not it is unstable. An ethical theory should explain why it is unfair, but EE has no principle by which this unfairness can be explained. EE's only principle is self-interest, and self-interest does not rule out parasitism.

7. EE puts its adherents in an *awkward position.* We have argued that egoistic reasons cannot be urged successfully in defense of the system of morality, and EE does not by a process of logic turn into its opposite. But this leads to a final argument. The EE's basic idea is that people should follow their own interests exclusively. But he has to admit that it is in his interest that other people be moral. Thus, he clearly cannot advocate his basic idea; if he did, people might believe him and act immorally. To follow his own interests, he must persuade

people not to follow their interests exclusively. This is awkward not because he must lie about his views, for his views allow him to lie when it is in his interest to do so, but because he is prohibited by his theory from defending the theory.

This recalls the public advocacy criticism, but with a difference. The fact that EE-ists cannot advocate their theory does not show the theory is mistaken, but does make it awkward for them to hold the theory, just because people who hold moral theories (like any other theories) like to advocate them; they want other people to believe the theory they favor. (Just listen to anyone argue about morality with someone who disagrees with him.) And the EE-ist finds that he has to give this up and tell people to act in ways he does not believe they ought to act.

This is not a contradiction in his view. It is perfectly consistent for him to *believe* that people ought to act immorally, yet *say* that they should be moral. Since the EE's theory is that everyone should act in their own interest, he must say that people should be moral, since talking is a form of acting and it is in his interest that people be moral. But he does not believe what he says and cannot (if he follows his own theory) say what he believes.

Another way of putting essentially the same problem is that the egoist does not want people to act as he thinks they should act. (He wants them to act morally, but thinks they should act selfishly.) But this odd consequence should not be blown up into a contradiction or logical error. It is possible even in everyday life not to want people to act as you think they should act: a lazy professor, for example, wants her students to do as little work as possible, but thinks they should do more. Of course, when you have a morality, you typically want people to act according to its principles; this is part of what is meant by saying that morality is supposed to be capable of being publicly advocated. But as we have seen, the immoralist must give up the pleasure of advocating his principles. This is a sacrifice he must make, but not a refutation of his theory.

From all this we conclude that critics have not succeeded in showing that egoism is in some way a mistaken theory. There is a price you have to pay to be an egoist: the risks of getting caught, the danger of antagonizing many people, and the necessity of silence about your true beliefs. But if you are willing to pay this price, it cannot be shown that you are making an error in reasoning. This is true even of immoralism, and since immoralism is a stronger theory than nonaltruism, if we cannot refute the first we cannot refute the second either. (This last point may seem strange, because ordinarily we say that what is stronger is easier to defend. But in logic, to say theory A is stronger than theory B is to say that if A is true, B must be true, but not the other way round. From this it follows that if you can refute B, you can also refute A, so that if you cannot refute A, you cannot refute B either.)

AN ASSESSMENT OF ETHICAL EGOISM

Because a theory cannot be refuted, it does not follow that we should adopt it: in philosophy, as in law, much depends on where the burden of proof lies. Where is the burden of proof with regard to EE? Since our ordinary beliefs regarding morality, fairness, generosity and such are fairly deep, EE would seem to have a considerable burden of proof to carry if it is going to persuade us. So let us return to the six arguments for EE and see how persuasive they may be.

1.   The first argument does not make EE itself a fundamental principle, but rather a means to an end. The opponent might argue that even if EE is correct in holding that universal selfishness is the best means to the end of greatest well-being for most people, it is too high a price to pay: helping others is itself so important morally that we should act accordingly, even if we lose some welfare in the end. But EE denies that helping others is of any value in itself, so this argument is a standoff.

2.   The "weak versus strong" argument does not sound very appealing to a contemporary person, since today we tend to be democratic and egalitarian and do not believe that there are weak and strong people by nature. (Apparently, so many Greeks in the fourth century B.C. did believe this that Plato considered it an important moral problem.) The difficulty of distinguishing between weak and strong, and of giving a definition of the strong, is brilliantly dissected by Socrates in Book I of Plato's *Republic*. But even if there are the strong and we could determine who are strong, it is clear that according to our own moral views the strong would have no special right to avoid ordinary morality. Because of our egalitarianism, we do not accept the proposition that the strong are by nature entitled to anything more than what the weak are entitled to. On the contrary, we would probably assign to the strong special obligations to help the weak.

3.   It should be clear from what has already been said that the argument about social conventions is a major argument and needs to be treated with respect. Plato devotes his major work to refuting it. Our long discussion of SEE was in effect a discussion of the third argument, but our conclusion was negative: the argument cannot be refuted. Egoists will give lip service to the social contract, but will never think they have a moral obligation to obey it, and will disobey it as their interests dictate. But this does not indicate necessarily that the third argument is convincing. Whether you find it convincing will depend on what you believe to be in a person's best interests. If you think it is in a person's best interests to achieve certain kinds of success, even by cheating and brutalizing others, then you will certainly see the point of the third argument even if you may not accept its conclusion that no one has an obligation to be moral. Plato thought the glitter of success was so alluring that he launched a major effort to prove that it is not in anyone's best interest to succeed no matter what the moral cost (we consider Plato's answer in Chapter Four). If you do not think that it is in a person's best interest to achieve success even when employing immoral means, then you must explain why it is not; if you cannot, you should at least be worried by the third argument.

4.   The "resource for others" argument supports nonaltruism and not immoralism: refraining from stealing and cheating would not seem to turn a

person into a resource for others. But even if an altruistic person does in a sense turn himself into a resource for others, it is not clear why a person should not have the right to do so if he or she wishes: maybe some people just prefer to be resources for others. And what exactly is it that is supposed to be wrong with being a resource for others? Note that the argument is not making the point that if people acted as resources for others, we would all be worse off in the end; this was the first argument for EE. What is being said is that being a resource for others is wrong in itself, apart from whether it leads to the best condition for anyone. But if you have already spent as much time or money on yourself as you need to, why not use some to help others? There does not seem to be anything attractive about spending vast sums of money to buy yourself trinkets while other people are starving. Finally, it might be asked whether being a resource for others is anything other than an unpleasant form of words: the reality behind the words is helping people, which does not sound like such a bad thing to do.

The attractive point behind the fourth argument is that someone who does become a resource for others simply disappears as a person, with no life of his or her own. Imagine a student who spends his time helping other students study, listening to their personal problems, taking messages for them when they are out, going to get them pizzas, and keeping them company on their study breaks. Such a person would be a pitiful figure, entirely at the disposition of others; he would seem to have no goals or projects of his own. To such a person we want to say: get a life! But this is just a common-sense argument that too much altruism may be too much of a good thing; it hardly convinces that one ought never act in a helpful manner.

5.   Similarly the "stand on your own two feet" argument contains an important kernel of truth, which seems to be wildly exaggerated. We can accept that independence, taking care of yourself, not being a burden to others, and so on are important character traits, without holding that people should never, or rarely, help anyone else. The argument against altruism seems to be that if people helped each other too much, they would come to rely on each other and not develop strength of mind. This may be true, but it hardly follows that people will lose their independence if they rely on each other to a certain degree: the best in life may be to strike a balance between helping yourself and relying on others. So even if we accept that standing on your own feet is good, we need not reject altruism, only put reasonable limits on it. There is also such a thing as helping people to stand on their own feet. It is not clear if the fifth argument would be opposed to at least this much altruism.

6. Finally, there is the "liberty" argument. The notion of maximum liberty needs to be clarified. If I am free not to rescue you when you are drowning, this may be liberty for me, but it is surely not liberty for you. It is not clear that there would be more rather than less liberty if we adopted the principle that people may ignore other people who are in need or in trouble. However, the central idea, that duties of assistance should not be considered mandatory but should be

voluntary, is admittedly an attractive one, if for no other reason than that it provides a basis for giving credit to those people who do decide to act generously (if you are required to be generous, it is not much credit to you when you are generous). And to a certain extent, perhaps to a very large extent, our ordinary morality does hold that generosity is a matter of charity, a kind of free gift, and not a matter of duty. (At the same time, our morality frowns on people whose generosity is insufficient, so perhaps we are a bit confused on this point.) Therefore, whether you find anything attractive about the sixth argument will probably depend on your prior thoughts about altruism. If you are inclined to believe that altruism should be a matter of a voluntary gift, then you will favor the sixth argument; but if not, it probably will not appeal to you.

We have now looked critically at arguments for and against EE. We have seen that EE cannot really be refuted, although its proponents must be prepared to make some uncomfortable sacrifices to maintain it. At the same time, we have seen that the arguments for EE are not terribly strong or convincing, so if the burden of proof is on EE, that burden has probably not been met adequately. In the end, no doubt, the strongest thing to be said about EE is what we said in the beginning, that a person holding this view would be regarded as a not very savory person, according to the principles most people accept. EE has not really given us any very good reason to change these principles.

A NOTE ON DETERMINISM

PE is not necessarily deterministic, but if it is true that people do not or even cannot form altruistic motives, then our options are much more limited than free-will theories would have us think. In any case, determinism is sometimes regarded as a challenge to ethics in its own right, so it may be useful to take note of it at this point. **Determinism** may be defined as the view that people do not have free will, which very roughly means that we are not really free to control our actions. Natural laws govern human beings as they do all other things. If an acorn grows into an oak tree rather than an elm, it is not because the acorn chooses to or decides to become an oak, but because given its internal constitution and certain external conditions such as sufficient rain, sunshine, and soil nutrients, natural laws determine what it will become. Similarly, natural laws and the conditions of our existence determine what human beings will become and how they will act; if a person decides to become a doctor rather than a hired killer, free will and choice have no more to do with it than with the acorn. A person is no more able to escape the power of natural law than is any other object in nature.

There are two questions about determinism: is it true? and, if it is true, does this mean that ethics is in some way fallacious or in need of reform? It is tempting, but imprudent, to react by saying that although ethics may be in need of reform, it is clearly not in need of the reform that determinism would require, so that if the answer to the second question is yes, the answer to the first must be no. This is not prudent, because it is possible that determinism is indeed true. It might be true even though it seems evident that absolutely everybody believes determinism is not true, at least not in their own case. The reason everybody believes determinism is not true in their own case is that it is impossible to understand how one would act if determinism were true. We cannot live without making choices: when you get up in the morning, you have to decide what to eat for breakfast (if you have gotten up, you have already decided not to stay in bed all day), and it is impossible to act other than under the assumption that what you decide is entirely up to you. Natural laws enter your decision as information ("If I eat bran flakes, I'll stay healthy and feel good all day") but not as governing factors (Imagine this: "Since I want to feel good all day, I'll just sit here and let the natural laws make me choose bran flakes." Having said this, what do you do now? Wait for the laws to make your arm reach out to the bran flakes box?).

Furthermore, everybody seems to know from their own experience that determinism is not true, at least if determinism is taken to mean that the decisions and choices we make are not the actual causes of our actions. For we do experience that what we do is within our own power, in the very simple sense that when we are presented with choices, we decide which choice to make. Sometimes this is not easy; we agonize over our choices, not knowing what to do, but when we finally make up our mind, we are certain beyond doubt that it is ourselves who have made the decision. We very easily could have made the alternative choice, but we did not. So real choice is possible; we experience it every day.

The difficulty is that determinism is very easy to believe about other people, and indeed about ourselves after we have done something. Determinism is a theoretical idea, not a practical one. This means that after someone has done something, you can try to explain why that person did what he or she did by invoking certain operative conditions and assumed natural laws. Thus, if you are a Freudian, you will explain someone's choice of bran flakes by noting something about her toilet training in infancy, or her feelings of guilt and low self-worth. What is most important is that you can apply these same ideas to yourself, to explain your own behavior, after you have done something: your own choice of bran flakes can be explained by the same operational causal factors. This can come as a revelation: "I thought I just liked bran flakes, but now I see that I like them because I think of myself as a rigid and uptight person who needs to be made looser," you say after your session with the psychoanalyst. The power of determinism is this: it always makes more sense to assume that a person's actions can be understood than that they "just happen, for no reason," and when you explain something, whether it be an action or a physical or biological event, you tend to explain it in terms of law-like generalities ("People who think of themselves in a certain way prefer bran flakes").

The other great strength of determinism is that it is difficult to explain what the alternative would be. If people do not do things according to natural laws, why do they do things? The free will position seems to rely on some kind of magic: people just decide to act one way rather than another. They do this by the power of free will they have. This sounds suspiciously like a cover-up; we evidently do not know what the causal principles are that control human action, but

rather than just admit our ignorance, we pretend we do know a noncausal principle, which we call free will. It sounds very much like a popular contemporary
explanation of evil: "The devil made me do it." If you ask a friend why she did
some particular thing and she answers, "No reason, I just did it," you are apt to
suspect that nonetheless there was a reason, but your friend may not know what
it was. "I just did it for no reason" sounds more like a dodge or a confession of
lack of self-understanding than an explanation of someone's action.

So when we agonize over a decision because we believe that we are presented
with real options between different actions, we may very well be under a bizarre
illusion. It could be—nothing in our experience of decision-making could rule
this out—that in fact the choice we made was made for us by the causal forces
acting upon us, and that our perception that another choice was possible was
just an illusion. It is a feature of illusions that they seem as real as reality itself.
(Consider some of the famous visual illusions, for example, the pool of water you
seem to see up ahead on a blacktop highway while you are driving in the summer. This looks so real that when you drive up to where you thought it was, you
often wonder where the water has gone.) For all our experience can discover, our
entire perception of freedom might be an illusion.

It is often pointed out, however, that there is a distinction between reasons
and causes. We explain the behavior of inanimate objects by causes ("Why did the
tree fall down? Because it was rotten inside and the wind blew"), but we explain
human actions by the reasons people have for doing things ("Why did you cut the
tree down?" "Because I wanted room to plant my vegetable garden"). A reason is
the explanation a person gives himself for his action. It is then suggested that
human freedom consists in our capacity to do things for reasons. To think of
yourself as acting for reasons is to think of yourself as acting freely. This point is
supported by the argument that the distinction between free and nonfree acts
depends on the distinction between things done for a reason and things not done
for a reason. You lie down because you are tired and want to take a nap (this is
your reason), but you fall down because you tripped; falling down is not something you do freely, because you do not do it for a reason.

This is an important point, but it is not clear that it proves as much as it is
said to. We can still ask why a person has the reasons he has. You lie down
because you are tired, but unless you are forced to lie down because you are so
tired that you cannot keep yourself awake (which would not be a free action), we
need to know why you choose to lie down rather than fight your fatigue and continue about your business? You may have a reason ("I've got nothing important
to do, so I might as well take a nap"), or you may not ("I just felt like a nap"), but
in either case sooner or later we will arrive at a point where you just wanted to
do something. There are generally other options available, and we choose the
option we prefer. If you were tired and had nothing important to do, why didn't
you watch TV or play a game? Because you didn't want to; you preferred to take a
nap. There was nothing on TV you wanted to watch, and games bore you.
Reasons seem to run out after a while as explanations of our actions; ultimately,
our preferences, tastes, ambitions, and so on seem to determine what we do, and

these are not reasons but the basis of reasons. (Your reason for working hard is that you want to succeed, but do you have a reason for wanting to succeed? No, you just do. That is the way you are.)

So if determinism seems to be difficult to avoid, does it threaten ethics? The worry here is that ethics depends on free will: if a person is not free, what is the point of preaching to him what to do? He will do what he must do, according to the laws of his nature. St. Francis preached to the birds, but he did not expect the birds to cast off their wicked ways and stop murdering worms. Neither should ethicists expect humans to cast off their wicked ways, if we are not free to do so but must act always from the laws of our nature. Ethics is supposed to work by persuasion, by showing people why certain actions (good) are preferable to other actions (evil), but if people no more act through moral sense and intelligence than animals do, then such appeals cannot work, and ethicists are only fooling themselves if they think they can persuade people to be good.

Further, ethics is said to have something to do with responsibility. This is a difficult idea, but we understand it well enough to see that if a person is not free to act, then she cannot be said to be responsible for what she does. "The devil made me do it" is a way of diverting responsibility; because I did not do it of my own free will, I am not to blame and cannot be held responsible. Children play this game all the time by blaming their actions on their friends ("Johnny told me to"). Adults do it too ("Congress caused the national debt"). The point of assigning responsibility is to evaluate merit and fault, but if no one is really responsible, then there can be neither fault nor merit and differential evaluations are impossible.

For this reason, determinism to many people seems like an appallingly easy way out for bad people. How often do you read in the newspapers about some murderer who pleads "temporary insanity" or "extreme emotional disturbance" or offers some other similar excuse for his acts? (Clever lawyers think up all sorts of brilliant excuses: "My client killed because he watched too many violent children's shows on TV," or "My client killed because he ate too much junk food and it affected his brain." These are from actual law cases.) If we accepted the general principle that people are not responsible for anything they did that could be explained by something that had previously happened to them, then if determinism is true, we could never have courts and justice at all, because everything you do can be explained by something that happened to you.

Determinists do not deny that ethics has its point: even if our behavior is determined, we are capable of altering behavior by changing the conditions that produce it, so it is important to know what behavior is good and what is bad. People act as they have been trained, therefore we want to train them to be kind and generous rather than to be murderers. (Determinists say that one problem with our society is that because we believe people are generous or murderous out of free will, we ignore the causes that make them what they are, preferring to preach futilely at them and then to punish them when they do not do what we want.) Even praise, blame, and punishment might have a point if it could be shown that these are effective ways of altering behavior. The reform in our ethical thinking comes from this: that if we accepted determinism, we would continue to praise, blame, reward, and punish, but not on any notion of "just deserts." For nobody can deserve anything if determinism is true. However, people think they do deserve rewards and punishment, and this false idea can be put to use to control their behavior. False ideas cause behavior just as effectively as true ones, perhaps more so. "Just deserts" would become a sort of socially useful fiction. Tell people that if they are kind and generous they are meritorious and deserve praise and affection, and they will become more kind and generous. This is not different than controlling their behavior by threats: convince someone that he will go to jail if he steals, and the fear you arouse in him will cause him to refrain from stealing. Convince him that if he gives money to the poor he is a noble fellow worthy of praise, and the pride and self-esteem you arouse in him will cause him to give the money. What you say to people affects their behavior just as much as what you do to them. Society uses its knowledge of psychology to control behavior and make people good.

There are many more things to be said about freedom, which is one of the great questions in metaphysics, but the relevant point here is this: there is almost certainly some acceptable definition of freedom that is entirely consistent with the principle that human actions are caused or determined. Therefore, the question whether determinism threatens ethics can be answered in the negative even if it is the case both that ethics depends on free will and determinism is true. This would be true if the sense of free will on which ethics depends is a sense that is consistent with determinism. There are many ways of making the case that this is correct. We shall end this section by sketching one of them.

Consider what we call willpower. What is willpower? It is the ability to overcome temptation in the name of some greater good. We have an opportunity to exercise willpower whenever we want very much to do something, but at the same time know that we should not do it. Your knowledge that you should not do it generates a certain desire not to; willpower is the ability we have to make this desire, the one supported by knowledge, to win out over the other. (Hence, willpower can be thought of as the ability to make some desire be stronger than it is.) If you have a strong will, your better judgment will win out and you will put aside the temptation. If your will is weak, however, you will do the bad action despite your knowledge that you should not.

Willpower is real, and appeals to willpower are certainly part of what ethics is all about. We know willpower is real, because we experience it every time we want to put extra butterscotch on our sundae. So to the extent that ethics requires us to exercise willpower, ethics is not threatened. Does this mean that determinism is false? No, because there might very well be a causal explanation why some person is able to exercise willpower while another is not. In fact, it would be a bit strange if there were no causal explanation; something must account for the fact that some people are strong-willed and others weak-willed. (It evidently makes no sense to imagine that a person could create a strong will simply by using free will to give himself a strong will. This seems as contradictory as bringing yourself into existence by deciding that you want to exist.) So willpower is the exercise of a freedom, but the ability to exercise that freedom has an explanation through natural laws. Determinism, free will, and ethics (at least the part of ethics that appeals to our willpower) are all compatible, so determinism, even if true, is no threat to ethics.

REFERENCES AND FURTHER READING

A good discussion of psychological egoism is found in James Rachels, *The Elements of Moral Philosophy,* 2nd ed. (New York: McGraw-Hill, 1986), Ch. 5.

Interesting essays on PE are found in Joel Feinberg's popular collection, *Reason and Responsibility,* especially the 7th ed. (Belmont, CA: Wadsworth, 1978).

Hobbes sketches his view in his masterwork, *Leviathan* (1651), of which there are several available editions. Selections from his various works are in Richard S. Peters, ed., *Body, Man and Citizen* (New York: Collier, 1962).

Robert G. Olsen, *The Morality of Self-interest* (New York: Harcourt Brace & World, 1965), is a defense of ethical egoism. A Hobbesean derivation of morality is defended by Kurt Baier, *The Moral Point of View* (Ithaca, NY: Cornell University Press, 1958).

Ayn Rand's books include *The Fountainhead,* (New York: Macmillan, 1943), *Atlas Shrugged,* (New York: Random House, 1957), and *Capitalism, The Unknown Ideal* (New York: Signet, 1967); her most philosophical work is *The Virtue of Selfishness* (New York: Signet, 1964).

A challenging defense of libertarianism is by Jan Narveson, *The Libertarian Idea* (Philadelphia: Temple University Press, 1988).

The wall metaphor is in David Hume, *An Enquiry Concerning The Principles of Morals* (1751), Appendix III.

Determinism

An excellent introductory treatment is found in Martin Curd, *Argument and Analysis* (St. Paul, MN: West, 1992). There are two books by Ted Honderich: a collection of essays, *Essays on Freedom of Action* (Boston: Routledge & Kegan Paul, 1978); and a comprehensive introductory text, *How Free Are You?* (New York: Oxford University Press, 1993).

Chapter Four

The Foundations
of Ethics

Whosoever heareth these sayings of mine, and doeth them, I will liken him unto a wise man, which built his house upon a rock. And the rain descended, and the floods came, and the winds blew, and beat upon that house, and it fell not, for it was founded upon a rock.
Matthew 8:24–27

WHY ETHICS IS SAID TO NEED A FOUNDATION

Reflecting, in 1637, on the knowledge of his day, René Descartes, in his *Discourse on Method,* compared the condition of mathematics with the moral writings of the ancient philosophers: "Above all I delighted in mathematics, because of the certainty and self-evidence of its reasonings, [but] I was surprised that nothing more exalted had been built upon such firm and solid foundations. On the other hand, I compared the moral writings of the ancient pagans to very proud and magnificent palaces built only on sand and mud." Now many people agree with Descartes that not only classical Greek and Roman moral philosophy, but ethics generally, rests on "sand and mud" and is badly in need of "firm and solid foundations." Mathematical ideas rest on proofs whose "certainty and self-evidence" can be demonstrated. Ethical ideas do not seem to rest on anything, which is why disputes in ethics appear to go round and round endlessly without reaching a conclusion.

Disputes about facts can usually be settled eventually by gathering evidence that sooner or later will persuade nearly everybody where the truth lies, but this often does not work in ethics. Suppose somebody nursed a grudge against her neighbor, and you wanted to convince her to forgive and forget. How would you persuade her that loving her neighbor is morally better than harboring grudges against her neighbor? Suppose you tell her she will feel a lot better about herself if she tries to forgive; she replies that hating this guy makes her feel fine, and she is very happy nursing her grudge. Or she might agree that she would probably feel better if she got over her grudge, but she says she has a moral reason for not doing so: "That man deserves to have someone hate him, and I am the one," she tells you. Try thinking of reasons why love is better than hate; they may be hard to find. You think carrying grudges is wrong, but your friend does not like her neighbor and wishes him ill, and there may not be much you can say to prove that she should not.

How can you be satisfied that your ethical ideas are good ones? This question raises the problem of justification in ethics. In this chapter, we study one general approach to that problem, **foundationalism.** The idea of foundationalism is this: ethical ideas can be justified by being derived from something that is not itself an ethical idea. Now people often wonder, "Where does ethics come from?" This sounds like a historical question, but people who ask this do not want to know how as a matter of historical fact ethical ideas originated, but what makes ethical ideas valid. They seem to think that ethics needs to be derived from something, which would then be regarded as its foundation. A foundation for ethics is thus some set of ideas, drawn from outside of ethics, which connects with ethics in such a way that ethics is justified because the foundational ideas are true.

What could serve as such a foundation? We consider three: religion, nature, and the self. Each answers the question, where does morality come from?—that is, what makes morality correct? (Some readers will think that morality comes from society, an idea we considered in the discussion of cultural relativism in Chapter Two.)

There are two basic points made by foundational theories. First, the foundational ideas are true. Second, the ethical idea is justified because the foundational idea is true. This second point is more interesting than the first. Take an example. People sometimes say that the first law of nature is self-defense. They think that nothing is more natural than to defend your own life, safety, property, and so on. And they think because it is so natural, it is also right to do so. But does anything become right because it is natural? Or consider religious ethics. Christian religion says, "Love your neighbor." One point to consider is whether religion is true in some sense. But even if it is, why is it good to love your neighbor, rather than hate your neighbor—because religion says it is good? These are the questions foundationalism has to answer.

It is desirable to examine briefly the terrain of justification in ethics. The question of justification is one of the more interesting aspects of ethical theory. There are other alternatives than foundational justifications or no justification at all. To make this clear, we shall briefly distinguish the following major groupings on the philosophical landscape.

1.   Some philosophers take the view that *ethics cannot be justified.* They reject not only foundational justifications, that is, the possibility of deriving ethics from something else, but any other kind of justification as well. As far as logic is concerned, people are therefore free to hold whatever principles they prefer; they cannot be condemned as ignorant, irrational, or mistaken. Some philosophers who take this view—and many who do not—see this lack of justification as a serous problem for ethics, but others do not. Among those who think the failure of justification is a serious problem are philosophers like Friedrich Nietzsche (1844–1900), who worried—or celebrated—that if God is dead, that is,

if there is no valid moral law, then all things are possible; and the existentialists, who think the lack of justification plunges honest people such as themselves into turmoil, anguish, and despair. Among those who do not see the lack of justification as a serious problem are the emotivists, who think that ethical discourse can go on even if ethical ideas cannot be defended; and the contemporary philosopher Richard Hare, who thinks that people can be relied on to choose decent moral principles they want so long as they are willing to apply their principles to themselves. Another group who also does not think that ethics can be justified thinks nonetheless that ethics can be explained, and that the explanation more or less serves the purpose—or at least some of the purpose—of justification, by making clear the role ethics plays in life, and why humans choose to behave ethically. The outstanding figure in this group is David Hume (1711–1776), whom we shall meet later in this chapter and again in Chapter Five. He has many contemporary followers.

2.   Other philosophers think that ethics stands on its own foundation, that is, it is *self-justifying.* They hold that the answer to the question "Why is such and such wrong?" is at bottom that it just is wrong, that everybody knows it is wrong, and that is the end of that. This idea is sometimes applied to particular principles such as not to lie or kill, but by other philosophers is applied only to certain basic ethical principles and not to derivative ones. The group known as intuitionists (we discuss this idea in Chapter Five and again briefly as the "no theory" theory in Chapter Nine) holds the first view; most of the utilitarians, including the great British utilitarians Jeremy Bentham (1748–1832), John Stuart Mill (1806–1873), Henry Sidgwick (1838–1900) and G. E. Moore (1873–1958), hold the latter. Mill, for example, says that you cannot really prove anything in ethics, but you can put forward certain "considerations" that are reasonable enough, and ought to convince just about everybody.

3.   Then there are those philosophers who think both that ethics needs justification and that justification is possible, but do *not agree that justification is derivation.* Their idea is that being ethical is being more logical or more rational than being unethical. These can again be distinguished into two groups. For the first group, there is an internal logic of "rational action" that distinguishes the ethical from the unethical. Immanuel Kant (1724–1804) is the outstanding example; he has many contemporary followers. For the second group, it is rational for people to form agreements and live up to them; ethics consists of the rules agreed to. This "contract theory" is found in Hobbes and also in John Locke (1632–1704); it also has many contemporary adherents.

4.   Those we study in this chapter favor *justification by derivation.* These are the foundationalists. Many great philosophers, including Plato and St. Thomas Aquinas, are among them. They claim that ethics can be derived from some foundation. We turn now to examine each of three supposed foundations of ethics, starting with religion.

RELIGION

Justifying One's Moral Beliefs by Appealing to Religion

Many people think ethics is founded on religion. And it is certainly true that many ethical beliefs people hold come from religion, either directly or indirectly. Some people seem to oppose abortion, for example, because their religion tells them it is wrong. The views of many people about marriage, extramarital sex, relations between parents and children, and no doubt many other topics come from what they have been taught by their religions.

Here we are interested in the idea that ethics is justified by religion. It is said that without religion there would be no reason to hold one belief rather than another, or to hold any ethical beliefs at all. Religion gives us our reasons to hold ethical beliefs, and explains why they are right.

It is important to be clear about the distinction between ethics *originating* in religion and ethics being *justified* by religion. When people explain their moral beliefs, they often say that they learned their morality from their parents, or from their religion, or (less frequently) from some teacher or other influential person. All this can very well be true: we derive our moral beliefs from many different sources, and parents, religion, friends, and school exert strong influence. But this answer to the question "Why do you believe that?" really explains how you came to believe that, but not why you continue to believe it. The fact that we may have picked up any given belief from a certain source is not in itself a reason to continue holding that belief. Maybe your parents happen to be bigots who are prejudiced against minorities, and maybe this fact explains some of your own prejudiced attitudes; but would you give this as a reason for continuing to be prejudiced? (You might explain your prejudices this way, if you have any, but you would likely reply that you are working on being more understanding of other people.) If you are going to continue to hold the moral beliefs that your parents taught you, you have to ask yourself, what reason do I have for thinking that the beliefs my parents taught me are correct, or are the best set of beliefs I might attain? It might be possible to give a good answer to this question (my parents have a lot of experience; my parents are very wise, and so on), but unless you can, then to continue to hold beliefs just because your parents taught them to you amounts to a willingness to let other people do your thinking for you. You are governed by the principle of inertia; once someone gives you the belief, you will hold it forever unless someone gives you a different one.

Now suppose your moral beliefs are founded on religion in the sense that you learned your beliefs from your religion. Your question now is, why should I continue to hold these beliefs? There are answers you might give to this: here are three, which we call affection, loyalty, and confidence.

Affection is the feeling that you have if you really like your religion and want to follow its teaching. Maybe you like the church services and the prayers, the rites and rituals, the special holidays; maybe you particularly like the people you meet. So you also come to like its moral teachings, since the morality is part of the package. Your feeling of affection toward the religion makes you feel that you support the morality as well. Or you might be *loyal* to your religion. You might want to be a good Catholic, for example, and you think a person who calls himself a good Catholic ought to support the Church's moral teaching. Even if you may have reservations about some points, you try to overcome these because you think it is your obligation as a loyal Church member. Third, you might have *confidence* in your religion: you think its leaders are pretty wise people, or that the religion is based on some unimpeachable source such as the Bible (which is itself supported by testimony and miracles, you imagine). So you reason that since you have confidence in the other parts of the religion, you ought to have confidence in its moral teaching as well. All these are reasons you might have for continuing to believe the morality your religion has taught you.

However, there is a problem with these reasons. None answers the question, "Is the morality of my religion really correct?" It is very difficult to hold a moral belief unless you think that belief is correct (in fact, it is impossible: try believing anything you think is not correct). So you now have to answer the question, "Is my church's teaching really right?" For example, is it really better to love my neighbor than to bear him a grudge? Suppose you ask yourself, why is it right? And if you are going to base your morality on your religion and continue to hold your moral beliefs because your religion tells you to hold them, then you are going to answer as follows. You will say that what makes something right is that your church says it is right. So the answer to the question "Why is it right to love my neighbor?" would simply be, "Because my church says I should love my neighbor." And "Why is it wrong to kill my neighbor?" Answer again: "Because my church says it is wrong."

But the reader will see that this is a very implausible answer. How can anything be right just because some human institution such as a church says it is right? It is not clear how any human institution can have the power to determine what is right and what is wrong: if a church can do so, why cannot some other institution, like the American Philosophical Association or the United States Congress? Most importantly, when an institution decides that something is right, it usually has reasons for its decision: it does not just decide, out of thin air. But if the church has a reason for saying that something is right, then the reason it is right, if it is, cannot be that the church says it is right; the reason must be the reason the church gives for saying so. (You may believe some theorem in geometry because your teacher once told it to you; but the reason that it is true is not that the teacher said so, but the proof that can be given.)

This is really a point about the concept of morality. Human institutions do not have the power to make anything right or wrong. If they did, they could change it, and how would they do that? By vote? Would it suddenly become wrong to love your neighbor if your church voted that it was wrong? There would have to be some reasons for their decisions, and then it would be the reasons that made it wrong, not the decision. So morality cannot be determined by the decisions of any human power, institution, or person.

Basing Morality on the Word of God

In fact, of course, no church simply declares anything to be wrong. A church always has a reason, and that reason is the word of God (no other reason would be a religious reason). We now turn to this. We shall skip over two obvious difficulties. The first is that it is questionable whether any church or person really knows what the word of God actually says, assuming that God exists and that God thinks about what humans ought to do. (Aristotle, who thought both that God exists and that God thinks—indeed, according to Aristotle, God *is* thought—also held that the only subject worthy of God's thinking is God Himself. In Aristotle's view, God thinks, but not about unworthy trivia such as how humans beings ought to act.) People believe that the word of God is found in the Bible, but it is unclear what grounds they have for holding that the Bible represents the word of God rather than the opinions of the authors of the Bible. (The argument that the Bible is the word of God because it says it is, or because of the miracles it recounts, is obviously circular, since we have only the Bible's word for it that these miracles ever took place.)

The second difficulty is that if morality is founded on God's word, then if God does not exist, morality is invalid. This point, though correct, is not going to impress those who believe that God does exist, so that to advance the discussion we shall simply assume we know both that God exists and what God teaches; let us say, the Ten Commandments. Some people think that these assumptions end the discussion, but in fact they only begin it. For there are two important claims to be examined: we ought to obey the Ten Commandments because God tells us to—that is, that God commands us to do something is sufficient reason to do it; and the Ten Commandments are ethical truths, just because God says they are—that is, God creates ethics by choosing to do so. Both propositions together constitute what is sometimes called the **divine command theory** of ethics.

God Says You Should   Presumably, many people think they ought to do things just because God has commanded them to do (or refrain from doing) them. Thus, Orthodox Jews and Muslims will not eat pork because it is written by God in the Bible and the Koran not to eat pork. Christians observe the Sabbath for the same reason. Other people cite the Ten Commandments as the reason not to commit adultery, or not to covet their neighbors' possessions. But why should we obey God?

Here are six possible reasons.

1.   One thing religious people say is that it is *blasphemous not to obey God*—or even to ask the question why we should obey. This, however, is not a reason but another way of saying that we should obey, since "blasphemous" means sinning by going against God. So the question becomes, "Why not be blasphemous?"

2.   Another thing often said is that if you do not obey, *God will punish you.* If He will, this is certainly a reason to obey Him; but is it a moral reason? To do

something merely out of fear of being punished seems to be neither a moral reason for doing it, nor the kind of reason God would want you to have, assuming God wants you to be moral; for if He does, then He must want you to do things, not because you are afraid of Him but because you think it is right to do them. In fact, it could be said that if your only reason to do something is fear of being punished, then from the moral point of view, you actually have a reason not to do it, since morality requires that we oppose those who threaten and coerce us.

3. and 4. Two other reasons given to obey God are that *God loves you* and *God created you.* Would you obey a person just because that person loved you? Your parents love you, presumably, but you do not necessarily obey them if you think they are wrong. It is supposed that God's love is greater and more perfect than any person's, which is a reasonable supposition, but how is it relevant here? That God loves you even with perfect love shows only that God's motivation toward you is favorable; it does not show that God knows any better than you do what's good, or what is good for you. Assume also that God not only loves you but created you (God created you because He loves you, according to theology); but why should you obey God just because God created you? Perhaps the reason is that we have a duty based on gratitude. But your parents also created you; this may give you a duty to respect them and even care for them (in both senses of the word), but no one thinks it puts you under an obligation to obey them.

5.   But perhaps we should obey God because *God is perfect.* This means that we should imitate God, trying to be perfect because He is perfect. God is said to be perfect in love, in justice, in mercy, and so on, and we should try to be so as well. There is nothing wrong with the idea that one way we learn is by imitating someone who is better than we are; and if the idea is to try to be perfect, then no doubt we should imitate someone who is perfect. Ted Williams was perhaps the most perfect baseball batter ever; if Ted Williams never swung at a pitch even an inch outside the strike zone, and strengthened his wrists by squeezing tennis balls for an hour every day, you might try these methods to perfect your hitting. So, if you believe that, for example, God loves everybody equally, even those who sin against Him, then you might try loving those who sin against you.

It might be said that this is slightly preposterous, since human beings cannot be perfect; but most ball players will never hit like Ted Williams, and imitating God may be an ideal to be aimed at (we could at least try to love sinners). A more important problem is the question, "Why should we want to be perfect?" If I do not care to be as good as Ted Williams, or to play baseball at all, then I would have no reason to squeeze those tennis balls. We cannot say that we ought to want to be perfect because God commands us to be perfect, since what we are trying to explain is why we should obey God's commands. The desirability of being perfect seems to be postulated by the argument rather than depending on God in any way. Thus, when Jesus says, "Be thou perfect, even as thy Father in Heaven is perfect," we have every right to ask him, why should the fact that my Father in Heaven is perfect mean that I ought to be perfect? Jesus cannot reply,

"You ought to imitate God because God is perfect," since that is the question we want answered. If there is some other reason for imitating God, it is not clear what it could be.

6.   Finally, it is said that we should obey God because *God knows what is right,* and we do not; in fact, it could be said (with some justice) that we cannot know what is right, unless God tells us, whereas God can know this, perhaps because He created right and wrong, or simply because He is God. There is no doubt that it makes sense to obey someone who knows something important that you do not know: we obey our doctors, who presumably know less about medicine than God knows about morality. So in a sense there is nothing intrinsically wrong with this argument. On the assumption that we can be confident that God really knows the difference between right and wrong, and we do not, it would be perfectly reasonable for us to obey God's commands. However, this argument has an important and unforeseen consequence: it conflicts with the other claim made by the divine command theory, that God creates morality, or that something is right just because God says it is right. For it is not clear how God can create morality and also know that morality is right.

Morality Is Created by God   This is the second claim of the divine command theory. Morality rests on the will of God, Who determines by His choice what is right. Thus, if the Ten Commandments are right, they are right because God determined that they should be right. This theory responds to the question already noted, "Where does morality come from?", by which is meant, "What makes it true?" It is thought, with considerable justification, that no merely human answer will suffice: if morality is established by society, or by some set of individuals, this would not really make it true; for how can human beings make anything true? Human beings can only discover what is already true. And if morality were established by some human agency (or, for that matter, by some natural agency), why should anybody who did not like what it required, obey it? Morality must therefore come from an agency greater than human beings (and greater also than nature), an agency endowed with both the power to create truths and the authority to make them binding. And there is no such agency other than God. (Any agency with these powers would *be* God.) The answer to the question "Where does morality come from?" must be God, because anything that came from some lesser agency just could not be morality, that is, could not be true and could not be binding.

As an illustration that morality depends on God's will, let us consider something that many religious people find to be quite important, forgiveness. Religious people point out that everyone needs to be forgiven for their sins. They say, quite reasonably, that unless you forgive those who have sinned against you, you cannot expect to be forgiven for your own sins. But this is not enough; they want to say that there is a connection between forgiveness and God. God wants you to forgive, and so He offers forgiveness to you, but only on condition that you repent, ask to be forgiven, and forgive others. The question is whether repentance and forgiveness are good things in themselves, or whether they are good because God wants you to do them. The religious view seems to be that forgiveness is a good thing because God forgives us and wants us to forgive others.

It may well be true that sinners want or perhaps need to be forgiven; God gives them this on condition that they first give the same thing to those who have sinned against them. So repentant sinners are forgiven by God even if not by the people they have injured, which must be gratifying to the religious believer. But that people want to be forgiven by somebody, and therefore have a reason to forgive others, is independent of anything God does. According to the religious view, sins against other people are also sins against God: you sin against God by disobeying His command not to sin against your fellow humans. However, this does not explain why it is morally better for God to forgive you than for God to roast you in hell. The answer is that God loves sinners, so He wants to give them what they need, provided they ask for it on His terms. But that raises another question: why is it better for God (and therefore us) to love repentant sinners than to hate them? Maybe it is better to bear grudges! The answer seems to be that it is better because that is the way God is. Repentance, forgiveness, and love are all good because they are made good by God, which is why they are good for us. This may mean that you should imitate God, or it may mean that it is good to forgive because God says it is, and God shows that He means it by, so to speak, practicing what He preaches. This is the argument that God creates morality.

The theory that God created morality must be very old, for Plato pointed out grave difficulties with it as early as the fourth century B.C. There are somewhat less interesting difficulties with which Plato did not trouble himself, but the reader should know what they are.

1. If God created morality, then *God could have made morality different,* indeed quite the opposite, from what He actually made it. Thus, God could have chosen to issue the anti–Ten Commandments, and if He had, it would be moral for us to commit adultery, desecrate the Sabbath, hate our parents, and murder and steal from each other. There is nothing logically wrong with holding this; however, some people think that murder, for example, is intrinsically wrong, so that nobody's saying so, not even God's, could make it right. The authors of the Bible seem to have been aware of this point, for it is illustrated in the story of Abraham preparing to sacrifice Isaac. The Bible itself evidently takes an ambiguous position on the question of whether God's commanding Abraham to kill his son makes it right for Abraham to do so: for just as Abraham is about to perform the sacrifice, God sends an angel to stop him (Gen. 21:1–14).

2. *Why should you obey God,* if God simply decides what's right and wrong? Why should God's decision be binding on you? (Suppose your friend decides that from now on it is wrong to chew gum. Why should that decision be binding on you?) We saw above that the only good answer to the question "Why obey God?" was the presumption that God knows better than we do. But now, we cannot say this, for there is nothing for God to know: things become right and wrong simply by His deciding, not by His knowing anything.

3.   If God simply decides what is right and wrong, *morality would be unintelligible.* For if God simply decides what is right, how can we understand why it is right? Using the divine command theory, the only reason that can be given for something being right is that God says it is. So why respect your parents? Because God says you should. Why not commit adultery? Because God says you should not. This repetition of the same reason becomes boring and pointless very quickly, and is unhelpful as an explanation. It will hardly satisfy anyone who wants to understand the difference between right and wrong.

4.   The problem that Plato points out is deeper than these. (You can read Plato's discussion in a wonderful dialogue called the *Euthyphro* about the meaning of religion.) Plato wonders if God Himself has any reasons for deciding which things are good and bad. With the divine command theory, *God cannot have any reasons:* God's will alone is the reason why some things are good and others bad. Plato thinks this view makes God out to be irrational, and thus unsuitable to God. God must have reasons why He makes some things good and others bad. But in that case, Plato notes, it is the reasons that determine what is good and bad, and not God's choice. God does not make things moral, He only knows which things already are moral.

This conclusion does not bother Plato, who is not committed to a Creator God, but who does believe in eternal moral truths. If the truths are eternal, God does not create them (nothing created is eternal), God simply knows what they are. (In fact, in Plato's cosmology, God does not actually create anything. What God does in bringing the world into existence is more like following a blueprint, or playing music: the music already exists, the player—God—simply realizes it.)

Plato's analysis of this problem is a major watershed in the history of theology. Either God has a reason for saying that killing is immoral, or He does not. If He has a reason, then what makes killing immoral is that reason: for example, if the reason that killing is immoral is that people have a right to life, then what makes killing immoral is that it violates the right to life. This is why killing is immoral; it is not immoral because God says it is. Hence, if God has a reason, then God is not the creator of right and wrong. If, on the other hand, God has no reason, then He can be said to be the creator of right and wrong; but He is also irrational and arbitrary, could have chosen differently than He did, and has not given us a reason to obey Him.

There is a response to this. The theologian might protest that the Plato-inspired argument misses the point. For what is true of God, just because He is God, is that He does have the power to make morality valid and binding on us, by a mere act of His will. God creates truth: because God says so, and for no other reason, $2 + 2 = 4$, yesterday precedes today, and the whole is equal to the sum of its parts. God's creative power really is unlimited: He creates truth by fiat, and He creates us to believe truth (like $2 + 2 = 4$) because it pleases Him to do so.

Now this argument is admittedly irrefutable: if you hold that God has the power simply to make it that you ought to obey His word, there does not seem to be any way to demonstrate that He does not. However, the irrefutability of the argument is an artifact of the fact that it is basically unintelligible: we cannot possibly understand what it might mean to have the power to make truths untrue, or to make it obligatory that we obey arbitrary commands. The theory rests on the use of words to which no meaning can be placed. That is a game which can be played, but no philosopher should be happy playing it.

NATURE

The theory that ethics must be founded on nature is possibly the oldest in the philosophical tradition. Greeks of the classical period (approximately the fifth and fourth centuries B.C.), including Plato and Aristotle, seem to have accepted the distinction between justice "by convention" and justice "by nature," and held that true justice must be by nature. Justice by convention was made up by human beings and was reflected in the laws of each country, which varied from place to place. Justice by nature, on the other hand, applied to all people alike and was the same everywhere, and is morally more compelling than mere human justice.

The classical Greeks disagreed, however, about what was just by nature. One well-known, if unpopular, theory, vigorously disputed by Plato, held that nature meant power and that what was just by nature was that the strong should rule (we have discussed this view in Chapter Three as an argument for ethical egoism). Later, the Stoics (primarily the third century B.C.) equated nature with law and reason, and taught that what was important was to live a life "according to nature." This they called wisdom. The Stoic theory, which, although enormously restrictive and disagreeable, is in its way quite interesting, and shows how flexible the concept of nature can be. By wisdom the Stoics seemed to mean the recognition that everything happens according to law, necessity, and the good; the wise person recognizes that things must be as they are, and attains happiness by learning to accept the necessities of things. Stripped of its metaphysical foundations about reason in nature, the Stoic view, if not carried to extremes, is good common sense; but the Stoics did carry it to extremes, arguing that the wise person will never want anything but what he or she can be certain of obtaining. This opinion leads to an acceptance of the status quo, a suppression of all desires except the most transparently attainable ones, and in general an unwillingness to put out effort to achieve anything difficult. However, the Stoics argued that what is truly difficult is not to attain your desires, but to master yourself so as not to desire what you cannot attain; thus, they stressed willpower and self-control as the ultimate goods. To the will they assigned the sole task of overcoming desire, holding, not implausibly, that the will is fortified in this task by the recognition that all human misery results from disappointed desires, so that the only certain way to avoid being miserable is not to desire anything in the first place. This attitude, which is inevitably encouraged by any philosophy emphasizing necessity or fate (the idea that things cannot be other than they will in fact be), may be wise or foolish, but despite the Stoic philosophy it is a far cry from anything that most people would regard as following nature; rather, it seems to be based on the possibility of denying nature by overcoming even the strongest natural impulses.

The Stoic transformation of nature into something very nearly its opposite should be taken as a warning to all those many people who seem attracted by such slogans as "Live naturally," "Live close to nature," "Follow nature," "Be natural," and so on. The idea behind all these slogans is that what is natural is good or right, whereas what is not natural may be neither good nor right. It is therefore of the first importance to make clear what is meant by nature. "Nature" is a notoriously ambiguous word; we will distinguish ten meanings, and there could be more. Whatever is meant by the term, "follow nature" theories must explain why being "natural" is better than being "unnatural." In some senses of nature, being unnatural is clearly the better choice; in other senses, whether to be natural or unnatural would seem to be a matter of taste or preference.

Senses of the Term "Nature"

Before examining whether what is more natural is more right, it is useful to examine several senses of the word "natural." John Stuart Mill (1808–1873), toward the end of his posthumously published "Essay on Nature," enumerated seven senses of the term "nature," arguing that none of these senses supports the idea that actions may be right or wrong "according to nature." We can distinguish ten senses. As might be expected, arguments recommending being natural do not always clarify which sense of the term "natural" is being lauded. We shall see that it is unclear that any of the senses can really support the view that being natural is better, morally or in any other way, than being unnatural.

Natural as Opposed to Being Designed by Human Intelligence   This is perhaps the most common meaning of the word "nature." In this sense, trees, tigers, mountains, and most of the things in the world are natural; books, cars, toothbrushes, and most of the things that constitute civilization are unnatural. Clearly, the advice to follow nature in the sense of putting aside everything designed by human intelligence is a prescription not for a good life but for an early death, since houses, warm clothes, and the controlled use of fire are only a few of the human contrivances without which our lives would quickly come to an unpleasant end.

Natural as Opposed to Learned   This is another common meaning: what is natural is what is innate. By nature, tigers hunt and rabbits flee; in contrast, most human behavior is learned. Unlearned human behavior includes (arguably) walking erect, shrinking from danger, crying when you are hurt, and laughing to relieve stress. Since learned behavior, from playing sports to studying philosophy, includes most of what makes human life enjoyable, any general program of replacing as far as possible learned with unlearned behavior would not seem to be a plausible prescription for improving life.

Natural as Instinctual, Spontaneous, or Coming from Feelings
Somewhat allied with the previous sense, here what is natural is regarded as what is spontaneous or instinctual, the realm of feeling; it is contrasted with the power of reason. Reason, identified with self-control and willpower, is thought to

be a kind of censor or traffic cop, regulating the expression of natural instinctual feelings. To the nineteenth-century Romantic writers goes the credit for "liberating feeling" and extolling the value of spontaneous self-expression; more recently, poets, bohemians, hippies, Freudian-influenced Marxists, and other upsetters of the status quo identify reason with capitalism, government, religion, morality, and the other suppressive powers of conventional society, and feeling with the liberating powers of the natural person. To them, reason is equated with internalized social control mechanisms and conventional values such as respect for law and working for a living; these stifle spontaneity and natural expressions of feeling. Such reason is, however, false and alienated; there is in addition a liberating reason, which enables radical philosophers and other advanced thinkers to see through the mask of rationality of alienated reason and achieve (or at least write about) the freedom of spontaneity.

The idea that control of emotions is less natural than expression of emotions may result from a confusion between having emotions and controlling them. Some emotions—for example, fear and anger—are evidently innate in the sense that we do not learn to feel them; other emotions probably do have to be learned—for example, shame and guilt. But the capacity to control emotions by reason would seem to be as innate as the capacity to express emotions spontaneously. What has to be learned is whether, why, and when to control the emotions, and possibly also certain techniques for controlling them (if you are angry, take a deep breath and count slowly to ten). But even if controlling the emotions were not a natural ability, this alone, as noted above, would not be a reason not to control them. Having a temper tantrum may be more natural than bringing your anger under control, but whether it is a good thing or not depends on many more important factors than mere naturalness.

Natural as Opposed to Conventional   Sometimes, unconventional behavior is regarded as better and more natural than conventional behavior. That unconventional behavior is admirable may well be true, if the unconventional behavior is a sign of independence of mind or native intelligence, which it often is. Conventional people tend to be dull, uninspiring, and limited. Unconventional behavior is also an expression of rejection of approved values and general revolt against society, which may be appropriate if social values are seen as oppressive. On the other hand, revolt or unconventionality for its own sake is frequently nothing more than a sign of immaturity and a failure to develop clear values of one's own; if you do not have your own values, you can always define yourself by rejecting everybody else's. Doing something just because it is unconventional is probably no better a reason for doing it than is doing something just because it is what everybody else is doing.

Unconventionality is thought of as natural because conventions are social rules; behavior which is free from such rules must thus be natural. But this is a mistake. Being unconventional means rejecting the prevailing standards, not conventions as such; it has little to do with being natural. Unconventional people get credit for originality, boldness, and independence, not for being natural. Men who first started wearing earrings defied convention but were not being more natural than those who preferred earrings on women.

Natural Identified with the More Basic or Simpler Part of Human Life   "Simplify, simplify," urged Henry David Thoreau, by which he meant remove from your life all extraneous details and concentrate on what is truly important. This is doubtless good advice, but what is truly important need not be identical with what is simple or what is natural. The most natural things may be the most complicated. The human brain is far more complicated than any computer, and no human machine is as complicated as the organic machinery that animates every living thing. Today, the ideal of simplicity appeals to those who have an aversion to certain aspects of our technological society, which they regard as overly complex. That the complexities of modern life have their disadvantages is evident when the elevator fails or when a storm interrupts electrical power to thousands of people, but, in general, complicated things such as telephones and computers save both time and money, and if simplicity were better than complexity, "Twinkle, Twinkle, Little Star" would be greater music than Mozart, and the bicycle would be the universal mode of transportation (as it still is in China). Complicated medical procedures such as organ transplants save the lives of thousands of people every year, and learning to enjoy what is complex and sophisticated, such as Shakespeare's sonnets, is one of the challenges and achievements of a good education.

Natural as Opposed to Synthetic or Artificial   This distinction underlies claims made for the alleged superiority of natural foods, organic farming, and natural remedies, under which is sometimes included medicinal herbs, folk remedies, and reliance on prayer and willpower instead of surgery. Some people support these preferences with quasimystical views about being "in tune with nature," though what that means or how one knows when one has attained it remain obscure. The aversion to synthetics seems to be based on a confusion between synthetic and poisonous. It may be true that many of the chemicals used to grow and process food are in fact unwholesome, and that many manufactured medicines have deleterious side effects. If so, the sensible person avoids them. But the class of poisons is not the same as the class of synthetics, and there is no guarantee that natural foods and medicines might not also be unhealthy. Nothing is more natural than a poisonous mushroom, which is poisonous all the same.

Natural in the Sense of "Close to Nature"   Here the idea is that civilization, by which is usually meant large cities, is a bad thing, to be avoided in favor of living in nature, that is, in the country or the wilderness somewhere. Part of the reason for this is the desire to avoid the stresses associated with urban life. These evils, such as noise, pollution, and crime, are real enough, and those who feel that they are intolerable, or that the advantages of city life are not worth these costs, by all means should find a quiet town or cabin in the woods somewhere. Many people find that escaping civilization for a few days in the wilderness, for example, on a backpacking or a rafting trip, can be a remarkably refreshing and rewarding experience. But this closeness to nature does not seem to offer enough to satisfy most people for very long; if it did, humankind would never have invented cities in the first place.

Natural in the Sense of Unaffected or Unpretentious We object to people who are affected or put on airs because they are trying to be other than they really are: they are disguising what they imagine to be deficiencies in their personality, background, or education and pretending to be superior to their actual attainments. It is this pretense that we find objectionable. Finding pretense objectionable, however, is one thing; finding naturalness preferable to unnaturalness is quite another. Whether we value naturalness as opposed to pretense depends on what kind of behavior is being displayed. If a person were naturally crude, rude, and boorish, we might very well prefer that he pretend to be other than he is, or at least try to appear so; this would at least show that he was striving to have good manners, even if he found it difficult to exhibit them. All education and most attainments are in this sense unnatural, in that people generally have to work hard to achieve any level of excellence; a person who is content to remain merely what she is will never achieve anything better.

Natural in the Sense of Easy to Do and Unforced Some people are natural athletes, or naturally friendly, or naturally good at music. Generally, people who are good at things like to do them, with the result that they become even better. People who have little talent for certain activities, on the other hand, find them frustrating and disagreeable. It is quite true that it is foolish to engage in activities that you do not enjoy and in which you are likely to accomplish little; "Do not beat your head against the wall" warns us not even to attempt something that is painful and futile. Whether we should follow nature in this sense of doing what you are good at and avoiding what you are not depends on what the activity in question is. Some people might be naturally good at lying and might enjoy deceiving people and getting away with it, but this is hardly an argument that they should go ahead and do so.

Natural in the Sense of Essential as Opposed to Accidental This is the most philosophical sense of nature, but it has many resonances in ordinary thought. We want to think that things have an essence, something that makes them what they are. This we call their natures. The nature of a thing is not merely those characteristics which it does not acquire from learning or from the environment; its nature is some inherent characteristic without which it would be something else, the characteristic by which it can be defined. Thus, all dogs bark, but "a barking animal" is not the definition of a dog, because barking is not the nature of dogginess. As Plato pointed out, people are featherless bipeds, but a one-legged person with feathers would be a person nonetheless.

If things have essences, then it can be said that they ought to express their essences, or realize their essences, or act in accordance with their essences. By so doing, they attain their good, it is thought. But this basic idea, which is at the bottom of natural law, which we shall study later, can easily be questioned. It may depend on your point of view: to the zebra, there is nothing good about the lioness expressing her inner nature!

This long examination of the term nature leads to a general conclusion: we have not found any meaning of nature from which one could draw a plausible conclusion that being natural or following nature is necessarily better than its opposite. And this is not the last of the difficulties facing this idea. Even if we had an acceptable sense of nature, there are further difficulties that "follow nature" theories have to resolve. Before looking at some philosophical theories, let us consider four of these.

General Problems with Naturalism

Many "follow nature" theories seems to suggest that nature intends that we act in one way and not in some other. The theories tell us that what is good, right, or wise is to act as nature intends we act. Here we point out four difficulties with this idea.

1.   Even if we grant that nature has intentions, it is *not clear why we should follow them.* For example, it might be thought that nature intends that sex be used for reproduction: if anything seems clear about nature, it is that all living things reproduce their kind so that their species can continue to survive. But maybe I do not want to reproduce, so I intend to use sex for personal gratification. Why should nature's intentions be binding on me? The reason given in classical natural law philosophy is theological: nature is created by God, whose purpose is to teach us, through nature, how to live. But this reason for following nature amounts to a demand to follow God's will, and reduces natural law to theological ethics, which we have already examined. Aristotle held a nontheological account of natural law that posits that each natural species, including humankind, has an essence that directs it how to act; whether Aristotle convincingly explains why any person should not act contrary to this human essence if it suits her purposes is open to question.

2.   If nature has intentions, it is *not clear that they reach very far,* hardly beyond some gross biological facts: preserve your life, reproduce your kind. So any ethics founded on nature's intentions will be incomplete, and will need another foundation for everything else. St. Thomas Aquinas and his followers held that nature's intentions were fairly wide—for example, that we should have sex with the same person all our lives, that people should obtain education, that parents should raise their children properly and children take care of their aged parents, that citizens should obey proper authority, and so on. No doubt these are all good ideas, but it is difficult to see how they can be deduced from anything intended by nature.

3.   It is clear that nature, far from being a moral teacher, can often be a rather *harsh guide.* Nature's intentions are not benign; quite the contrary. Animals kill each other with the greatest cruelty, many animals eat their young

or practice other forms of cannibalism, the weak are dealt with mercilessly, and, in general, nature's only constant seems to be that every living thing will eventually meet its end in a fairly gruesome manner. Nobody believes that we should follow these teachings, if that is what they are; human morality does just the opposite and calls for nature to be renounced and rejected in regard to such matters as helping the weak, regretting the loss of loved ones, and so on. (Of all animals, only the elephant seems to have a sense of helping its fellows in trouble. Some people actually admire the elephant for doing this; they seem to think the elephant is more moral than mere lions or giraffes.) In fact, it seems plain that those who would follow nature are deceiving themselves (people who think they are following the Bible often deceive themselves in the same way). They do not think something is good because they find it in nature; rather, they independently decide what is good, and then follow only those practices in nature that correspond to these principles, ignoring the rest.

4.   There is a confusion that even great philosophers such as Aristotle seem to have fallen into. It is the *distinction between means and ends*. It is true that unless you follow nature in your choice of means, you will not achieve your ends; but it does not thereby follow that you can choose your ends by following nature. For example, suppose you want to be healthy. Nature teaches us that fatty foods, excessive smoking, and poor exercise do not produce health, so if your goal is to be healthy you had best follow nature and avoid these evils. But "follow nature" theories would be not very interesting if all that was meant by following nature is that we should select the best means for our ends. They want to claim that we can learn what our ends ought to be by following nature. They think that if you consult nature, you will find out that you ought to be healthy, or that you ought to value certain other things, such as peace of mind over success and competition. (A cherished idea of many modern followers of nature is that the competitive turmoil of Western civilization is unnatural because it inhibits peace of mind and serenity.)

There is nothing more important in life than choosing your ends wisely. But nature can never show us anything other than the means; ends have to be chosen on the basis of a person's fundamental values, not on what is or is not natural. Suppose someone likes junk food so much that he chooses to risk his health rather than sacrifice his daily Big Mac, fries, and shake. (Many hard-working people risk their health to achieve success; professional athletes make physical risk-taking part of their job.) This may be a mistake, which he will come to regret later in life when he has his first heart attack. But you do not discover the importance of good health by consulting nature, but by thinking about what you value most. People come to regret their decisions made earlier in life, not only because as they grow older they become wiser, which they like to tell themselves, but also because as they grow older their values change. By the time they are 40 and nursing aching muscles and a weak back, they can no longer understand how playing sports could have meant so much to them at age 20. "Follow nature" theories seem to hold that what makes a choice foolish is that it is unnatural, when in fact what makes it foolish is that it does not fit in with other things that we value more. If success and competition are what is most important to a person, and if that person understands the sacrifices pursuit of these goals may require, there is no reason in nature why he should not make that choice.

Two Kinds of Naturalism

Many theories are called naturalistic or are varieties of **naturalism.** These theories should be divided into two groups since they are quite different. What justifies the common classification is that both kinds of theories base ethics on nature; but they do so in two very different ways. Here we are going to discuss only one of these two kinds of naturalistic theories. We begin by explaining the difference between these two ways of basing ethics on nature.

The term "basing on" can mean either "explaining by" or "justifying by." Any naturalism bases ethics on nature; but it is one thing to explain ethics by nature, another to justify ethics by nature. Consider the example of war. We might think that war can be explained by human nature, in that people are naturally aggressive, given to holding grudges and seeking revenge, and too easily provoked into wanting to vindicate their rights; but we might be reluctant to justify war by human nature. When we feel entitled to justify going to war, we appeal to our national interests, the defense of liberty, human rights, or something like that; we would not say, "We are justified in going to war because it is our nature to do so."

However, the distinction is commonly overlooked, because sometimes we do justify something by appealing to nature. These justifications do not always wash however. A dog chases a cat. The cat's owner complains to the dog's owner, who says, "It's his nature to chase cats." Needless to say, the cat's owner does not find this reply adequate; she wonders whether it is the dog owner's nature not to control his animal. Expressions such as "Boys will be boys" (especially when applied to grown men) "Business is business," or "That's the way it is in the army" are attempts to justify activities—rather dubious ones, usually—by appealing to the nature of the beast. We do not find these justifications persuasive, precisely because we expect people to rise above their natures when the occasion requires. But perhaps this is not always the case. There may be times when we do accept appeals to nature as a justification, as when it is said to be natural for parents to love their children and want to protect them from harm. In saying this, we are not simply recording a fact, but commending an attitude. We endorse the parents' attitude on the grounds that it is natural, and we scorn parents who have a different attitude toward their children. The theories we are considering here justify ethics precisely by appealing to nature in this way.

We shall discuss theories that justify ethics by appealing to nature, but the reader should be aware that there are theories whose primary emphasis is on explaining ethics and not on justifying it, and these theories may also be called naturalistic. They would be so called if their explanation appealed to natural facts, rather than to religion or to what philosophers tend to regard as metaphysics. We have already seen a theory that explains ethics naturalistically—subjectivism. According to this theory, ethical principles cannot be justified, since they are only expressions of people's attitudes. It does not make sense to say that one attitude is better than another; if you said that, you would only be expressing your attitude. However, ethics can be understood: sophisticated subjectivism claims to explain what ethics is, why we have it, and what we are doing when we use it. Since this explanation appeals only to natural terms (no religion, no metaphysics), sophisticated subjectivism is regarded as a form of naturalism. We shall return to explanatory naturalistic theories in Chapter Five.

After this long introduction, we now turn to three naturalistic theories, natural law, evolutionary ethics and sociobiology, and pragmatism.

Three Naturalistic Theories

The three theories we discuss approach nature differently. Natural law reflects the understanding of nature prevalent in Greek and medieval philosophy. Evolutionary ethics and sociobiology purport to be based on Darwinian-oriented biology. Pragmatism uses general empiricism and scientific method.

Natural Law   In the Middle Ages, the idea that ethics derives from nature, and that human beings should be governed by **natural law,** was virtually a given of philosophy. The philosophy of natural law articulated by Aristotle was developed by the medieval theologians in the context of ideas about reality and knowledge that often seem quaint and even bizarre to the modern mind. Nonetheless, the thought that, for example, it is natural for mothers to love their children and unnatural for people of the same gender to have sex together, has a certain appeal in some quarters. The thought here is not simply that most mothers love their children or that most people prefer sex with a partner of the other gender. The idea is that we can learn by nature what we ought to do and not do because nature intends that certain things be done or not done. Mothers ought to love their children because that is nature's purpose.

Nature is not a person, so nature cannot literally intend that anybody do anything; however, this is perhaps not a fundamental objection. For, however we unpack the metaphor, we can certainly see the point of saying that nature intends the eyes to be used for seeing or sex to be used for reproduction. We do not in practice seem to have much trouble knowing what the purposes of natural entities are. An acorn, to use Aristotle's favorite example, is the seed of an oak tree, and its purpose in nature is obvious. Every animal reproduces, takes nourishment, flees from danger, and so on; all these actions are natural and part of nature's purposes.

But even if there are purposes in nature and if, as Aristotle thought, it does not begin to make sense to talk about certain natural objects (such as the heart or the eyes) without explaining what their purposes are or what they are good for, it is still a long step toward developing an ethics. Aristotle took the heroic tack of basing his ethics on a search, not for purposes of this and that but for the purpose of human beings. Religions typically say that the purpose of human beings is to glorify God, or to participate in God's plan about the battle between good and evil, or some similar idea; but Aristotle had never heard of such purposes and would not have known what to think of them if he had. He had to look for purposes in nature itself. If acorns have a purpose, he thought, so must everything else in nature, and hence so must human beings. But if the purpose of an acorn is to produce an oak tree, what is the purpose of the oak tree? To produce more acorns? This was not in fact Aristotle's view; he held that the purpose of any fully developed entity is simply to be itself. An object's purpose, or "final cause" in Aristotelian terminology, is the same as its essence, that is, what it truly is; the essence (and purpose) of an acorn is to become an oak tree, but the essence of an oak tree is simply to be what it is, namely, an oak tree.

So the purpose of a human being is simply to be human, but what is that? And what must humans do to be what they already are? In answering these questions, Aristotle is nothing if not ingenious. The essence of something is not just static existence, as the example of the oak tree might indicate. According to Aristotle, the essence of a thing is an activity, something the thing does; this he understands as its characteristic function, that is, that which it does uniquely or better than other things. This is why the essence of the heart is to pump blood; nothing else in the body can perform this function. Therefore, in looking for the purpose of a human being, we must ask what is characteristic about the human being, what can the human do uniquely or better than any other thing. This activity constitutes the human essence.

Aristotle points out that some functions, such as growth and reproduction, humans share with all living things; other functions, such as perceiving the environment and moving around in it, we share with animals. The unique human function, or at least the function humans do far better than any other thing, is the use of intelligence. Hence, Aristotle concludes that the function of the human being, our essence and nature, is to use our intelligence in suitable ways. And, therefore, this must be what it is natural for us to do; and if natural, then also good and right.

Aristotle was nobody's fool, and his reasoning to this point is fairly impressive. But we may seem far from ethics, since evidently intelligence can be used in innumerable ways, only some of which are ethical. Here Aristotle introduces an idea about excellence. Clearly, the kind of activity that it is right to do cannot be bad activity or activity done poorly; it must be excellent activity or activity done as excellently as possible. If the function of the eye is to see, it must follow that seeing is a good thing to do and that the eyes should do it as well as possible. No one would think that any natural thing has a function that it is bad for it to perform (only the heart can be stricken with a heart attack, but we do not thereby think that giving you a heart attack is the function of the heart); or that its functions should be performed badly, as if the eye should see myopically. Activities—for example, playing at sports—are things we want to do well; who would say that she is trying to be the worst tennis player on the team? From this it follows that the function of a human being—to use intelligence in some way—must be something that is done as well as possible, some activity that could be called excellent.

However, at this point Aristotle's reasoning breaks down, and he abandons it. For instead of telling us how we can determine what excellent activities are, or how we distinguish between doing something well and doing it badly, he launches into an investigation of the virtues, such as courage, temperance, and generosity. This discussion, although interesting enough in its own right, appears to be based largely on the orthodoxies of Greek morality and not on any analysis of the human essence. In Aristotle's favor, it must be said that to the Greeks, virtue *was* excellent activity, and the particular virtues were regarded as forms of human excellence. Aristotle's theory requires him not simply to accept this as a conventional point of morals, but to demonstrate it by tracing the virtues to the human function, to human beings acting in accordance with their purpose or their specific activity. He has to show how courage, for example, or generosity, rather than their opposites, cowardliness and stinginess, enable us to fulfill our human function (actually, for Aristotle every virtue has two opposites). Unless he does this, he has not succeeded in showing how his theory about human function leads us to even a single good or right action. Aristotle's theory amounts to an implicit promise to show that being courageous and having the other virtues are excellent, just because the virtues are more natural, more in line with our function, than being cowardly and unvirtuous. And it seems difficult, indeed impossible, for him to make good on this promise. His argument falters, and he simply assumes that the virtues are more or less as the Greeks took them to be, without even trying to show that these particular points of character are closer to our essence, or more in accord with our specific function, than their opposites. (There is more to Aristotle's theory. He says the virtues make you flourish. We shall see this in Chapter Seven.)

Despite the rather calamitous collapse of Aristotle's natural law program, his theory was revived nearly a thousand years later by the great theologian-philosophers, notably St. Thomas Aquinas (1225–1274), who grafted Aristotle's naturalism onto a Christian theological foundation and worked hard to make the theory more precise. Aquinas had an enormous advantage over Aristotle: he had the idea of God as creator of the universe and lawgiver to human beings (as we have noted, Aristotle held no such ideas; his God neither creates nor legislates). He had a second advantage also, though relatively minor: he believed in the human-centered cosmology, that is, in a theory of creation according to which the entire point and purpose of creation was to set the stage for a stupendous drama involving us. (The medievals, who were nothing if not literal, reinforced this human-centered cosmology with an appropriate astronomy: they imagined that the earth rested at the physical center of the universe, in real space, surrounded by the orbits of the sun and moon and the sphere of the stars). Thus, St. Thomas was able to assume that nature is created by God for the purpose of instructing us in our role in the drama.

Aquinas relied heavily on the idea of an *inclination*, which he took to be not just any random desire or preference but some deep-seated thrust of the human person. Inclinations are what nature, working as God's instrument, teaches each living thing to do to achieve its proper good. Thus, a dog has a natural inclination to chase cats, a squirrel to bury nuts, and an acorn to grow into an oak tree: these are the things the organism will naturally do, unless prevented by outside interference. Such interference is regarded as unnatural according to this view, as only the essential inclinations constitute a thing's nature. Because of his belief that God creates out of the abundance of His Goodness, Aquinas could be confident that each thing both had a natural good and was naturally instructed how to achieve it. When it follows its inclinations, as it will unless prevented, it achieves its natural good.

Being natural entities, human beings also have natural inclinations that lead them to their natural good, which we call happiness. Unlike animals and plants, however, human beings do not pursue their inclinations directly by instinct, but must understand what they are through reason, the instrument God gives us to enable us to know how to act. (Also, unlike animals and plants, humans have a supernatural good, which is salvation; but this is a subject not to be learned from nature through reason, but from revelation, that is, through scripture and faith). By reason, we act through free will; first we must know what to do, and then choose it. Because we are sinful, however, we often ignore our reason and make the wrong choice. God created us with this double nature so that we may be the instruments through which the struggle between good and evil unfolds. What is called the law of nature are the rules God has created for us to follow. These rules are written in the heart of every person; we learn what they are by using reason to understand our deepest inclinations.

Inclinations thus play a twofold role in Aquinas' ethics. First, they set before us our most basic courses of action, teaching us what we ought to do to attain our happiness. This would not, however, give us morality, but only rules to happiness. Morality in the Biblical view, which Christian philosophers follow, consists of commands imposed on us by a lawgiver. So, inclinations also function as the operations of the law, which commands us, through God, to do our duty. Morality is based on God's commands, but God speaks through reason directed at our natural inclinations (God reinforces the natural law by His explicit commands in the Bible, so that His commands may be unmistakably clear. God has foreseen that some people will not get the message if it comes only from the inner voice of their reason).

What are the deepest human inclinations? Aquinas identifies remarkably few of them (see his "Natural Law," *Summa Theologica,* Q. 94, art. ii), but we can amplify somewhat: to preserve our own lives; to harm no one and to live in peace with our neighbors; to reproduce our kind and to educate our children; to seek knowledge, especially knowledge of God. These inclinations are good precisely because God builds them into us for our own benefit; by following them, we shall attain happiness, which is our earthly reward for virtuous living and whose attainment is entirely within our own power. Salvation, on the other hand, cannot be attained by our own power, but requires grace, or God's good will. Moral principles, the precepts of the natural law, are based on these inclinations.

Survival being the deepest instinct of all natural entities, suicide is morally wrong; as sex is the instrument of reproduction, having sex without the intention to reproduce is forbidden, and marriage is for the purpose of producing children; peace being the condition of well-being, living in peace is required by nature; love of children being natural to all animals, nurturing and educating one's children is commanded by the law of nature.

The Christian synthesis probably carries the natural law philosophy as far as it can be carried; but its limitations are evident. First, Aquinas simply overlooks the fact that humans have bad inclinations as well as good ones, inclinations to hate as well as to love, to destroy as well as to heal, to oppress as well as to liberate. Nothing in his theory enables us to distinguish the good ones, which should be followed, from the bad ones, which should not be. Second, he is far too optimistic in assuming that the path of virtuous action and the path of happiness are the same; like Aristotle, he assumes that the performance of virtuous actions will in general make you happy, an assumption not necessarily borne out by experience. Third, Aquinas gives no reason other than the theological one to justify morality; ultimately, his argument is that we should follow our good inclinations because God puts them into us expressly for us to follow. But as we have seen in the section on religion, this raises without answering the question, why obey God?

This examination of natural law enables us to see how difficult the project of justifying ethics by nature turns out to be. We shall now turn to some other varieties of naturalism, as naturalism seems to be not only among the oldest of ethical theories but the most varied. It is understandable that those who think that ethics needs to be supported by something other than itself would return again and again to nature to provide that foundation. The other candidates, after all, do not seem too promising, and beyond that, it can hardly be denied that the idea of being natural, not only in what you eat and what you breathe, but more generally in how you live, does seem to have a considerable appeal.

Evolutionary Ethics and Sociobiology   The theories of Charles Darwin in the middle of the nineteenth century led certain philosophers to suppose that the theory of evolution might provide a foundation for ethics, a foundation which would at last base ethics on science, and so make it secure from personal preference and mere speculation. It was the best known of these philosophers, Herbert Spencer (1820–1903), and not Darwin himself, who coined the expression, "survival of the fittest." The basic idea was that nature itself, through evolution, makes a distinction between those forms that are better, and those less good; the former are those that are chosen by nature to survive. As it happens, these better forms turn out to be those that are more advanced in the sense of being more complicated, more capable of self-control through choices, and more intelligent. It was thought, therefore, that evolution gave a certain stamp of approval to human behavior that had these characteristics.

Evolutionary ethics (EvE) turned out to be not especially benign, but a particularly vicious form of it was called social Darwinism. This view emphasized the fact of struggle and competition to survive: only the strong, or the "fit," are able to triumph and succeed. That the strong survive and the weak fall by the way was taken to be a kind of iron law of nature; like all natural laws, human beings have no choice but to obey it, and can only create problems for themselves if they try to counter its effects.

The proponents of this view concluded that it was therefore scientific to believe that those people who had in fact triumphed, who occupied the top positions in the social system, were more fit than those who occupied lower ranks. The rich and powerful thus claimed a kind of natural foundation for their position. If they were there, it was because they were more fit to be there; nature had in effect chosen them to occupy the positions they held. As for the poor and powerless, they too could be said to have been chosen, or perhaps rejected, by nature, and so had no legitimate claim to anything other than what they already had. Since some of the people who were rich and powerful had in fact achieved their success through their own skill and effort (and since most people who are on the top like to think that their success is merited by their talents), the view in question had a certain charm to some.

The vicious aspect of social Darwinism was the conclusion sometimes drawn that no attempt to help the poor should be made, or could ultimately succeed if it were made. Since the poor are those who have lost out because of their own unfitness, it is not a bad thing that they are at the bottom of the social scale; that is where nature intends them to be. Because of this, to help such people would be fruitless: you cannot improve the condition of those who are naturally unfit. Furthermore, even if you could make fundamental changes in the lives of the unfit, it would be a mistake to do so. Nature progresses at the expense of the weak: unfit individuals and unfit species must disappear to make way for those more advanced. To impede or prevent this process would in the end retard the improvement of the human race, and not only freeze development at its current stage but possibly reverse the direction of development as more and more unfit individuals survive and reproduce. An ethics that teaches the contrary can be condemned as unscientific: what if, through some idea about ethics, someone in geological times had managed to repeal the law that "Big fish eat little fish"? The result would be that there never would have evolved any big fish.

The ideas of competition, struggle, and survival seemed to be predominant in Darwinism, and no human activity exemplifies these characteristics more than war. EvE thus tended to be associated with the glorification of war. Hence, militarism ("War is the health of the state") seemed to be given a foundation in science: war is the activity by which the fit eliminate the less fit. The victory of a country in war could be taken to be proof of that country's natural superiority, and proof of the superiority of its values as well. Thus, values such as courage, obedience, and loyalty tended to be regarded as endorsed or even required by nature, while values such as independence of mind, artistic sensitivity, and compassion tended to be regarded as weak and contrary to nature. Patriotism and even superpatriotism were held to be high values: a country at war is something like an ant colony, in which each individual plays his or her assigned role without asking any questions. The wisdom of all this was thought to be a more or less straightforward consequence of the theory of evolution.

There are major confusions about evolutionary theory in EvE. "Fit to survive" does not mean more complex, more intelligent, or more advanced, but only more capable of adapting to surrounding conditions. It is evident that the cockroach is at least as fit to survive as any human being, but that does not make the cockroach superior in any moral sense. Perhaps, however, the worst error in the theory is its assumption that human beings have no control over the direction of evolution, and therefore must simply obey its laws, whatever they may be. Human history, however, has shown the opposite: our effect on the natural world alone, by the creation of new species, elimination of old ones, and the alteration of the conditions under which every living thing evolves, has been to change the direction of evolution in ways whose magnitude cannot be measured. Although human beings have not in the past perhaps been very prudent in using this power, it cannot be said that we lack capacity to alter evolution in directions we ourselves choose. If this is true, then we are not slaves to evolutionary processes but have some freedom to direct evolution in accordance with our moral ideas.

Sociobiology is the study of animal behaviors, which includes human behavior from a biological point of view. Many animals exhibit interesting specific behaviors, for example, territoriality, marking off their territory by certain stratagems, and excluding others of their species. Certain conclusions about human behavior are drawn from these animal behaviors. People are territorial too; individuals as well as nations mark off their land and uninvited strangers are kept out. From this it can be surmised that nonterritorial arrangements such as collective farms or world government will not work because they violate basic human behavior patterns.

Of course, it is true that any ethical principle that people cannot or will not follow is in a sense pointless and perhaps should not be advocated. It does not follow that such a principle is morally wrong, or even that hopelessly idealistic principles cannot have any effect. "Love thine enemies" might be a high moral ideal even if very few people are likely to follow it, and perhaps its advocacy will at least cause some people to treat their enemies less harshly than otherwise. Principles that people actually advocate rarely enjoin actions that are strictly impossible; no one says "Fly by flapping your arms," because if they did they would be advocating something that is physically impossible. Sociobiology seems to suggest that some activities are biologically impossible, but this idea is problematic; human behavior is much more flexible than animal behavior because humans do, but animals cannot, control their behavior through their conceptions of what is right and wrong. Nothing is stronger than the desire for self-preservation, yet martyrs go to their deaths and heroes risk their lives out of moral conviction.

Both evolutionary ethics and sociobiology strive to be scientific, but seem to support conclusions that would invalidate some of our most cherished ethical norms. In this they are strikingly different from natural law, which tries to show that ethical norms are founded in human nature. A naturalistic view that also tries to make ethics scientific, but without sacrificing ethical values, is pragmatism.

Pragmatism   The philosophy known as pragmatism originated in the United States in the late nineteenth century and has attracted many able philosophers, especially Americans. As its name implies, **pragmatism** is about practice and the practical; the emphasis is on doing, action, and concrete results rather than abstract thought. Ideas are regarded as "instruments" for action, really no different from tools such as saws and hammers; they are the means by which we construct, or reconstruct, the world around us. Abstract thought that has no results in the world of practice pragmatism rejects as not only useless but literally without meaning; for it holds that the meaning of any idea is what difference would be made if someone took the idea seriously enough to act as it requires.

The application of pragmatism to ethics is primarily due to John Dewey (1859–1952). Like the evolutionists, Dewey wanted to make ethics scientific, which to him meant that propositions in ethics ought to be empirically verifiable. He thought he could achieve this with his view that propositions are instruments whose value is to be measured by the consequences of using them; like all other tools, ethical ideas are evaluated by how well they perform the function assigned to them. At bottom, the logic of ethical thinking is the same as the logic of carpentry, dog grooming, or any other activity. In all such activities, skills are learned and problems arise; when a problem occurs, what you do is analyze the problem and proceed according to the most effective means the analysis suggests.

What distinguishes ethics from thinking in general is that while all thinking is about action and its consequences, ends and means, ethics concerns the best action and the best consequences. All propositions according to pragmatism state means by which ends can be achieved; but the particular task of ethics is to state, not any means to any ends, but the best means to the best ends. "True" is what works, but "good" is what works best. It is true that if you want to drive a nail, you can use a rock; but it is better to use a hammer. Just as carpentry tells you that hammers are better nail-drivers than rocks, ethics tells you that certain actions are better problem solvers than others.

If ethics states means to ends, how are ends themselves to be evaluated? Before we know how to achieve an end, we have to know which ends we ought to try to achieve. Some philosophers think they can give a definitive statement about ultimate human ends—whether these be identified as pleasure, happiness, wisdom, love, freedom, personal enrichment, commitment and service, or something else—but all such accounts must be rejected on Dewey's view. There is no such thing as *the* set of ultimate human ends. This is not because different people choose different ends for themselves, but because of what an end is. An end is a link connecting one set of means to another set of means; a statement of an end is a hypothesis that constructing such a link will prove a satisfactory resolution of the problem at hand. Because life is ongoing, and problem solving never comes to an end, there are going to be as many ends as there are problem-solving moments in life. Each end has its job to do, and must be assessed by how well it does that job.

Thus, any view of what ought to be done can be expressed as a tentative verifiable hypothesis, saying, "If I do this, then I will achieve that." These hypotheses can be verified by doing the action and seeing whether the expected result occurs. If you achieve what you are aiming at, your idea has been verified, and your action has been proved to be a good thing to have done. This is as true for ends as it is for means because any end is only part of the means to something else. No end is valuable for its own sake, apart from the means required to produce it and the consequences that ensue from attaining it.

How do ethical principles fit in? Dewey is not opposed to abstract principles, ethical or otherwise, provided they are understood in terms of their real concrete consequences. Every tool must be judged by how well it works. No idea has value in and of itself; the value of any idea, even of an ethical idea, is exactly what it does for us when we use it. If principles help us construct good solutions to problems, they are useful tools; when they do not, their use can be pointless and even harmful. Nobody would use a sledgehammer when driving a nail, for no better reason than that a sledgehammer is a nobler and better instrument than a mere claw hammer.

So far, Dewey's theory seems to be about the logic of ethics. It is naturalistic in that ethical ideas are supposed to be validated in experience. But Dewey was also keen on giving to human values a natural foundation; in his view, values are not transcendent, but arise out of human life. He held a theory of human action strongly rooted in biological psychology. He regarded human beings as essentially problem-solving organisms; unlike animals, whose problems essentially consist in finding food and avoiding enemies, human lives contain innumerable and varied problems to which we must find solutions. Problems impede our lives by interfering with our ongoing activity. Normally, our activity continues in an orderly manner, but from time to time difficulties arise that interrupt the normal flow. Human beings have developed intelligence as an instrument to resolve such difficulties. Investigating, gathering evidence, drawing conclusions, putting forth theories, and so on take place when problems are created and need to be resolved. I am lost in the woods; I postulate that this path will lead me out; my idea is a prediction that by following this path, I will get out of the woods. My idea is true if the prediction is fulfilled; the path is good if it leads me where I want to go. Were I not lost in the woods, I never would have had the idea that this is the shortest path out. Good ideas are those that work to best advantage, which means not only solve the problem at hand, but do not lead to further problems down the line. A good idea allows activity to continue; a bad idea leads to further problems and confusion.

But Dewey's theory does not seem to be as successful with regard to ethics as it is with regard to meaning and truth. Here are some criticisms.

1. His theory about means and ends seems to be based on a *confusion between two senses of ultimate.* (The word "end" lends itself to this confusion,

since it has the same two senses.). In one sense, something is ultimate if it is the last point or termination of some process, like a journey (your ultimate destination is where your journey comes to an end); in another sense, however, to say that something is ultimate is to say that it is valued for its own sake. In this sense, a person's ultimate end is the basic goal the person is trying to achieve, as when you wonder what your ultimate end is in studying philosophy. Dewey's contention that no end is ultimate since life goes on, is of course correct. This is the first sense of ultimate: life's journey never ends, so no end is ultimate. But it does not follow that all ends must be evaluated as means only. Some ends might be valuable for themselves, quite apart from what they lead to; studying philosophy is an excellent example.

2. *It is unclear what is meant by "practical."* It is difficult to see what Dewey has in mind when he calls on thinking to be practical. In the narrow sense, practical refers to the immediate problems of everyday life. But in a wider sense, practical refers to anything that can be the subject of an activity, even the activity of thinking itself. If the term "practical problem" is taken in a broad sense, so as to include anything one can think about, then to say that thinking should be practical is only to say that thinking should be thinking. If the term is taken more narrowly, so as to exclude something, then it seems arbitrary to make that exclusion. For example, it might be difficult to see any practical value in certain problems in astrophysics; how could there ever be any practical good in knowing whether the sun is going to burn out in five billion years or only in five million? But it would seem narrow and dogmatic of Dewey in effect to banish these problems from our thinking. Some ideas just are interesting for their own sake, it would seem, and if an idea is interesting, nobody is going to refuse to think about it just because it might seem to have no connection to everyday life.

3. *What does Dewey mean by an "activity"?* It is probably not very clear in our ordinary thinking what we would call an activity (is listening to music or getting a massage an activity?), but nothing much rests on this. In Dewey's theory, however, everything rests on "restoring normal activity," so it is important to know what an activity is. If an activity is any state we happen to be in, even sleeping, then restoring activity is an empty and useless notion. If certain states are not to be regarded as activities, then it is not clear why such states are to be avoided. The word "activity" suggests the expenditure of effort rather than a state of calm and repose. But that it is better to be active rather than inactive would seem not to be a general truth about conduct, but a proposition relative to specific situations. Taking a nap is important enough at certain moments. So either "activity" covers any state, and Dewey's criterion tells us nothing, or it covers certain high-energy conditions, and his criterion seems arbitrary and often incorrect.

4. A similar ambiguity affects the idea of a problem. Ethical thinking for Dewey consists of solving problems, but *what is a problem?* Is a problem anything

someone takes to be a problem, or is it real in some sense? Suppose an adult bookstore opens in your neighborhood. The neighbors may think there is a problem, but the bookstore owner claims it is they who are the problem, because they do not happen to like his merchandise. Since according to Dewey problems occur in behavior, not in thought, it would look like the neighbors have no problem since their behavior is not affected by the bookstore's presence. They are just as free as before to do whatever they want. But many people will not agree that this issue can be dismissed so easily.

5.   Dewey claims that problem solving is the criterion of ethical behavior: if we attend to problem solving, we will thereby attend to ethics as well. But can this really work as a theory of ethics? Ethics not only has to help us to solve our problems, but to do so in a morally commendable way. What makes morally questionable actions sometimes tempting is that they do seem to be useful in resolving problems. If, for example, my problem is an unhappy marriage, walking out on my family might solve my problem, but it is not necessarily the best solution ethically. It is not even clear what is to count as a solution to a problem, as opposed to simply an abandonment of it. If I do walk out on my marriage, have I solved my problem, or escaped from it? It is not clear how Dewey could make the distinction, nor why, if he could make it, he would say that solving problems is better than just quitting on them, since the problem goes away in either case and normal activity is restored. Thus, problem solving all by itself *cannot be the sole criterion of right and wrong.*

6.   Dewey seems to retreat to some broader criterion such as reducing problems for everyone. Walking out on my marriage would not be acceptable because it creates greater problems for everybody else. But here Dewey seems to be *abandoning his position* that correct ethical values can be defined as those that lead to the best solutions of life's problems; instead, he seems to be defining best solution in terms of previously understood correct ethical values. Why should I, as a problem-solving organism, care whether I create problems for anyone else, if I solve my own problems in so doing? After all, animals create problems for other animals all the time, as when the wolf eats the mother sheep. The reason seems to be, basically, that creating problems for others is morally wrong. But if that is so, then Dewey has not defined morality in terms of problem-solving, but has defined what is to count as a solved problem in terms of whether the result is morally acceptable or not. And this means that his whole project of understanding ethical thinking as a problem-solving activity has been in effect abandoned.

The Naturalistic Fallacy

We turn now to the most important logical criticism of the idea that morality should be based on nature. This idea is called the **naturalistic fallacy**. Nothing is more important for an understanding both of the logic of morality and of moral theory in the twentieth century.

The naturalistic fallacy is of two types. The first is due to David Hume (1711–1776) and usually goes by the unpoetic but completely informative name of the **is-ought fallacy** or the **fact-value fallacy,** also called **Hume's Law.** The second is due to the twentieth-century British philosopher G. E. Moore (1873–1958), who called it the "naturalistic fallacy" but should probably have called it the **definitional fallacy.** Both arguments describe the same thing, which is that there is no way to use argument containing nothing but statements of fact to support conclusions of morality. Hence, you cannot argue from "is" to "ought." The two branches support each other in the following way. Whereas Hume said you cannot argue from "is" to "ought," Moore said you cannot get there by definition either.

The Fact-Value Fallacy   Let us illustrate how Hume's Law works. Suppose you point out that all people want to be happy, and then note that there are certain things you can do to help people become happy: do not tell them lies, help them when they are in trouble, act friendly and courteously, and so on. You conclude that you ought to act in these ways. According to Hume's Law, this conclusion doesn't follow. Hume's Law says that if you are going to have an "ought" in your conclusion, you will need an "ought" in your premises somewhere. To make the conclusion follow, you will have to add a premise: "I ought to act in such a way as to make people happy." Without this premise, or something like it, you will have simply stated a list of facts, which by themselves do not entail that you should (or should not) do anything.

Hence, no "ought" statement can be derived exclusively from statements about facts. To have an "ought" in the conclusion, there has to be an "ought" in the premises. But from what is that derived? And the answer can only be, either from nothing at all or from still another "ought" premise. Hence, there cannot be any "ought" that rests ultimately on statements of fact alone.

This conclusion has sometimes been challenged by people who give examples such as the following: "This is thin ice, therefore you ought not to go on it"; "You bought that sack of potatoes, therefore you ought to pay for it"; "Picking your nose in public is rude, therefore you ought not to do it." All these examples are supposed to illustrate that "oughts" follow directly from statements of fact. Concepts that allow this to happen are sometimes called *thick* concepts, since they contain both a descriptive (or fact-stating) aspect, and a prescriptive, what-you-must-do aspect. Dangerous, rude, and property, are said to be thick concepts, as are ethical concepts generally. Treachery, brutality, promise, courage, lie, coward, and gratitude could be examples of concepts that both state facts and prescribe behavior. Thus, to say that some action is brutal is not only to give a brief description of that act but to evaluate it negatively.

That there are thick concepts no one can deny; that their existence defeats the naturalistic fallacy is another point altogether. Those who say that it does claim that the descriptive element already gives you a reason for action: to say that this act is cowardly, which is to describe it, is enough to give somebody a reason not to do it.

It seems fairly clear, however, that the fact that some act is considered rude is not by itself a reason not to do it: we need also accept that it is wrong to act in ways that are considered rude. It will not meet the point to hold that the word "rude" already means that it is wrong, so that the description of the act as a rude act is enough to tell us not to do it. For anybody might describe the act in exactly the same way and even admit that it was rude, and yet say that it was not wrong. If the word "rude" contains a negative evaluation, this is a function of the word, not of the factual description of an action. There may be some actions that are, let us say, so gross that anyone would call them rude, as no doubt anyone would call certain acts cowardly, shameful, and a disgrace to the person who does them. Yet all this point shows is that we have as a matter of fact universal, or near universal, agreement about some basic evaluations. It does not show that this agreement is forced on us either by how we use ethical terms or by any set of facts.

The Definitional Fallacy   The other form of the naturalistic fallacy involves definitions. Suppose somebody thinks he can avoid Hume's argument by proposing a definition: morally right just means, he might say, those acts that serve human happiness. He might put this forward as an analysis of the meaning of morally right. Or suppose he wants to do this in the way actually analyzed by Moore, by proposing a definition of "good." (For purposes of the analysis, it does not matter which term in morality is the subject of the definition.) So suppose he offers as his theory of what the word "good" means that good means pleasure. His basic idea might be that being pleasant or causing pleasure is what people mean when they call something good. Now if we took this as our definition of good, we might think the following argument amounted to an argument from facts to values: "Good means pleasure; this thing causes pleasure (or, is pleasurable); therefore, this thing is good." The premises of this argument consist of a definition and a fact. The definition, though not exactly a factual statement, is rather like a factual statement in reporting what a word actually means. At any rate, the definition does not seem to be a value statement, at least not in the ordinary sense that a statement that says that something is good or bad would be a value statement.

Of course, we might dispute the purported meaning of the word "good": presumably, many people would not accept that good means pleasure. But good must mean something, and whatever you take it to mean gives you your definition, and thus the possibility of arguing from facts to values.

Against this, Moore makes the following simple argument. Suppose we grant that good means pleasure. But suppose we then want to say that pleasure is good. We could not say this with meaning because of our definition. If good just means pleasure, then when we go on to assert that pleasure is good, what are we saying? By the basic principle of logic that a definition can always be substituted for the word defined, the sentence "Pleasure is good" turns out to mean, "Pleasure is pleasure"! But this last sentence does not seem to assert anything, or at least not anything very interesting; it is a tautology, a simple logical truism of the form a = a.

But, argues Moore, such an outcome is not admissible. "Pleasure is good" cannot mean the same as "Pleasure is pleasure" because the former raises what

Moore calls an open question, that is, one whose truth needs to be debated; if pleasure is good (which Moore does not deny), this is not true simply because of what the word "pleasure" means. But "Pleasure is pleasure" clearly is not an open question, since it is a form of a = a, about which there is nothing to debate. Since these two sentences have different logical properties, the definition "Good means pleasure" cannot be correct.

One could put the problem in the following way. Why should anyone want to propose this definition of "good" in the first place? Presumably, it is because one wants to defend the theory that pleasure is good, or perhaps the stronger thesis that pleasure is *the* good. But if one does put forward such a definition, then this turns out to be precisely what one cannot do if Moore's argument is correct. If you are going to argue that something is good, you cannot do so on the basis of a definition. Presumably, therefore (since exclusively factual premises will not get you there either), you will have to have some evaluative statement mixed in with your premises somewhere.

But this argument has the most profound consequences for any attempt to found ethics on nature. It shows that it cannot be done! No matter how sophisticated your theory about nature and nature's intentions, if these are taken to be strictly statements of fact they will never entail any moral principle whatever. We will always need some basic evaluative principle (such as, "It is good to follow nature's intentions"), which is not itself derived from any facts about nature. Evolutionary ethics, for example, rests on the unstated assumption that the superior ought to survive; Dewey's theory, on the assumption that we ought to solve our problems. Neither of these principles follows from any facts one could learn about nature. Since this is true of any form of naturalism whatever, the naturalistic fallacy, if it is correct, shows that any naturalism rests on a fallacy and therefore cannot be correct.

THE SELF

The final foundation for ethics is the self. What can it mean to found ethics on the self? It seems clear that nobody would regard anything as valuable unless someone wanted it. This is obviously true of economic value (something nobody wants is worth zero dollars), and seems true of moral value as well: would justice have any value if nobody wanted to be treated justly? So if we had some theory about what people really wanted—really wanted, not just thought they wanted—we could try to make this the foundation of value. The principle would be that what people really want is what is good. But is there something that people really want? We examine two answers. According to Plato, what people really want is mental and emotional health. According to self-realization theories, they want to make real their inner nature.

Plato: The Healthy Soul

In his *Republic* (iv, 444), Plato argues that justice is the health of the soul. Since nothing is more important than having a healthy soul, nothing is more important than justice. The idea of a healthy soul is not meant as a metaphor. Plato, who probably deserves credit for inventing the concept of mental health and by implication the science of "soul medicine" (psychiatry), holds that just as bodies can be healthy or sick, so can souls. He supports this with a fairly elaborate psychology, which we shall not try to explain other than to say that for him the soul consists of parts or elements that may relate to each other either well or poorly. In a healthy soul, these parts are in "harmony" (this musical reference *is* a metaphor) or "balance," which means that each part has its proper place or role in the "symphony" of the human person. A healthy soul, he maintains, is one that enjoys mental stability or emotional maturity, a condition that occurs when each psychological function is performed appropriately under the benign guidance of reason informed by wisdom. In a harmonious or well-ordered soul, desires, emotions, and what Plato calls the "spirited" element of the personality all cooperate under the mastery of reason. (In another dialogue, Plato offers a striking image: the soul is a chariot drawn by horses; reason is the driver. The horses of desire, emotion, and spirit provide the moving power, but unless they are controlled by reason they will run wild and the chariot will come to grief.)

Why should a person who loves justice be mentally healthier than someone who does not? The answer is found in Plato's psychology of wickedness. He argues that a person who is violent, consumed by hatred, bears grudges, or commits vile crimes suffers from a problem of self-control: his desires have gone out of control and overcome the power of self-discipline *(Republic,* viii, ix). Wickedness occurs when the desires, which ought to be under the control of reason and therefore subject to restraint, get loose, act like untamed horses, and run free. Lacking all self-restraint, the desiring person takes what he wants and does what is pleasing. To him, all desires are equal: to have a desire is to want to gratify it. He knows no proportion, rule, or morality. He is the slave of his desires, rather than their master. His life has no purpose other than to gratify whichever desire happens to afflict him at any given moment. In another striking metaphor, Plato compares such a person to a leaky vessel, which can never be filled no matter how much is poured into it *(Gorgias,* 494). Such a person cannot be emotionally secure, for only a person governed by restraint and proportion can enjoy mental and emotional health. And since justice means governance under rule and restraint, the person who is slave to his desires cannot love justice.

You cannot be emotionally healthy by seeming to be moral; you must actually be moral if you wish to be healthy. Thus, it will not do to act justly if you do so from a motive of gain or reputation. A just person is one who loves justice, that is, who is just for the sake of justice and not for the sake of what he or she can obtain through justice. Justice is loved as an end, not as a means. But although the just person is happy in the sense of having a healthy soul, this is consistent with the person not being happy in the sense of having lots of good things in life, including loving friends and material comforts. Plato admits that being just is no guarantee of happiness in this sense, though no doubt the just person is more likely than the unjust to benefit from loving friends, if not necessarily from material wealth. But a healthy soul is more profitable, more valuable to anybody, even than wealth and friends.

There is certainly a great deal of good sense in Plato's analysis of the psychology of wickedness, but it is limited and one-sided. No doubt some wicked people are wicked just because they are out of their own control: their desires rule their lives. They possess no internal censors or conscience—no super-ego, as Freud put it many centuries later. Violent people perhaps can be so described, as can those who suffer from an inability to delay their gratifications. Such people do not strike us as very healthy mentally; we might even regard them as mentally ill in a clinical sense. But not all wickedness can be so described. Plato takes no account of the cool and collected criminal, who is wicked as a result of rational calculation: the forger, the art thief, the embezzler, or the man who murders his wife to collect the insurance. Villainy comes in many psychological garbs. In Shakespeare's *Measure for Measure,* the villain is the apparently upright and morally rigorous Angelo, governor of Vienna, who conceives a lustful passion for the virtuous Isabella. The plot is about Angelo's cold-blooded attempt to coerce Isabella by threatening to execute her brother, who has been convicted of some minor crime. What is damaging for Plato's theory is that people like Angelo do not seem to suffer from their wickedness; on the contrary, successful villainy brings them enormous gratification. Angelo is, of course, ultimately exposed and punished, as are all villains in Shakespeare, but there is no suggestion that he is emotionally weak, psychologically unstable, or mentally ill. (In this regard, Angelo differs from other Shakespearean villains such as Iago and Richard III, whose intense hatred has its source in some deep emotional deprivation.) Of course, it must be the case that there is something that explains Angelo's wickedness, but it is not necessarily something we would consider mental illness. So Plato is not convincing in arguing that the wicked person is necessarily mentally ill, and that unless you love justice you cannot enjoy mental health.

Angelo's case does support one of Plato's points, that injustice may be the result of strong desires or emotions (lust, in this case; but greed, hatred, and jealousy can have the same effect) overcoming reason and moral principle. The difficulty is that Plato wants to generalize this into a hypothesis that all immorality is the consequence of overly strong desire. And this appears to be not the case. Two students may have exactly the same desire to pass a test, but one cheats and the other does not. Why? There can be many reasons; perhaps the cheater does not have much confidence in her knowledge; or does not want to risk losing her sports eligibility; or is afraid of her parents. There is no reason to suppose that the cheater cheated because she was overcome by one of these emotions; maybe she cheated as a result of a calculated decision. The only generality we can make is that if a person cheats, her motivation to pass the test must have been stronger than her motivation to be honest. But this is a tautology; it does not prove that immoral people are always overcome by strong desires.

The conclusion that only the person who loves justice can have a healthy soul largely follows from Plato's definitions. He defines justice as "having your own," so that it follows that a just soul is a soul in which each part does or has exactly what it is supposed to do or have. And he defines a healthy soul as one in which the elements are properly balanced, each in its proper place. But nothing really follows from definitions: a critic could say that an unjust person, though he cannot have a healthy soul in Plato's sense, might have a soul that is perfectly healthy in some other sense, namely, not suffering from any mental disease. So Plato's argument fails in two respects. First, he should not simply define mental disease as an imbalance of the soul's elements; he has to argue, with evidence, that anything we recognize as a mental disease consists in such an imbalance. Second, he has to show that no mentally ill people love justice. This proposition is an empirical claim, and a false one at that. Hence, we must conclude that even though Plato might be correct in saying that what we all want more than anything else is mental health, he has not shown that having mental health and loving justice—being a moral person—are one and the same.

Self-Realization

The idea here is that what is important in a person's life is self-development, self-expression, or self-realization. Slogans such as "Be yourself" and "To thy own self be true" express this thought. But what is a person's own self? Are we to imagine that a person has a kind of hidden inner nature or real self that should be allowed to emerge? If so, some theory is needed to explain what this is and why it is good to be true to it.

Any such theory has to solve the problem that Plato faced, that of connecting the inner self with morality. Plato was aware that our anarchistic and destructive nature is just as real and even more powerful than our creative and loving nature, and therefore sought internal controls rather than uninhibited self-expression. Self-realization ethics can not merely assume that a person who realizes his or her nature will be a morally good person, since people can be aggressive, selfish, unjust, and cruel; if self-realization is the only standard, it is unclear how these evil aspects of human personality can be controlled.

Here we will consider self-realization as part of a philosophical theory called *absolute idealism,* a metaphysical view first formulated in Germany that became popular in England and the United States in the late nineteenth century. The leading figures are the English philosophers T. H. Green and F. H. Bradley, and the American philosopher Josiah Royce. (The staying power of the movement is noteworthy: Green was born in 1836 and Bradley lived to 1924, when he died at the age of 88. Of lesser power but perhaps more topical in his views was Royce [1855–1916], who typified late Victorian self-confident religiosity. An interesting but no doubt minor figure is the American, Brand Blanshard, often thought of as the last of the absolute idealists, who died in 1987 at the age of 95.) Their metaphysics appealed to a certain "spiritualizing" sensibility of the late Victorian era that was made uncomfortable by the thought that the universe was constituted by the dead, purposeless matter portrayed by physical science. The idealists wanted a universe that suited our highest aspirations, as they imagined them: meaning, unity, goodness, thought, logic, and infinity needed to be real, not simple byproducts of human brain chemistry. So they likened the universe to a living organism, or even a sort of person or self, rather than to a lifeless machine. As a self, the essence of the universe is said to be thought, mind, or purpose. Since it is an organism, the universe does not consist of independent material things externally related by physical laws, but of interconnected elements united organically, that is, connected in such a way that each part or element of the universe depends on every other part and on the whole.

According to the idealists, nothing is intelligible other than by being connected to other things, so that what is most intelligible, and hence most real, is what is most connected or coherent with everything else. Unity or coherence is thus the same as reality.

The idealists tried to reproduce or incorporate these ideas in their ethical theory. The main ideas are coherence, organic unity, and the principle that parts depend on the whole. They vigorously opposed what they saw as the atomistic and mechanistic view of the psychology of their day, which regarded the self as a collection of independent mental states loosely associated with each other. An unorganized collection of impulses, desires, thoughts, and perceptions do not constitute a self. These need to be integrated into a unity of personality, and are organic in that each part depends on every other, each getting its meaning by the place or function it has in the total life of the self. In the coherent self, no element is without its role; there are no stray thoughts or random impulses, but all are organized into a total personality.

The organizing of the self is a rational process conducted by the will. We will many things, not all of which we can or should have. An irrational will is inconsistent; by willing one thing you are prevented from obtaining other things that you will. What is rational is to will in such a way that as much of your will can be realized as possible; in that way, we can obtain a single unified will that is perfectly consistent with itself. But this can only be done if all our willings are brought together under a single principle or universal law. So the point of life is to create for yourself a coherent self in which everything hangs together, made intelligible by a universal principle. When you have accomplished this, if you can, you have made yourself into what you really are, a mirror image of the Absolute. The elements of the self must be made subordinate to the self as a whole: no element has any value for its own sake, but only for its role in the economy of the entire personality. This is self-realization, for when you achieve this you have given yourself an intelligible self that is therefore real.

But what is the connection with morality? The idea of a coherent personality is more than a little reminiscent of Plato, but the idealists added an important dimension present but not emphasized in Plato's philosophy: the social. Both the self and morality itself are social, in their view. They opposed the liberal view that society is a kind of collection of individual people whose ideas and desires precede society. They did not regard the social whole as the sum of the individual parts, for there are no individuals apart from society, and society is not an outcome of interactions between separately existing individuals. I am nothing apart from my social roles and relations; I am what I am because I am what society makes me. Like organs in an organism, individual people are defined by the roles they play in the social entity.

But in that case, self-realization is not the making real of some individual's personal identity, but of society as expressed in that person. To have a coherent self is to have a self that coheres with all other selves. The goal is therefore not the greatest coherence of each individual, but the greatest coherence of society as a whole; individuals cannot adopt coherent selves that are in opposition to social coherence. This is what Royce called community: people united with each other in a coherent social union. Hence, Royce holds that the greatest virtue is loyalty, commitment to a community that transcends the individual self and thereby gives one's life its meaning. The ultimate loyalty is not to some particular community but to all communities and to the entire moral progress of the human race, which means loyalty to a community in which each member is loyal to all the others. In the end, loyalty must be to loyalty itself, that is, to the idea of the unity of all people. Morality in the end comes down to social unity.

So the idealists solve Plato's problem of connecting individual self-realization with morality by defining the individual as a social entity. In a sense, there cannot be a conflict between the individual and morality, since morality requires social unity and the individual becomes real by becoming social: self-realization consists in internalizing the commands of morality by forging social ties with others.

Apart from its somewhat dreamlike metaphysics, there are important difficulties with the idealist position.

1.　The picture of the coherent self is less attractive than the idealists imagined it to be; it seems to leave no room for spontaneity, impulse, chance, or purposeless playfulness. A person with a totally coherent personality might be rigid, overly disciplined, stiff, excessively logical and focused, and too self-controlled. She might never have any fun nor allow any to anyone else.

2.　Some idealists, notably Bradley, argued that one's moral obligations are defined by the role one plays in the social economy. This seems to be a form of social relativism that leaves no room for UMTs, nor for the individual conscience in conflict with the demands of the community. Bradley was aware that his theory tended to exaggerate the social at the expense of the individual conscience, but was unclear how to avoid this.

3.　A point that Bradley seemed not to be aware of was the extent of the complicity of his theory with the social status quo. Making duty depend on social role seems to be a static view that imposes on people only the duties that their society endorses at any given moment. It is not clear how the moral progress that idealists endorse can come about, if there are no universal moral truths and individuals have no moral obligations other than to obey the rules of the current stage of social development.

4.   Criticisms 2 and 3 cannot be made of Royce, since his ideal of loyalty to the universal community provides a kind of UMT, and avoids the reduction of morality to social roles. Royce recognizes that neither community nor loyalty can be ultimate values, since communities go wrong morally and the value of loyalty depends on what you are being loyal to (would you be loyal to Hitler?). His idea of loyalty not to this or that community but to the universal community excludes communities such as the Mafia that use loyalty for the purpose of preying on people. Nonetheless, even a universal community might engage in horrific practices, and if it did we would not admit that loyalty alone would be enough to give the community highest moral value.

5.   It is ironic that self-realization at the hands of idealists turns into a theory of social morality rather than one of individual self-affirmation. This seems a far cry from the robust individualism expressed by authors such as Ralph Waldo Emerson (1803–1882), who is celebrated for stressing the ideals of individuality, independence of mind, and self-reliance. The quirky individualism of Emerson's younger friend Henry David Thoreau (1817–1862), escaping from the stress of civilization by retiring to the wilderness of Walden Pond, seems closer to the spirit of self-realization than the theory that an individual is only a moment in a social organic unity. Whether or not the social whole is greater than the sum of its individual parts, unless there is some room for individuals to be individuals and not just parts of wholes, self-realization seems an empty promise of a theory. But if you do allow individuals to express their individuality, then it is not so easy to see how morality can be identical with self-realization, and the self sinks as a foundation of ethics.

To make the self the foundation of morality, it is necessary to show that what is good for the self and what morality requires are the same thing; thus, a person who seeks the good for the self necessarily seeks to be moral. And the difficulty is that it is quite unclear that this equation is true, and implausible that it might be true. In effect, self theories say that moral people are happy and happy people are moral, and while this is not untrue if you look at the right examples (many moral people are happy, and many immoral people are unhappy), there seems to be plenty of evidence that it is not true necessarily: there are far too many people who are immoral but who do not suffer from it.

And why is this not what we would expect? The purpose of morality is open to debate, but it seems unlikely that it is to enrich any individual; if morality has a purpose, it is more likely to be to enrich society as a whole. There is no reason to think, and much reason to deny, that social well-being requires some sacrifice of individual well-being. As Freud put it, a truly healthy and contented person might be someone who is not afraid to gratify every one of his or her most anti-social urges. If that is even close to the truth, it will not be possible to base morality on any conception of the self.

REFERENCES AND FURTHER READING

Religion

There are two anthologies: Gene H. Outka and John P. Reeder, eds., *Religion and Morality* (New York: Anchor, 1973); and Paul Helm, ed., *Divine Commands and Morality* (New York: Oxford University Press, 1981).

A convenient edition of Plato's "Euthyphro" is in *Five Dialogues of Plato,* by G. M. A. Grube (Indianapolis, IN: Hackett, 1981).

A challenging defense of religious-based ethics is Philip Quinn, *Divine Commands and Moral Requirements* (New York: Oxford University Press, 1978).

Kai Nielsen, *Ethics Without God* (London: Pemberton, 1973), makes the case announced by its title. There are, of course, many other books with the same mission.

Nature

Aristotle's *Nicomachean Ethics* is one of the great books of the philosophical tradition. An accessible translation, under the title *The Ethics of Aristotle,* is by J. A. K. Thompson (London: Penguin, 1953). An excellent commentary is J. O. Urmson, *Aristotle's Ethics* (Oxford: Blackwell, 1988).

A selection of essays is in Amelie Rorty, ed., *Essays on Aristotle's Ethics,* (Berkeley, CA: University of California Press, 1981).

A convenient edition of St. Thomas Aquinas is *Treatise on Law* (Washington D.C.: Regnery, 1988). D. J. O'Connor, *Aquinas and Natural Law* (New York: Macmillan, 1968) is a good, short critical introduction. More sympathetic to Aquinas is A. P. d'Entreves, *Natural Law* (London: Hutchinson, 1951), Chs. 1 and 2.

Classical texts of evolutionary ethics are Herbert Spencer, *The Principles of Ethics* (London: Williams & Norgate, 1892), and T. H. Huxley, *Evolution and Ethics* (London: Pilot Press, 1947; first published 1894). Anthony Flew, *Evolutionary Ethics* (New York: Macmillan, 1967), is a devastating critique.

Edward O. Wilson, *Sociobiology* (Cambridge, MA: Harvard University Press, 1980) is the standard text; a popular presentation is Richard Dawkins, *The Selfish Gene* (New York: Oxford University Press, 1976). There is an anthology by Arthur Caplan, ed., *The Sociobiology Debate* (New York: Harper & Row, 1978). A good critical discussion is Michael Ruse, *Sociobiology: Sense or Nonsense?* (Dordrecht, Netherlands: Kluwer, 1979).

Dewey's views have to be culled from his voluminous writings. The most theoretical is *The Theory of Valuation* (Chicago: University of Chicago Press, 1939). Many of his books contain chapters on ethics, notably *The Quest for Certainty* (New York: Minton, Balch, 1929).

Hume states Hume's Law in his *Treatise of Human Nature,* Book III, Part I, sec. i (p. 469 in the revised ed. by L. A. Selby-Bigge and Peter H. Nedditch, (New York: Oxford University Press, 1978).

G. E. Moore's naturalistic fallacy is found in his *Principia Ethica* (London: Cambridge University Press, 1903), Ch. 1.

An anthology on the subject is by W. D. Hudson, ed., *The Is-Ought Question* (New York: St. Martin's Press, 1969).

W. D. Hudson, *Modern Moral Philosophy* (New York: Macmillan, 1983) contains a good, clear discussion of the problem. So do G. J. Warnock, *Contemporary Moral Philosophy* (New York: Macmillan, 1967), and Mary Warnock, *Ethics Since 1900* (New York: Oxford University Press, 1966).

"Thick" and "thin" concepts are discussed sympathetically by Bernard Williams, *Ethics and the Limits of Philosophy* (London: Fontana, 1985), Chs. 7 and 8. A related way of overcoming Hume's Law is advocated by John R. Searle, *Speech Acts* (London: Cambridge University Press, 1969), Ch. 8.

The Self

In addition to the *Republic,* the beginning student of Plato's ethics should become familiar with his *Gorgias,* in which Plato contrasts self-control with pursuit of pleasure and power. The image of the soul as a chariot is found in the *Phaedrus.* (There are many adequate translations of Plato's various writings).

Josiah Royce's works include *Religious Aspects of Philosophy* (Boston: Houghton Mifflin, 1885) and *The Philosophy of Loyalty* (New York: Macmillan, 1908). Like F. H. Bradley's once celebrated work, *Ethical Studies* (Oxford: Clarendon Press, 1924), these books have very likely lost most of their once considerable power to inspire readers. A good brief treatment is Ch. 1 of Mary Warnock's book noted above.

Chapter Five

Moral Facts

The naked truth of it is, I have no shirt.

Love's Labour's Lost, V, ii, 716

We say that cruelty is bad and kindness good, but what do we mean when we say that? Is it a fact that cruelty is bad? Is it really true? (It's a fact that fire burns. This is really true). Suppose someone changes a moral opinion (from antiabortion to prochoice, let's say). Has that person simply changed his or her opinion, or is the new opinion possibly closer to the truth than the old opinion (or perhaps further away)? In Chapter Two, we puzzled over the possibility that there might be universal moral truths. In this chapter, we turn to the related idea that there are moral facts. **Moral facts** are supposed to be real facts, just like scientific facts or historical facts. The chief property about any fact is that it is what it is, independently of what human beings want, feel, or believe. You may think that cruelty is bad, but unless you believe that the badness of cruelty is independent of what we people think about cruelty, then you don't believe in moral facts. The theory that there are moral facts is called **moral realism** (MR).

The question whether there are moral facts may strike you as puzzling, so to understand MR we first are going to compare morality to two areas with which we are familiar, history and literature. Ask yourself whether you think morality is more like history, or more like literature, and you will begin to understand what is being debated between realism and antirealism. We present some reasons why MR seems plausible to some philosophers, and then look at three arguments against MR, followed by arguments that support it. During these explorations we shall introduce the idea of projectivism, an antirealist idea first proposed by David Hume. Next, we turn to a recent theory, quasirealism, which is a kind of compromise between MR and antirealism. The chapter ends by considering three advantages of projectivism.

HISTORY OR LITERATURE?

Let us begin obliquely. What is the difference between history and literature? The answer may be obvious, but we are looking for a specific difference. Consider two famous kings: Macbeth and Henry VIII. You may not know much about each, but if someone asks you a question about Henry VIII, what you do know is that there is an answer, even if neither you nor anyone else knows what it is. For example, what color was Henry VIII's hair? Since Henry was a real person, you know his hair had some color, though you probably do not know whether or not history records what it was. But what color was Macbeth's hair? Nobody can say, for the very good reason that Shakespeare does not tell us. We call the question "What was the color of Macbeth's hair?" an *open* question because there is no correct answer. The question about Henry's hair is a *closed* question because there is a correct answer, but possibly not one that anybody today can discover.

For any question one might ask about history there is some correct answer, even if people today might not be in a position to know what the answer is. The reason for this is that history is a domain of fact, and there is some truth about every matter of fact. We can say that the difference between history and literature is that all questions about history are closed, but most questions about literature are open. Ask any question you like about any event or any person; if the event or person is historical, there is a correct answer, but if literary, probably not. For example: "What did Henry eat for breakfast three days after his eighteenth birthday?" Pigeon's eggs? Roast boar? Nobody knows, but you do know that either he ate breakfast or he did not, and if he did then he must have eaten something, so there is some fact of the matter and some answer must be the correct one. But what did Macbeth eat? There is no answer. Every answer is equally wrong, because there just is no fact of the matter to make any answer correct. Literature is full of gaps: authors do not fill in all the details because authors only tell you what you need to know to enjoy the story. But there are no gaps in the facts.

(If you do not believe this, try to think of anything that could have happened. It is either a fact that it did happen, or a fact that it did not. There is no such thing as saying that it neither happened nor it did not happen. This is a way of saying that every proposition is either true or false. In logic, this idea is called "the law of excluded middle," meaning there is no middle ground between truth or falsehood. This law does not apply in literature.)

It follows from this that if you are dealing with a domain in which some questions are open, then that domain is not a domain of fact. There are no facts in that domain. This is what we would say about literature. This may seem surprising, since we might be tempted to say that there are facts in fiction—for example, it is a fact that Macbeth murdered King Duncan and became King of Scotland. But it is best to say this is not a fact; if we must use the word, it is best to say that it is only a "fact" that Macbeth became King of Scotland (or: it is a fact that "Macbeth" became "King of Scotland"). The simple reason for this is that Macbeth is a character in a play and therefore incapable of becoming king of a real country. (In some movies, movie characters jump off the screen and interact with "real" people; but of course these aren't real people, only more movie characters.) (Don't get confused here by the fact that there was a real King of Scotland named Macbeth, who did murder his predecessor Duncan.) There are no facts in literature, though there are facts about literature. What really is a fact is that Shakespeare wrote a play in which Macbeth becomes King: "facts" in literature are, as philosophers say, "reducible" to facts about authors.

But we have to make a distinction that may seem to you to be a quibble. Though there are no facts in literature (only "facts"), there are correct answers to some questions. It is not the case that *all* literary questions are open. Did Macbeth become Thane of Fife or Thane of Cawdor before he became King? If you do not remember, you can look it up; it is in the play. So just because some domain is not a domain of fact, it does not follow that there are no correct answers in that domain, or that all questions are open. And there is another factor as well. Open questions can be important; in literature, the interesting questions are the open ones. Was Macbeth motivated by love of his wife, or ambition, or both? Had he always been ambitious, or did the witches put ideas into his head? And what about those witches; were they only figments of Macbeth's imagination? (Banquo saw them too, so they probably were real.) This is where interpretation comes in. Shakespeare does not answer these questions, so they are open, but it might be the case that some answers make more sense of the play (and are better supported by what Shakespeare does tell us) than others. We might be able to produce interesting, even logically compelling, reasons to support one interpretation rather than another. Some answers are better than others; never the less, it would be wrong to say that some given answer must be correct.

It might be thought that history also admits open questions, since history certainly admits to interpretations. But interpretations in history are always answers to closed questions. Suppose you wondered why Henry VIII divorced two of his wives. (Contrary to popular misconception, Henry VIII did not cut off the heads of all six of his wives. He cut off the heads of two, divorced two others, one died, and the sixth survived him.) This is not something you can look up, such as which wives he divorced and which he executed; any answer you give will be an interpretation. Nonetheless, there must have been a reason, or several, why he did this, and therefore some interpretations will not only be better or worse than others but will be closer or further from the truth. Suppose you said that Henry divorced his wives because his brother-in-law was a lawyer and needed the business. This would not be close to an acceptable answer, even if in fact Henry had a brother-in-law who both needed and received the business. Some interpretations are far off the mark, others closer to the truth, but all interpretations other than the one that is true are in fact wrong. Hence, in history even questions that can only be answered by interpretation are closed. That interpretations are necessary therefore does not prove that some domain is not a domain of fact, but only that not all the important facts can be discovered.

To summarize: if some domain is a domain of fact, then all questions are closed; interpretations are possible, but only because some closed questions can not be answered. If, on the contrary, there is any open question in a domain, then it is not a domain of fact, even though there may be closed questions, and interpretations are needed to answer the open questions.

What does this have to do with morality? The question is whether morality seems to you to be more like history, or more like literature. Is morality full of open questions that can only be answered by interpretation, or do all questions already have correct answers? Some people might think that moral questions are closed; after all, there is not much room for interpretation if you want to know whether you should break your little brother's arm because you do not like the way he is sassing you. But what about questions such as: "Should you forgive injuries or try to avenge them?" "Do you have a right to tell a lie if you really do not want somebody to find out something?" "Do terminally ill people have a right to kill themselves?" Would you want to say that there is a correct answer to these questions? Or would you say that there is room for interpretation and, though some answers might make a lot more sense than others, no answer is really correct?

If you think that morality admits of *any* open questions, then you are implying that morality is not a domain of fact, and you must conclude that there is no such thing as a moral fact nor a moral truth. It is not a fact that you should not break your brother's arm, nor is it true. If, on the other hand, you think this is a fact, then you admit that *all* questions in morality have answers, though we may not be able to discover what they are. You think interpretations in morality are like interpretations in history, responses to questions for which there are factually correct answers and not merely better and worse answers. You are a moral realist.

Why believe in moral facts? There are two very good reasons.

To Make Morality Secure and Firmly Grounded   The theory that there are no moral facts should make you uncomfortable. If there are no moral facts and all questions are open, then morality, like literature, would be a work of the human imagination, and we can make it contain anything we want. (Shakespeare could have made Macbeth an innocent victim of his scheming wife and the malicious witches, but he did not.) If you admit that it is up to human choice to decide whether it is wrong to break your brother's arm, then some humans might choose differently, and then it would not be wrong, at least not for them.

Things have to be *really* right and wrong, otherwise it does not *really* matter what you do. If it is not a fact that breaking arms is wrong, then why not break arms if you are so disposed? Morality has to be *binding,* which is to say obligatory on everyone, whether they like it or not. If morality is not really binding it is pointless, for there would be no reason why immoral people should not do whatever they please. That is one reason why morality is important: to provide reasons why immoral people should not do whatever they please. If there are no moral facts, then nothing is really right or wrong, and immoral people are not really doing anything wrong. And there is no real reason why the good people should do the right thing either. If all of this could be true, then morality would lose its point and might as well disappear.

It is better to hold that some things are just wrong, as a matter of fact. Facts are what they are independent of what people want or think. If it is a fact that

Henry had red hair (which he probably did, since his daughter Queen Elizabeth I had red hair), then there is nothing anyone can do to change it. If it is a fact that hurting your brother is wrong, then there is nothing you or anyone can do to change that.

Moral Facts Are Implied by Evaluations   There is no way to think morally or to make moral evaluations, which everybody does, without assuming that there are moral facts. When you say something is wrong, what you mean is that it is really wrong; you do not mean that you think it is wrong, or that it is wrong because society says it is wrong. (If you mean that society says it is wrong, you would say so; you would not say that it is wrong). And to say that it is really wrong is the same as saying that it is true that it is wrong, or that it is a fact that it is wrong. Everybody already believes in moral facts, at least implicitly, no matter what their philosophical views may say, so moral realism is only reporting, or making explicit, what people already believe and what our evaluative language necessarily commits us to.

Of course, even if our moral thinking and evaluative language commit us to some idea, it does not follow that the idea is true. When we look at morality philosophically, we might very well conclude that this presupposition of moral thinking is not true. Whether there are moral facts is a theoretical question about morality, and no theory is bound to accept an idea simply because we assume it apart from theory.

To this the realist replies that if in our moral theory we were to conclude that there are no moral facts, we would create an unfortunate conflict between our moral theory and what we believe when we practice morality. There would be an inconsistency between our theory and our practice. It is better to choose a moral theory that avoids such conflict, if one is available. And since the belief in moral facts is inevitable, in that this belief is a presupposition of our moral thinking, we can avoid the conflict only by adopting a theory about morality that accepts moral facts.

This argument is sometimes buttressed with a point about the burden of proof. Philosophy is neither a sporting event nor a courtroom drama, so it does not make much sense to worry about who wins philosophical arguments, but because MR is consistent with our moral thinking, it is sometimes said that antirealists have the burden of proof. This means that the realist does not have to prove MR is correct; unless its opponents can prove it wrong, MR should be accepted. Our analogy with history and literature is meant to put this claim in perspective. If you think morality is more like history than like literature, then you will agree with MR and look to see if MR can be refuted; if it cannot, you will conclude that MR is the better theory. If, however, you find that the comparison with literature is more persuasive, then you will not accept that the burden is on the opponents since MR will seem implausible to you from the beginning. You will not accept it without good convincing arguments that MR is true. There is no absolute burden of proof; you will have to decide for yourself where the burden lies.

ARGUMENTS AGAINST MORAL FACTS

Despite the realist considerations, moral facts seem more or less mythological to many philosophers. Suppose you wanted to describe some situation you regard as highly immoral: torture, for example. You go about describing the torture chamber in all its gruesome detail: the whips, the thumb screws, the rack. Let your medieval imagination roam. You imagine a poor victim being slowly crushed to death by heavy weights placed on his chest; or maybe his flesh is torn from his body by hot pincers. Enough! You have described something terrible. But what fact is the fact that it is terrible? Once you have described the whips and the weights and so on, and described the victim being tortured (do not forget to include the victim's suffering, his screams, and his pleas for mercy), it would seem that you have described all the facts that there are to describe. Is the fact that torture is evil an additional fact to those mentioned? Imagine drawing a picture of the torture scene; you can put just about everything in your picture other than the wrongness. If the wrongness is a fact, it is certainly a very different kind of fact from the "natural" facts that can be described or drawn.

Let us now examine three arguments against moral facts: the argument against moral knowledge; the argument from supervenience; and the argument from moral motivation.

Is There Knowledge of Moral Facts?

If something is a fact, then at least in principle it is knowable; there is no point in asserting that a certain domain is a domain of fact and at the same time saying that the domain is not, even in principle, knowable. This is true even of history, where, it might be thought, since the facts belong to the past and the past cannot be revisited, many facts must be forever unknown to us. But we can always suppose what we would need to know to discover such facts: we could discover the color of Henry VIII's hair if we should happen to find some long-lost document, for example. We can not say this could not occur, no matter how unlikely it may be. In principle, if something is a fact, then it is knowable.

Facts are typically known by methods with which we are all familiar: making observations, collecting data, and conducting experiments. Other than facts of mathematics and logic, which present special problems, any fact whatever is known this way—for example, historical facts such as the fact that Henry VIII died in 1547, scientific facts such as the fact that the orbits of the planets Pluto and Neptune intersect, and ordinary facts such as the fact that sugar makes foods taste sweet. Moral facts, however, are not; we do not observe the wrongness of torture, nor do we discover that torture is wrong by collecting data or devising some clever experiment. So knowledge of moral facts would have to require some special method or special power of knowing. MR must therefore claim that there exists a special power of knowing that we can use when we want to know what the moral facts are. What we do observe or imagine are the natural facts; we then use the special power to know the associated moral fact. Realists call this special kind of power *intuition,* and the knowledge it gives us *intuitive knowledge.* And the first argument against moral facts is that there is no such thing as intuition or intuitive knowledge.

Antirealists make four related arguments against knowledge of moral facts and the alleged power of intuitive knowledge.

No Power Discovered by Philosophers   There cannot be a power of knowledge that needs to be discovered by philosophers. No one needs to be told that we have the power of knowing by opening our eyes, looking around, and seeing the world; or by learning new ideas from listening to what people say; or by understanding logical proofs as in mathematics. If we really have any power of knowledge, no one would need to be told about it; and especially not by philosophers, who are not in a position to discover new truths about human powers. The realist argument is a bit inconsistent: that there is a given power of knowledge is a natural fact about the human mind, so it can only be discovered by empirical methods, not by philosophical theory. To this the realists reply that we do in fact know that we have such a power—we use it whenever we make a moral judgment. But this reply seems to beg the question, since the power has been postulated to explain how we know moral facts, the existence of which is the point in question. You cannot, therefore, prove the existence of the power by saying that you discover its existence in the process of knowing moral facts.

***Ad Hoc* Hypothesis**   Realists argue that since there are moral facts, and since these facts can be known, there must be a power of intuition. Antirealists argue that the alleged power is not known to exist through observation, but is assumed to exist. They claim the assumption is an *ad hoc* hypothesis. An *ad hoc* hypothesis is an idea introduced into a theory for the express purpose of making the theory work, even though there is no evidence independent of the theory that the hypothesis is true. The only reason to believe the hypothesis is that without it you cannot believe the theory, and you want to believe the theory. Such hypotheses should be avoided if some other explanation of the facts can be discovered. For example, suppose I keep losing my pencils, so I explain this by thinking that there is a "pencil ghost" who steals them. Why not? Something has to explain what happens to my pencils, and if there is such a ghost that would explain it. But the ghost has been created expressly for the purpose of explaining something, and there is no evidence that such a ghost exists other than the fact that my pencils are missing, which is the very fact I am trying to explain. This does not prove that there is no such ghost, but it does show that the ghost explanation ought to be avoided if something better is available. Suppose I discover my cat playing with a pencil; the hypothesis "The cat takes my pencils" would explain why they disappear and is supported by independent evidence, namely, that the cat plays with pencils. As between the two explanations, "Ghosts take my pencils" and "The cat takes them," we should prefer the second because the first is *ad hoc.*

The alleged "power of intuition" is an *ad hoc* hypothesis, for there is no evidence that such a power exists other than the need to explain how we know moral facts. "Intuition" makes the theory of moral facts work; without intuition we would not have moral knowledge and so could not accept moral facts. But suppose we can explain our moral judgments some other way, without the double hypotheses of moral facts and intuitive powers. Such an explanation, if it were based on what we already know without assuming things we do not know, would be preferable to the facts-intuitions theory.

No Distinction Between Moral Knowledge and Moral Belief   If something is *knowledge,* then there has to be a way to distinguish it from mere *belief.* For example, you believe that the ice on the pond is thin. But do you know that it is thin? Well, you could go out on the ice and see if it cracks. If you have not done this, or anything else to test your belief, then you cannot say that you know the ice is thin, only that you believe that it is thin. Even in the case of facts that are unavailable to us, such as most historical facts, we can still imagine what we would have to do to turn our beliefs into knowledge. Suppose I believe Henry's hair, like Elizabeth's, was red. I do not know that this is true, but I can imagine what it would take for me to change my belief into knowledge, for example, the discovery of a reliable portrait or document.

But what is the difference between knowing some moral fact and simply believing it? Do I know that torture is wrong, or do I believe that it is wrong? The difference between knowledge and belief has to do with evidence; if I do not possess enough evidence, then my belief is a mere belief and not knowledge. But what is the evidence that would prove that torture is wrong? That it hurts people? That people do not like to be tortured? That I would not want to be tortured myself? That practically everybody agrees that torture is wrong? This is all true, but none of these facts seem to provide evidence that torture is wrong without some other additional assumption, which itself needs to be shown to be knowledge. For example, if it is wrong to hurt people, then it follows that torture is wrong, but how do I know that it is wrong to hurt people? It is at this point that realists want to introduce intuition, but this begs the question, which is not *how* we know that torture is wrong but *whether* we know it. Where there is knowledge about some domain, there has to be a way to distinguish the knowledge from belief, but as there does not seem to be a way to distinguish moral knowledge from moral belief, there cannot be such a thing as moral knowledge.

Here is a related argument. Whenever we have knowledge about some domain, then it is appropriate to say that we also have beliefs about that domain. If you are a great expert on something, then almost all of your beliefs about it are true. Whenever you can distinguish beliefs from knowledge, you can say what information you would have to have that would cause you to change your beliefs. For example, if I believe Henry's hair was red because his daughter Queen Elizabeth's hair was red, then I can say that were I to obtain certain information (you discover a hitherto unknown document: it is a sworn statement from Henry's barber describing his brown hair), I would change my belief. Having obtained the new information, I now know better.

But what information would lead me to change a moral belief? This is a subtle question, since moral beliefs do seem to be subject to change. The celebrated author of *1984,* George Orwell, used to support capital punishment until he actually witnessed an execution; he was so appalled at seeing a living person in the prime of life suddenly put to death that he changed his opinion. Was it his moral belief that changed, or was it his factual beliefs that changed? Evidently, he had not thought much about capital punishment; maybe he had naively assumed that execution was something like erasing a figure from a drawing: a few quick clean strokes and it is gone. He overlooked the fact that the prisoner is not a lifeless drawing but a living person. So what changed was Orwell's factual beliefs; his moral beliefs only changed because the facts were not as he thought. Consider torture. You believe that torture is wrong. Why? Because it hurts people. But suppose you found out that people really like to be tortured. Do you change your belief that torture is wrong? Yes, but not because your moral belief has changed, but because you have learned a fact about torture. You still think that it is wrong to hurt people, but no longer think that torture hurts. Your moral belief that it is wrong to hurt people is not subject to change based on new evidence. But if that is true, then morality is not a domain of knowledge.

Inert Hypothesis   A hypothesis is *inert* if it does no work, that is, if it is not needed to explain anything. Antirealists say that "moral facts" is an inert hypothesis. What needs to be explained, according to antirealists, is the fact that we make the evaluations we do make, and give the reasons we give in support of our evaluations. But all this can be explained by psychological, historical, and sociological theories that are scientific, that is, subject to empirical verification. Given these theories, nothing further is explained by postulating that we make evaluations in response to the moral facts.

Suppose, for example, I make the judgment "Hitler was depraved." I may believe that I make this judgment in response to the very evident fact that Hitler really was depraved, but the antirealist holds that such an assumption is not necessary. The actual facts are that Hitler acted in such and such a way, and that I react to his actions by making a moral judgment. The complete explanation for my judgment can be given by reference to certain important facts about me (what I value, how I think people ought to act), my culture, our history, and so on. These explain why I regard Hitler as depraved. No further postulate of real moral depravity is necessary.

Supervenience

This is a somewhat technical concept that philosophers have crafted for the purpose of analyzing certain puzzling relationships. **Supervenience** expresses a relation of dependence between two things. "B supervenes on A" means that B depends on A, or is based on A somehow. One way of saying it is "B because of A." Morality is said to supervene on natural facts in that the moral status of something depends on the natural facts about it. Suppose it is cruel to kick your dog. We would want to say, "Kicking the dog is wrong because it is cruel." Being cruel is the natural fact, being wrong is the moral status, and the relation between them is that the moral status depends on the natural fact.

The supervenience of moral status on natural fact is not itself a controversial point; it only becomes interesting when what we have called "moral status" is said to consist in "moral facts." For moral facts are alleged to be just as real as natural facts; they are real facts, real parts of the world, independent of human beings. Therefore, the realist has to explain how such facts can supervene on natural facts; what is the "because" which connects the fact that this is cruel with the fact that this is wrong? What kind of a relation can this be?

If two things are related in some way, we can say one of three things: either the relation is a coincidence, or it is based on some causal principle or law of nature, or it is based on logic. For example, suppose you went to ten parties in a row and Jane was at every one of them. This probably would be a coincidence: Jane just happens to get invited to the same parties you do. Most of the important relations between things are not coincidental but causal: if you step on the gas and the car accelerates, this is not a coincidence but the result of the fact that the car is built in such a way that stepping on the pedal causes gas to be injected into the engine that in turn causes the car's wheels to turn. Finally, some relationships are based not on laws of nature but on logic. These are relationships that follow from definitions and methods of computation. Suppose you fail every test in your philosophy class; it would not surprise you if you also fail the class. Is this cause and effect? No. The relationship of "Fail the tests, fail the class" is not a law of nature but a logical consequence of the fact that your final class grade is a composite of your test scores. This is a matter of definition and computation, not of cause and effect.

The problem for moral realists is that the supervenience between natural and moral facts does not seem to be any of these three relationships. It certainly is not a mere coincidence that cruelty is wrong; and it is not a causal or logical relationship either. Causal relationships are generally thought of as being based on natural laws, which explain them. Thus, the fact that stepping on the gas causes the car to accelerate can be explained by various natural laws about the volatility of gasoline, the mechanics of piston engines, the inertia of bodies at rest, and so on. But there are no natural laws governing the relationship between, say, the natural fact of being cruel to someone and the nonnatural fact that it is bad. (Check your science textbooks to see whether you can find a chapter on "Laws governing moral facts"). Only natural facts enter into natural laws.

There is another way of explaining causal relationships. In a causal relationship between two facts, the existence of one fact brings into existence the second fact: the fact of stepping on the gas produces the fact of the car's acceleration. We might say here that the fact of cruelty existing brings about the fact of badness existing. The difficulty with this way of putting it is that there is no way of explaining how this occurs. When we say that one thing brings something else into existence, we generally think that there is some explanation available that explains how this happens, which we could express by saying that the resulting fact is due to some kind of causal power in the causative agent. For example, gasoline has the power to explode when ignited, releasing considerable heat and energy; this is what provides the power to drive the car. But there seems to be no way to identify any causal agency by which natural facts produce moral facts: what is there about cruelty, for example, that produces badness?

Here the realist might want to say that the badness is a property of cruelty. Cruelty just *is* bad; badness is one of its properties (hence, it is a fact that cruelty is bad). But this gets us nowhere either, for there can be no explanation of how it is that a given natural fact has a given moral property. We can explain the volatility of gasoline by gasoline's molecular structure, but we can hardly explain the badness of cruelty by cruelty's molecular structure! If you understand the structure of gasoline, you would understand why it is volatile. But if you understand a cruel act—say, wantonly kicking a dog—do you understand why it is bad and not good? Not at all. We would just have to accept as an inexplicable fact that certain natural things have certain moral properties, even though as far as we can explain anything they could just as well have the opposite moral properties.

Finally, supervenience is not a logical relationship either, since a logical relationship is such that there would be a contradiction asserting one of the terms and not the other. But there is no contradiction in asserting that cruelty is not bad; to produce a contradiction, you would need some intermediate premise—for example, "Wanton infliction of pain is bad"—about which the same problem would arise. (This point is what in Chapter Four we called Hume's Law.) There is a looser sense of logic, according to which, for example, logic tells us that you cannot torture someone by beating him with strands of moist spaghetti, since the purpose of torture is to inflict pain and spaghetti beatings do not hurt. Logic tells us that it is preferable to use a barbed whip; but it is not logic that tells us that beating someone with a barbed whip is evil.

There is, however, another way of looking at supervenience. Since none of the proposed elucidations of the relationship between natural and moral facts seems to be plausible, it is said that supervenience should be understood not as a categorical relationship but as a *hypothetical relationship*. A categorical relationship says: "This is torture, therefore this is evil." It is a relationship between two facts, the fact that this is torture and the (alleged) fact that this is evil. What is meant by a hypothetical relationship? A hypothetical relationship says that *if* something is evil, then any comparable thing is evil. "If this torture is evil, then any comparable torture is evil," says the cautious hypothetical relationship. It is said that the peculiar relationship between natural and moral facts that is called supervenience ought to be understood hypothetically: morality stands to natural facts in such a way that all natural facts that are similar to each other have the same moral status, whatever that status may be. So supervenience is not the name of the relationship that holds between a natural fact and a moral fact; it is the name of the relationship that holds between any natural fact–moral fact construct and all comparable natural fact–moral fact constructs. It is hypothetical, in that it does not say that torture is evil but only that if one act of torture is evil, then any comparable act is evil.

This is a perfectly reasonable way of looking at supervenience, but it does not help the realist. For the problem of the relation between moral and natural facts persists even in the hypothetical interpretation of supervenience. How can the realist explain why it is that if *any* act of torture is wrong, then *every* such act is wrong? When we are dealing with natural facts or with logic, it is clear why it is that comparable things have comparable properties. If this bucket of gasoline will explode if you drop a lit match into it, then so will all buckets of gasoline; but the reason for this is the underlying molecular structure of gasoline which makes it a volatile substance. If this triangle has angles totalling 180 degrees, so does every other triangle because of the structure (definition) of triangles. Again, when we deal with natural and moral facts related hypothetically, only two alternatives present themselves to explain the hypothetical relationship: either it is a coincidence that all torture is bad (not a very attractive theory), or there is a causal or a logical relationship between torture and evil. So we are right back where we started.

The conclusion is that supervenience cannot be a relationship between two kinds of facts, natural and moral. To hold that there are moral facts, therefore, is to make their relationship to natural facts impossible to explain. You would have to resort to an *ad hoc* assumption again: there just *is* a special supervenient relationship that the two sets of facts have, a relationship that cannot be explained as either coincidental, causal, logical, or anything else.

One chief attraction of antirealism is that if morality consists in what we believe and not in some set of real facts, supervenience is not difficult to explain. Suppose there are no moral facts but only beliefs. Nothing is really good or bad, according to antirealism; what there is, is human beings who think that things are good or bad. So supervenience amounts to a relation between something being torture and human beings believing that it is bad. But there is nothing mysterious about this at all: it is absolutely elementary that human beings believe torture is bad, and you do not have to search very far to figure out why we think it is bad.

If morality consists in people holding beliefs about things, then morality is no different from other beliefs people have. Consider natural beauty. Suppose you think the sunset is beautiful. We typically say that beauty is in the eye of the beholder, so perhaps "beauty realism" is not as attractive a theory as moral realism. But if there were beauty realists, they would have to say that the beauty is a fact as much as the sunset, and they would have the same supervenience problems we just described. If you think, however, that your belief that the sunset is beautiful is simply a belief, and that there is no corresponding beauty fact, then it is not surprising that a natural fact (colorful sunset) that appeals to your sense of beauty causes you to have that belief. Nor is it surprising that if you think this sunset is beautiful, you think that all similar sunsets are beautiful. This shows nothing more mysterious than that your beliefs about beautiful sunsets are consistent.

But your beliefs may not be consistent: people do not always have consistent beliefs about beauty, or about morality, or about most things perhaps. The hypothetical interpretation of supervenience would be then no more than a way of saying that people ought to be consistent. There would be no need to introduce some special supervenience relationship to explain how moral status relates to natural status.

Summary: Morality supervenes on natural facts, so if there are moral facts they must supervene on natural facts; but there does not seem to be any way to explain this supervenient relationship other than to say it is unique and inexplicable. On the other hand, if there are no moral facts and morality consists in beliefs people have, then the supervenience of morality is not mysterious, since it is common that our beliefs should be founded on our knowledge of natural facts. Hence, moral realism is not the preferable theory.

Does Morality Motivate?

Socrates was perhaps the first philosopher who observed that morality motivates. His view was that no one does wrong voluntarily, by which he meant that all that it takes for you to want to do what is right is for you to come to think that it is right. You cannot think that something is right and not want to do it. (This does not mean that you actually will do what is right, since you may be motivated even more powerfully by something else, such as emotions or desires.) Socrates' observation of the motivational power of morality was developed by Plato into part of the argument that there is such a thing as moral knowledge, which consists in apprehension of eternal moral truths. Plato was, of course, a moral realist—perhaps he should be thought of as the ultimate moral realist—so it is one of the ironies of philosophy that the same observation can be used as an element in a major argument against moral realism. This argument was first proposed by Hume in the same landmark chapter of his *Treatise of Human Nature*—Book III, Part I, Section I—containing Hume's Law.

Hume's Argument   Hume does not argue against moral realism as such, but against the even more sweeping theory that moral distinctions are "founded on reason." This theory is related to moral realism in such a way that its rejection is tantamount to rejecting moral realism, as Hume notes in passing. What Hume takes aim at is the view that morality consists in factual beliefs; Hume wants to argue that morality does not consist in any kind of beliefs. In this he goes too far, but his argument does point up a major difficulty with the realist view that morality consists in knowledge of moral facts.

Hume's argument centers on the question of motivation. Let us look at this by making a simple observation. People do things for reasons. But what is a reason? A reason is a consideration why you should or should not do something. It is a reason not to kick the dog that the dog will be hurt. But we should distinguish between something's being *a* reason, and something's being *your* reason. Something is your reason only if you in some way adopt or endorse it. That the dog will be hurt may be a reason not to kick the dog, but this is not necessarily your reason, since you may be indifferent to whether the dog is hurt or not. If you are indifferent to the dog's feelings, many people would think that you are probably not a very nice person, at least as far as animals are concerned, but this opinion may not move you in any way. You have not adopted or endorsed the reason that the dog will be hurt as your reason.

The fact that something is a reason does not necessarily motivate anyone, but if something is your reason, it necessarily motivates *you*. What this means is that it enters into your deliberations when you make up your mind what to do. You may of course have conflicting reasons for doing things, in which case not all of them can actually be reasons that move you to act; but if something is one of your reasons, it has to be a factor in your deliberations. For example, you may not want to hurt your dog, but you may think it needs to be taught a lesson about something it did of which you disapprove. If you also think that a good way to teach dogs is by kicking them, you might kick the dog even though you are sorry to hurt it. You consider all these factors and decide to kick the dog. When some consideration enters your deliberations, it becomes a factor that determines your action. So we can say that some consideration is a reason you have if that consideration is among the factors that ultimately produce your action.

Why is this an argument against the existence of moral facts? Let us put another question. Suppose you recognize something as a reason to do or not to do some action; do you thereby recognize this as your reason? The answer would seem to be no, unless—and this is a crucial point—the reason is a moral reason. For example, suppose you admit that it is a reason to buckle your car seat belt that it is safer. This is a reason; but is it your reason? Not unless you want to be safe, one might think; otherwise you would say no more than that it is a reason for someone else, but not necessarily for me. But now the case seems to be different with regard to morality. If you think stealing is wrong, for example, does that mean that you think that *you* have a reason not to steal? It would certainly seem so: your reason is that it is wrong (in your opinion). Hume argues that morality is motivating in exactly the sense that if you hold a moral opinion, you necessarily have a reason for acting. This is just what it is to hold a moral opinion, according to Hume: to hold a moral opinion is to give yourself a reason for action, that is, to have a motivation to do something. So if you think it is wrong to steal, you will not steal for this reason, unless of course you have other and even stronger reasons why you want to steal (you may be in a store and suddenly be tempted to take something; the temptation is so great that it overcomes your belief that stealing is wrong). A way of saying this is that having a moral opinion disposes or inclines you to act in accordance with that opinion. Therefore, a person who claims to hold a moral opinion, but is never moved to act according to that opinion, does not in fact hold the opinion; that person is what is known as a hypocrite. (You claim to think it is wrong to gossip, but you love to spread stories behind people's backs and never hesitate a moment to do so. You are a hypocrite: you only say you think gossip is wrong, but you do not really believe it's wrong. Your actions, not your avowals, indicate your actual beliefs.) To hold a moral opinion is to have a reason for action, and a reason for action is something that enters into the factors causing you to act. The idea that morality is necessarily motivating is called **internalism.** (This word indicates that there is a necessary, or internal, connection between having a moral opinion and having a reason to act.)

There is one more point that completes Hume's argument. He distinguishes between what he calls "passions," which are emotions and desires, and "reason," which is basically beliefs or opinions. Reason never motivates, he asserts; only passions motivate. Suppose you have a belief: you think dogs resent being kicked. This belief all by itself will not move you to do one thing rather than another. All beliefs are alike, in Hume's view, in being utterly cold and incapable of causing us to do anything. Suppose you believe the sun's rays are hot, or the moonlight is romantic, or snow is cold and wet; what do you do? Nothing: beliefs as such do not make you act. To act, what is required is some passion: you must want the dog not to resent you, or you must want to get hot or want not to get hot, or be in the mood for romance, or dislike being out in the cold and the wet; only then will you do one thing rather than something else. Reason can do no more than supply the information that enables us to fulfill our desires and satisfy our emotions. So there are two factors in action: desires, which make you want to do something, and beliefs, which give you the information you need to carry out your desires. Hence, this part of the account is called the **belief-desire theory** of action. It divides the thinking part of our actions into a motivational side, which is desire (or sentiment or passion), and an informational side, which is belief. (It does not matter for the purposes of prompting you to action whether your beliefs are true or not, by the way; if you have the belief, you will think it is true, which is enough to get you going even if it is not in fact true.)

Let us summarize so far. Hume makes three points: to have a reason is to have a motive to do something; to hold a moral opinion is to have a reason (internalism), and beliefs are not motives (the belief-desire theory). This enables Hume to draw a conclusion about moral opinions. What, we ask, does it mean to say that someone holds the opinion that kicking the dog is wrong? We might think that a moral opinion is a belief that something is either right or wrong; we often use "opinions" and "beliefs" synonymously. But from Hume's three points it follows that *moral opinions are not beliefs.* And this is what Hume wants to prove: whatever a moral opinion is, it cannot be a belief.

So what is it? According to Hume, moral opinions are what he calls "sentiments"—that is to say, attitudes of "approbation and disapprobation," to use his lovely antiquated terminology. To hold a moral opinion about something is to have a sentiment, a pro or con attitude, toward it. The significance of this distinction is that beliefs are mental states that can be true or false (have truth values), but attitudes cannot be true or false, hence cannot be "correct" or "incorrect." And this is why Hume's argument amounts to a case against moral realism, because according to moral realism we do hold moral beliefs, and they are true or false depending on whether or not they correspond to the relevant moral facts. If our moral ideas can be true or false, then it is possible that we might be able to know which are true and which are false; we could have moral knowledge. But if moral opinions do not consist in beliefs, then there can be no moral knowledge since you cannot know something without believing it; therefore, there can be no knowledge of moral facts, which, even if they exist, are consequently irrelevant to moral thinking.

Note that Hume's argument would not prove that there are no moral facts. (How can you prove that there are no moral facts? Maybe they exist out there somewhere, in Platonic Heaven, or in Metaphysical Space, or even in the Absolute Mind; anything is possible.) His argument is an extremely clever way of showing that we cannot know moral facts, if there are any. The reason we cannot know moral facts is that we cannot know any fact without forming a belief about it, and we cannot form beliefs about moral facts. This has nothing to do with psychology, but with logic. Our moral opinions are not the kinds of things that could be beliefs, just because moral opinions motivate and beliefs cannot motivate.

You should recognize the affinity of this argument with subjectivism, a theory that Hume defends in the same chapter of his *Treatise*. Hume was the first philosopher to identify the major points of the subjectivist argument, and is therefore rightly regarded by contemporary subjectivists as their patron saint. (Hume published Book III of his *Treatise* in 1740; he was 28.)

Realist Replies   Can the realist reply to this? Of course, but perhaps not without some sacrifice. The realist can reply by rejecting either the belief-desire theory or internalism.

1.   The belief-desire theory says that beliefs do not motivate; only desires motivate. The realist can argue that Hume's claim that beliefs do not motivate is excessive. What is true is that *factual* beliefs do not motivate: that you think the sun is hot does nothing by itself to motivate you to go out or come in. But one could say that it is exactly a characteristic of moral beliefs that moral beliefs do motivate. This is indeed what we ordinarily think, and what Socrates believed. If you believe that something is wrong, to that extent you are motivated not to do it. Your belief that it is wrong is your reason not to do it. Hume agrees that if you *think* that something is wrong you have a reason not to do it, but as he holds that only passions motivate, he has to say that "thinking that something is wrong" is not having a belief that it is wrong. Instead, he explains "thinking that something is wrong" as having a certain passion, which he explains as a "sentiment" of disapprobation. (This slippage from "passions" to "sentiments" is a weak spot in Hume's theory.) But why should we accept this, asks the realist? To think that something is wrong is to believe that it is wrong. Moral beliefs do motivate, so the belief-desire theory is mistaken.

However, it is not clear that this reply will serve the realist's purposes. Remember that the realist holds that beliefs about morality are beliefs about facts, and are not different in that regard from ordinary factual beliefs. So why should it be just the moral beliefs that motivate? This is really a difficult dilemma for the realist. If realism holds that moral facts are real facts just like natural facts, then it is not clear how it can be that knowing such a fact can motivate us to act. Suppose the realist is right and I know that it is wrong to kick the dog. I add this piece of information to my store of knowledge, along with several million other facts I already possess. Now I know lots of facts: facts about astronomy, facts about geography, facts about history, facts about morality. Each fact is no more or less a fact than any other fact, but—here is the strange part—my knowledge that snow is cold motivates me to do nothing whatever, but my knowledge that stealing is wrong motivates me not to steal. How to explain why it is that only moral facts motivate?

This shows that even with respect to MR, there is a significant difference between moral and factual knowledge: one motivates directly, the other motivates only through the mediation of desire. So now the question is whether MR explains this better than antirealism. And it certainly seems as if MR cannot explain it at all; that only moral beliefs motivate just seems to be a fundamental datum, not to be explained but simply accepted. But antirealism explains the difference very well by holding that so-called moral beliefs are not really beliefs. They are sentiments. They are not informational. They are already on the motivational side of the belief-desire division.

2. The realist's other move is to reject internalism. This move enables the realist to assert flat out that having a moral belief is just like having any other factual belief: moral beliefs are not motivating. Only desires motivate. If you take this view, you will hold that a person can believe that stealing is wrong, yet not have the slightest reason to avoid stealing. She can, without any hypocrisy or "cognitive dissonance," go about merrily shoplifting everything not nailed down, all the while believing with total sincerity that stealing is wrong. To have a moral belief by itself gives you no reason whatever to act one way rather than the other. You also must have a desire. That stealing is wrong may be a reason not to steal, but it is not your reason not to steal unless you have the desire to act morally. You do not get this desire simply from your moral belief; the desire must be in some important (but perhaps difficult to specify) way independent of the belief. You must be a moral person, with a good character, who wants to act morally; your belief merely tells you what acting morally would be (not to steal, for example).

The important idea here is that even if you do not have this good character and have no desire whatever to do what is morally right, you can still know or believe that actions are right. This is crucial if MR is to be maintained. According to MR, right and wrong are matters of reason and knowledge, not of desire, so it would be arbitrary to hold that only those people with the appropriate desires could attain the knowledge. You can learn physics or history or anything else no matter what desires you have (of course, you must have a desire to learn those subjects, otherwise you will not even study them; but you do not need to have any other special desires), so why should the case be otherwise with regard to the knowledge of right and wrong? Right and wrong is just another subject of study that you can master if you choose; mastering it has no effect on your life. (If you think this sounds like what you read in Chapter One of this book, read it again. There it was said that learning moral *theory* will not make you moral; it was not said that learning *morality* will not make you moral.)

Realists believe that there is such a thing as knowledge of right and wrong. Unless they are willing to argue that the knowledge of right and wrong is arbitrarily different from all other knowledge, they have to allow that the knowledge of right and wrong is one thing, the desire to do the right and shun the wrong is another. Those realists who are internalists think that the knowledge of right and wrong motivates directly; they therefore reject the belief-desire theory. But realists who prefer the belief-desire theory must reject internalism, and hold that a person can have moral beliefs but not be motivated to moral action. This view is called, perhaps not surprisingly, **externalism.**

Many philosophers find externalism almost ludicrous, as our illustration of the merry shoplifter suggests, but that is perhaps not an argument since externalists claim to produce *empirical evidence* for their view. They appeal to backsliding, to wickedness, and to moral indifference.

The *backslider* is the person who knows that something is wrong, but does it anyway due to weakness. This shows that mere knowledge of right and wrong is not much of a motivator; one needs also a strong will, at least when temptation enters the picture. However, the backslider is consistent with internalism, at least if the backslider is to be understood as a person who wants to do the right thing but is not able to make himself do it. He has motivation to do what he regards as right, but not very much motivation.

Wickedness is more interesting. The wicked person is the person who does evil deliberately, that is, knowingly and willfully. He not only knows that something is wrong and chooses it anyway, but the fact that the thing is wrong is his very reason to do it. He chooses to do what is wrong precisely because it is wrong. To be wicked, according to externalists, is to be motivated to do something because it is wrong. Wickedness defeats internalism; since wicked people exist, it cannot be correct that believing that something is wrong necessarily motivates you to shun it.

No doubt wicked people exist, but is their motivation what the externalist imagines? The character of the wicked person comes to us through the Christian religion. Christianity defines wickedness as falling away from God, which can only occur through an evil and corrupt will since God takes care to see that everybody knows the difference between right and wrong (God writes this in your heart, so you cannot plead ignorance). Thus, Christian religion has a stake in defeating internalism. Christianity also has a theory about free will that it needs to protect: evil is attributed to the free choice of human beings, not to any failing or defect in God. To make this plausible, externalism is the preferable view. But despite its impressive pedigree, externalism may not be a correct doctrine. If a person does something that he knows to be evil, it may be doubted that he really believes it to be evil; very likely what he thinks is that it is commonly taken to be evil but really is good (the ethical egoist, for example, knows that people generally believe selfishness to be wrong; however, the egoist thinks selfishness is not wrong). Or perhaps the wicked person might admit that some action is evil from a certain point of view (society's, maybe), but not necessarily from his own point of view. For example, Satan in Milton's *Paradise Lost* is depicted as revolting against God, knowing that to do so is forbidden; but it is fairly clear that Satan does not concede to God the right to determine what is right and wrong for him,

Satan. This is actually an interesting case, since there is reason to think that Milton wanted to portray Satan as pure evil, that is, as revolting against God out of sheer pride and arrogance and just for the love of evil. However, it can be said that Milton did not succeed in doing this, which would not be surprising if internalism is correct. What Milton actually portrayed is a Satan who simply denies that God has the authority to make rules binding on him. Satan in his own eyes is not acting out of love of evil; he is simply asserting his right, which he thinks is properly his, not to be bound by laws made by another.

The example of satanic wickedness is perhaps too dramatic; can there be an ordinary person who nevertheless does not care for morality? The answer is very obviously that there not only can be but are many such people: they care for convention, for success, for fashion, for advantage, for reputation, for anything, more than they care for morality. These are the people who are *morally indifferent.* So it is argued that the existence of such people proves that internalism is wrong.

Not so, replies the internalist: morally indifferent people do not believe that morality is for them. People who are indifferent to morality believe that morality may be good for other people, but not for them; they do not regard morality as being a reason why *they* should do one thing rather than another. It is not that they recognize the authority of morality, but refuse to follow it; rather, they simply do not recognize that morality has authority for them. Hence, they are not a counter example to the internalist's claim that it is impossible to recognize the authority of morality and yet not be motivated to act morally.

Summary: The debate between internalists and externalists continues a discussion that was introduced into philosophy by Socrates, the first internalist. Note the distinction between **realist internalists** (RIs), such as Socrates himself, and **subjectivist internalists** (SIs), such as Hume. Realist internalists hold that you can know or believe that something is right, and it is this knowledge or belief that motivates you to do it. Subjectivist internalists hold that you neither know nor believe that anything is right; instead, it is your attitude of approval that motivates you. The difference between RIs and SIs is that SIs hold, but RIs deny, the belief-desire theory of motivation. SIs say that belief alone cannot motivate; therefore, if moral ideas do motivate, they cannot be beliefs. SIs think that it is easy to understand how pro or con attitudes would motivate someone to do or avoid some action, but they cannot understand how a mere belief would motivate anyone to do or avoid anything. RIs reject the belief-desire theory; according to them, mere beliefs can motivate, at least if they are moral beliefs.

And, finally, there are the **realist externalists** (REs). Like the SIs, REs accept the belief-desire theory and so hold that only desires can motivate. Since they are realists, they hold that moral beliefs are beliefs, not attitudes, which can be known to be true or false. And, therefore, they are forced to be externalists, and to hold that you can have the moral belief without the moral desire and so not be motivated to act morally.

Thus, only the subjectivist can hold both the belief-desire theory and internalism. Realists must reject one or the other. But if these two theories are more plausible than the contradictory theories, subjectivism is more plausible than either version of realism. The price subjectivism pays for this triumph, however, is that it holds that our moral beliefs are not really beliefs at all but something else, "sentiments" as Hume says (somewhat vaguely). Realists find this conclusion itself somewhat implausible.

THREE POINTS THAT SUPPORT MORAL REALISM

It is now time to look at arguments supporting realism. We discuss three: the implausibility of error theory; a problem with logical configurations; and the possibility of morality.

Error Theory

There is a very major misfortune that strikes subjectivism. It turns out that something we very deeply believe about our morality is not true. Worse, we reassert this belief whenever we make moral judgments, so that in a sense every moral judgment we make is false, even apparently inconsistent ones. (Two inconsistent judgments cannot both be false, logic tells us.) This is not a happy situation for any theory to be in.

What we believe when we make a moral judgment is simply this: the moral judgment is true. Nothing could be simpler. And when we say that something is true, what we mean is that there is some fact that makes it true, because what it is for any judgment to be true is that there is something (a fact) that makes it true. (If there is no such fact, the judgment is false.) Subjectivists have had to admit this, however reluctantly; as Bertrand Russell put it, "Suppose . . . that someone were to advocate the introduction of bullfighting in this country. In opposing the proposal, I should feel, not only that I was expressing my desires, but that my desires . . . are right, whatever that may mean. . . ." However, if subjectivism is correct, the subjectivist's desires cannot be right, and right means nothing; or so it would seem.

The realist, of course, answers that if the subjectivist's desires are right, it is because it is a real moral fact that bullfighting is wrong. But what can the subjectivist say? There are two ways to go. Either the subjectivist can stick to his guns and deny that anyone's moral feelings are right, in which case he has to explain the rather extraordinary fact that everyone thinks otherwise; or he can attempt to devise some theory according to which we can explain how moral opinions can be "right" and "wrong," within the framework of subjectivism. The first route is called **error theory** (ET) and is taken by J. L. Mackie. The second route is called quasirealism and is taken by Simon Blackburn; we turn to this later in the chapter.

Mackie makes the very important observation that the fact that just about everybody thinks a certain thing does not mean that that thing is true. As philosophers we are free to follow our theories where they lead and not be bound by what is normally called "common sense" or "self-evident truth," which generally means what most people regard as true without having thought about it very much. Therefore, we should not be intimidated by the admittedly universal belief that moral judgments really are true or false. But we do need to explain this belief. There are two explanations: projectivism, and the social account.

Projectivism   The belief might be a kind of historical accident, like the once almost universal belief that men and women are psychologically different in some very important way. But it might be the case that the belief is built into us in some way and that we are incapable of not thinking it. Hume himself notes this about some of our metaphysical beliefs, and suggests that something of the sort might also be true about moral beliefs.

The human mind has a propensity, Hume says, to "spread itself on external objects," taking its own inner workings to be real properties of nature. We think the fire is really hot, when in fact we know that the heat is a sensation caused in us by the fire's energy radiated onto our flesh. We think that the sky is blue, when we know that it only looks blue due to the reflection of light by the atmosphere. In fact we think that grass is green and snow is white when we know that any color is nothing but the property of surfaces to absorb certain wave lengths of light and reflect back others into our optic nerves. We spread our own perceptions back onto nature. (Hume's own contribution to this analysis of "spreading" is his theory of causation, which you study in a general introduction to philosophy.) The important point here is that we do not make these "projections" by free will or by ignorant mistake; they are built into us in such a way that we cannot help but make them. We are born to think this way. No matter how much I learn about the physics of heat, in my real life, when I get too close to the charcoal grill, I will not only say but think, "That grill is hot!"

We do the same thing with evaluations. Thus, we think that the sunset is beautiful, that maggots are disgusting, that elephants are wise and lions courageous. So the first part of error theory is **projectivism,** the claim that our belief that right and wrong are facts in the world is still another example of the mind's tendency to project its own thought processes onto the outer world. The tendency may be incorrigible, yet as philosophers we can unmask it for what it is.

The Social Account   Mackie offers this as a second explanation of our belief that right and wrong are real. (Mackie is not clear whether in his view both the social account and projectivism are needed to explain the phenomenon, or whether each explanation is sufficient.) The **social account** makes three points. First, it is in our interest, collectively, to give our moral judgments a certain authority, greater than they would have if we were to believe that moral judgments were only expressions of attitudes. We want to be able to tell those who dissent from our morality that their dissenting attitudes are just wrong. Second, society functions best when people internalize moral values, that is, come to believe that their values are really correct. And third, everybody wants his or her moral opinions to be generally accepted, which we could not expect unless we supposed that our own values were the correct ones that everyone else ought to adopt. For all of these reasons, we come to believe that there really is such a thing as right and wrong. And so it happens that even if we disagree about what the correct values are, we all arrive at the belief that there really are correct values.

Problems with Error Theory   If projectivism is true, then our belief that values are real is simply part of the way we are made to think and we have no choice but to believe it, even while we know that it is false. This is Hume's view: "Nature," he says, meaning how we are made, "is always too strong for principle." (By principle here he means philosophical discoveries.) But Hume is not very happy with this conclusion; he thinks it introduces an inexplicable and irreconcilable division into our thinking between what we think "in our study" and what we think in "real life." We would prefer not to compartmentalize our thinking, but Hume cannot figure out how we can avoid it.

Hume does not try to explain this tendency to "spread," taking it to be an ultimate fact about human nature. But by Hume's day the problem of "double-thinking" had been troubling philosophers for over a century, when learned opinion had come to the conclusion that our common-sense beliefs about the natural world were for the most part very far from the truth (example: uninstructed by science, we think the sun is a round hot ball not terribly larger than and not very far away from the earth). René Descartes just a century before Hume worried about the theological implications of accepting a God who creates human beings with strong propensities to believe falsehoods about nature; Descartes to his own satisfaction managed to explain that God did this for our own good, so that He is exonerated from the accusation of deceiving us.

It would seem that ET has to follow either Descartes and explain why we make the projections we do, or it has to follow Hume and admit that the mind's tendency to spread itself on the world is an inexplicable misfortune. But of these alternatives the first would seem difficult to accomplish and the second not terribly attractive. It is better not to need an error theory in the first place.

Problems with the Social Account   The social account ought to, but does not, distinguish two historical epochs: before the discovery of ET and after. For once our errors have been exposed as a kind of socially induced self-deception, it is difficult to see how we can go on making them. Who in Russia today believes that Stalin was a hero, after the revelations of the past twenty years? And how could anybody believe that there are moral facts, once error theorists explain that we only believe this because it is socially desirable that we do so? Unless we are constrained by nature to believe something, then once we find out that it is false we simply stop believing it. Social accounts may explain why we used to believe something, but cannot explain how we continue to believe it once we have come to regard it as false.

So ET has its weaknesses. But if we are not to regard our belief in moral facts as an error, then either we shall be realists, or we shall search for an alternative theory that explains some way that our belief can be "correct." Such an account exists and is called quasirealism, and we shall turn to it later. Quasirealism rejects both realism and subjectivism. It is a "have your cake and eat it too" theory: it wants to say that there are no moral facts, yet we may go on talking and thinking as if moral judgments are true (and false). It needs to explain how moral judgments can be true although there are no moral facts that make them true. This is a challenging task.

Logical Configurations

A very clever argument against subjectivism is due to the English philosopher P. T. Geach. He is willing to concede for argument's sake that when we assert a moral judgment ("Lying is wrong") we are merely expressing an attitude. But he points out that we do not confine ourselves to asserting moral judgments; we also use them in other logical configurations. We say, for example, "If lying is wrong, it is wrong to get your little brother to lie." The expression "Lying is wrong" looks as if it had the same meaning in both sentences, but in the second sentence we are not asserting that lying is wrong and thus not expressing our negative attitude toward lying. In fact, we do not seem to be expressing any attitude toward anything in the second sentence. The sentence seems to be a very ordinary hypothetical proposition that states that if one thing is true then another is true. But this would not be possible if the sentence "Lying is wrong" merely expresses an attitude and is not the kind of thing that could be true or false.

Further, Geach points out that we can make logical arguments with the configurations, and that these arguments seem to be valid. So we could say:

(a) Lying is wrong;

(b) If lying is wrong, then it is wrong to get your little brother to lie;

(c) Therefore, it is wrong to get your little brother to lie.

Presumably, anyone would accept that this is an elementary valid argument. But it is not valid if subjectivism is correct, Geach argues, because (a) is merely an expression of an attitude toward lying, whereas (b) is an assertion of a connection between two propositions. In other words, "Lying is wrong" is not being used the same way in (b) as in (a). In (a) the sentence "Lying is wrong" does nothing but express an attitude; but no attitude is expressed in (b). So the simple little argument turns out to be convicted—by the subjectivist—of committing the fallacy called *equivocation* (using the same word with two different meanings, as when you say "If Tom works in a bank, Tom's feet must be wet all day"), and is therefore invalid. Since this conclusion is evidently not acceptable, the subjectivist interpretation of (a) must be incorrect.

To this Simon Blackburn has attempted an ingenious response. The problem as he sees it is to interpret (b) so that it too expresses attitudes. So what can the subjectivist understand by a hypothetical sentence like (b)? Blackburn proposes that (b) is to be understood as expressing a complicated conjunction of attitudes of approval and disapproval. Sentence (b) expresses an attitude of approval of: [making disapproval of getting little brother to lie] follow on [disapproval of lying]. In other words, a person who utters (b) is expressing his approval of connecting two attitudes of disapproval. (Try and figure out how Blackburn is interpreting (b). We have used the [ ] signs to distinguish the parts of the sentence.)

If this is good enough as an interpretation, logical configurations can be understood as expressions of attitudes rather than assertions of propositions connecting other propositions. This seems to be an answer to the charge of equivocation, in that "lying is wrong" is made to express an attitude in both its appearances in the argument. But what about the entire argument: (a) and (b); therefore, (c)? Has Blackburn succeeded in preserving the logical validity of this argument, which is the point of his reinterpretation? Possibly not; the solution to one problem seems to generate another. For in the original argument, what is being said (which is what is said in any argument) is that if the two premises (a) and (b) are true, the conclusion (c) must be true. The conclusion is proved on the basis of the premises ("proved" means shown to be true). But on the attitudinal reconstruction, there is no question of truth, so what is being said by the argument? Blackburn is a bit unclear about this: he seems to vacillate between saying that the argument says that anyone who holds the premises actually must hold the conclusion, and that anyone who holds the premises ought to or is committed to holding the conclusion. Neither of these interpretations can be quite right, however.

The first interpretation would say that anyone who has the attitudes expressed by the premises must have the attitude expressed by the conclusion; but this would seem to be a question of psychological fact, which presumably cannot be determined by logic alone (people are notorious for having illogical and contradictory attitudes). The second interpretation is more promising, but even here it is not quite clear what is being said. Someone who has the attitudes in the premises is committed to having the attitude in the conclusion, but what is the sense of "committed"? One can be committed to something either morally or logically. Since we are interpreting a logical argument, presumably the conclusion must express a commitment based on logic. To say that if you hold the attitudes expressed in the premises you are committed to holding the attitudes in the conclusion is to say that it would be illogical to hold the attitudes in the premises without holding the attitude in the conclusion. But what does that mean? Normally, when we say that it would be illogical to hold two different ideas at once, we mean that both of the ideas cannot be true: if one is true, the other must be false (it is illogical to hold both that the earth is flat and that you can sail in any direction without falling off the edge). But there is no question of truth in our attitudinal argument. In what sense of logical would it be illogical to hold two different attitudes?

There is an obvious answer to this: your attitudes are inconsistent if you have both a pro and con attitude toward the same thing (you both favor and oppose abortion, let us say). This would be the attitudinal analogue to both believing and disbelieving the same proposition. However, Blackburn has to explain what it means for attitudes toward *different* things to be inconsistent with each other. What is the attitudinal analogue to believing that this figure is a triangle and disbelieving that its angles equal two straight angles?

Attitudes that are inconsistent must "clash" with each other somehow, as Blackburn says, but in what does this clash consist? Not in the impossibility of holding both the attitudes; that would be the psychological interpretation just rejected. Not in the moral undesirability of holding them both; that would be a moral point, but the argument is supposed to prove the moral point, not assume it. What Blackburn actually suggests is that someone who has the attitudes expressed by the premises but not the attitude expressed by the conclusion would be in a psychologically undesirable mental state, a "fractured sensibility" of which no one would approve. However, this seems to beg the question also, since the argument is supposed to demonstrate that the resulting mental state *is* "fractured," and so undesirable. The argument has to show that it is fractured by showing that it is illogical: what makes the resulting mental state fractured is precisely that the state is illogical. Blackburn cannot assert that the mental state is fractured in order to show that it is illogical.

Blackburn's attempt to solve the problem of configurations is part of the theory he calls quasirealism. The idea is that we can hold an attitudinal theory of moral judgments without sacrificing normal logical manipulations. We see that this is not so easy to accomplish. Most importantly, Blackburn wants to rescue the entire apparatus of "truth," that is, the principle that some moral opinions are correct and others incorrect. We shall shortly see how he tries to do this.

The Possibility of Morality

It has been said that the question whether there are moral facts is not only pointless but unintelligible. Making moral judgments, R. M. Hare points out, is an activity that would occur even if there are no moral facts, since what is required to make moral judgements is that people care about certain things. If you care about animals, you will regard treating them cruelly as wrong, whether or not "Treat animals kindly" is a moral truth. Moral judgments depend on the fact that we humans value certain things; since we would continue to value these things whether or not there are moral facts, to say that there are moral facts adds nothing to what we do or how we think.

This sounds like an argument against moral realism (Hare is, in fact, an antirealist), but Hare means it to be a "plague on both your houses" argument. He wants to say that the entire controversy is unintelligible, taking as his standard of "intelligibility" the effect something has on what we do. The difference between "p" and "not-p," Hare thinks, consists in the difference in what we would do if we believed "p" or if we believed "not-p." (Think of the difference in what you would do if you believed "There's a tiger in the next room" versus "There is no tiger in the next room.") Since our moral practice would be the same whether or not we believed that moral facts exist, the question itself makes no sense. Hare's point is not that there are no moral facts, but that the question whether there are should not arise.

However, this conclusion gives aid and comfort to the subjectivist and will be resisted by the realist, since Hare thinks that morality can be explained in subjectivist-sounding terms such as "caring for things" and "valuing some things more than others." But if everything about morality can be explained by the subjectivist, there is no need to posit moral facts, and MR is useless. We can, however, turn Hare's point against the subjectivist by noting that the important question is not whether there are moral facts but whether people believe there are. The belief that there are moral facts does make a difference; if people came to believe that there are no moral facts, they might eventually cease to care for anything, with the result that if morality is based on caring, morality would disappear.

Why might people cease to care for things if they came to believe that there are no moral facts? Because when we care for something we often think that it is really valuable, and we give this as the reason why we care for it. It is true that we sometimes care for things out of sheer love, which is indifferent to whether the loved object is really valuable. These two kinds of caring are sometimes difficult to disentangle, but insofar as we can disentangle them, morality seems to be the kind of caring which depends on the belief that the thing cared for is worth caring for. Let us give some examples. Parents who care for their children may love the child even if the parent believes the child is really not worthy of much love. This is the kind of caring based only on love. But consider the environment. Many people care for the forests and streams, and value clean air and water. Their caring is not based on sheer love, because if they did not think that these things were truly valuable they would not care for them. And morality seems the same way. If you care for justice, it is not because you just happen to love justice as a parent loves her child, but because you think that justice is truly valuable. If you came to the conclusion that there was nothing to justice other than the fact that you and other people cared for it, you probably would stop caring; after all, why should you care about it if it is not truly valuable?

It is correct, as Hare says, that if you do care, then you make moral judgments ("Do not hang this innocent man! It is unjust!"), and that unless you cared you would not make moral judgments; given that you care, it is irrelevant whether there are moral facts or not. But what Hare overlooks is that unless you believed in moral facts you would not care in the first place. And so in another of those philosophical ironies, belief in moral facts supports the subjectivist idea that morality is based on caring. Unless we believe in moral facts, we cannot have a caring-based morality. The belief in moral facts makes morality possible, even by the subjectivist interpretation of morality.

A MIDDLE GROUND? QUASIREALISM

It seems as if there is a lot to be said for both sides of this dispute. Whenever that happens in an intellectual debate, someone will conclude that there is truth on both sides, and therefore there must be some kind of middle ground between the two competitors. If you think that morality essentially is based on our attitudes, yet you think there must be some kind of moral facts and moral truth, you will be interested in exploring a middle ground. So let us see if it is possible to have your moral truth and hold an attitude theory too. **Quasirealism** is the position that there are no moral facts, and so moral judgments only express attitudes; yet moral judgments have truth values (can be true or false), and each moral judgment actually is either true or false. In other words, there is moral truth (that is the "realist" part) even though there are no moral facts (that is the "quasi-" part; it is really an attitude theory). Quasirealism begins with the projectivist theory of moral qualities (we spread them out onto the world, but they are not really there), but unlike error theory, it does not hold that projectivism implies that we are in error when we regard our moral judgments as true. Thus, quasirealism sets itself the task to show that truth in morality can be explained in terms of attitudes.

Obviously, what we are going to have to do is find a sense for the idea that a moral belief can be true even though there are no moral facts that make it true. The first thing we will have to note is that our theory of truth is not going to be the standard and time-worn, even if much attacked, idea that a proposition is true if it "corresponds" to the facts, because there are no moral facts to which moral beliefs can correspond. The second thing to note is that since we are working with nothing but attitudes, truth is going to be defined in terms of attitudes. In other words, we are going to have to say that an attitude is "correct" and the beliefs expressing the attitude "true" if they connect in some way with other attitudes and beliefs.

The problem of truth is a classical philosophical issue; the reader must study general philosophy for a review of the several theories. Quasirealism tries to avoid theories of truth by simply looking at what is happening when we use the word "true." If someone says, "It's a hot day today," and you reply, "That's true," what you are doing is expressing your agreement with what was said. If you yourself say, "It's true that it's a hot day today," what you are doing is asserting that it is a hot day. Hence, what it is to say of some proposition that it is true, according to quasirealism, is nothing other than to assent to or to assert the proposition. "P is true" is just a way of asserting P. This may not seem like much of a theory, but a "no-theory" theory is exactly what the quasirealist wants, since any other theory is going to point beyond the proposition asserted to something that makes it true. But on the "no-theory" theory of truth, there is nothing that makes any proposition true, because it is not something for a proposition to be true. All that needs to be explained is what is being said when we *say* that some sentence is true. And the answer is: when we say that a sentence is true, we are asserting the sentence. But subjectivists can admit that we assert sentences: to admit this is to admit no more than that we say, "Lying is wrong." So when we say, "It is true that lying is wrong," what we are doing is reasserting that "Lying is wrong."

This shows that we can call our moral ideas true and false. But remember that the quasirealist wants to avoid ET as well as the implication that no moral attitudes are any better or worse than any other attitudes. Therefore, he needs a theory that explains how moral sentences can be true and false. Morality must be a domain of truth, like history. But statements in such a domain must satisfy certain conditions that we impose on true and false statements generally. These are called *constraints on truth*.

Let us look at two constraints on truth. The first constraint is that truth must be *complete*. If any domain contains truth, then (according to the argument earlier in the chapter) every proposition in that domain has a truth value. The second constraint is that truth must be *consistent:* if any proposition is true, then no proposition inconsistent with that proposition can be true. The problem for the quasirealist is to show that these constraints can be met in a domain populated by attitudes and not by propositions. Here the quasirealist exploits the fact that among our attitudes is the attitude that not all of our attitudes are as good as they could be; we all recognize that it might be possible to improve our attitudes. (We cannot but recognize this about ourselves since we recognize it about other people: "He has bad attitudes" implies that his attitudes, or some of them, could be better. It would be illogical to think that someone else's attitudes could be better but that my own are necessarily already perfect.) The move here is then to imagine a set of the best possible attitudes, that is, the attitudes about which it could not be said that they could be improved. Then we can say that a proposition that expresses any attitude that is a member of this set is true. So, if the attitude "disapprove of hurting little brother" is among the set of the best possible attitudes, then the proposition "not to hurt little brother" is an ethical truth, and it is a fact that you ought not to hurt your little brother. Since every possible attitude either will or will not be included in the set of best possible attitudes, every ethical proposition will be either true or false.

But how about the constraint that there cannot be inconsistent truths? Translated into attitude sets, this would require that there can only be one best set. But could it not be that there might be conflicting attitudes, neither of which is better than the other? For example, I oppose polygamy, but you favor it. All our other attitudes are identical. Might it not be the case that neither of the resulting total sets is better than the other? Yes, but then neither set would be the best possible set. For as soon as I recognize that your attitude is no less acceptable than mine, my own attitude must change; if it is not unacceptable to favor polygamy then it cannot be admirable to oppose it. Hence, toleration of both is better. Whenever I regard two attitudes as inconsistent, then either I must regard one or the other attitude as inferior, in which case both are not members of the set of best attitudes; or if I regard both as equally admirable, then as a matter of logic I must recognize that neither is the best attitude, but rather an attitude of toleration that embraces them both is better. So if I think it is equally acceptable to favor polygamy or oppose it, I should hold that "To each his own in matters of marriage" is closer to the ethical truth than is "Shun polygamy" or "Practice polygamy," and the set of attitudes containing the attitude of toleration is a better set than either of the others. In principle, a single set of best attitudes is possible.

Nothing in all of this helps us to understand which set of attitudes actually is the best, or for that matter what would count as making one attitude better than another, but that is not the quasirealist's point. Quasirealists will let you adopt any theory you please about what is morally good or what is morally bad; their interest is in the purely theoretical conception of moral truth. They wish to avoid error theory, the claim that our moral language is fundamentally mistaken because moral judgments have no truth value. With the idea of the unique set of best attitudes, they can argue that even though there are no moral facts because all is attitude, it is possible to explain how moral judgments do have truth values. The set of best attitudes is like the set of true propositions: complete and consistent. A judgement expressing an attitude in this set is true; any other judgement is false. No error theory is needed.

Quasirealists must make an assumption: they assume that truth can be separated from fact. The quasirealist compromise consists in rejecting the notion of moral fact yet rescuing the idea of moral truth. They have to hold that when we regard moral judgments as true or false, we do not make the false assumption that there are moral facts that make the judgments true and false. But to some people it sounds very odd to hold that we can assume truth without assuming facts, since in their view to think an idea true just *is* to think that there are facts that make it true. After all, if it is true to say that torture is evil, then there would seem to be something that torture really is: evil.

How odd is the quasirealist compromise? Remember that projectivism is a view held originally outside of ethics: we "project" colors onto objects and (if Hume is correct) "project" causes and effects into the world. Consider colors. The projectivist tells you that the sky is not really blue, but does the projectivist tell you that when you say the sky is blue you make an error? Not necessarily; we should distinguish *pure projectivism* from *quasirealist projectivism*. (Pure projectivism would be in ontology what error theory is in moral theory.) The quasirealist projectivist approach is to "save" our ordinary talk about colors by arguing that, even though colors are not in things but are our own reactions to light, it is nonetheless correct to say that the sky is blue, the apple is red, and the grass is green because that is how they appear to the normal eye under standard conditions. Our color talk can be true even though there are no real colors to make it true. Perhaps something of the sort can be done for our talk about right and wrong.

Quasirealist projectivism has extremely interesting consequences, not only for general philosophy but for projectivism itself. We cannot go into these consequences here, other than to note that according to the quasirealist interpretation of projectivism, the ultimate projectivist would be Immanuel Kant, according to whom *all* the "categories" by which the human mind understands reality are merely projections of our own mental processes. We find them in the world because we first put them there, says Kant; but we find them nonetheless. Kant calls his view *transcendental idealism,* to which quasirealist projectivism seems a very close counterpart. Applying this to ethics, we can say that we find value in the world (we can say this because our evaluations are sometimes true), but we find it there only because we project value onto the world through our own attitudes.

Whether we choose quasirealist projectivism or pure projectivism depends on whether we think the best theory "saves" moral truth. We shall close this chapter by giving some reason to think that this is not the best theory. If this is correct, projectivism is a preferable theory to realism, and pure projectivism is preferable to quasirealist projectivism.

THREE ADVANTAGES OF PROJECTIVISM

Realism and projectivism can be put to three tests: Which has the most plausible account of what morality is? Which has the most plausible account of moral disagreement? and Which has the best account of the significance of the question, "Why be moral?"? Let us assess realism by considering each of these challenges.

Realism holds that morality is essentially an intellectual enterprise, a search for moral truth. It therefore involves crucially cognitive skills—in a word, logic. This is what Plato thought: for him, moral thinking involves a search for definitions and principles which, like all truth, need only to be discovered to be accepted. Is this the most plausible picture of morality? We shall see what morality looks like on an attitude theory by describing the view of David Hume.

Hume's Theory

The reader will recall from the discussion of naturalism in Chapter Four that a distinction was made between *explaining* morality "by nature" and *justifying* morality "by nature." We pointed out that there are theories that can be called "naturalistic" because they explain ethics by appealing to nature, rather than to, say, God, an afterlife, metaphysical principles such as Plato's Ideal Forms, or alleged "nonnatural" moral properties and facts. Such naturalist theories do not try to justify ethics, that is, try to prove that ethics is "valid" or "a good thing" or "binding on everybody," or anything of that sort.

To explain ethics in ordinary, naturalistic terms is Hume's explicit goal in his moral philosophy. This he tries to do by tracing ethics to what he regards as fundamental facts about human nature and about our situation in this world. Given these fundamental and ultimately inexplicable facts, it is understandable why we have the ethics we have. It is also plausible to think that each person has a powerful motivation to follow ethical principles, or would have if they thought about it. So that, in a certain sense, Hume's naturalistic explanation of ethics does provide a sort of justification, in that his naturalistic theory describes the ethical principles that best fit human nature and the conditions of life, and explains the reasons why people should accept them.

We have already noted two contributions of the first order Hume makes to ethical theory. First, there is internalism, the claim that moral opinions motivate and must therefore be attitudes and not beliefs. Second, there is projectivism, the claim that moral properties originate in our attitudes and are imposed on the world by the human mind. As we have seen, one option open to projectivists is to try to "salvage" our prephilosophical commitment to moral fact; this is quasireal-ism. But rescuing common sense from philosophical criticism is no part of Hume's philosophical project (although some commentators think otherwise). His project is to explain morality, that is, to show what our moral attitudes would be, given certain facts about us. He regards this as a sufficient explanation of morality. It is not Hume's argument that we ought to have such attitudes but that, since most of us are rational, most of us will have them because we would be better off if we did.

Hume makes four postulates about human nature; these he regards as con-firmed by experience.

Limited Benevolence   Hume firmly opposed the fashionable psychological egoism of his day; he admits that self-interest is a powerful motivation, but denies it is the only motivation or even that it is always dominant. People do act benevolently, taking pleasure in the pleasure of others.

Sympathy   This is not the feeling of pity or compassion we have when we observe another's misfortunes, but the power we have to put ourselves in other people's shoes. We can see the world as other people see it, through our imagina-tion. A rich man may feel embarrassed or uncomfortable in the presence of the poor, but even if he has never actually been poor himself he has the power to imagine what it must be like to be poor. A perfectly healthy person can imagine (at least to a certain extent) what life must be like for those who are sick, blind, or confined to wheelchairs.

A Sense of Fair Play   We are disinterested. That is, we do not necessarily see the world from our own perspective, but are able to take a more universal per-spective, seeing things as anybody might see them. This enables us to take a "moral point of view," from which we see things from the point of view of an impartial spectator. For example, if I think of someone as my enemy, I see him from my own point of view; for all I know, he is kind and loving to everyone else. But when I think of him as "vicious, odious, and depraved," as Hume says, I view him not from my own point of view but from the point of view of anyone. This is disinterested, for I think of him not as being an enemy to me (he might actually be quite pleasant to me personally), but potentially to anyone at all. I am judging impartially because I am giving my own interests no greater place than the inter-ests of anybody.

Reason
People have enough reason to understand the effects of their actions and to guide their behavior so as to obtain the goals they seek.

With these assumptions, Hume can give an account of morality based on our attitudes of approval and disapproval. Morality for Hume consists in taking a point of view that is disinterested, that is, which belongs to anyone. Our approval of an action is moral approval if we approve the action without regard to the people involved in the action; what we approve is doing this *kind of thing,* rather than doing it to such and such a person. You are generous to me or to my friend; I approve, but my approval is not moral approval, because I love my friends and approve generous actions toward them for that reason. But because I am benevolent and fair, I can be disinterested, and approve of generosity no matter to whom it is addressed, even to people I do not know. This makes my approval moral approval; the actions we approve when we take the disinterested point of view are those we can regard as morally good. Given his premises about benevolence, sympathy, and rationality, Hume supposes that just about everybody would approve the same kinds of actions. Which? Those that promote friendship, prosperity, and harmonious social relations, for these appeal to our benevolence and sympathy. Which would we censure? Those actions that have the contrary effect.

Given the prevalence of such sentiments, Hume thinks, it is fairly clear what the moral values would be: people would favor generosity, courage, kindliness, modesty, emotional moderation, and a long list of other similar virtues. They would favor rules requiring respecting other people's lives and property, keeping your word, and dealing fairly with others. These virtues and rules would be in a certain sense "conventions," in that they are entirely constructed by human beings, but like the rules of law they are neither arbitrary nor unintelligible. They reflect our natural and learned preferences and prompt us toward well-being, which is what sympathetic, fair-minded, and reasonably benevolent people would naturally approve.

Hume supports his theory with acute observations about social reinforcement mechanisms that, as he explains, work to strengthen the generous and impartial attitudes and to weaken our natural attitudes of avarice, self-love, and partiality. We need not report all this here, since we are arguing that there exists—and has existed for over two hundred years—a powerful theory based on attitudes that explains morality. If this is true, there is no need for MR's appeal to moral facts and intuitions.

Moral Disagreement

The second criterion by which we compare realism and projectivism is their view of moral disagreement. Which theory seems to fit best with what we know about moral dispute? Moral disagreements exist, and moral debate occurs. Yet discussion of moral issues sometimes leads to agreement, sometimes brings the parties closer together, and sometimes enables each side to see the other's point of view, all of which would happen more often if people obeyed basic principles of civilized discourse. However, sometimes agreement is not reached and the sides may remain as far apart as ever. For various reasons, not all moral disagreements can be resolved by reasoned discussion.

Given this, we can say:

1. Moral disagreement can be reduced by intelligent discussion.
2. It is possible to come to see the other side's point of view.

3. Moral disagreement is often over the importance to be given to competing values.

4. Disagreements about basic moral principles are frequently not resolved by discovery of new facts.

5. Some moral disagreements are intractable, which means some moral disputes cannot be resolved.

1.   There are certain basic rules you must follow if you expect to resolve moral disagreements intelligently. Distinguish the moral issues from the factual issues, and be clear you know what the facts really are; think through your own ideas before presenting them; reason logically from premises to conclusion; do not assume your opponent is stupid or immoral until proved otherwise; make an honest attempt to understand the arguments that can be made for the other side. You must be able to identify and avoid basic "informal" fallacies: *ad hominem* (attacking the opponent rather than the argument); arguments to or against *authority,* also known as guilt by association, which means accepting or rejecting a point because you do or do not like its origins or others who advocate it, such as: "The Pope is against birth control, therefore birth control must be [good/bad]"; changing the subject, irrelevant counterexamples, and equivocation (subtly or not so subtly changing the meaning of words in the middle of the argument), all of which amount to *confusing the issue* or throwing dust in the opponent's eyes; *begging the question,* as in "The Bible is the Word of God, which is proved by the miracles it reports"; pounding the table ("By God, I'm right about this!") and other forms of *emotional outbursts; innuendo and intimidation,* as in, "Of course you would defend homosexuals"; *poisoning the well,* for example, by calling some theory "racist" rather than refuting it; and other ways of arguing fallaciously, all of which you will learn about in your logic and critical reasoning courses.

2.   Debaters who follow these rules scrupulously will be able to discuss difficult and emotional issues thoughtfully and with considerable civility. Even if no accommodation of views occurs, both sides will understand where and why they differ, and come to "agree to disagree" intelligently.

But meeting these conditions does not guarantee that moral disagreements will be resolved. Why not?

3.   One important reason is the necessity of balancing values. There is no formula for this, so judgment is required, and different people will judge differently. Your friend who is under the age of 21 asks to borrow your driver's license—you are "legal"—so he can go to the bar that night; do you lend it to him? You know your friend has been going to the health center for treatment of a sexually transmitted disease; do you ask him if he has told his girlfriend? Loyalty, friendship, honesty, and privacy are values everybody accepts, but which are the most important, and how do you decide what to do if they conflict? If you talk to your

friend about his girlfriend, he may accuse you of butting into his business; is it worth the risk? If you discover that your friend has not told his girlfriend, do you tell her yourself? You can talk these problems over with your peers and spiritual advisor, but in the end what you do is a question of your own judgment and values. If your friend objects to your decision, you can talk about it with him, but assuming he sincerely would not have done what you did were he in your position, the two of you may never wind up seeing eye-to-eye.

4.   This illustrates that even when all the facts are known, including the consequences of alternative actions, agreement may be elusive. It may be that the facts are often not entirely known, especially since it is difficult to predict how people will react to what you do, for example, whether your friend will be angry or secretly relieved if you tell his girlfriend; but even if the facts are clear, the moral problem might remain. You might think it is not your business to interfere in your friend's relationship, yet you think the girlfriend has a right to know. This cannot be solved by finding out new information.

It is sometimes said that most people agree about basic values, and moral disputes are mostly about facts, but this appears to be far from the truth. Some people want to work and succeed, others prefer to have a good time; some people respect the law and will not violate it, others think the law is a nuisance; some people believe in settling disputes amicably, others resort to violence. When they disagree, they are appealing to different values, none of which can be proved by appeal to factual information.

5.   Some disputes seem unresolvable because the sides argue from different premises, holding conflicting moral beliefs that they cannot support but see no reason to reject. There is often no clear proof that one belief rather than another is morally superior, because a proof in logic is a valid argument starting from premises either known or agreed to be true; where the premises can be rejected without obvious error, no proof is possible. "If a fetus is a person, abortion is murder" is not a proof, though it is a valid argument, because there is no known argument that can show that the fetus is (or is not) a person. (The counterargument, "A woman has a right to do anything she wants with her own body, therefore abortion should not be regulated by law," begs the question, since if a fetus is a person a woman does not have the right to do anything she wants with her body. This illustrates the importance of avoiding the fallacies just mentioned.) We all agree that settling disputes with your fists is wrong, but basic values cannot really be proved. If you refuse to help someone cheat in a class and they look at you as if you came from another planet, it might be difficult for you to prove to them that cheating is wrong.

Given all these considerations, which view, MR or projectivism, has a more plausible account of moral disagreement? The picture of morality we have sketched contains open questions, to which there are no correct answers but for which there may well be answers that are better or worse. This makes morality more like literature than like history. This is an antirealist point, since MR holds that there are no open questions in morality. Of course, it is not possible to prove that MR is wrong; the facts of moral disagreement and dispute are consistent with the presumption that all moral questions are closed. Yet as Ralph Waldo Emerson said with a far different connotation, mere consistency is the hobgoblin of little minds. In philosophy, where theories are never proved with anything approaching rigor, mere consistency with what is known is at best a minimal condition for acceptance of a theory. What is needed is a robust plausibility, a deep sense of the credible given the known facts. If the known facts about moral disagreement are those just discussed, then the theory that morality, like literature, contains open questions that can fruitfully be debated but never finally resolved, seems more credible than MR or even quasirealism.

Why Be Moral?

Moral theory should give us some reason why we should be moral, but there is a paradox in the question. What could count as a reason to be moral? Assume reasons for doing anything are either self-interested reasons (if you are moral you will gain something: love, friendship, respect, happiness) or moral reasons (be moral, because being moral is the right thing to be). Now somebody says, "Give me a reason to be moral." If you tell her she will benefit from being moral, you are giving her a self-interested reason, but it is a reason to be un–self-interested, which is contradictory. If you tell her that it is right to be moral, you are assuming she should do what is right when she wants to know why she should do what is right, which is question begging. So neither self-interested reasons nor moral reasons can be reasons to be moral. Therefore, the question "Why be moral?" cannot be answered.

There is another approach. Perhaps the question cannot be answered because the question does not make sense. "You ought to do what is moral" tells you nothing, because to say that something is moral is the same thing as to say that it ought to be done. Hence to ask, "Why ought I be moral?" is to ask, "Why ought I to do what I ought to do?" There is no answer to this question because there is no question: if something is what you ought to do, then you ought to do it, otherwise it would not be what you ought to do. It would be a contradiction to say that you should not do what you ought to do.

Another way to put the point is this. Suppose there are moral attitudes and immoral attitudes. The question is, why are moral attitudes better than immoral ones? But what is meant by better? If you mean morally better, then by definition moral attitudes are morally better than immoral ones. But if you mean better in some other way ("I'll get rich with my moral attitudes"), then the question is irrelevant to morality.

This dismissal of the question "Why be moral?" is an evasion. Once you label something as "moral" you also label it as "what you ought to do," but nothing follows about what it is that we ought to label "moral" or what we ought to do or what attitudes we ought to have. The question "Why be moral?" asks, "Why ought I to do certain acts or assume certain attitudes?"—namely, those that we label "moral"? And this question is not senseless. If someone wants to know whether they ought to be dishonest, what they are asking is why dishonest conduct is wrong. It will not answer this question to point out that "dishonesty" is wrong by the very meaning of the word.

However, the "senseless question" response does make an important point. This is that the question "Why be moral?" has no special importance of its own. What is important is to determine which acts are the moral ones. Since this is the same thing as determining which are the acts we ought to do, there is no further problem about why we ought to do the moral ones.

So the question behind "Why be moral?" is, why ought I to do certain actions and not others? Take kindness to animals. Suppose you give moral reasons for being kind to animals: animals suffer; they are our fellow creatures; all living things have a right to be treated kindly, and so on. Anyone can still ask, why should I be bound by these reasons? Look at this from the point of view of the superenlightened egoist. What is his view about honesty? He is happy to acknowledge that there are excellent reasons why people ought to be honest. But he does not see why *he* should be honest. His honesty will not benefit him (he assumes), and he does not care about benefitting anyone else.

It is for this reason that Plato tried to show (as we saw in Chapter Four) that the moral person enjoys something more valuable than worldly goods, namely, a healthy soul. Plato is trying to argue that there is a self-interested reason to be un–self-interested. We have called this a contradiction, but Plato has anticipated this criticism. His point is that a healthy soul is a self-interested reason to *be* moral, but it is not a self-interested reason to *act* morally. The reason to act morally must be that you love justice. If you act morally because you want a healthy soul, and not because you love justice, you are self-interested, not moral, and do not have a healthy soul. Healthy soul is not a reward, but a condition you must be in to love justice, that is, to act morally for its own sake.

But Plato's argument involves a paradox of its own. If you aim at a healthy soul and not at loving justice for its own sake, you will find yourself loving justice, but you will love justice because you want a healthy soul and not because you love justice, which is contradictory. If you aim at loving justice for its own sake and not for the sake of a healthy soul, you will have no reason to aim at loving justice, since a healthy soul is the reason to love justice. In effect, Plato concedes that there is no reason to love justice for its own sake. There is a reason to have a healthy soul, because a healthy soul is good for you, and if you do have a healthy soul you will love justice for its own sake. Paradoxically, if you are self-interested and aim at a healthy soul, you will be un–self-interested and love justice for its own sake. (This is a bit like saying that if a sentence is true, it is false, and if it is false, then it is true. A famous example of such a paradox is the sentence, "This sentence is false." Try working this out if you do not see it right away.)

This is the same paradox that anyone falls into who claims that the reason to do good is for the reward. If you do good for the reward, then you are not worthy of having the reward, but if you do good for the sake of doing good, then (if the reason to do good is for the reward) you do not have a reason to do good. What this shows is that goodness is its own reason; there is no other reason to be good. But if there is no other reason to be good, because goodness is its own reason, then the bad person cannot be convinced to become moral. The bad person does not accept moral reasons, and you cannot prove to her that she should. If your arguments could convince her, she would already be moral. You cannot prove to someone that she should adopt a disinterested point of view or cultivate sentiments of benevolence. If you tell her that she is unfairly partial to herself, she will admit it but see no reason why she should not be. If you accuse her of being hard, cold, and uncaring, she will admit that as well, but see nothing wrong with it. How can you prove that she ought to feel certain sentiments that she happens to lack?

This is a rather uncomfortable conclusion. If you cannot convince the immoral person to be moral, does that not imply that there is no reason for her to be moral? If there were a reason, why could she not be convinced of it as well as anybody else? And if there is no reason for her to be moral, that would seem to mean that she has no obligation to be moral. That is bad enough, but it gets worse: if the immoral person has no obligation to be moral, then in acting immorally she is not violating any moral obligation, so she is not being immoral!

And it gets worse still. If there is no reason why the immoral person should be moral, then there is no reason why anybody should be moral. Morality appears to be a prejudice, an irrational preference for one thing over another. "Morality totters," to paraphrase what a famous logician once said about arithmetic. (Bertrand Russell had shown that there is a paradox in set theory, which was thought to underlie arithmetic.) This certainly will not do: there has to be some reason why morality is better than immorality.

How does Hume handle this problem? Hume insists that as far as ordinary matters are concerned, anyone has all the reason one can possibly want to be moral, that is to say, to be kind, honest, friendly, generous, humane, beneficent, moderate, decent, and indeed to cultivate and practice all the other virtues. The reason is your own happiness, to which everybody may be presumed to have a favorable attitude. This attitude creates an obligation to virtue, but it is an "interested obligation," as Hume puts it.

Hume may exaggerate the attractiveness of virtue, for his argument seems to prove too much; if morality were as tied to happiness as Hume makes it to be, there would be very little immorality in the world. Even Plato, who takes the line that immoral people are irrational in not being able to understand their own best interests, explains immorality by referring to the strength of the passions, which can easily cloud reason, defeat self-control, and make immediate pleasure seem more important than emotional health. That this can happen is not surprising in Plato's theory, since for him true happiness is something rather arcane and requires a good deal of philosophy to understand. But if, as for Hume, happiness is right on the surface and tied so closely to virtue, how to explain the evident preference some people have for vice? It would seem that we must admit that the connection between virtue and happiness is perhaps not as clear nor as uniform as Hume would have it.

Hume admits that in at least one case virtue is not tied closely to happiness. Dishonesty can be profitable. Hume imagines (*Enquiry Concerning the Principles of Morals,* Sec. IX, pt. ii) what he calls a "sensible knave" who sees how he can profit from trickery. The sensible knave is honest when he has to be, but cheats when he sees how he can get away with it (he is the prototype of the superenlightened egoist). Why not? Hume admits that it will be "a little difficult" to answer the knave "if he feels no reluctance to the thoughts of villainy or baseness. . . ." But Hume gives two answers, both appealing to self-interest. First, it is not as easy to get away with villainy as the knave might think, so before he enters into his villainy he would be well advised to consider the trouble he may cause himself. Second, the knave deprives himself of one of life's greatest pleasures, the satisfaction derived from the consciousness of one's own integrity, a pleasure that Hume declares to be incomparably greater than the possession of material wealth ("the acquisition of worthless toys and gewgaws . . . the feverish, empty amusements of luxury and expense"). (This last passage could be sour grapes. Hume was trained as a lawyer but would not practice; he wanted an appointment as a philosophy professor but could not get one due to his nonconformist religious views; instead he had to settle for law librarian at the University of Edinburgh. It was not until late in life, when his writings began to produce an income, that he became financially comfortable.)

Hume's two answers are not very effective. The first answer appeals to the knave's prudence, but the knave, being sensible, has already considered this point and has no need for advice from Hume. Hume's second answer is circular, which is not surprising since the response to the question "Why be moral?" was seen to be circular. If the knave feels no reluctance to villainy, he will neither suffer from a guilty conscience nor will he suffer from the lack of the pleasures of integrity, since these pleasures mean nothing to him. Hume has no convincing answer to the knave who lacks a conscience, that is, who is not equipped with moral attitudes to begin with. So, as he circumspectly acknowledges, his response falls short of giving the knave a reason to shun knavery.

But it does not follow that the good person has no reason to shun knavery. There are reasons in abundance to shun knavery. The knave is a thief. He is indifferent to the rights of others. He hurts innocent people. He gets his bread without earning it. How many reasons do you need?

Projectivists argue that Hume's failure to answer the knave is in no way an indication of a shortcoming in the attitude theory. We cannot give bad people reasons to be moral, but that does not mean that there are no reasons to be moral, or that we cannot give good people reasons to be moral. The imagined collapse of morality is averted.

Realists are not so sure of this. They argue that the answers given may satisfy the good person, but not the philosopher. Suppose the good person is also a bit of a skeptic; he will then want to know why he ought to care about these things. Why should I care about innocent people, or the rights of others, or being a thief (so long as I am not convicted), or earning an honest living? These reasons to be moral are all expressions of certain attitudes, but they do not justify themselves, as the sensible knave proved to Hume. The skeptical good person will want to know why she should maintain the attitudes that make morality possible.

At this point, the cat begins to chase its tail as the poignancy of arguing in a circle is demonstrated. The good person follows along as the moralist hopelessly tries to convince the knave to abandon knavery. "Your reasons, Jack," the knave challenges the moralist. The moralist replies, "You will hurt innocent people, you will gain your bread without honest labor." The knave is not impressed: "My gewgaws mean more to me than all your principles." The moralist tries again: "You ought not to want things purchased at such a price." "Why not?" asks the sensible skeptical knave. Moralist: "You will be a cold, callous, indifferent subpar human if you do." Knave: "Words. What is that to me?" "It is wrong," announces the moralist. "But that is what you are trying to prove," points out the logical, sensible knave.

And the good person can only agree. If morality cannot be proved to the knave, it cannot be proved at all. The good person has no better reason to be moral other than that morality appeals to her current attitudes. And that is why temptation is so powerful.

Now the realist argues that MR can provide a way out of this quandary, but projectivism cannot. The problem with the attitude theory is that according to it, there are no real obligations. There are only attitudes; obligations amount to someone's attitude that someone ought to do something. The attitude theory wants to make out that the problem of bad attitudes is a social problem, a question of motivating people and assuring that they have the right attitudes. But MR says that the problem is a theoretical one, of explaining why good attitudes are preferable to bad ones. If this is not solved, morality will be in danger: if there is really nothing wrong with bad attitudes, then there is nothing right with good ones, so good attitudes are put at risk. The attitude theory cannot say that good attitudes are better than bad ones, as Hume reluctantly admits. The best it can do is point out, somewhat lamely, that good attitudes are preferred by good people.

But when the question is not which attitudes good people prefer but whether a person has an obligation to be moral, the realist can make a reply but the projectivist cannot. Realists can say that there is a real obligation to be moral. It is just a moral fact that everyone has an obligation to be moral. This fact is independent of any attitudes anyone may have. Projectivists cannot say this, because for them there are no moral facts that are independent of people's attitudes. All projectivists can say is that they approve of people being moral. But that they approve of something does not make what they approve of binding on anyone else. It does not give anyone else an obligation to be moral.

Let us be clear about what the realist is claiming. MR does not claim to be able to prove that there is an obligation to be moral, for it is not evident what that proof might be. All that MR claims is that if MR is true, then it must be a fact that one ought to be moral. If it is a fact, then the skeptic, who holds that there is no reason to be moral, is mistaken. But according to the attitude theory, there can be no such fact because there are no moral facts. It does not even make sense to say that the skeptic might be in error. There would not be an obligation

that the immoral person should be moral. The most there can be is the attitude
of moral people that the immoral person should be moral. And this, according to
the realist, is a moral and intellectual disaster.

So long as the attitude theorist works within the standpoint of morality, that
is, the attitudes of good people, he can say that everyone ought to have moral
attitudes. Having moral attitudes is what good people approve. But the realist
wants to say that there has to be some standpoint from which the standpoint of
morality is preferable to the standpoint of immorality. This is a standpoint that
has to be neutral as between all attitudes, a standpoint that anyone should take
regardless of their attitudes. The realist worries that unless there is such a neutral standpoint, then there is no way to say that the standpoint of morality is
preferable to the standpoint of immorality. The projectivist cannot admit that
there is such a standpoint, since to do so would be to admit that morality consists of something other than attitudes.

We saw that in Hume's account of morality, being fair-minded meant taking a
point of view from which all interests are regarded impartially. But one has to
want to take such a standpoint, and this desire is a moral desire. The realist
thinks that morality requires a standpoint that one takes even in the absence of
moral desires, and from which one sees that moral desires are preferable to
immoral ones. Because there is no way to acknowledge such a standpoint according to projectivist theory, morality is ultimately unjustified, and there is no
answer to the question "Why be moral?"

But perhaps that is as it should be. The realist acknowledges that it is not possible to give the knave a motive to be moral, and also acknowledges that it is not
possible to prove that anyone has an obligation to be moral, so it seems that all
that realism can do is keep alive the bare possibility that there may be a neutral
standpoint. This seems little better than empty posturing. It is not possible to
answer the question "Why be moral?" other than by appealing to the conscience
of a person who already is moral, and that is circular, so the realist has no better
answer to the knave than does Hume. The realist's assertion that sensible knavery is wrong in fact, and would be wrong from a neutral standpoint, amounts to
nothing more than the assertion that it is wrong. But the projectivist says this
too. Neither can convince the knave, and both acknowledge that the good person
does not need to be convinced, so it is not at all evident how the realist's position
is superior in protecting morality other than by offering assurances to the good
person that it is really better to be good. (The same argument can be made
against the quasirealist's postulate of a "best set" of attitudes.)

So where does this leave us? Hume explains morality by assuming that in general people are moderately benevolent, fair-minded, and sympathetic. These people will develop moral attitudes and will feel an obligation, based on these attitudes, to virtue. But what of the people who lack these qualities? Happily (if
Hume is right), they are not numerous, for it is evident that they will not feel any
such obligation.

But how can we explain the obligation they have? Ought they not be virtuous whether they feel it or not? And here the attitude theory can only follow its

principles and say, yes, according to the attitudes of the good people already described. But if this answer is thought insufficient, and if an answer is wanted that is embedded in reality itself—if we need to say that the wicked people "really ought not to be wicked"—then the attitude theory cannot supply one. But what theory can?

REFERENCES AND FURTHER READING

David McNaughton, *Moral Vision* (Oxford: Blackwell, 1988), is an admirably lucid and concise book on moral realism that is written as a general introduction to moral theory.

Texts advancing projectivism are: J. L. Mackie, *Ethics: Inventing Right and Wrong* (New York: Penguin, 1977), and Simon Blackburn, *Spreading the Word* (New York: Oxford University Press, 1984). Blackburn especially has written extensively on the question of supervenience. See Part II of his *Essays in Quasi-Realism,* (New York: Oxford University Press, 1993).

Essays defending moral realism are found in Geoffrey Sayre-McCord, ed., *Essays on Moral Realism* (Ithaca, NY: Cornell University Press, 1988). A celebrated defense is David O. Brink, *Moral Realism and the Foundations of Ethics* (New York: Cambridge University Press, 1989).

"Intuitions" are classically defended by H. A. Prichard, *Moral Obligation* (New York: Oxford University Press, 1949, reprinting essays from earlier decades), and D. W. Ross, *Foundations of Ethics* (New York: Oxford University Press, 1939). John Stuart Mill, *Autobiography* (1873, many editions), was an early critic; another is R. M. Hare, *The Language of Morals* (New York: Oxford University Press, 1952, 1961).

David Hume is one of the most creative of Western philosophers. He is also one of the most lucid, though contemporary readers may have difficulty with his majestic but anti-quated style. His views on various topics in ethics are found in his *Treatise of Human Nature* (1735–1736), especially Bk. II, Pt. III, Sec. iii (the belief-desire theory), Bk. III, Pt. I, Secs. i (internalism) and ii (the attitude theory). A shorter and more readable version of his general theory is *An Enquiry Concerning the Principles of Morals* (1751). Of the many editions of both works, those edited by L. A. Selby-Bigge and revised by Peter H. Nedditch (New York: Oxford University Press, 1975, 1976) are regarded as standard. (Any edition of the *Enquiry* must include the four Appendixes. The first contains Hume's clearest statement of projectivism).

Mackie has written an excellent introduction, *Hume's Moral Theory* (London: Routledge & Kegan Paul, 1980).

Most books on ethics say something about moral disagreement and moral debate. An interesting book is Albert Jonsen and Stephan Toulmin, *The Abuse of Casuistry* (Berkeley, CA: University of California Press, 1988).

A particularly lucid discussion of "Why be moral?" is in Paul Taylor, *Principles of Ethics* (Belmont, CA: Wadsworth, 1975), Ch. 9. The idea that the question is senseless is argued by Prichard in *Moral Obligation,* Ch. 1.

The "history or literature" analogy is adopted from Ronald Dworkin, *A Matter of Principle* (Cambridge, MA: Harvard University Press, 1985), and Richard Posner, *The Problems of Jurisprudence* (Cambridge, MA: Harvard University Press, 1990).

Part Two

Substantially Normative Issues

Chapter Six

Lying

Lord, Lord, how this world is given to lying.

Henry IV, Part I, V, iv, 148

Imagine this (or you can read it: it is a summary of a short story by French writer Marcel Aymé called "The Proverb"). Your name is Lucien Jacotin, you are 13 years old, an indifferent student, and not much interested in anything really. Your father loves you in his fashion, but it is a clumsy fashion—he is a bully, insulting, nags you about your schoolwork, is never satisfied with your grades, and suspects that you are not studying as hard as you might. The top student in the class, Béruchard, of whom your father is terribly jealous for his good grades, is the son of your father's junior colleague, a man inferior to your father in rank, prestige, and ability. At the office, M. Jacotin must swallow his pride and listen to M. Béruchard boast of his son's achievements. M. Jacotin devoutly wishes that your grades were equal to Béruchard's, but you are just not up to it.

One day you come home with an assignment: write an essay on the proverb, "Haste makes waste." You can't think what to say; you procrastinate. Your father first is angry, then decides to help you. He gives you ideas, furnishes whole sentences, and finishes by dictating the entire essay.

M. Jacotin is very proud of his essay, but you are not so sure; you do not think it is really the kind of essay your teacher will like. But you have confidence in your father's superior knowledge, and you turn it in. M. Jacotin is mistaken; his essay is full of faults. When the teacher returns the graded essays, he ridicules yours, condemning it as "six pages of sermonizing irrelevant to the subject" and reading it out loud to the class as an example of what not to do. Your grade is 3 out of 15. You have never been so humiliated.

M. Jacotin is anxious to learn how his little effort succeeded. Day after day he inquires at dinner whether the essays have been returned. Finally, you can put him off no longer.

"What grade did you get?"

158

—13.

"Not bad. And Béruchard?"

—13.

"And the top grade?"

—13.

M. Jacotin is delighted. His face lights up. "You see, my son, when you set your mind to do some job, everything depends on thinking it out. You must learn this lesson. From now on, we will do all your work together."

The story of Lucien Jacotin begins our discussion of lying. Popular newspaper accounts of immorality, such as the savings and loan officer who embezzles the depositors' money, or the politician who accepts free vacations and other favors from corporations doing business with the government, are the subject of intense public moral indignation, but most people are not tempted personally by such activities because (among other reasons) most people are not in a position to embezzle money and are not offered favors to influence their votes and decisions. Most people do not commit murder or rape either. But there can hardly be a human alive who has not been tempted to tell a lie at one time or another, and it may be doubtful if there are many people who have not actually told lies, perhaps not often but at least occasionally during their lifetimes. At the same time, just about everybody thinks lying is morally wrong, at least generally speaking; the trouble is, we do not always think it is wrong when applied to ourselves, or at least to ourselves in the position we find ourselves in now. Lying is an easy way to avoid trouble, or to get out of it if we are in it, and we all want to avoid trouble as easily as possible, even if the trouble we are in is of our own manufacture. Thus, lying may well be everybody's number one moral concern.

Think about the Lucien story, or discuss it in class or with your friends. What are Lucien's motives for lying? Is his lie justified? If you think he should not have lied, explain what you would have had him do, or what you would have done in his shoes. If you think he was right in lying, explain why he should be an exception to the general rule that lying is wrong. Can you generalize this exception into a theory of when it is permissible to lie? Or do you want to go further, and question whether lying is really as wrong as it is made out to be? And while we are on that question, what is wrong about lying anyway? Just why is lying generally thought of as a moral wrong? We shall try to investigate some of these questions in this chapter.

A DEFINITION OF LYING

It is well to begin with a definition of lying. This is not without controversy. We define a lie as *a false statement that the speaker believes to be false.* There are basically two alternative definitions: a lie is any intentional deception; and a lie is a statement made with the intent to deceive. There is authority in the philosophical literature for all three definitions, and sometimes the same philosopher waffles between them. Kant, for example, defines a lie as "an intentional untruth as such," which seems to support our definition that a lie is a statement you believe to be false; but Kant also says, "a lie requires a second person whom one intends to deceive," which seems to support the second alternative. Whatever the authority, however, both of these alternative definitions are inadequate.

Let us compare the three definitions. They differ in four points.

1. Our definition and the second alternative refer to *statements,* whereas the first alternative does not.

2. Our definition refers to *falsity,* whereas the two others do not.

3. Our definition holds that the speaker must *believe* the statement to be false; the alternative definitions say nothing about the speaker's beliefs.

4. The two alternatives refer to *intentional deception,* whereas our definition does not.

We defend our definition by explaining each of these four points.

1.   According to our definition, a lie is a false statement, so it follows that a lie must be a *statement.* But must a lie be a statement? Can you not lie without stating anything—for example, by actions and gestures? If you ask me which way is the door and I knowingly point in the wrong direction, have I not lied without making a statement? Most important, can you not lie by not saying, that is, by omitting, something? Consider this remark by psychologist Paul Ekman in his book *Telling Lies:* "There are two primary ways to lie: to conceal, and to falsify." But clearly concealing alone is not lying: if you ask me with whom I went out last night and I won't tell you, I have not lied to you. Can there be an example of concealing that might be considered lying? Consider a surgeon who accidentally cuts a blood vessel during surgery and does not tell the patient. The surgeon's failure to tell the patient what happened is morally wrong. But the fact that this is wrong does not make it a lie, as if the only kind of wrongful deception were lying. Concealment itself can be wrong if the victim has a right to know. We would not regard the surgeon's silence as a lie, precisely because the surgeon has said nothing; "not saying" is not the same as lying. Hence, to lie is to make a statement. (But what constitutes a "statement" is another problem, as we shall see.)

We should also note here the importance of discretion. There is nothing commendable about blabbing or spilling the beans. If a stranger phones when a child is home alone, the child is instructed never to say "My mother isn't home," but "My mother can't come to the phone right now," which though less than the whole truth is all the truth the caller needs to know. Discretion means knowing how much truth to tell, when, and to whom. If silence were a form of lying, discretion would not be the virtue it is.

2.   By our definition, a lie must be a statement that is *false.* The alternative definitions imply that something might be a lie even if it is not false; this implies that a statement is a lie if the speaker thinks the statement is false, even if it happens to be true. This is sometimes said, by *Newsweek* magazine for example: "A

true statement can be a lie. Imagine a dishonest agent telling a client 'the check is in the mail' and then discovering that his secretary has actually mailed the check. The agent intended to lie" (October 5, 1992). Here the last sentence gives the case away. The agent did intend to lie, but did not succeed in lying.

We should distinguish between successful lies and attempts to lie. When I tell you something that I think is false, but in fact I am mistaken and what I say is true, my intention may have been to lie, but I did not succeed in lying just because I told you what is true. I cannot be accused of lying if I have passed on correct information to you. Of course, if I say something that is false but which I believe to be true, then I am not lying but merely making a mistake.

3.   We require not only that the statement be false, but that the *liar must believe it to be false*. This may seem obvious, but the alternative definitions, which understand lying as intentional deception, imply that it is irrelevant what the speaker believes; whether he is lying or not depends on the effect—deception—he intends to produce.

The definition of lying must make some reference to the speaker's mental state, but which one, her belief or her intention? The alternative definitions have chosen intention; by our definition, this is the wrong mental state. Let us test this by examples. In 1958, in the midst of the Algerian revolution, French President Charles de Gaulle went to Algeria and said to the French settlers there, "I have understood you." What he said was something he knew to be true. For he *had* understood them: he knew they wanted him to pursue vigorously the war against the Algerian revolution. But he also knew that he had no intention of doing so, and that the settlers would think otherwise. De Gaulle intended to deceive, but as he believed what he said, he did not lie to the settlers. (The result of de Gaulle's abandonment of the settlers was the assassination attempt depicted in the movie *Day of the Jackal*.) Or take another example. Suppose I believe you are an idiot, and I say to you, "Jack, you're an idiot." In saying this, I intend to make you believe that what I said is a joke, and that I do not really think you are an idiot. So I am trying to deceive you. But according to our definition, since I am in fact passing to you information I believe to be true, I cannot be accused of lying. The liar expects that if you believe what she says, you will believe something false; she does not expect that if you believe her you will acquire truth. Hence, the liar must herself believe that her statement is false. So de Gaulle may have tricked the settlers, but he did not lie to them.

4.   The fourth point also has to do with belief and intention. This is very important for what follows in this chapter. We should distinguish between *lies* and various kinds of *intentional deception*. Not all intentional deceptions are lies, and not all lies are intentional deceptions either, as we shall see. You can deceive in all sorts of ways—for example, by telling part of the truth, by not saying something at all, by coloring what you say, or even by acting in a certain way. None of these are lies. If I fail to tell you something important, and you are thereby deceived, your complaint against me is not that I lied to you but that I failed to tell you something. Similarly, if I tell you a half-truth, or deliberately distort,

your complaint is that I deceived you, tricked you, or misled you. We reserve the word "lie" for false statements, not for half-truths and evasions. The proper complaint to make against President de Gaulle was not that he lied to the settlers, but that he misled them.

Oddly enough, it is possible to lie to make someone believe what is in fact true. This happens when you know that you will not be believed. For example, suppose you were the boy who cried "Wolf" in the famous story, how would you convey to your fellow townspeople that the wolf had really arrived? You know that if you cry "Wolf" they will not believe you. So what do you do? Well, one tactic is to stroll nonchalantly into town and say, "No wolf today, folks." You say this not to deceive, but to cause the townspeople to believe what is true, namely, that today there really is a wolf. By our definition, what you said is a lie (a false statement that you believe to be false), yet you did not say it with intent to deceive, so it cannot be classified as an intentional deception.

Hence, there can be intentional deception without lies, and lies without intentional deception. Intentional deception is no part (neither a necessary nor sufficient condition, as the logicians say) of the definition of lying.

This point is normally overlooked, because the usual purpose of lying is to deceive. But to build this into the definition is to fuse the action with what one is trying to accomplish by doing the action. We often do make such a fusion. If I flip the light switch, my intention is to turn on the light, and my action can be described as turning on the light. But for clarity we might prefer to say that I turned on the light by flipping the switch, which makes clear that I did something (flip the switch) with a further intention (to turn on the light). It would be a mistake to define "flipping the switch" as "intentional light illumination." Similarly, it is better to say that one lies to deceive (or one deceives by lying), rather than to define lying as intentional deception.

Another reason the distinction between lying and intentional deception is often not made is that people tend to be as strongly opposed to deception as they are to lying. This is not only a conceptual confusion, it is also a moral mistake, as we shall argue in this chapter. Deception may be morally bad, but generally it is not as bad as lying. This difference, which is an important though neglected part of our moral thinking, is concealed by definitions of lying that equate it with intentional deception.

Let us return to the first point and consider statements. We said a lie has to be a statement. What is a statement? In particular, how is a statement distinguished from certain other utterances of declarative sentences? Suppose someone says, "Once upon a time, many years ago, in a kingdom far away across the sea, there lived a beautiful princess." Or suppose someone said, "Did you hear what the Pope said to President Nixon? He said. . . ." Now the first of these is a fairy story, the second a joke. The words are false, and the speakers believe them to be false; yet no one would accuse them of telling lies. Why not, if our definition is correct? Our answer is that these fictions are not lies because they are not statements.

How is a statement distinguished from other utterances? It might be tempting to answer that the joker does not intend or expect that anyone will believe him, but this won't do in the case of practical jokes, where the fun is that the listener-victim does believe you ("Unless you call the Dean immediately and report what you just did, you'll be in big trouble." "There's an ugly green bug on your shoulder").

To define a statement is a problem of some difficulty in philosophy of language, which we cannot resolve here. For our purposes, we take the word "statement" to have the force of the word "assertion." That is, when we assert something, we not only say it but we endorse it, we put our own authority behind what we say. In telling stories we do not do this; hence, it would be wrong to say that Tom *asserted* that once upon a time there was a princess, although correct to say that Tom *said* that there was a princess. When we tell a lie, we are putting our authority behind the proposition we state, just as we are when we say something we know to be true. We are in effect saying: you can take my word for it.

We can now define lying by the following Liar's Table. Suppose your statement is "p." Then:

If "P" Is:	You Believe "P" Is:	Result:
T	T	Truthful assertion
T	F	Attempt to lie
F	T	Mistake
F	F	Lie

Having given and defended a definition of lying, we shall briefly distinguish the kinds of lies. There are five: scheming lies, malicious lies, self-serving lies, altruistic lies, and paternalistic lies. Our moral response is not the same to lies in each category.

1. Most people do not engage in *scheming lies,* since most people do not scheme, and when they do, they try at least to be honest about it. Scheming lies are what perjurers tell on the witness stand, and what a dishonest stockbroker tells you when he sells you a stock he knows is worthless. A schemer is a wicked person who cannot be trusted and is out to harm you for his own profit. Scheming lies are universally condemned, and are philosophically the least interesting kinds of lies.

2. Scheming lies are told with some further objective in mind; lying is a means to achieve something. But *malicious lies* are told for their own sake, or rather for the mere pleasure of speaking ill of another person. Everybody enjoys gossip, and some people are not too scrupulous about whether their gossip is true or not. The malicious liar enjoys saying bad things about other people, just for the nasty fun of saying so; or his motive might be more complex, founded on

dislike of someone or on resentment or on a generally malicious disposition. Malicious lies may be told without any ulterior motive, for the pleasure of speaking evil about another person, or they may be told precisely because they are harmful, to lower the victim in the opinion of the listener.

3.   *Self-serving* lies are the lies even good people tell, often to avoid some trouble for themselves ("My dog/computer ate my term paper"). A lie which you tell to avoid some difficulty would be self-serving, as when you praise something you don't really like (your friend's clothes or poetry) just because you don't need the hassle of making someone angry at you. These lies seem harmless, which is why self-serving lies are so tempting (we shall discuss this further at the end of this chapter).

4.   Altruistic and 5. paternalistic (or, "parentalistic") lies are lies told with a good motive, namely, the desire to help another person. Unlike self-serving lies, which may be excusable but are hardly commendable, these lies may even be commendable, from their good motivation.

Altruistic lies are told to a third person with the intention to help someone else. Your friend's alarm clock does not go off and he misses a test; you cover for him by telling the professor that he is sick. Your willingness to take a risk to help your friend is praiseworthy, even though your method of doing it is not.

Paternalistic lies are told to the very person you are trying to help. You know your friend's boyfriend is going out with other women, but you tell her it is not true. Your desire to protect her from being hurt by bad news is a good motive. (Everyday social lies are partly parentalistic, partly self-serving.)

Like self-serving lies, altruistic and paternalistic lies might easily be thought to be harmless. What harm does it do anyone if your friend takes the test tomorrow? If they are harmless (they may not be), we may wonder why they are wrong. We may even wonder whether they are wrong. Hence, these kinds of lies raise the question, what is wrong with lying? We turn to this later in the chapter.

IS IT ALWAYS WRONG TO LIE?

Some people evidently think it is never permitted to lie. They take "Do not lie" to be a rule for which there are no exceptions. Even if they engage in socially necessary "white lies" ("How do you like my new dress?" "Oh it looks so good on you"), they feel a bit ashamed of themselves, seeing this as weakness of character and wishing they had the strength of mind to say what they really believed. Such people are **absolutists:** they hold that it is *never* permitted to lie.

Absolutists need to be challenged by more interesting counterexamples. To start, so to speak, at the top, would it really be wrong to lie to a maniacal killer who comes looking for his victim? Nobody would say, "He's hiding in the closet" (the truth), if there were a way to deceive. Or suppose the killer wants *you.* "Where are you hiding?" he demands. "In the closet," always truthful you reply. ("I cannot tell a lie," said George Washington.) This looks like a situation in which a lie would not only be justified, but would even be mandatory; you would be morally at fault if you did not lie.

Or consider this example. It is World War II and a downed American flyer is fleeing a German army patrol in France. A French farmer hides him. Five minutes later the Germans arrive and demand of the farmer, "Have you seen anybody come this way?" Even a wily peasant gifted at evasion and subterfuge is going to have a hard time avoiding a lie in this case, and who could say a lie would not be justified? (If you were watching a movie, you would want the Frenchman to say, "Yes, off in the woods over there.")

One philosopher who is often said to have held an absolutist position is the celebrated Immanuel Kant (who uses the would-be killer example). Kant's words certainly lend themselves to this interpretation: "The duty of being truthful . . . is unconditional. . . . To be truthful (honest) in all declarations, therefore is a sacred and absolutely commanding decree of reason, limited by no expediency. . . . [T]he duty of truthfulness . . . is an unconditional duty which holds in all circumstances. . . ." Nonetheless, a closer reading brings into doubt that Kant actually does or intends to say that it is always wrong to lie; rather, what he intends is the quite different point that a lie is always a wrong. Kant's point is that you commit a wrong even when you lie to the murderer (you wrong everybody else, he thinks); but this is consistent with saying that what you do is not wrong. Kant believes that there is always something important at stake when we tell a lie, and that we should never lose sight of the moral loss that even a justified lie entails, assuming there is such a thing.

Perhaps the absolutist would be willing to qualify his position a bit by allowing an exception: you may lie when strictly necessary to save a life. This principle seems reasonable, but the absolutist will fear, correctly, that it opens the door to still more lying; for suppose the maniac does not intend to actually kill his victim, but only to thrash him within an inch of his life; or perhaps not even as badly as that. Why should we not be allowed to lie to prevent that? In fact, once you get thinking along these lines, why should we not be allowed to lie to prevent any wrongful harm from happening to anyone? This is the problem of the slippery slope: one kind of absolutist thinks it is better not to get started on the slope, because once you are on it, there is no principled way to get off again. (You can always say arbitrarily, "I'll go this far and no farther"; but why not? If you will lie to save a life, why will you not lie to prevent some lesser harm?)

Some absolutists who want to retain the absolutist position, yet allow certain "untruths," say that when a person has no right to certain information—as the murderer has no right to know where his victim is hiding—then telling him a falsehood is not really lying. By this move, one can retain the absolute principle "Never lie," yet deny that you must tell the truth to murderers. This solution distinguishes absolutism from nonabsolutism only by changing the name of what you may do. You are allowed to do the same thing that the nonabsolutist allows you to do, which is to say something you know is untrue to the murderer; but you will not call it a lie but something else (an untruth maybe). This is a solution only for those who prefer names to reality.

If someone has no right to certain information or is going to misuse it, you can refuse to tell him; but as we have seen in the French farmer example, this is not always so easy. If the farmer says to the German officer, "I will not answer," it is obvious what conclusion the officer will draw. But not every potential misuse of information justifies a lie; the misuse must be serious. Perhaps we should say that relatively unimportant anticipated misuses of information do not justify any departure from strict veracity; more serious misuses justify withholding information or other forms of deception; and only serious misuses justify lying.

Some of the most interesting questions about lying are raised by the justification of "reasons of state." At the height of the CIA-organized Bay of Pigs invasion of Cuba in 1961, the American representative to the United Nations, Adlai E. Stevenson, asserted to the General Assembly that no United States forces were involved in the operation. Stevenson was not lying; he believed what he said was true, and he believed it because President Kennedy had allowed him to be misled. Stevenson had not been told about the extent of CIA involvement in the Bay of Pigs because he was not trusted, and he believed Kennedy's public statement that the fighting was "between the Cubans themselves." And Kennedy, for "reasons of state," did not want American involvement in the invasion to become known, in part because the success of the invasion depended on the Cuban people rising up to overthrow the Castro government, and this was thought to be unlikely if it were known that the invasion was an American production.

Many interesting questions are presented here. Should Kennedy have lied in public? Should Stevenson have been willing to lie before the United Nations? Should Kennedy have been unwilling to deceive a man who was, after all, not only a distinguished American statesman, twice his party's candidate for President, but also a member of Kennedy's inner cabinet (though not a close friend or advisor)? Many people, of course, opposed the invasion on moral grounds, holding that the United States had no right to attack a small neighboring country no matter how offensive its government (many people who asserted this view, however, did not find the Castro government offensive, but actively supported it). Our question here, however, is this: given the belief, correct or not, that the truth would doom the success of the operation, does this alone show that the invasion was not justified on the grounds that no policy initiative can be justified if lying is necessary to enable it to succeed?

This question shows how strong and implausible is the position taken by those who hold that "Never lie" is an absolute rule. They are forced to claim that lying is not only wicked, but is so wicked that nothing can justify doing it. With regard to some government operation, for example, which must be carried out in secret and which therefore may need to be protected by a lie, their view is that no such operation can ever be justified; better to abandon the operation than lie to conceal it. This view, however, seems difficult to defend: consider military operations. The Allied armies invaded Europe by landing in Normandy on June 6, 1944; success of the very risky plan depended on concealing from the defending German forces the exact date and location of the invasion, and stratagems were taken to accomplish this. (The ruses were so successful that the German commander, Field

Marshal Rommel, was away on vacation when the invasion began.) Would even an absolutist complain if Allied officers told lies, as perhaps they did, as part of the concealment? In the Irangate scandal in the 1980s, the Sultan of Brunei gave the United States several million dollars to pay for certain weapons President Reagan wanted sent to Iran. The whole operation turned out to be a farce and a disaster, but the revelation of the role of the Sultan was particularly embarrassing since Brunei is a small but oil-rich state that is in the position of needing to be friends with everybody in its region. It is easy to say that what this proves is that the entire Irangate operation should never have taken place, and that the Sultan should have stayed out of it; but morality is always easier in hindsight. Given that the Sultan, wisely or not, did not stay out of it, someone then had to decide how far to go to protect him from the consequences. And if those consequences were serious enough, both for him and for the United States (imagine the possibility of the Sultan's government being overthrown by a local ayatollah) then it is not so clear that lying would be impermissible to prevent those consequences.

Two Types of Absolutists

There are two types of absolutists, who give different arguments for their positions. Let us call them the **strict moralist** (SM) and the **slippery slope–ophobe.**

The Strict Moralist   He holds that a lie is such a moral evil that nothing can justify telling one; no good can possibly be so important that it overweighs the evil of the lie. In his view, it is necessarily morally better for a person to tell the truth (or to avoid telling a lie) than to prevent any other evil whatever. The SM, in other words, is forced into holding the following. Suppose there are two bad things: telling a lie, and failing to prevent some evil. According to the SM, the former is always morally worse than the latter, no matter what evil the latter is. This must be the SM's view, since he asserts that when you have to choose between the first and the second course, you must always choose the second.

SM makes two points. The first is that the SM position is morally *rigorous,* whereas nonabsolutism is morally lax. SM takes due regard of the moral evil involved in telling a lie, which nonabsolutism underestimates. The second is that morality is not voluntary or a matter of free choice but *imposed* from outside; SM holds that because lying is wrong we have no choice but not to lie, regardless of the consequences.

However, it is not necessarily moral laxness to hold that some lies are justified, provided you also hold that it is wrong to lie. This sounds like a contradiction, but it is not. Here we introduce a distinction well known in philosophy but not sufficiently incorporated into ordinary moral thinking. It is the distinction between what philosophers call *prima facie* duties, and what they call duties all things considered. A *prima facie* **duty** is an act that would be your duty, unless it is overridden by something more important morally. You must (morally) do the act in question unless there is some good reason not to. A **duty all things**

considered is what results after you consider everything that needs to be considered. For example, since you are a student it is your obligation to come to class; cutting classes is wrong. But this obligation is *prima facie.* Maybe you have a terrible headache; all things considered it is more important to stay in bed, and you are entitled to cut class.

With this distinction, we can say that not to lie is a *prima facie* duty, and therefore it is morally wrong to lie. But not to lie is not necessarily a duty all things considered, and so it is not necessarily wrong to lie in every given case. In the situation in which you must either lie or fail to save a life, it is wrong to lie, but only in the *prima facie* sense; in the "all things considered" sense, it is not wrong to lie.

This terminology enables us to see that the difference between the SM and the antiabsolutist is not that one is strict and the other lax. For they both take a strong position against lying; but the antiabsolutist recognizes that other things might be worse. Therefore, some lies might be justified; lying under those circumstances is *prima facie* wrong, but not "all things considered" wrong. The antiabsolutist does not underestimate the wickedness of lying, as the absolutist fears he does, but puts lying in its proper place in a scale of wrongs. Its proper place may be high up in the wickedness ranking, but not necessarily at the top.

As for the claim that morality should be regarded as something imposed from the outside, the nonabsolutist is not precluded from taking this view of things. The nonabsolutist opposes making decisions based on a hard-and-fast rule, thinking that this method is not necessarily morally preferable to basing decisions on analysis and judgment. He may also hold that the duty not to lie is imposed, but then add that there are two other duties that are equally imposed, namely, the duty to prevent harms when you can and the duty to reflect on each situation and use judgment to reach a moral decision.

Slippery Slope-ophobia   This is the second form of absolutism. The SS-ophobe admits that not saving a life may be worse than lying, but he counsels not lying nonetheless. Because he admits that some evils might be worse than telling a lie, the SS-ophobe cannot be accused of holding an implausible scale of values. But how can he be an absolutist, since there will be occasions when he decides to do what he thinks of as the worse of two wrong actions?

The reason is that the SS-ophobe fears, above all, the slippery slope. His position is that if there were nothing else involved, then it would be better to tell the lie and save the life; but there *is* something else involved, and because there is, it is better to tell the truth even if that has the consequence that you fail to save the life. What else is involved, which causes this difference? The answer is, the slippery slope. If you tell a lie in this situation, where it is arguably justified, then you are in danger of sliding down the slope and telling lies in all sorts of other situations in which they are not justified. Better not to lie in the first place than to take this moral risk, says the SS-ophobe.

Why does the SS-ophobe think that if we allow even a single lie, we are in danger of sliding down the slope? We should distinguish two reasons: *the absence of principle* and the *presence of temptation.*

1.   If we think it is permissible to lie in one case, there is no principle by which we can hold that it is not permissible to lie in other cases. As we have seen, if I may tell a lie to save a life, then possibly I may tell a lie to prevent other, lesser evils, or even to accomplish certain good things. This argument relies on consistency: if you allow me to lie in the given case, then if you are consistent you will allow me to lie in the other cases. And since we do not want to allow you to lie in those other cases, we must prohibit you from lying in the first case.

The argument is that any line we draw is going to be arbitrary, so that it is better not to try to draw lines, but simply to prohibit the entire class of actions. However, this point seems self-contradictory. For the SS-ophobe himself admits that it is legitimate to lie in certain cases—for example, to save a life—but not legitimate in others—for example, to avoid petty annoyance or embarrassment. So how does he draw the line? If we really cannot draw any lines, then the SS-ophobe has no argument; his case collapses into that of SM, which claims it is not legitimate to lie under any circumstances. So there seems to be no slippery-slope argument here at all: if we cannot draw any lines, then we ought to hold that all lying is wrong, which is SM; or if we can draw lines, then there is no danger of sliding down the slope for lack of principle.

Another problem with the "no principle" argument is that the fact that a line may need to be drawn at an arbitrary point does not mean that the difference it marks is not real and important. For example, children become adults. The fact that it is arbitrary where we put the dividing line (age 18 or age 21?) does not mean that there are no real and important differences between children and adults. Everybody knows the difference between a calf and a bull, and even though the line between them is arbitrary, nobody would say that we can play with the bull the same way we might play with the calf! The fact that we might not be able to state a good reason why the line between acceptable and unacceptable lies should be in one place rather than another does not show that we might not have good reason for prohibiting most lies but allowing some nonetheless. We might very well allow the lies that are necessary to prevent great harm; how necessary is necessary, and how great is great, might be left to individual judgment.

2.   According to the "presence of temptation" argument, even if you can draw lines, the temptation to ignore them, once you allow some lies, will be too great. People will cross the line and lie even when they are not permitted to. You are led down the slippery slope from one lie to another until you routinely resort to lying to solve your problems, ignoring all the lines even when they have been clearly established. (This is how bad habits are formed; it is not so bad if you fail to study for one day, but after you neglect your studies the first day it is easier to neglect them the second day, and the third, and so on until you are in deep trouble.) Even if there are legitimate lies that do some good, the evil of allowing them is that people will be tempted to cross the line into illegitimate lies that do nothing but harm. Therefore, it is better not to allow any lies at all, so as to eliminate the temptation to cross the line.

This argument makes a very important point, which is sometimes overlooked by moralists. It is that in making our moral rules, we ought to take into consideration not only how good the rules look on paper, but how people will actually act were the rules to become accepted. Here the fear is that were we to introduce a rule saying, "You may lie for such and such good reason," however appealing this rule may look in itself, people would abuse the privilege: they would use the rule as an excuse to lie in other situations that the rule does not cover. And this result would be so undesirable that it would be better not to have the rule.

It is clear, however, that this fear rests on many assumptions about how people would behave, not all of them entirely plausible. We can acknowledge that were people to behave as the SS-ophobe fears they will, there would be a powerful argument against allowing *any* lying. But is it really plausible to suppose they will? We are asked to believe that if people are allowed to tell good lies, they will then be tempted (irresistibly) into telling bad lies: they will become liars, for this reason alone. So just imagine that you, whom we assume to be an otherwise truthful person, are faced with a situation in which a lie is arguably permitted: your aunt gives you an ugly tie for your birthday, and you tell her how much you like it. Does this make you into a liar? Does it mean that you will be tempted to tell more and more lies until no one can trust you about anything? These consequences seem farfetched, and if they are, then the fears of the SS-ophobe are exaggerated.

There is also a kind of *reverse slippery slope* argument that is often heard: if you tell one lie, people will never trust you again (assuming you get found out, that is). This is certainly good advice, if not made into an absolute rule; for even if it were true that no one would trust me as a result of my lie, it might still be morally desirable for me to lie in certain situations. But it is most implausible, to say the least, to suppose that people will not trust you if the lies you have told are good lies. Remember the French farmer who hid the fleeing airman and then lied to the German soldiers. If he goes home and tells his wife what he did, need he be afraid that she will never believe another thing he tells her? ("I know you, Pierre, you're the self-confessed liar. You lied to the Germans once, how do I know you're not lying to me now when you tell me you're not sleeping with Babette?") What makes people think you may be untrustworthy is that you have told bad lies, lies they do not think are justified. But bad lies should be avoided just because they are bad.

Despite all this, there is good sense in the absolutist position, provided it is not taken too absolutely. What absolutists are probably thinking of is not the kind of lies we have discussed to this point, which are mostly altruistic lies, but rather self-serving, scheming, and malicious lies. These they wish to banish absolutely. This is a morally attractive view, but perhaps it is not much different from saying that bad lies, suitably defined, should be prohibited. And although we might well agree that you should never promote your own interests by means of lying, and that you should never use lies to harm another person, we might (by stretching a point) find exceptions even to these rules. Whether this gives us an absolutist position or not is perhaps a question more of terminology than of ethics.

LYING AND DECEPTION

To this point, we have argued that the prohibition against lying should not be considered absolute. We have not said anything about why we have, or should have, this prohibition in the first place: we shall turn to this in the next section. Here we develop the important, but controversial, distinction between lying and deception.

Some people think there is no difference, or if there is, it is morally insignificant. They think this either because they think that lying is a form of deception, or they think that what is wrong with lying is that it is done to deceive. However, as already noted, lying should not be regarded as a form of deception because it is possible to lie without intending to deceive. The fact that typically, or indeed virtually always outside of philosophy books, people tell lies to deceive someone does not mean that lying should be classified as "deception." But even if lying is a form of deception, and even if it is wrong for that reason, it does not follow that all forms of intentional deception are equally wrong. If lying is a form of deception, we ought to say that some forms of deception are worse than others.

Our common morality does make a distinction between lying and deception by means not involving lying. Just about everybody would prefer to evade or mislead rather than lie. Even people who would not dream of telling a lie will occasionally resort to ambiguity, memory lapses, mishearing, or even true statements they know will be taken to mean something else when they are pressed and want to avoid revealing something. We have already noted "discretion," a praiseworthy form of deception. We praise people as well for their tact and diplomacy; what are these virtues but the skill at concealing or at least sugar coating your true thoughts so that people do not become angry with you? There are many other examples.

Both saints and moral philosophers seem to accept the distinction between lying and deception. There is a story about a certain St. Athanasius, who was pursued by persecutors. The persecutors did not recognize him, however, and demanded, "Where is that traitor Athanasius?" To which the saint replied, "Not far away." This story has been related with approval by a contemporary Christian philosopher, who says it illustrates "the cunning of the saints," which seems to mean the ability to achieve your ends without actually lying!

Another philosopher who accepts the difference between lying and deception is none other than Kant, who is doubtless the strictest moralist among the great philosophers. For Kant says that if you want your neighbors to think that you are about to go on a trip, you may pack your bags and leave them in plain view. You are not responsible for whatever inferences your neighbors draw; after all, you are perfectly within your rights in putting your bags wherever you please!

Of course, these examples will not convince those who reject the lying–deception distinction; they think it is wrong (at least *prima facie;* they are not necessarily moral absolutists) to deceive anyone, and that the means by which you do so are irrelevant. They think a person, such as St. Athanasius, who prides himself on never lying, although busily deceiving people when he has to, is a hypocrite and morally muddled; since he has a right to deceive the persecutors, they think, he might as well go ahead and lie to them. The fact that what the saint said was actually true cuts no ice; only his intention matters, and that was to deceive.

In making the distinction between lying and deception, ordinary morality does not hold that deception is a good thing; what it holds is that deception is less of an evil than lying. Or more precisely, ordinary morality holds:

1. Where it is legitimate to deceive someone, it is morally preferable to do so without lying: the St. Athanasius story.

2. There are times when it would be wrong to lie, but not wrong to deceive without lying: the Kant example.

Let us consider the St. Athanasius example. St. Athanasius, though he preferred not to lie, was entitled to lie to the persecutors if necessary. Imagine this dialogue.

> **Persecutor:** Tell us your name, you dog, or you die!
>
> **St. Athanasius** *(trying gamely to stick to his principle that a saint never lies):* My name? What significance can the name of a poor sinner like myself be to a brave soldier like you?
>
> **Persecutor:** You're not that traitor Athanasius, cursed be he, are you?

At some point in the grilling, even the cunning saint might run out of evasive tactics. At that point, he is morally within his rights to lie to avoid being killed; these are persecutors, after all. But is it correct to say that since the saint had a right to lie, he might as well have lied straightaway, that there was nothing to gain by trying to restrict himself to the (intentionally deceptive) truth? Let us note here the very important distinction between *prudential gain* and *moral gain*. We can certainly see that it was safer for St. Athanasius to deceive by telling the truth, since the persecutors would have been even angrier with him were they to discover that he had lied to them. So does this show that what St. Athanasius gained by telling the (misleading) truth instead of a lie was entirely prudential, namely, a decrease in risk to himself? Not necessarily, for we must ask why the persecutors would have been angrier. The answer is, obviously, that people do not like to be lied to; they prefer to be deceived, other things being equal. That the persecutors may be slightly irrational in this preference (given, after all, that they intend to kill him), does not change the fact that their sentiments are representative: we all feel more offended by lies than by deceit.

So Athanasius' prudential gain is based on a moral sentiment: the reason the persecutors would be angrier with him is that by lying he would have offended them more than by simply deceiving them. The lie is the greater offence; hence, there is a moral as well as prudential gain in avoiding the lie where possible. Now if this is correct, it follows that what is wrong with lying cannot be only that it is a form of deception, for if the only evil were deception, all forms of deception would be equally evil. There must be something else wrong with lying that makes it worse. What this is needs to be explained.

To this point, we have supported the lying–deception distinction with arguments based on common moral opinion, moral sentiment, and the authority of saints and great philosophers. Such arguments can never be decisive, nor ultimately convincing against someone who holds a contrary opinion. What is needed is some theoretical explanation or justification of the distinction; we must show why lying is worse than deception, that is, we must explain the reasons that support the two propositions of ordinary morality mentioned above. We shall return to this in a later section.

WHAT IS WRONG WITH LYING?

Everybody is against lying, but not everybody has a theory about what is wrong with lying. We are going to provide three theories: social contract, respect, and bad consequences.

Social Contract

Suppose you go to a party and meet a stranger. You tell each other about your backgrounds, your interests, what you do for a living, and so on. Each of you assumes that the other is speaking the truth. Neither of you promised to speak the truth, so why is it not just as likely that at least one of you is lying (if you know that you are not lying, does that not make it more than likely that the other person is lying, given that lying and truth telling are equally probable?) The reason is that although neither of you has explicitly promised anything, you share an understanding of how to act, that is, you have each made an implicit promise to be truthful (and to respect many other social conventions as well, for example, not to get too angry over political disputes, and so on). Being truthful is among the social conventions that we all agree to practice. Because of this, it is perfectly reasonable for anybody to assume that any other person will be truthful; only if you have some special knowledge about a person (which you do not if the person is a stranger) would you have grounds for suspecting that what the person says might not be fully truthful.

Telling the truth might be considered part of the **social contract,** that is, the set of rules, unwritten and even in a way unstated, that everybody in society has implicitly agreed to live by. As a member of society, you agree to abide by the rules, and expect everyone else to obey them as well. In a general way, everybody knows what these rules are, and everybody has a right to assume that everybody else will act in certain ways, because the rules exist and are generally understood and accepted. Morality, according to this view, consists in such a set of generally accepted rules.

Social contract is based on the idea that we have an obligation to obey those rules we want everybody else to obey, provided we have good reason to think everybody else wants the same thing. My right to anyone else's obedience to the rules depends on my own promise to obey them; unless I agree to obey, I cannot expect anyone else to obey either. Since I want everyone else to obey, I do promise; and since I have reason to believe that everyone else wants more or less what I want, I can be confident that everyone else has promised also. These promises and reasonable expectations reinforce each other as moral obligations.

An ingenious social contract argument is suggested by Kant. He thinks that lying is precluded by our agreement to use language. Speech, Kant thinks, is founded upon an implicit agreement that words will be used to convey what is the case; any other understanding would make speech impossible. Indeed, we could not even learn how to speak correctly unless people who already knew how to speak told the truth. How would a child learn the language if adults lied? (A cat goes by. "What's that, Mommy?" "That's a cow, dear," says the lying mother.) Simply by using speech, therefore, we make a promise, not to any particular person but to everybody in general, that we shall use words to mean what they say, that is, that we shall speak the truth. Every lie is a violation of this promise, and is therefore not only a sin against language but a breaking of faith with all our fellows.

It is for this reason that Kant holds that every lie is a wrong. Even where the lie might not be a wrong against the victim, as in cases in which the victim will abuse the knowledge and so is not entitled to have it, a lie is nonetheless a wrong against all other people, for it is a violation of the premise upon which language—and, therefore, society itself—is built. This is the conclusion that has evidently misled commentators into thinking that in Kant's view every lie is wrong. So terminology is important. Had Kant thought of the *prima facie* terminology, he could have said that every lie is *prima facie* wrong and have avoided giving the impression that he thought that all lies are impermissible.

Are the rules of the contract conventional, or are they necessary in some way? It may be thought that there is no difference, for even social conventions impose obligations based on reasonable expectations. In some countries, it is expected that a dinner guest will bring some little present for the hostess—usually flowers or candy, but some small object will suffice. A guest who fails to bring something is considered rude. Everybody knows the custom and most people are rather fond of it, so everyone has a reasonable expectation that everyone else will perform, and this creates the obligation to do so. Nevertheless, there is no really good reason why the practice should continue; it is simply considered a nice tradition. Hence, it is a convention, a custom but not part of morality; the rules of morality, we want to say, are more important than mere custom and are supported by good reasons. We should be able to explain why it is desirable to have any given moral rules; the explanation must be stronger than "We like it," or "We've always done it this way."

Do we have such an explanation for a strict rule against lying? It seems clear that a very strict rule against lying would be a convention; the rule could be relatively relaxed. For example, it is said that certain peoples in the South Sea Islands practice recreational lying, a game we might call "Make a fool out of somebody." The object of the exercise is to tell a preposterous lie in such a convincing way that somebody believes it. Some people develop great skill at this, and have scored notable triumphs in making their friends look like fools. They are not shunned and disliked for doing this; on the contrary, their skill is appreciated and they are rewarded with admiration. A notable victim of the game is said to have been the American anthropologist Margaret Mead, whose adulatory reports of the relaxed sexual habits of the native youth were evidently based to a certain extent on wildly exaggerated stories she was told. It may not have been very nice to play such a trick on the soon-to-be-famous anthropologist, which is an argument against playing the game on strangers; but that is not an argument against the game itself.

Respect

The concept of *respect* has deep roots in our thinking. Everybody wants to be treated with respect, and everybody wants to earn the respect, not of anyone you please but of the people whom you yourself respect. To be regarded with contempt, especially by people whom you yourself respect, is about as wounding, and damaging to the ego, as any kind of psychological blow.

Kant, as we shall note in Chapter Nine, takes the view that ethics, at least in large part, was founded on the idea of granting respect to all rational agents. This is his way of expressing the idea of the intrinsic worth everyone possesses as a human being. Contemporary Kantians argue that "Respect other people," or "Treat everybody with respect," is a fundamental principle of morality. And it is certainly true that not respecting someone is almost a prerequisite for acting immorally toward him: you do not normally lie to, cheat, or steal from someone you respect. If all immorality entails disrespect, then the respect to which people are entitled is the reason why we must do nothing immoral.

"Respect" is a difficult term to define; Kant himself acknowledges that he could be accused of "hiding behind an obscure emotion." Even good dictionaries define respect in terms of such near synonyms as esteem, honor, and high regard: in ordinary language, respect means something like, "have a high opinion of someone due to that person's good qualities." The term "respect" is often misunderstood as meaning basically fear. People think that when it is important to get other people to respect you (let us suppose you are in charge of a crew of workers, for example), you must make them afraid of you. But fear is not part of respect; fear alone breeds hate and contempt, not respect. People also think that if you respect someone, you want them to think well of you (which is true), but it is sometimes overlooked that if you respect someone, what you also want is to be worthy of that person's respect. Thus, respect is an elevating emotion; it makes you want to be better than you might be otherwise.

Let us examine the connection between respect and lying. It is sometimes thought that you might lie to a person you respect to conceal facts from them that would lower yourself in their eyes. This is the excuse people often give for lying to their parents. But if you have to lie to maintain your parents' high opinion of you, it would seem that you do not trust them very much. You think they will make undeserved trouble for you if they know what you are doing, so you have to pretend you are not doing it. Lack of trust is not an indication of respect.

To lie to someone is to manipulate that person, by trying to make her believe what you want her to believe rather than what is true. Manipulation implies contempt: you do not manipulate someone you respect. To lie is to imply that to a certain extent the victim is not entitled to have a mind of her own, nor any rights and interests; she is thought of as an object for the liar to control as he wishes. This is why people who are manipulated feel used, or "feel small." They have been treated as if they have little worth for their own sake, and exist only to serve the purposes of the manipulator.

That lying is a form of contempt explains why everyone gets so angry when they discover they have been lied to. Even a minor lie makes you angry, which is why liars can often accuse their victims of reacting irrationally: the victim's anger seems excessive in light of the trivial nature of the lie. But it is neither the contents of the lie nor the harm the lie may have done to you that prompts your anger, but the insult that the lie expresses. You realize that the liar is contemptuous of you and probably thinks you are weak and stupid.

Support for this theory comes from the anger we feel at parentalistic lies, lies made to us for our own good. The fact that it was the speaker's intention to benefit us—even the fact that the speaker may have actually benefited us—at best mitigates, but does not erase, the sense of betrayal we feel at having been lied to. If lies were wrong just because they were harmful, why should we feel anger at someone who lies to help us? Such lies express the liar's belief that the victim needs to be protected against some piece of knowledge. The victim is perceived as weak and vulnerable; to have the knowledge would be harmful. This is quite different from thinking that the knowledge will make the victim unhappy. Bad knowledge of a serious nature—you learn that you have a debilitating disease or you learn that your girlfriend is in love with someone else—will make anybody unhappy. But most of us think that happiness based on ignorance is not very valuable; better to face the truth and suffer than to live merrily in a world of illusion. The parentalistic liar not only makes this decision for the victim, he reverses the judgment: he says to the victim, in effect, you are better off living the illusion than suffering with the truth. And what else can this show but that in the opinion of the parentalist, the victim is a weakling incapable of coping with reality?

This is not to say that parentalistic lies are always unjustified. Some people, at certain points in their lives, are unable to cope and would be better off not knowing unpleasant truths. This is especially true of people who are very ill or emotionally distressed in some way. Compassion might dictate that they be spared painful knowledge. But even justified lies give us grounds to resent the liar and to claim to have been mistreated. We think this not because we have been harmed, but because we have been insulted by being told that we are not competent to deal successfully with troubling knowledge. So even if a parentalistic lie is not wrong all things considered, it is always *prima facie* wrong.

Finally, there is a sense in which a liar shows contempt not for others, but for himself. (Kant makes much of this.) The liar demeans himself by his lie, for he shows contempt for his own rationality, preferring to put his immediate ends ahead of his essential personality: "A liar. . . throws away his own personality; his behavior is vile, he has transgressed his duty toward himself," says Kant, adding ". . . man is a person and not a thing. . . . It is absurd that a reasonable being . . . should use himself as a means." Since a lie is an offense against reason, the liar, misusing reason for mere personal gain, dishonors what is most valuable about himself.

Bad Consequences

A fundamental argument against lying is that lies produce *bad consequences.* Morality tells us that we should act in such a way that we produce good consequences, not bad ones. Lies produce bad consequences in two ways. First, the victim is harmed by being made to believe something that is not true; in general, we are better off believing truth than falsehood. Consequences that fall on the parties to the lie we call *direct* consequences.

Second, lies cause bad consequences *indirectly,* that is, to people who are not parties to the lie, in that each individual lie adds to a climate of suspicion and mistrust. Suspicion and mistrust are not only uncomfortable emotions in themselves, their presence makes life more difficult. Suppose Margaret Mead had come to learn about the game of recreational lying; even if no one actually lied to her, she might have found it necessary to verify the reports of her informants, which would have been difficult, embarrassing, and even dangerous (since she could not trust her informants, she might have felt it necessary to snoop around visually verifying their tales of sexual exploits).

The indirect bad consequences of lies affect everybody, not only the person who is the direct victim of the lie. Suppose I visit a country of liars; I am lost, so I ask someone for directions. Should I believe what they tell me? Perhaps they will lie and send me out of my way. Even if I know that only a fraction of the people lie and the rest are honest, I am going to have to worry about this. So lies affect me in a bad way, even if I have never been lied to myself.

Now it is clear that if lies are going to be excluded solely because of bad consequences, it is indirect bad consequences that will have to be the reason. Most lies produce some good consequences for somebody, usually the liar: the scheming liar advances his scheme, the malicious liar enjoys his malice, the other kinds of liars might well produce more direct good than harm, or might produce no direct harm at all. It cannot be said that the liar necessarily will not benefit more than the victim suffers: there is no general argument that lies do more direct harm than good.

But all lies produce indirect bad consequences, even parentalistic ones (will you trust your doctor if you suspect that doctors sometimes lie to patients?) and even those lies that are not found out (because the liar's lying behavior is reinforced if he gets away with it). It is very likely that these indirect bad consequences outweigh any good the lie does for anyone. Yet even indirect consequences cannot be the reason lying is prohibited by morality. We do not think lying is wrong because it has bad consequences, but because the bad consequences fall on someone on whom they should not fall, namely, innocent victims. We would not be at all unhappy if it were the liar who suffered the bad consequences. In other words, lying is wrong not because someone suffers bad consequences, but because someone suffers bad consequences wrongfully. But what makes it wrong that consequences fall on a victim and not on the liar is that the victim should not have been lied to. So it would be circular to say that it is the bad consequences that make it wrong to lie. You cannot say that it is wrong to lie because a victim suffers bad consequences, and then say that it is wrong for the victim to suffer bad consequences because it was wrong to lie to him!

THE CONNECTION BETWEEN
LYING AND DECEPTION

We need an explanation of why lying is wrong, but we also need an explanation of why deception is wrong but not as wrong as lying. It would be pleasing if the two explanations turn out to be the same.

It seems that the three reasons we gave for prohibiting lying would also be reasons for prohibiting deception. Thus, if they provide good reasons why lying is wrong, they also provide good reasons why deception is wrong. But can we explain why lying is more wrong than deception? We shall offer a theory to explain not only why deception is wrong, but why it is less wrong than lying. We give two answers; we call them *lesser burden* and *blame the victim*.

Lesser Burden   Let us suppose that we can measure a wrong by the extent of the burden it imposes on its victim; the greater the burden, the greater the wrong. If deception imposes a lesser burden than does lying, then deception would be wrong, but not as wrong as lying is.

But it is clear that deception does impose a lesser burden on truth seekers than does lying, for the following reason: it is easier to discover the truth if you have been deceived than if you have been lied to. Suppose I want to know where St. Athanasius is, and you tell me, "Not far away." How difficult is it for me to discover that you are St. Athanasius? I immediately realize that I do not quite know where he is. And then I see that all I have to do is ask you, "But where exactly is he?"

Contrast this to the situation in which you tell me a lie: "He is in the closet." Now I think I know where he is; but even if I suspect that you are lying, what can I do? I have already asked you the direct question, so there is nothing for it but to go search for myself, or perhaps put my dagger at your throat and ask you to rethink your answer. But both of these tactics are far more difficult and unpleasant than asking you a direct question. So lying imposes the greater burden on truth seekers.

Blame the Victim   We may measure a wrong by the extent to which the victim brings his victimization on himself. The more the victim is to blame, the less the wrong on the part of the wrong doer. But in deception the deceived person to a certain extent participates in his own deception. For suppose I ask the saint, "Where is St. Athanasius?" and he responds, "Not far away." Whom but myself do I have to blame if I assume that the stranger to whom I am talking is not the saint himself? Of course, St. Athanasius' words are misleading, but I am making an inference from what he says, and this inference could be mistaken (it is the shrewdness of the saint that he understands that his questioner will not realize that the conclusion—that this man is not St. Athanasius—is only an inference and has not been asserted as fact). Every case of deception is characterized by the fact that the deceived person has made an inference from what he has been told, and has assumed without evidence that the inference is justified.

But this is not so of lying; if you believe a lie, you are not inferring anything, you are simply accepting what you have been told. Of course, you may be to blame even for that, for not being suspicious enough. But the deceived person also accepts what he has been told, so he is also culpable on that score. If the saint tells the persecutors, "You'll find St. Athanasius in that closet over there," then the persecutors can perhaps be blamed for believing what they were told, but they cannot be blamed for also assuming something that they were not told. Because he makes this assumption, the victim of deception is in part responsible for his own deception. This is not true about the victim of lying, so the liar is more responsible for the victim's coming to have a false belief than is the mere deceiver. If the liar is more responsible for the injury to the victim, then lying is worse than deceiving.

We have tried to explain why both lying and deception are wrong, and for the same reason, and why lying is worse. We have provided two explanations that meet all three goals. Each explanation shows that lying is wrong, that deception is wrong for the same reason, and that lying is worse. Lesser burden says that both are wrong because they impose burdens on the truth seeker, but deception imposes a lesser burden; blame the victim says they both are wrong because they prevent the truth seeker from reaching the truth, but that in deception the truth seeker is partly to blame. We may conclude that the proposition of morality, that lies are worse than deception, has been vindicated by moral theory.

WHY LYING IS SO EASY: SELF-SERVING AND OTHER HARMLESS LIES

"'Tis as easy as lying," says Hamlet bitterly to Guildenstern. Our final task is to explain why lying is so easy. The reason is that certain lies seem not only harmless, but on the whole beneficial; these include many self-serving and altruistic lies and all parentalistic lies. (Rosencrantz and Guildenstern were spying on Hamlet for the King to find out whether Hamlet was really mad or only pretending. Their deception was self-serving, scheming, altruistic, and parentalistic all at once.) Either the liar or someone dear to him benefits and nobody is hurt, it may seem. Let us consider only self-serving lies. You fail to complete a class assignment on time, largely because you foolishly got sucked into a TV movie the night before; you tell the professor you had to study for a big test in another class. Why not? You think that it saves you a lot of hassle and doesn't hurt anyone. Or you are supposed to read six books for your research project, but you only read four; nevertheless, you list six titles in your bibliography. Why not? You think, "I learned all I need to know about this topic, and the professor won't know the difference. Who's harmed?" Of course, the worst kind of self-serving lies ("I love you") may be said to be wrong just because they do harm the victim; but you may know young people who would not dream of telling anyone "I love you" when they do not, but who will nevertheless keep their options open by telling their regular girlfriend or boyfriend that they have to stay home and study when in fact they are on a date with someone else. What you don't know can't hurt you, they reason.

It would be too simple to say that many self-serving lies have no bad consequences, because they can have indirect ones. If it becomes known that one can lie to a professor and by so doing get away with derelictions, students will be tempted to take advantage, and honest students will become demoralized. Even if it does not become known, the risk that it might is great. Another kind of indirect bad consequence is that getting away with lying reinforces lying behavior. The successful liar learns that lying is a useful way to solve problems. This is almost inevitably going to cause trouble for someone later, if not for the liar himself then for other people. Bad habits such as lying may seem easier to control than they actually are. The liar is like an alcoholic: he thinks he knows just how far he can go without causing any problems, but this self-confidence may very likely be self-deception. So self-serving lies may be the first step on a slope that really is slippery and that really does lead to nasty messes at the bottom.

Nonetheless, these consequentialist reasons may not carry us very far, because the possibility of somewhat remote bad consequences may not seem sufficient to deter behavior that avoids a real and present danger. What about our other reasons, disrespect and social contract? Suppose you lie to your professor. Professors do not like to be lied to, not only because (as students may think) they see themselves as the enforcers of official morality, but because like anyone else they do not like to be manipulated and treated with contempt. Some contempt is thoughtless, as when you read the newspaper or talk in class; you find these activities more interesting than the professor's boring lecture. But you show contempt deliberately when you shortcut assignments, cheat on tests, and lie, for here you are saying that the professor's assignments are not worth your time and trouble and that you are able to manipulate her and the system to your own advantage.

However, this very argument reinforces the perception that lying is easy. The self-serving liar may recognize the disrespect involved in lying to his professor and yet not grant it much importance; so what, he may think, if the professor is made to look somewhat foolish, when my grade (therefore, my future) is at stake? And since he does not expect that the professor will discover the lie, the point will seem even stronger that the tradeoff is justified; if the professor doesn't ever know she's been fooled, what harm is there, even to her? "Some good to me as opposed to no real harm to anybody" is a hard argument to beat.

Let us consider social contract. It is an interesting fact about our social conventions that lying to get yourself out of trouble is prohibited; if you get yourself in trouble, you are expected to face your problem and deal honestly with it, even if this means taking your medicine ("like a man," as we used to say). We admire people who show strength of character, that is, who respect principles even at personal cost. Our conventions do not allow lying as a legitimate means of handling a problem.

Why do we have such a convention? Is there something behind it, or does it just express a social value preference? Imagine a different convention. Instead of promising to tell the truth in exchange for everyone else promising to do the same, suppose we made such a promise but allowed exceptions in certain circumstances (namely, when a lie would help the liar a lot and not seem to harm anybody else). People who told such socially acceptable lies would not be punished in any way, even informally by bad opinion. The results of this convention would be fairly obvious. People would doubt what was said to them when the exceptional conditions obtained, and would have to protect themselves by requiring verification. This would make life more complicated for everyone. It would also make the convention permitting lying somewhat pointless, because the verification requirement would lead to the exposure of most lies. Liars would not be punished, but they would not accomplish anything either. Since nobody wants to be lied to, and everybody will take steps to prevent lies from being effective, it seems best to accommodate this by making a generally sweeping rule against lying in the hope that most people will obey voluntarily and many others will obey from fear of being caught. The rule not to solve your problems by lying is justified as a moral rule, not a mere social convention or value preference.

These are the moral considerations that count against even the harmless or victimless lie. There is always a moral cost in lying, as Kant takes pains to note. But there could be a personal gain as well. What will you do? Here, as elsewhere, philosophy does not give answers, but it does help you think about the questions.

SUMMARY

Let us briefly summarize the results of this chapter. We have given a definition of lying and clarified the distinction between lying and intentional deception. We have argued that there are good reasons to hold that a lie is always *prima facie* wrong, but that the prohibition on lying is not absolute. We have examined three reasons against lying: bad consequences, respect, and social contract. Of these, bad consequences seems the weakest. These same considerations explain our prohibitions against deception. However, intentional deception, although wrong,

is not as bad a moral wrong as lying; we have defended and explained this proposition. Hence, there might be circumstances in which it would be wrong to lie,
but not wrong, or not as wrong, to deceive. Finally, we pointed out that lying is
often easy because the lie seems to promise some gain for the liar without any
loss to anyone else. We have argued that there are good moral reasons for not
lying even in such cases, but noted that in the end each person must make a
decision whether the gain from lying is worth the moral cost.

REFERENCES AND FURTHER READING

The murderer example is from Kant's celebrated essay "On a Supposed Right to Lie from Altruistic Motives," available in several collections, and most conveniently in the book by Sissela Bok noted below.

The St. Athanasius story is taken from P. T. Geach, *The Virtues* (London: Cambridge University Press, 1977).

Kant's example of packing one's bags is in his *Lectures on Ethics,* trans. by Louis Infield (New York: Harper & Row, 1930, 1963). Also see *The Metaphysics of Morals,* trans. by Mary Gregor (New York: Harper & Row, 1964), Pt. II, Ch. 2, "Concerning Lying."

The Margaret Mead incident was reported in the *Chronicle of Higher Education,* August 2, 1989, p. A6. President Charles de Gaulle's policy in Algeria is described in Brian Crozier, *De Gaulle* (New York: Scribner, 1973), pp. 481–519; the "Je vous ai compris" statement, characterized by Crozier as "guileful," is on p. 485. For Adlai Stevenson, Kennedy, and the Bay of Pigs invasion, see Kenneth Sydney Davis, *The Politics of Honor: A Biography of AES* (New York: Putnam, 1967), p. 456; Trumbull Higgins, *The Perfect Failure: Kennedy, Eisenhower, The CIA and the Bay of Pigs* (New York: Norton, 1987), p. 130; and Thomas C. Reeves, *A Question of Character: A Life of JFK* (New York: Free Press, 1991), pp. 266–69.

A well-known discussion of some features of lying is Sissela Bok, *Lying* (New York: Pantheon, 1978). This book usefully reprints some classic but hard-to-find material.

An interesting treatment with some pretense of philosophical rigor is Warren Shibles, *Lying, A Critical Analysis* (Whitewater, WI: The Language Press, 1985). He attempts to set out conditions of a lie in truth-table form. My "Liar's Table" derives from this.

The *Berkshire Review* published a special issue, "Lying and Deception," vol. 15, 1980.

Social contract theory derives from Thomas Hobbes, *Leviathan* (1651), and John Locke, *Second Treatise on Government* (1690, many editions). The most advanced contemporary statement is David Gauthier, *Morals by Agreement* (New York: Oxford University Press, 1986).

Chapter Seven

Good Character

Dost thou think, because thou art virtuous, there shall be no more cakes and ale?
***Twelfth Night,** II, 3, 124*

VIRTUE ETHICS

Good character is something people ought to want to have, and what it is and why it is desirable ought to be part of the subject of moral theory. The Greeks, many medievals, and certain early modern philosophers did not emphasize questions of rules and obligations but studied what they called "virtue"; for them, the principal question of ethics is not "What obligations does one have?" but "What kind of a person should one want to be?" The study of obligations, duty, and moral rules may be called **duty ethics** (DE); the study of the virtues is called **virtue ethics** (VE). Virtue ethics makes good character, or the virtues, a central part of ethical theory. Some contemporary philosophers would like to restore virtue ethics to its central place in ethical theory.

What is good character? The *Oxford English Dictionary* defines "character" as a person's "moral and mental qualities." We can be more specific. A person's character consists of his or her values, beliefs, attitudes, dispositions and inclinations, wants and desires, sentiments and emotions, all of which are, as it were, lying in wait ready to emerge into thought, word, and deed under suitable provocation. Character can be subdivided into character traits, such as friendliness, honesty, sense of humor, ambition, and so on. The *virtues* are those traits that are considered good ones, especially if they are morally good; the bad ones are called *vices*. Trustworthiness, fairness, and compassion are virtues; cruelty, indifference, and egotism are vices.

Virtues and vices are the subject of the first two sections of this chapter. Specific aspects of good character are studied in the subsequent sections: saintliness and heroism, caring and compassion, and independence of mind.

184

The Importance of the Virtues

Why is it important to study the virtues? Here are five reasons.

1.   Virtue ethicists think that ethics is largely about *assessing character*. Thus, Hume says, "If any action be either virtuous or vicious, 'tis only as a sign of some quality of character. It must depend on durable principles of the mind, which . . . enter into the personal character. Actions themselves . . . are never considered in morality." (*Treatise on Human Nature,* III, III, i.) We dislike a thief, according to this view, not because he steals but because he is dishonest; we dislike a liar, not for the lie but for the untrustworthiness that the lie reveals. We do not appraise actions for their own sake. Two students cheat, one because he is too lazy to study, another because she falls into a last-minute panic. The lazy cheater reveals bad character; the panicky students perhaps only lacks self-confidence. We assess the action, in Hume's view, so that we can assess the character the action reveals.

2.   DE *misunderstands the place of duty* in morality. It makes it seem as if the only commendable moral motivation is the sense of duty: a person who is morally good is a person who is motivated by a desire to do what is morally right. But this is a distortion.

Suppose two adult children telephone their mother to wish her a happy birthday. One does so because she has a strong sense of duty and thinks that she is obligated to call her mother; the other does so because she is genuinely fond of her mother and wants her to feel good on her special day. Duty-oriented ethics suggests that the dutiful daughter acts in a truly moral fashion, whereas the affectionate daughter simply acts naturally, as her inclinations lead her, and so is not acting morally at all. But this seems wrong; we are inclined to regard people who act from feelings of affection as, if anything, morally better than those who act primarily from obligation.

It is better to regard duty a backup when sentiments are lacking. Even a person who is not generous might force herself to do something generous because she thinks it is morally right (one can even force oneself to be affectionate and friendly). Suppose you are tired of hearing about the homeless, and no longer care what happens to them. But you consider that it is your duty to help those in need, so you help them. You would be a better person if you were more compassionate, but since you are not, it's better that you have a sense of duty than that you don't.

3.   DE makes it seem as if moral decision making consists in choosing and following rules (that state moral obligations). This overemphasizes the role of deliberation, and makes moral decision making more of a logical or rational process than it really is. VE emphasizes the importance of *sentiments and affections* in reaching moral decisions. A morally good person may often act on the basis of feelings rather than as a result of rational deliberation. She enjoys doing good acts and does not enjoy doing bad ones. She acts from her character, not from her conceptions of right and wrong. A person who is generous or honest

does not need a rule or a conception of duty to do generous and honest actions. She does these actions because she likes people and does not want to hurt them, not because she thinks there is a moral rule. She acts from sentiments, not from conclusions based on logic.

4. DE makes morality seem much more *difficult and onerous* than it really is. DE even suggests that it is morally preferable not to enjoy doing good actions. You go to visit your ailing grandmother in the nursing home; this is very unpleasant, but you think you owe it to her. The more unpleasant it is, the prouder you are that you have done it. No pain, no gain—morally speaking.

VE does not think that morality must be a burden people ought to shoulder. It is better to enjoy being moral and to get pleasure and satisfaction from doing what is right. If you are affectionate, generous, loyal, hard working, and so on, then actions flowing from these traits will give you pleasure. A well-developed moral personality enables you to get much satisfaction from your moral actions: your generosity, kindness, and friendliness please you as much as they please others. As a result, you feel satisfied and content when you do the right thing; your life is enriched by morality.

5. DE suggests that the way to teach people to be moral is to preach at them, telling them what their duties are and urging them to act as duty requires. This method is less than effective. VE by contrast suggests that people may be taught to be moral through the use of *role models*. Role models are admirable people whose lives and character can inspire others to follow their example. They appeal to our moral imagination, and make us want to be like them. We learn morality by imitation, not by absorbing rules. As every child knows, it is what his or her parents do, not what they say, that shows what they really believe about right and wrong. We respond to character and personality. We want our own character to be admirable and worthy of emulation. VE emphasizes the importance of good moral character in moral education.

The Priority of the Virtues

We are apt to overlook all of this unless we study the virtues; this study is therefore a necessary part of moral theory. But how important is it? Some virtue ethicists hold that virtues are more important than obligations and duties. They hold either (first thesis) that obligations can be explained through the virtues, or (second thesis) that obligations are morally important only because virtue is morally important. We call this view the **priority of the virtues.** We shall examine both its theses.

Virtues Prior to Obligations in Definition   According to DE, our moral obligations are defined in terms of some theory about duty. A virtuous person is merely a person who fulfills his or her moral obligations, so defined. That is, DE defines virtue in terms of duty. But according to the first thesis of the VE priority view, obligations are defined in terms of virtue. There is no theory that explains what our obligations are. VE explains what the virtues are: courage, justice, moderation, friendship, and the rest. A person who is virtuous will act as virtue dictates, in the appropriate circumstances: a friend, for example, will help you out when you are in trouble. Our moral obligations are to do those things which virtuous people do: thus, it is our obligation to help our friends when they are in trouble.

This seems to be Aristotle's view. He does not think that moral obligations can be defined by a set of rules, because rules are general, obligations specific. It is good to be generous, but no rule tells you how generous you must be, and to whom. Nor is there any rule which determines how to be friendly, or kind, or loving. The answer lies with what Aristotle calls (*Nicomachean Ethics,* II, 9) "perception," our power of knowing specific cases. The virtuous person has good perceptions; she sees what to do, because she is virtuous. So what is virtuous is nothing but what the virtuous person does in the appropriate circumstances. If you are not virtuous, there is no rule which will tell you what to do; you must ask or imitate the virtuous person.

Here are three objections to Aristotle's view.

1. Right action is to be defined as what the virtuous person does in the circumstances, but how does the virtuous person know what to do? Aristotle's reliance on perception does not seem to take him very far; how does the virtuous person know that her perception is not misleading her (as sight and other perceptions sometimes mislead us)? Does the virtuous person simply react to the situation without thinking about it, or rely on her conscience? Why should these methods prevent her from making a mistake?

In fact, Aristotle does not hold that virtuous action is nothing but perception, for he somewhat confusingly notes that virtuous action involves "right principle" and "reasoned desire" (*Nicomachean Ethics,* II, 2; VI, 2). This makes it seem as if the virtuous person knows what duty is, in which case duty can be defined independently of what the virtuous person perceives.

One thing Aristotle is clear about is that virtuous action is a matter of habit and training. Virtuous people know what to do because they have been trained properly. It is important that people develop good moral habits, but saying that an honest person knows what to do through being trained properly only turns the problem of what to do into the equally difficult problem of what a person should be trained to do. Should she be trained to lie to the murderer or to tell the truth, to fight when outnumbered or to run away? It would seem there must be a moral duty that guides either the virtuous person, or her trainer, so the duty cannot be defined as whatever the learner learns or the trainer teaches.

2. The view that virtues are prior in definition also seems circular. It defines moral obligation as the actions that a virtuous person would do, but how does it define a virtuous person? Not as a person who honors moral obligations, for that would contradict the view. But it is not clear that there is any other way of

defining the virtuous person. Further, suppose you wanted to take Aristotle's advice when you were puzzled about what to do, and sought out a virtuous person to emulate. How would you know who is the virtuous person? People do not come with labels reading "virtuous person." One person stands and fights, the other runs away. Which one to imitate? Aristotle himself says that we must not assume that anyone who takes risks is thereby brave; excessive risk taking is sometimes—not always—simply foolhardy. (Aristotle notes that professional soldiers are more apt to run away when they are outnumbered than are new recruits. The professional does not want to risk his life unless he has a fair chance of winning, whereas the recruit is full of enthusiasm and underestimates the danger. On the other hand, the professional is not alarmed at incidents that may frighten the novice since the veteran can tell what is really dangerous and what only seems so.) So if you are new to the game, how can you tell who is the one whom you should imitate, the soldier who fights or the one who runs away? If you have learned a rule ("Fight if you are outnumbered three-to-one or better; otherwise, run") you can use it to know who is brave; but if you have learned the rule, you do not need to imitate anybody.

3.   A person who is not virtuous might define virtue as what virtuous people do, but this cannot be the virtuous person's definition. Suppose it is a question of bravery. The brave person reasons as follows: "I am brave; act B is what brave people do; therefore, I will do B." But if the first thesis is correct, this reasoning is circular. A brave act is what brave people do, so if the brave person decided to do something else, let us say act Z, then act Z and not act B would be the brave act. So the brave person has to define brave acts other than as the acts that brave people do.

Virtues Are Prior to Moral Obligations with Regard to Value   DE holds that you should develop good character so that you will honor your moral obligations. This makes obligations prior to virtue in value: the importance of being virtuous is explained by the importance of honoring one's obligations. But the second thesis of VE's priority view says that what is important is that you be virtuous, and explains honoring obligations in terms of being virtuous. Hume thinks that honoring obligations is important because it is a *sign* that you are virtuous; whereas Aristotle contends that honoring obligations is important because by so doing a person *becomes* virtuous.

Here are three arguments for this thesis.

1.   What counts morally is not what you do but why you do it. This is Hume's claim: acting from virtuous motivation is good for its own sake. We have already seen that virtue ethics stresses the importance of motivation, but the priority view carries this argument further by claiming that morality says that we should act from good motives and not that we should do good acts. Motivation is what morality is all about, and it is for this reason that we ought to cultivate good moral traits and habits. It does not matter whether a person does the right thing, provided that she always has the right motives.

Remember the two adult daughters who phone their mother on her birthday? Suppose there is a third daughter who is even more attentive to her mother than the first two. Let us say she telephones faithfully every week. Her motive is simple: she wants to assure her inheritance. Her motive is so bad that it might be better if she never phoned at all. It is better to do the wrong thing for the right reason than the right thing for the wrong reason. If you have a bad character, it does not matter that you do good deeds; it is no credit to you, and the beneficiary would not be pleased if she knew your real motive.

2.   Virtue provides reasons to act morally. DE seems to provide no reason why anyone should obey the rules, other than the rules themselves. If you ask why you should obey the rules, the answer is that otherwise you will not do your duty, which is circular (as we noted in Chapter Five). But if virtue is desirable in itself, there are at least two reasons to act morally. One is that you should act morally because acting morally is what a virtuous person does: you cannot be a brave person without doing brave acts. The other is that by acting morally, you develop good character, or retain the good character you already have. If you are not yet brave but want to be, you must do brave acts; you cannot become brave by acting cowardly.

3.   Developing virtuous character is the *summum bonum*. Once philosophers thought that they ought to explain what the *summum bonum*, or chief good, was. They reasoned that if some things were better than other things, there must be something that is the best of all; a wise person would be someone who strives to understand what this is, and attain it. But philosophers did not do a very good job at explaining the *summum bonum*. Plato thought that the *summum bonum* required an intuitive grasp of something inexplicable that he called the Form of the Good; Aristotle allowed himself to wonder whether the *summum bonum* did not consist simply in studying philosophy; the Stoics thought that it was accepting fate or the order of nature; theologians tended to make the *summum bonum* consist in union with God, so sublime that it was beyond comprehension; and other philosophers gave other interpretations, equally mystifying and unlikely to be attained by most people. Contemporary philosophers abandoned the search for a *summum bonum*, but virtue ethicists want to revive the tradition. They think the chief good consists in attaining virtue. What is really important in life is to develop good character. The wise person, in pursuit of the chief good, will act morally because the development of good character is the highest goal in life.

There are also three criticisms to be noted.

1.   The second thesis of the priority view claims that acting morally is not important for its own sake but only because of its connection with being virtuous. But even if being virtuous is something that should be desired for its own sake, it does not follow that acting morally is not something that also should be desired for *its* own sake. That we should act justly, for example, for no other reason than that justice ought to be done for its own sake, is a standard moral idea

dating at least to the Hebrew Bible. The priority thesis does not prove that this principle is mistaken.

2.   Even if the thesis that acting morally is not important for its own sake were correct, virtuous people could not accept it, since a virtuous person is someone who acts morally just because she thinks it is right to act morally. We would question whether a person who did not think morality was important for itself was really a virtuous person. But if a virtuous person could not accept the second thesis, there is a paradox, for according to virtue ethics we ought to be virtuous people, from which it follows that we ought not to accept the second priority thesis.

3.   The priority thesis claims that what is important is to be a person who wants to have good character, rather than a person who is motivated by a sense of duty. But this rests on a misleading view of the motivation of the virtuous person. The virtuous person is the person who does not want to cheat, or to be unkind or unfair, and so does the right thing from character rather than from duty. But part of the reason the virtuous person does not want to cheat is that she does not want to do anything immoral. If she did not think cheating were wrong, apart from any connection with bad character, she would lose this part of her motivation and might no longer not want to cheat. Since part of what makes a virtuous person virtuous is that she believes that some things are right and others wrong, independently of any connection with virtue, a virtuous person who came to believe the second thesis might become less virtuous.

It seems then that the virtuous person could not accept either of the priority theses. The virtuous person thinks that what is morally important is to honor our obligations, so the virtuous person thinks that obligations can be defined and that acting morally is important apart from being virtuous. If we managed to make virtue prior to obligations, we would have managed to eliminate virtuous people.

The upshot of all this is that neither priority thesis is convincing. The priority view overstates the case. We cannot have morality without moral rules and obligations. We could not know what traits are virtuous and what are not without rules to tell us which acts are right and which wrong. We could not even have virtuous people without moral rules to guide virtuous people to act virtuously. Virtues are not, therefore, more important than obligations, duties, and moral rules. They are not more important; but they are important. Good people want to be virtuous and consider which traits of character they ought to cultivate. They try to develop good habits so that acting morally is easy and pleasurable for them. Doing virtuous acts is an end in itself, but so is being virtuous.

What Good Are the Virtues? The Flourishing View

Why is it a good thing to be virtuous? Aristotle considers the virtues to be those character traits anyone needs to do well in life, by which he means, not to succeed in merely conventional ways but to live well and to prosper in some philosophically commendable sense. Aristotle's word for "living well" is *eudaimonia,* which is often translated as "happiness" (the Greeks had no other word for happiness) but literally means "good spirit." Although this idea cries out for definition, Aristotle supplies only a vague and unsatisfactory one: "activity of soul in accordance with virtue" (*Nicomachean Ethics,* I, 8). Contemporary Aristotelians regard the virtues as the traits connected with what they call "flourishing," and therefore, hold the **flourishing view** (FV): the virtues are desirable because they are linked to flourishing.

What is it to flourish? Flourishing is a "condition of the soul," as Aristotle puts it, which anyone would want for its own sake. It is, to use another Aristotelean term, a "final end": you do not want to flourish to attain something else, but you want other things so that you may flourish. Flourishing is a condition of the soul that would be chosen by any rational person who is in a position to choose.

FV has to solve two problems: to explain flourishing in such a way that it appears to be something which any rational person would desire; and to show that virtues and vices are good and bad respectively just because of their special connection with flourishing. It is questionable whether FV solves either of these problems.

The Definition of "Flourishing"   There are two states of the soul associated with flourishing but that cannot be identified as flourishing. They are *contentment* and *being virtuous.* Contentment, or the enjoyment of your life, is certainly a desirable condition of the soul that any rational person would want for its own sake. But for purposes of FV, contentment is not connected closely enough with virtue. Will virtue make you content? Possibly; but also possibly not. It depends on what you like. Some people are content to pig out on junk food or to skewer their enemies. Flourishing must involve contentment, because a person who is not content cannot be said to flourish; but if flourishing were simply identified with contentment, the connection between flourishing and virtue would be too loose for the purposes of virtue ethics. Contentment is desirable for itself, but does not support the view that virtues are desirable because of their connection with flourishing. Hence, FV cannot define flourishing as contentment.

Nor can we define flourishing as living in accordance with virtue. As contentment is desirable in itself but not necessarily linked with virtue, living virtuously, though identical with virtue, is not obviously desirable in itself. The definition fails to explain why flourishing is desirable or why the virtues are good traits to have, and of course it makes the proposition that virtuous people flourish circular. Unfortunately, Aristotle himself does not succeed in avoiding this circularity, as his definition of *eudaimonia* shows.

Hence, for FV flourishing must include both contentment and virtue, but cannot be defined as either contentment or virtue. Fortunately, there is a third conception, and it is Aristotle's. According to him, to flourish is to lead a rich, full life, a life that engages many skills and capacities in a deep way and provides ample and varied satisfactions and fulfillments. A person who flourishes is happy and content, but content in the special way that comes from the full use of one's talents and capacities. He is not content in the way the couch potato is content. The essence of flourishing is full use of one's capacities. Contentment, Aristotle says, is a natural consequence of a full and satisfying life. You also need favorable external circumstances, Aristotle very sensibly points out, such as good health, friends, physical and financial security, and—we might add—education and a decent job.

Aristotle's conception of flourishing is attractive and would appeal to many people. But it is too much to assume that it would appeal to all rational people. For not every person who is rational wants a rich, full life. Some people are hermit-like and deliberately try to narrow their lives to a single point, whether it be contemplation of God or development of their stamp collection. Other people choose high-intensity careers like investment banking that demand great concentrations of energy rather than full use of capacities. Still others would prefer a life filled with much leisure, relaxation, and good times in which their capacities are frequently left to idle. No one can say that such people are irrational, and if they get what they want perhaps they are content, but they do not seem to be flourishing in the sense required by FV. It would seem to be difficult to state a sense of flourishing that is both universal enough to appeal to everybody who is rational and which at the same time is not reduced to a mere state of contentment. But if there is no universal idea of flourishing that is going to appeal to everyone, FV cannot establish its case that the virtues are desirable because they lead to flourishing. Even if the virtues do lead to flourishing in Aristotle's sense, this will not impress those who prefer some other kind of life.

The Connection Between Flourishing and the Virtues

1.   According to FV, the virtues are said to be desirable just because of their close link to flourishing; the vices, on the other hand, are connected with the opposite of flourishing, which we can call "withering." Now why should it be the virtues that make you flourish and the vices that make you wither, rather than the opposite, or neither? There are three possible answers. The ancient Hebrews took a straightforward view of the matter. They though that flourishing was the *reward* of virtue. They reasoned that if you obey God's laws, God will give you a rich, full life, and you will die in old age amid your fig trees, your cattle, and your numerous servants, wives, and progeny. The first Christians, having noticed perhaps that God rarely fulfilled His promise, were more sophisticated, and determined that God delayed His reward until the life to come, perhaps because the virtuous person would then be in a better position to enjoy it.

2.   For Aristotle, there is an *intrinsic connection* between flourishing and the virtues. The Hebrews made flourishing a consequence of being virtuous; for them, there was nothing intrinsic connecting virtue to flourishing. Aristotle does not hold that the virtues are rewarded with flourishing. For him, the virtues are the constituent elements of flourishing, as vices are constituent elements of

withering. Exercising the virtues is just what leading a rich, full life is. By exercising virtues you flourish, and by exercising vices you wither.

Aristotle's method to reach this conclusion is in principle inductive: he begins with a list of acknowledged virtues and then in effect asks why these are the traits which are considered virtuous. His answer is that these are the traits that, when activated, constitute flourishing. People who have and exercise the virtues are, from that alone, living a rich, full life; they flourish, and nobody else can flourish.

It is interesting to explore Aristotle's thinking by looking at the vices. Think about such traits as jealousy, envy, vengefulness, or avarice. What is wrong with these qualities? The dispositions they involve are crippling and the associated emotions unpleasant and destructive. The traits are not good to have, and the more you have of them the worse off you are. The avaricious person is never satisfied, no matter how much he has; he is, to apply a striking metaphor of Plato, like a vessel with a leak that can never be filled. The jealous person is inclined to be suspicious of trifles, and to misinterpret everything; he is easily fooled, obsessed with mistrust, and led astray by his irrational suspicions (think about Othello). Someone who is vengeful and vindictive broods over imagined wrongs, magnifies every slight, and gloats over fantasies of revenge. To have these traits does not lead to unhappiness; if you have them, you are already unhappy. No one would voluntarily make herself jealous, envious, and the rest; like all the vices, we would want to avoid these conditions if we could, and would try to get over them should they strike us.

Interesting support for the conception that vices constitute withering comes from envy, and especially from the distinction between envy and treachery. Shakespeare's Iago is both envious and treacherous. His envy withers his life, for though he is a man of great ability and courage, he is obsessed by his imagined grievances and throws away all chance for honorable achievement and promotion. But it might be said that treachery, which is a worse vice than envy, does not cause unease but pleasure. Iago is guilty of treachery against his benefactor and patron, Othello (as well as against his comrade Cassio), and had his treachery proved successful, it would have made him happy, even ecstatic (it does prove successful, but he does not live long enough to enjoy it—villains in Shakespeare are always punished, for Shakespeare believes that the wicked cannot flourish). Treachery contributes to Iago's happiness, indeed it constitutes his happiness and sole joy, but only because of his original envy. Without this, treachery would give him no pleasure. So we can conclude that some vices make you miserable, and even those that make you happy do so only by relieving the misery of some other vice. Vices are not pleasurable in themselves; the pleasure they provide comes from the removal of pain. You only get pleasure from a vice like treachery if you are already suffering from a vice like envy. Hence, nobody would want either vice for its own sake.

But as bad character is its own punishment, so good character is its own reward. To be pleasant, cheerful, and friendly is not to be rewarded with happiness; these dispositions constitute happiness. A person endowed with such qualities enjoys being generous, open, interested in others, and concerned about their well-being, and has a life that is rich and rewarding.

So Aristotle is right in thinking that virtues are constituent parts of flourishing, and vices of withering. Nonetheless, this argument does not show that virtues are good because of this, since there may also be virtues and vices that do not contribute to flourishing and withering. Everything seems to depend on what you want. No one wants to be consumed by jealousy, but it is less clear that no one wants to be deceitful and overbearing, or that if they are they will suffer from it. The thief's life is not necessarily diminished because of his thievery, nor is it necessarily less full, interesting, challenging, and fulfilling than the honest person's. If you are honest you will not get fulfillment from stealing, but if you are a thief maybe you will not get fulfillment from not stealing. The tightwad delights in being cheap, suffers at the very prospect of spending money, and regards generous people as fools and wastrels (Scrooge would be an example were it not for the fact that Dickens tries to make just the opposite point; but could we not imagine a Scrooge who did not have guilt-ridden nightmares?) The bully enjoys bullying, and flourishes by pushing his weight around; the ruthless, ambitious person flourishes by trampling on people who get in his way. If there are vices that do not cause us to wither, and virtues that do not cause us to flourish, then it is not correct that all the virtues and vices are intrinsically connected with flourishing, and therefore, flourishing cannot be why virtue is good and vice bad.

There is another point that defeats the claim that there is an intrinsic connection between virtue and flourishing. This was understood by the Hebrews, who invoked God to reward the virtuous because they had little confidence that virtue would be rewarded in the natural course of events. They did not share Aristotle's blithe assumption that it must be the virtuous person who will have the good life. Two centuries before Aristotle, the prophet Jeremiah had complained, in a book Aristotle had never heard of: "Wherefore doth the way of the wicked prosper? Wherefore are they all happy that deal very treacherously? Thou hast planted them, yea, they have taken root; they grow, yea, they bring forth fruit: thou art near in their mouth and far from their reins." (Jer. 12:1, 2.) (The Hebrew Scriptures were not translated into Greek until about fifty years after Aristotle's death.)

It may be worth noting why the connection between virtue and flourishing seems stronger to Aristotle than it does to contemporary philosophers.

We have already seen in Chapter Four that Aristotle's philosophy is based on the view that natural things have natural ends, and flourish by attaining these ends, as nature has ordained. For Aristotle, the virtues are the excellent expression of our natural ends or basic natural capacities, so it is easy for him to equate flourishing with acting virtuously. It was even easier for the medievals, who believed that both nature and human ends were established by the loving Creator. But the postulate of a human nature with ends ordained by nature is not accepted by many contemporary philosophers, including contemporary followers of Aristotle, who adopt only the idea of flourishing and the corresponding idea of intrinsically worthwhile activities, leaving these conceptions largely unsupported. For them, virtues are no more natural or part of our natural ends than any other character traits. Therefore, they have difficulty explaining why it is the virtues, and not some other activities, that constitute flourishing.

Interestingly, Aristotle does not actually have a word for virtue; the word he uses is *arete,* which does not mean virtue but "excellence." (Because of Aristotle's word *arete,* the term "aretetic ethics" is sometimes found as a name for virtue ethics. It would be better if this rather ugly neologism were not to clutter the minds of philosophy students.) Throughout his treatment, he is referring not to virtues but to excellences of character. This may be an advantage. To be excellent is to be able to do something well, and to do something well is intrinsically rewarding. Whatever we do, as Aristotle points out, we prefer to do well, not for the sake of some external gain but simply for the sake of doing things well. No one cultivates bungling and ineptness. Given this terminology, it is perhaps easier for Aristotle to hold that all virtues are intrinsically desirable for their own sake. When we exercise our capacities in an excellent way, we experience pleasure, feel satisfied, and enjoy our lives, so if excellent use of capacities is virtue, virtue gives us a full, rich life.

3.   The notion that there is a *strong contingent connection* between virtues and flourishing allows that you might not flourish even if you are virtuous, and might not wither even if you are racked with vice, but holds that you probably will, given psychological and social facts that happen to be true or are very likely to be true. Hence, though being virtuous is not part of what constitutes flourishing, nor is it rewarded by flourishing, it does increase the odds of flourishing.

It is not mysterious how this happens. In the first instance, the virtues enable other people to have a good life, not their possessor: if you are honest, this benefits primarily those whose property you do not steal. But the virtuous person also receives a benefit from being virtuous, due to the fact that we like people whose character is such that other people benefit from them. You are honest, so I benefit because I do not have to protect my property against you. I consequently like and respect you because of your honesty; you benefit from my affection and good opinion. So you receive a secondary or consequential benefit, not from your honesty itself but from my reaction to your honesty. This is likely to add to your happiness, since most people need the affection and respect of other people to be happy.

There is another kind of consequential benefit from being virtuous. People admire their own moral goodness; a considerable part of one's proper self-respect is a consequence of thinking of oneself as a good person. Justifiable pride, as Aristotle holds, is itself a virtue: a person who has certain talents and accomplishments is entitled to feel proud of them, and the same might be said of desirable traits of character. We might say that being proud of one's virtue is an additional secondary benefit of being virtuous, but a secondary benefit that is of the first importance. Proper self-respect is a significant and necessary element of flourishing, so in this way also, having virtue makes it more likely you will flourish.

In these ways, virtues help us flourish because of what it takes to make us happy. Since much depends on your character and your tastes, which vary from person to person, there is no single set of traits that will constitute or lead to well-being for everyone. All that we can say is that under "standard" conditions, which means if you are a more or less normal person living among typical normal other people, you are more likely to flourish if you are virtuous than if you are not. You can try to flourish through vice if you are so inclined, and some people who try it will succeed; but your are more likely to have a successful and happy life if you are virtuous.

If this rather modest theory is correct, the best virtue ethics can say is that most of the time, most people will flourish because of their virtue. But some will flourish without virtue. People may obtain rewards—friends, honors, self-esteem—from talents and traits that have little to do with virtue. People might like you and you might like yourself because of your musical talent, or good looks, or social charm, or sex appeal, especially if they all came in a package. Even the vices can make some people happy. Gluttons enjoy gluttony, seducers enjoy seduction, and villainous people get pleasure from the success of their villainous schemes. As for pride, people who are villains or scoundrels can obtain satisfaction from their evil deeds and even take pride in being evil, as Shakespeare's villains often remind us (Richard III, Edmund in *King Lear,* and others). Furthermore, you can sometimes obtain the rewards by fooling people, a fact that worries Plato: perhaps you are really a scoundrel at bottom but can fool people into thinking you are virtuous. You can even fool yourself: some people are quite good at self-deception and imagine they have the most noble motives, when in fact they are utterly selfish, so they like themselves for possessing a virtue that is entirely imaginary.

This somewhat lugubrious conclusion exposes what is wrong with the flourishing view. It puts the cart before the horse. Virtue may lead to flourishing, may even constitute part of flourishing, but this is not the reason why virtue is desirable. Virtue is desirable because it is morally good to be virtuous; it is not desirable because it is connected with some other good thing. So even if it were true that virtue is part of flourishing and that everyone wants to flourish, it is not true that you should want to be virtuous because what you really want is to flourish. You should want to be virtuous because you should want to be a good person, and being virtuous is what it is to be a good person. It is enough reason to cultivate the virtues that it is morally better to be a good person than to be a bad or indifferent person. The flourishing view puts the cart before the horse since it holds that virtue is good because it leads to flourishing; on the contrary, it is because you ought to be virtuous on moral grounds that it is highly desirable that you enjoy being virtuous, that you like yourself as a morally good person, and that your virtues come to constitute part of what it takes for you to flourish. If being virtuous is not part of what you need to flourish, you will be virtuous but miserable, and in that case you will not likely remain virtuous for very long.

WHAT ARE THE VIRTUES?

Which Traits Are Virtues?

The ancient Greeks seem to have held that there were four **main virtues,** namely, *justice, temperance, courage,* and *wisdom;* so testifies Plato in the *Republic,* although in fact Plato in other dialogues discusses many others—for example, piety, patriotism, and loyalty to friends. Plato himself seems to regard the four traditional virtues as a kind of given, so much so that in what surely is one of the more bizarre twists in the philosophical literature, he makes the entire argument of the *Republic,* including its psychology and political theory, depend on the assumption that these four virtues are the very ones the theorist must discover in the soul and exemplify in the state. Medieval theology followed Plato in accepting the four natural virtues, transforming Plato's wisdom and courage into their near cousins, *prudence* and *fortitude,* and adding the three theological virtues, *faith, hope,* and *love* (Greek *caritas,* often mistakenly translated as "charity"). All other virtues are supposed to be derived from these seven. (St. Thomas Aquinas thought that all four natural virtues were forms of love.)

The medievals, or at least their theologians, also valued humility, meekness, chastity, and obedience, none of which would have appealed to the Greeks. Nor do they appeal very much to the modern Westerner. Nonetheless, our society is far different from that of Athens 2400 years ago, and Athenian tastes and point of view would make modern Westerners uncomfortable. The Greeks of the Golden Age (mid-fifth to mid-fourth centuries B.C.) had come a long way from the gangsters and ruffians depicted in Homer's *Iliad* (the date is uncertain; probably about 700 B.C.), having added to the art of war—music, theater, poetry, mathematics, astronomy, architecture, sculpture, history, and of course philosophy, most of which they had either invented outright or (like mathematics and astronomy) adopted and developed; for all of these accomplishments, they were inordinately but justifiably proud. Cultural pride in fact is one of the unstated but paramount virtues that constitute Aristotle's conception of the good life; he would have been shocked at the contempt for their own culture that passes today for wisdom and virtue among some intellectuals and young people. But despite or because of its accomplishments, Greek society was xenophobic, chauvinistic, racist, elitist, militaristic, sexist, and riven by class antagonisms and political instability; its intellectuals and aristocrats were fascinated by politics but mistrusted and feared the common people. Aristotle's discussion of the virtues is addressed to a group of embattled intellectual aristocrats who know their own worth, are keenly conscious of their superiority in matters of learning and taste, and set themselves high ideals in questions of personal conduct, but feel threatened by and alienated from the masses, and are torn, as was Aristotle himself, between a desire to lend the state their talents by participating in politics and a desire to retreat into a secure and satisfying private sphere of study and learning. (Aristotle, who was not a native Athenian, toward the end of his life evidently came under suspicion of being insufficiently patriotic, and found it prudent to retire into exile to his native region, where he died.)

Our contemporary conception of virtue is heavily influenced by Christian ideas, with which Aristotle and his compatriots would not have sympathized. Not for them the thought that the meek shall inherit the earth, or that a rich man can no sooner enter heaven than a camel can pass through the eye of a needle. Jesus' injunction to sell all you have and give to the poor (*Matt.* 19:21) would have provoked mirth and derision among Aristotle's circle. (Ask yourself what the conventional Christian thinks of Jesus' injunction.) Aristotle appreciates wealth and social standing, and does not see the attraction in poverty, weakness, simplicity, and humble origins. Indeed, our contemporary sense that we owe generosity and compassion toward those who are poor, ill-favored, and ill-treated is quite absent in Aristotle. The entire idea of responsibility mixed with guilt toward those less favored than oneself, which is a pervasive aspect of contemporary American social morality, is lacking in Aristotle.

What attracts Aristotle is *magnificence,* by which he means spending large sums of money on public projects without being ostentatious or vulgar about it. In his view, "shabbiness" or spending less than one ought is unworthy of someone with money. The examples he gives are fitting out a naval ship and subsidizing a diplomatic mission to a foreign city, but he also applauds magnificent private occasions like a big wedding. What distinguishes magnificence from mere vulgar display of wealth is the appropriateness of the object; a rich man who spends as much on dinner for the members of his club as he might spend on his daughter's wedding exhibits vulgar ostentation in Aristotle's eyes. For those who are not rich but merely comfortable, Aristotle counsels *liberality,* which means spending appropriately on suitable persons such as, presumably, one's friends: the Greeks were party animals and each member of a "set" was expected to do his share in playing the host, as lavishly as means allowed. Not moved by our religious sensibility, Aristotle does not commend charitable works or good causes, such as giving money to the homeless or helping the mentally ill and the physically handicapped.

Aristotle thinks *proper ambition* is a virtue, but he confines this to desire for honor, which he says we can want too much of or in the wrong way. Surprisingly, he does not discuss ambition for success, or accomplishment, or love, or friends, or money, or many other things for which people can be ambitious. He thinks that the virtue of ambition depends first on its object—there are some things you should not be ambitious for, such as becoming the biggest crook on Wall Street—and second on how you go about attaining it; it is all right to want to get rich, but not to want to get rich by embezzling money from a savings and loan company.

Temperance is one of the classical Greek virtues to which Aristotle devotes several chapters (*Nicomachean Ethics,* III, 10–12). Temperance has to do with the control of physical pleasures. A person who never felt such pleasure is such a *rara avis* that we have no name for him, says Aristotle (incongruously launching into Latin in one standard English translation); the problem is with the person who is excessively fond of the pleasures of the senses. Temperance prevents you from becoming disgusting by overindulging. The Greeks had no conception of the Christian idea of "mortification of the flesh," and would have been mystified at the idea that "the flesh" is a trap set by the devil to ensnare the innocent. The Greeks enjoyed creature comforts, sensual experience (who could live in Greece and not love sunbathing?), good food, and drink. What they deplored was animal-like behavior, "shovelling it in," addiction, and losing control through overindulgence. Denial of physical pleasure and self-infliction of mild self-torture (medieval monks used to wear itchy shirts to prove that their spirit could overcome their flesh) would have struck the Greeks as mental imbalance. (One wonders what they would have thought of the contemporary craze for punishing physical exercise such as long-distance jogging.)

A very important virtue is *justifiable pride* in one's own merits, what Aristotle calls "greatness of soul." The great-souled person knows his own worth and will not let anyone else forget it. This is not to say that he is boastful; on the contrary, boasting he regards as vulgar and beneath him. He acts always with a consciousness of his own dignity, concerning himself above all with honor and what is honorable. He will therefore never perform any vile or dishonorable deed. But he accepts no praise from those who are below him; such people are beneath his notice. He loves truth (concealment is a sign of fear), and scorns flattery, for flatterers pretend to an admiration they do not feel and praise not from truth but for gain. He cares not for fortune, good or bad; he is self-contained and reluctant to call on others for help. He is restrained in admiration, never gushing forth praises due to others. He is neither irritable nor excitable, harbors no resentments, never hurries—there is nothing he finds worth getting excited about or hurrying for—but is always in command of himself, his emotions, and his actions. Above all, he never loses his dignity.

Other moral virtues Aristotle analyzes are *veracity, modesty, courage, gentleness* or *good temper, sincerity* and *frankness,* and *justice* (so important and complex as to deserve an entire book). It is interesting to compare Aristotle's virtues with those listed by Benjamin Franklin in his *Autobiography* (written between 1771 and his death in 1790): *temperance* (moderation in food and drink); *silence* ("Avoid trifling conversation"); *order* (in both your personal life and business affairs); *resolution* ("Resolve to perform what you ought; perform without fail what you resolve"); *frugality; industry; sincerity; justice; moderation* ("Avoid extremes; forbear resenting injuries"); *cleanliness; tranquility* ("Be not disturbed at trifles"); *chastity* (which for Franklin means not abstinence but restraint); and *humility,* which he defines cryptically as "imitate Jesus and Socrates," rather a tall order that Franklin disappointingly explains as meaning not to belittle those who disagree with you. (The student who has read Plato's Socratic dialogues may wonder why Franklin thinks one would develop such admirable restraint by imitating Socrates.) Franklin is sometimes derided for having no more inspiring objective than worldly success (in contrast, it is said, to Aristotle), but his list of virtues, though interestingly different from Aristotle's, is not unattractive, and the criticism is parochial and prejudiced. The reader should decide which virtuous person you would prefer to be, and to have as a friend: the virtuous person depicted by Aristotle, or that of Franklin.

An interesting point is that there are some virtues for which we seem to have no name, though we identify their counterpart vices. People who are surly and quarrelsome, or get angry too easily, notes Aristotle, make bad company; but there is no name for the opposing virtues. We have no name for someone who is not boastful. We might add that cruelty is a vice, but there is no name for its counterpart virtue other than kindness and gentleness, which perhaps do not quite describe what is meant. Excessive concern with or fondness for one's self, egoism, self-absorption, excessive ambition, and indifference to the needs and feelings of other people are all moral vices; there may not be a name for the counterpart virtues, though thoughtfulness, helpfulness, and cooperativeness come close.

Is There Any Principle by Which a List of Virtues Can Be Generated?

Aristotle certainly gives none, and it is difficult to see what the principle might be. Hume takes the view that virtues are those traits that are agreeable or useful to their possessor or to other people (*Treatise on Human Nature,* III, III, i). This is probably as good a principle as one can have. The truth of the matter is that there seem to be certain qualities that just about anyone would call virtues; these include courage, honesty, and fellow-feelings. Many of the other traits we regard as virtues because they appeal to our tastes: we like and admire people who are modest, for example. Certain other traits ought to be considered virtues because of our moral theory: if we think that altruism is a great moral principle, or that doing good for others is the essence of morality, then traits such as fellow-feeling, compassion, benevolence, and so on would be considered virtues, since they are the traits that people ought to have to act as the moral theory would have them act.

Alasdair MacIntyre claims that there can be no principle by which a list of virtues is generated, since virtues can only be understood in terms of certain activities or *practices,* and that therefore, there is no such thing as virtue as such. The virtues of a soldier, which include loyalty, physical (though not necessarily moral) courage, and ability to endure hardships, are quite different from those of a lawyer, for example. A virtue is a trait needed to succeed in some specified practice or activity; each practice has its virtues, and no virtue can exist without some specific practice.

There is some truth to this view, but it is an overgeneralization resulting from understanding virtues as if they were skills. It is true that different activities require different skills: the skills you need to be good at playing shortstop are very different from those you need to be good at playing the violin, so no doubt it would not make much sense to talk about skills and talents without specifying the associated practices. (Although, strictly speaking, it does not follow that because every practice has associated skills, every skill must be associated with a practice. Some skills might be useful independently of any practice.) But confusion results from assimilating virtues to skills, since virtues are traits of character and not talents or abilities. As such, they are activated not by choice but by circumstance. The ability to endure hardship, for example, is a character trait that, fortunately, most of us do not have to rely on, and may not even possess to any great degree; but in time of difficulty—for example, natural disaster or civil disorder—those who have this trait will make it through more successfully than those who do not. This virtue is not specific to some practice in which people engage; suffering through tough times is not a practice. Virtues such as loyalty, reliability, and self-confidence are not skills and are not specific to any practice, though perhaps some traits are regarded as virtues partly because they are useful in mastering most practices: if you want to be good at just about anything that is difficult, it is desirable to possess self-confidence, perseverance, and a high tolerance for frustration and disappointment.

There is an important similarity between virtues and skills, which is that to a certain extent, which varies from person to person, virtues, like skills, are achievements. It is not so easy to be good; the virtues have to be learned, practiced, and retained by repetition. Like skills, the more you exercise them, the better you become. The same is true of vices: it gets easier and easier to tell lies the more lies you tell. Virtues and vices are both habit forming, so you have to decide which habits you want to form and then keep at it until it becomes easy. Unlike other achievements, however, to acquire the virtues you do not possess you have to begin by wanting to acquire them. Most people develop good character from earliest childhood as part of their basic personality, but if you do not have good character, you can develop it by deciding that you want it and then working to acquire it. This is one reason people may be proud of their virtue. Honesty is a good example; if you feel you tend to embellish the truth, practice stating the facts exactly and cut yourself short when you begin to make things up, and you may develop the habit of honesty.

Moral and Nonmoral Virtues

Aristotle distinguished between intellectual virtues and what he called "moral" virtues (*Nicomachean Ethics*, II, 1), but this latter term is his cover term for all the nonintellectual virtues. We would not normally think that proper ambition or liberality with money are moral virtues, which shows that Aristotle's two-category classification is too limited. Perhaps we should have three categories: *intellectual virtues* such as strong understanding, quick wit, good memory, and sound judgment; *moral virtues* such as fairness, compassion, honesty, integrity, generosity, and reliability; and *desirable personal qualities* such as a sense of humor, kindliness, courage, good cheer, and friendliness. Personal qualities based on physiology such as athletic ability, good looks, graceful carriage, and sexual attractiveness make people good companions and desirable friends, but are not virtues since they are not traits of character.

Desirable personal qualities are not always consistent with moral virtues. A person who always tells the truth would have the virtue of honesty, but he might make dull company if he never contributes anything interesting, clever, or amusing. A somewhat mendacious teller of tall tales might make a more desirable companion. Shakespeare's Falstaff is a drunkard, a liar, a rogue, and a thief, but he is a better companion than many a deacon! There is such a thing as being "too good"; for the most part, we prefer someone whose moral virtue is tempered by the virtues of good companionship, though there is a limit to how far we would allow someone to violate rules of morality in the name of fun and friendship.

To some extent, what we consider a desirable personal quality is a question of taste: some people find sarcasm and bluntness virtues, others find them painful. But everybody admires intelligence, quick wit, and personal delicacy. As Hume points out, there are some character traits that are naturally pleasing, and others that we learn to like due to their evident utility. Loyalty to friends and preference for self are natural character traits, but since we prefer to live in a society where people are not unduly partial, we learn to admire fairness or impartiality. But even courage to some extent is a matter of taste, for not everybody admires courage, at least if Falstaff's frequent jibes ("The better part of valour is discretion": *Henry IV, Part I*) are to be taken at face value.

It is not an easy matter to draw the distinction between moral virtues and admirable character traits such as courage and loyalty. The concept of "morality" is not sufficiently refined so that we can decide with confidence whether a given failing is immoral or a character flaw, and for practical purposes such as assessing conduct and deciding how to treat people, it may not make much difference since the nonmoral traits can be just as important as the moral in our assessment of character. The Greeks considered courage to be one of the four chief virtues, and a person who acts in a cowardly way is certainly disgraceful and even despicable; but courage is perhaps better thought of as a personal quality that we greatly admire, having a moral side only when its absence leads people to abandon their principles, betray their friends, or evade their moral duties. A person who simply lets herself be pushed around we would regard as weak, mousey, and far from admirable, though not immoral.

Or consider stinginess. Anybody has the right to spend or not spend his money as he pleases, so a tightwad is not immoral unless he defaults on his debts; but we look with disfavor on someone who is "cheap," will not spend money even if he can afford it, and calculates the cost of everything too carefully. Another example is gluttony, which is included among the famous "seven deadly sins" of theology, even though we do not regard overeating as a moral vice but as a personal weakness that renders its possessor either ridiculous or contemptible depending on how disgusting he appears. On the other hand, lust, another "deadly" sin best defined as inappropriate (not as excessive) sexual desire, leads to immoral actions when it prompts its victim to engage in infidelity, betrayal, or sexual harassment.

Self-Control and Motivation

Another distinction worth noting is that between what has been called motivating virtues and the virtues of self-control, such as patience, perseverance, diligence, the ability to delay or forego gratification, and what is called "willpower," or the ability to control one's desires and impulses. The **virtues of self-control** are cool, calculating virtues, which look beyond the present moment to the broader picture and to long-range consequences. They are of first importance in the formation of good character, and to a large extent constitute what we think of as strength of character. A great part of one's moral education, and of the entire process of maturity, consists in learning these virtues.

Motivating virtues are traits, such as generosity and compassion, which make us want to do things. These are the "warmer" traits, and sometimes they need to be restrained by the virtues of self-control. Suppose you are moved by a mail appeal illustrated with a picture of a cute puppy dog to send money to an animal rights organization; but then you reflect that the money will be used to hinder medical research that might save human lives, including maybe your own some day. Here your natural and commendable compassionate impulse gives way to prudent reflection. Before you act, you think; perhaps you investigate. Only when your healthy skepticism about mail propaganda has been satisfied do you decide whether to send the money. Though generosity is a virtue, impulsively giving away your money is a folly, which can be corrected by the cool, self-control trait of skepticism.

Aristotle and Plato do not make a distinction between motivating virtues and the virtues of self-control because they held that there is always a self-control component in any virtue. Hence, for them motivating virtues are not virtues at all. In their view, a virtuous person is not someone who is moved in morally good ways, such as through compassion or generosity, but who thinks things through intelligently. They do not find anything virtuous about unthinking action. Compassion, to the extent this means feeling sorry for someone and acting spontaneously on the feeling alone, is not a virtue. They would find nothing commendable about the person who, moved by pity for the poor little puppy, rushes her check off in the mail without inquiring about what will be done with her money. Because in their view one's motivations are not in themselves virtues, they do not regard self-control as a set of virtues separate from the motivating virtues. To be virtuous is already to exercise control with regard to what to do, when and why to do it, how much, how often, and so on.

For this reason, Plato holds that ultimately there is only one virtue: wisdom *(Protagoras,* 361). His argument is that no other virtue, such as courage, does you or anyone else much good unless you know how to use it properly. This is a sensible enough point, although it hardly establishes Plato's conclusion that nothing but wisdom is a true virtue, as Aristotle quickly pointed out *(Nicomachean Ethics,* VI, 13). But Aristotle agrees that the virtues cannot exist without wisdom. Plato's doctrine that at bottom all the virtues are the same thing is called **the unity of the virtues,** a doctrine that also is attributed to Aristotle, though Aristotle does not hold that at bottom there is only one virtue. For Aristotle, a person who has one virtue has them all. This seems a bit implausible, however: a person can be honest, for example, without being kind, though it might be said in Aristotle's defense that virtues do seem to come bunched together—for example, a person who is kind is more likely to be honest than a person who is cruel.

Another doctrine sometimes attributed to Plato is that there is a **master virtue,** a superior virtue that holds the others together. For Plato this would be justice, for he says *(Republic,* 441–443) that a person who is just would also be wise, courageous, and temperate, since the just person has all of the "parts of the soul" in good order, and these other virtues express the good condition of each part of the soul. (Wisdom is when your intelligence is in control, temperance is when your passions are moderated, and courage is when your "spirit" is strong and enables you to face adversity.)

Despite the authority of Plato and Aristotle, it seems contrary to experience to hold that moral goodness comes in an all-or-nothing package, and equally contrary to experience to hold that virtues are "have it or not" propositions. In fact, virtues come in degrees: some people are more honest than others, some are kinder, others friendlier, more just, more brave, more self-controlled, and wiser. Perhaps no one is entirely devoid of all the virtues, though one could imagine as an extreme on a continuum a totally virtueless individual whose numerical ranking on the virtue scale is zero for each virtue. We could call such an imaginary person a "beast." A "saint" would be someone who has a high score on the virtue scale for each or most of the virtues. Presumably, most people would fall somewhere between the saint and beast.

The Golden Mean

The reader may be surprised to learn that for Aristotle, all virtues have a common form. They are a midpoint between two extremes, one of excess and the other of deficiency. This is Aristotle's famous doctrine of the **Golden Mean.** Courage is perhaps the most celebrated example. Contrary to what might be the modern view, Plato and Aristotle both hold that courage is to be distinguished not only from cowardliness, which is a deficiency of boldness, but also from what they call foolhardiness or rashness, which is an excess of boldness. The courageous person is not the person who simply rushes in whenever there is danger or distress. (But Aristotle admits that courage is closer to rashness than to cowardice.) Rather, the courageous person is like the hero of many a popular movie, who not only is willing to put himself in danger to protect or rescue others, but also knows how to accomplish the rescue. Competence at being brave was for the Greek philosophers an essential part of being brave. They would have enjoyed the likable but inept character often seen in movies who tries to help but does not have what it takes to help; when this fellow rushes in to perform the needed rescue, he gets himself in trouble and has to be saved by the hero. He overcomes fear and takes a risk, but would not be regarded as courageous; he is said to be foolhardy because he does not know his limits, and his rashness endangers others. Given his low skill level at performing rescues, he should not try them.

Can we defend the idea that for every virtue there are always two opposed evils, an excess and a deficiency? It is certainly true that you can be too friendly, with the wrong people, for the wrong reason and so on, as well as not friendly enough. Or you can be too liberal with your money, spending more than your means allow, or making foolish gifts. Modesty perhaps is in between boastfulness and false humility. Justice is wanting neither more nor less than what you are entitled to have. Aristotle gives many examples to support his case. Honesty is an interesting problem: can there be too much honesty? Perhaps Aristotle would say that the virtue is *discretion*. Discretion is telling neither too much nor too little, knowing what to tell, and when to tell it, and to whom. An indiscreet person is one who tells too much, which we call blabbing; a person who will not tell or tells too little, we call secretive.

Look for counterexamples to the theory that every virtue is in between two vices. Honesty in the sense of not cheating seems to be one. There certainly can be a deficiency of this, but what is the excess? Would Aristotle say that the virtuous person knows when to cheat, and whom, and how much? Or is there some other excess the honest person avoids? Aristotle's generalization seems a bit overdrawn.

Vices

From virtue we turn to vice. Law-enforcement "vice squads" deal with illicit sex, gambling, and drugs, but the term "vice" in moral theory covers anything wrong, evil, or a sin. The "deadly sins" are those that are not only considered the worst but are thought to be the origin of all the others. The **seven deadly sins** of theology are *pride, envy, lust, gluttony, anger, covetousness,* and *sloth*. This may seem a haphazard list. Many obvious sins are missing, and there is no evident principle by which the list is drawn. The reader may be surprised that the two great sins of childhood, greed and selfishness, are not listed (greed: "Don't be greedy, Johnny, you already had five candies"; selfishness: "Don't be selfish, Johnny, let Irma share your toys"). None of the deadly sins seem terribly immoral other than anger and envy; the rest are more like personal failings than moral faults. There is no obvious parallel between the sins and the virtues; if hope is a virtue, despair ought to be a sin. If prudence is a virtue, rashness or folly ought to be a sin. Some of the sins amount to a failure of self-control, such as, lust, gluttony, and anger. Students who do not like to study should notice that sloth—the combination of laziness and sloppiness—is on the list. Students who prefer to complain than work can take comfort that griping is absent, rather surprising in view of the importance given to the virtue of fortitude. Avarice or greed, which is missing, is perhaps covered by covetousness, but they are not the same; avarice is wanting more than you need or more than your fair share, and covetousness is wanting what belongs to someone else.

Pride is perhaps the most interesting sin. We are proud of pride. "School pride" is pushed on students by overpaid cheerleaders working in university administration; public schools, which evidently are run by people who think children are too humble, put out propaganda to induce children to feel proud of themselves. But for orthodox theology, pride was the Original Sin; it inspired

Satan to revolt against God, and Adam to eat of the Tree of Knowledge. Pride means puffing yourself up, wanting to be better than you are, thinking that you are entitled to more than belongs to you. Theology demands that we recognize that we are miserable sinners and utterly dependent on God, without whose Grace we cannot even begin to be good (the best we can do is pray that God will give us the moral strength to struggle against temptation). Weak and sinful as we are, we have nothing to be proud about.

Aristotle considers pride a virtue, and perhaps apart from theology only excessive or overbearing pride should be regarded as a sin. This is the same as *arrogance*. The arrogant person respects no one and makes no attempt to disguise his contempt. He insults you by his manner; he wants you to know that he is doing you a favor by admitting you to his presence. Though he may not actually do any harm and does not mean to be unpleasant, he is insufferable; we often dislike the arrogant person more than we do others who are really evil.

Another form of pride is *obstinacy,* the refusal to admit that you have made a mistake or may be in the wrong. Bertrand Russell's famous declension of the pretend verb "obstinate" makes the point that it is hard to distinguish the sin of obstinacy from the virtue of principle: "I am a man of principle, you are obstinate, he is a pig-headed fool." The Biblical Hebrews were notoriously obstinate; they called themselves "stiff-necked" because they were too stubborn to heed the warnings of God's prophets. But obstinacy served their descendants well during two millennia of persecutions, when a less stubborn people could have avoided much suffering by abandoning their faith.

Benjamin Franklin says that pride is the most difficult passion to subdue. His point is a matter of logic: "Even if I could conceive that I had completely overcome it, I should probably be proud of my humility." We might put it this way: you cannot believe that you have attained a virtue without being proud of yourself; but to be proud of humility is a contradiction. A person who conquers pride is humble, but a person who believes he is humble is proud of his humility; so a person who thinks he has conquered pride, has not. Therefore, you can never believe you have attained the virtue of humility. But pride is a sin, and one should struggle to subdue it. Therefore, whether you think you are proud or whether you think you are humble, you should struggle to be humble. Hence, you can never cease struggling against pride.

The term "deadly" is a mistranslation of the Latin *capitalis,* which does not mean fatal but being at the head of the list. But the term is well chosen, since capital sins are those which, unless repented of, send you to Hell, at least if they are done deliberately and in full knowledge of what you are doing (the same evil deeds done in ignorance are not capital but venial.) Roman Catholics hold that capital sins must be forgiven formally, that is, after repentance and penance (which is a kind of self-inflicted punishment) under the direction of a priest who, acting as God's representative, assesses the repentance, imposes the penance, and grants absolution; less serious (venial) sins can be forgiven without the priest's direction if the sinner sincerely repents, asks forgiveness, makes amends, and does penance. (Be sure to distinguish "venial" sins from "venal" behavior, which is often a capital sin.) But you must make amends; merely feeling sorry will not absolve you. And you have to be punished for your sins, one way or another. If you do not punish yourself voluntarily through penance, God will do it for you later. Forgiveness is a virtue and God is merciful, but the theologians who were in charge of morality for nearly 1500 years were not about to let any sinner escape unpunished.

Making lists of sins is fun; you can safely try it at home. See if you can think of others. Ask yourself this: for any supposed vice, would you really be unhappy, or badly off, if you possessed that vice instead of a corresponding virtue? What would you think if many of the people you lived with possessed the vice; would you prefer to make new acquaintances? If the answer is not yes to at least one of these questions, then it is problematic that you regard the trait as really a vice.

SAINTS, HEROES, AND SUPEREROGATION

From sinners we pass to saints. Virtue ethicists sometimes say that morality should be learned through the inspiring models of heroic, noble, or saintly people. This is the method of emulation or role modeling. Candidates for the role of sainthood include Socrates, Jesus Christ, Mahatma Gandhi, Abraham Lincoln, and Martin Luther King, Jr., people whose lives are said to be capable of inspiring moral idealism. Virtue ethicists also suggest that we can determine which conduct is virtuous by observing the actions of these role models, but this point is clearly circular since some standard is needed by which it is decided which are the people to be emulated. If you asked most ordinary Americans who they would like to be or whose lives they would like to imitate, they would probably mention "tough guys" like Clint Eastwood or Arnold Schwarzenegger, glamorous celebrities like Elizabeth Taylor or Michelle Pfeiffer, and perhaps certain athletes who (if their boasting can be believed) have managed to sleep with thousands of women. Virtue ethicists would be aghast at some of these unwholesome types as role models, which shows that you cannot first pick out role models and then deduce standards of good and bad from their behavior.

What Is a Saint?

Here are two methods for conferring sainthood, based on assigning "saintliness points" and electing to sainthood those who have a given quantity of such points. Assume we know what the virtues are, and assume that virtues come in degrees (some people have more, some less, of the same virtue), so that we can assign points to indicate how much of each virtue a person has. One method is to define a "saint" as someone who attains some arbitrary high score for each virtue. If there were ten virtues, and a very high score for any virtue were 100, then we might fix (say) 1000 total points as the threshold for saintliness.

This method is based on the assumption that sainthood should be defined absolutely: if you possess so much virtue, then you are a saint. A saint scores so many saintliness points, so in principle any number of people could qualify for sainthood, and we could have a whole population of saints, as the Puritans imagined. There is another way of looking at saintliness: a saint is someone who is much more moral than most people. This requires a different method for determining sainthood, based on comparing candidates for sainthood with the average person. Grant that we can determine how much of each virtue the average person possesses; we take this to be the norm for that virtue. We then measure how much more of each virtue than the average is possessed by any given candidate for sainthood, and compute an overall virtue score based on this percentage. A candidate might be, say, twice as virtuous as the average person, so his or her virtue score would be 200. We can now proceed in two ways. One method is to determine how much more virtuous than the average person a saint should be. Let us say a saint should be twice as virtuous as average; hence, we confer sainthood on all people who score 200 or more. The second method is to base sainthood on a person's standing in the population. We confer sainthood on all those who fall into a top percentile of the population. (If we decide that a saint ought to be in the top .02% of the population virtue-wise, there would be as many as 50,000 American saints. If this is too many, proceed in reverse: decide how many saints you think there ought to be, and adjust the qualifying percentile accordingly. If you think there should not be more than 500 saints in the United States, the sainthood percentile would be .0002.)

The argument for the first method is that saintliness should not be defined so as to make it necessarily rare. If saintliness is something to be emulated, as virtue ethicists say it is, then saintliness ought to be attainable by everyone who tries, and should be defined by some absolute measure. This assumes saintliness is a good thing for everyone. If saintliness is not desirable for everyone, then the percentile method of defining saints would be preferable.

Why is it that saintliness is considered to be a condition we should all attain and yet is thought to be rare? Our fantasy exercise in measuring sainthood enables us to see something virtue ethicists rarely note. Perhaps we should recognize two kinds of saintliness, ordinary saints and heroic saints. **Ordinary saints** are those people who have the standard virtues to a large degree. They attain high levels of morality, not by any extraordinary or heroic deeds but by living their normal lives decently. They are not usually considered saints because they do not claim any special virtues, but by our first definition of saintliness as possessing the virtues to a high degree, they would qualify. They raise their children, work at their job, pay their taxes, love their friends and family, take part in civic activities, and manage to do these everyday activities without stealing, cheating, imposing on their neighbors, or deliberately causing trouble for anybody. Since they possess many of the virtues to a large extent, their score would be high on our first saintliness measure. There may well be large numbers of such people.

Philosophers do not seem to think of ordinary good people as saints; what philosophers call saints are what we should call **heroic saints,** people whose lives are dedicated to something, either to moral perfection or a heroic goal such as liberating their people or comforting the sick. There are also saints whose lives are marked by deeper spirituality than most people can experience. These are the ones who are put forward as models of inspiration, and they are few in number.

But it may be questioned whether perfection is a goal to which everyone ought to aspire. Dedicated or spiritual people are certainly admirable, but do we really want to emulate people who dedicate their lives to some moral ideal or heroic cause? Perhaps there is something to be said for a less intense, less focused existence. Would we like to live surrounded by dedicated people? Saints are inspirational; either by explicit teaching or simply by how they live, they set high standards and challenge you to be better than you are. But such people tend to be more interested in people in the abstract than in real particular people; they see you as a potential recruit or soldier in the moral struggle. Spiritual people perhaps worry too much about the condition of their soul; what is worse, they worry about the condition of your soul. Such people are intimidating without meaning to be. They make other people uncomfortable, and though a certain amount of discomfort is good for you and you should learn to profit from it, too much discomfort can be debilitating.

There is no reason to imagine that saints cannot be good company and fun in ordinary ways; judged by most standards Lincoln was as much of a saint as any American leader, but he loved to argue, swap stories, and tell (often raunchy) jokes. So we might want to be in the company of saints, but perhaps we would not want to be in the company of nobody but saints. We need people who keep us up to high standards, but we also need some ordinary people with whom we can let our hair down and relax. The Puritan community of saints might strike us as stuffy and intimidating, and in any case we might discover, as Benjamin Franklin confesses to discovering, that striving for perfection is a time-consuming matter that is easily pushed aside by more pressing daily business.

Supererogation

One question moralists sometimes put is whether morality requires that we do our moral best, or allows us to get by with doing less than our best. **Rigorists** hold that we are always required to do our moral best. This view makes no distinction between different types of morally commendable actions, taking all morally commendable acts to be morally required. In effect, it holds that we are required to be moral saints, and ought to cultivate all the virtues to the highest degree. Here, however, we shall distinguish between three different kinds of morally commendable acts. These are ordinary duties, supererogatory acts, and heroic duties.

Ordinary Duties   These set the standards of what is expected of everybody. Basic honesty, for example, is required of everybody. Acting in accordance with ordinary standards is morally commendable but does not entitle you to any special praise or merit: you do not earn praise because you did not tell any lies today. If, however, you fall below ordinary standards, you are subject to criticism, reproach, and chastisement. Hence, an **ordinary duty** is a morally commendable act that (1) you are morally required to do; (2) earns you no special praise if you do it; and (3) earns you condemnation or rebuke if you fail to do it.

Supererogation   This can be thought of as acts that are aspirations and ideals, for example, heroism. A hero acts "above and beyond the call of duty" by doing something that is morally commendable but not required by ordinary standards. To be heroic is an aspiration or an ideal, not a requirement. For heroism, the hero earns praise and special recognition. Since no one is required or expected to be a hero, no one can be blamed for not performing some daring rescue or other risky feat; but the person who does rush into the burning building to save the baby justifiably gets his picture in the newspaper and a medal from the mayor. Thus, a **supererogatory** act is a morally commendable act defined as the negation of each of conditions (1), (2), and (3). (Stop and work this out to be sure you see it.)

Heroic Duties   There is a problem with the concept of the supererogatory. If an act is commendable, why should you not be condemned if you fail to do it? Suppose you do not save the baby from the burning building and it dies before the rescue units arrive. Are you simply off the hook morally? Would a decent person not suffer guilty pangs of conscience and regard himself partly responsible for the baby's death? We say that at certain moments a person is called on to act, or is put to the test; these are occasions that call for heroics. Classical examples occur during wartime, or when something horrific is happening. At these times, acting according to ordinary standards seems insufficient. Heroics are required.

Take the Germans who looked the other way when the Nazis carted off Jews to be slaughtered. What could they do about it? Had they interfered, they would have been carted off too. Sheltering even a lone Jew for a single night might have led to prison or death; such an act would be heroic, so by our definition of supererogation, not doing it does not earn you any rebuke.

But this does not seem right; people who fail to be heroes may earn rebuke, perhaps even harsh rebuke. Some acts are difficult and require courage, but invoking supererogation when courage is required may sometimes be an excuse for not having courage. This is the moral danger of the concept of supererogation. During the Nazi persecutions, there were Germans and other Europeans in occupied countries who did risk their lives by aiding Jewish fugitives (they numbered in the tens and perhaps hundreds of thousands; the state of Israel memorializes several thousand by name). We want to be able to say that such heroes deserve special commendation and remembrance, without excusing those who failed.

Sometimes rising to the occasion when heroics are called for is morally required, and failing to meet the challenge is a moral blemish. Hence, we need a third category of commendable acts. We call these heroic duties. **Heroic duties** are commendable acts that are like ordinary duties because—conditions (1) and (3)—doing them is required, and failure to perform subjects you to condemnation and rebuke. But they differ from ordinary duties like paying your debts and keeping your word because of the risk involved. They are like supererogatory acts in that—negation of condition (2)—they earn you special praise.

Heroic duties require moral courage. Let us say you know your boss is stealing from the company. It is easy to make excuses ("It's not my job to police this company"), and difficult to act. But there is no physical danger: whistleblowers and others who stand up against powerful interests risk loss of job, money, friends, social position, and even health, but are not typically attacked by Mafia hit men. The category of legitimate supererogatory acts may be limited to acts of physical courage like rescuing plane crash survivors from icy waters: some people just are not strong enough, or cannot swim well enough, or cannot keep their wits about them, or lose their nerve. These acts are not duties, not even heroic duties. They are simply too difficult for all but the best endowed to perform. They are supererogatory: it is no disgrace not to do them.

Heroic duties can be assessed on a dimension called stringency: how bad is it if you fail to perform your heroic duty? Heroic duties are typically far more urgent and important than ordinary duties; they involve life or death or some matter of great importance, so failure to perform them is a more serious failure than failure to perform ordinary duties. On the other hand, what is heroic is difficult and so cannot be demanded as forcefully as what is ordinary. This creates a conflict that is not easy to resolve. It is generally very important that you do the heroic duty, so that failure earns condemnation; but at the same time, because of the difficulty, it is excusable if you fail.

We can distinguish two reasons for failure, fear and indifference. Indifference is not an excuse. Most Germans were not Nazis and would not have murdered anyone, but many did turn away out of indifference; they told themselves, "It's not my business" or, "What can I do, I'm only one person?" (Many of them did not like Jews very much anyway.) They were guilty of bad faith, the sin of Pontius Pilate. They washed their hands before evil. They invoked supererogation to evade their responsibilities.

Suppose you do not report your thieving boss, telling yourself that it is not required that you be a hero. Are you acting from fear or indifference? Probably some of both, but as there is no physical danger, a large part of your motivation might be indifference. You ignore the wrongdoing because you are not sufficiently concerned to confront it, not because you fear the consequences. To call this supererogatory is bad faith. You share some of the responsibility for the wrongdoing and are complicit in it.

On the other hand, where fear is the chief motivation, as where there is physical danger, those who do nothing do have a certain excuse, and are in a morally more ambiguous position. The person who recognizes his duty but is too fearful to do it at least has the merit of knowing what he ought to do; he punishes himself for his failure by feeling guilty. He deserves credit for not searching for excuses to shelter his culpability: courage is by definition difficult, so failure to show courage can be excused to a certain degree. Yet, since courage is a personal strength and a chief component of personal merit, those who do not show courage suffer from a character flaw that is particularly notable and deserving of reproach.

So if you fail to report your boss out of fear for your job, you are culpable for having violated your heroic duty, but as you have an excuse you are in a better position morally than the person who fails to report his boss because he tells himself that to do so would be supererogation and supererogation is not morally required. Of course, "better and worse position" may not mean much; we are not talking about judgment by other people, but what you ought to think of yourself when you look in the mirror. If you are indifferent to evil, you may also be indifferent to making harsh assessments about your own moral status.

THE MORAL CHARACTER OF MEN AND WOMEN

Consider the following passage from Jane Austen's novel *Emma* (1815):

> **Mr. Knightly:** If Frank Churchill had wanted to see his father, he would have contrived it between September and January. A man of his age—what is he ? Three or four-and-twenty—cannot be without the means of doing as much as that. It is impossible.

> **Emma:** You are the worst judge in the world, Mr. Knightly, of the difficulties of dependence. . . . It is very unfair to judge of anybody's conduct without an intimate knowledge of their situation. . . .

> **K:** There is one thing, Emma, which a man can always do if he chooses, and that is, his duty . . . it is Frank Churchill's duty to pay this attention to his father.

> **E:** You have no idea what is requisite in situations directly opposite to your own . . . I wish you would try to understand what an amiable young man may be likely to feel. . . .

> **K:** Your amiable young man is a very weak young man, if this be the first occasion of his carrying through a resolution to do right against the will of others. It ought to have been a habit with him, by this time, of following his duty, instead of consulting expediency.

> **E:** We are both prejudiced! You against, I for him.

> **K:** Prejudiced! I am not prejudiced.

> **E:** But I am very much, and without being at all ashamed of it. . . .

This passage might be cited to illustrate the difference in morality between women and men. Emma tries to put herself in Frank's place, understands his problem, and is forgiving and makes light of his alleged transgression, but Mr. Knightly will not make allowances or listen to excuses, since he knows what duty requires and demands strict obedience to duty's claims. Emma, we might say, is more "person-oriented," whereas Mr. Knightly is focused on moral principle. If these values are representative of men and women, there might be something interesting to be discovered about morality. Let us see what can be made out of possible differences in moral styles of men and women. Though it is difficult to describe these styles without skirting stereotypes, some moral philosophers think these differences are important enough to take the risk. These philosophers attribute to men a morality based on "principle," and to women a morality based on "relationships."

Men: Morality of Principle

Men believe in *principles*. They think morality consists in abiding by rules that apply to everyone. Men are said to operate in a world of more or less anonymous strangers, who relate to each other through impersonal rules. Rules enable men to hold people at arm's length and avoid personal involvement. Hence, men prefer impartiality, fairness, and treating everybody alike, and respect people who set high moral standards by acting according to principles that are fair to everybody.

Men's morality is *merit-based*. They honor achievement and have little patience for people who fail and make excuses. Men believe in individual responsibility. They think people who violate rules ought to suffer consequences. Men are reluctant to forgive transgressions because they think people profit from being held to standards. It is unfair to the people who try to follow the rules and to the transgressors themselves, and in the end undermines the entire system of rules, when transgressors avoid the consequences of their misdeeds. Men are disciplinarians.

Men are *competitive* and value creativity, individual achievement, and self-reliance. They want to think of themselves as strong-willed and independent in mind and spirit. They respect individual accomplishment, success against the odds, achievement of difficult goals, and victory over competition. They value "toughness," and are suspicious of signs of weakness, in which category they tend to place emotions and personal intimacy. They take pride in keeping their emotions under control, in maintaining their composure under difficult circumstances, and in getting the job done despite personal distress. They are contemptuous of those who are "soft" or "weak."

Women: Morality Based on Relationships

Women are said to operate in a world of friends, neighbors, and family, and their morality is said to be based on cultivation of *personal relationships, sharing, and caring* for others. Women take genuine interest in other people, respond to their needs, and value closeness and warmth. Their morality is not based on following principles but on affection, trust, compassion, and sympathy, so they are said to be "emotive" rather than "logical."

Women's morality is *nurturing;* they want people to grow and prosper. They think it is better to bring out the good in people rather than to criticize or punish; they seek to give people what they need to thrive and flourish, offering support, sympathy, and encouragement. Forgiveness, understanding lapses and weakness, patching over quarrels, and starting again are more important than winning moral victories and keeping score. They accept human weakness, thinking that to err is human. Their morality makes good intentions more important than actual achievement.

Women value group rather than individual success, *cooperation* rather than self-assertion and victory. They are willing to sacrifice their own interests, identify with groups, and submerge their individuality into the group's goals and identity. They value the support they get from other people, and define success as developing close and warm relationships; they believe in compromise. They value agreeable personalities, "niceness," and people who are easy to get along with rather than those who are challenging, hard-driving, or prickly. Their self-worth is founded on sustaining ties with other people, not standing on principle or asserting their rights.

Some readers will regard these two styles of morality as mere stereotypes; others may see in them considerable truth. Let us assume for the sake of discussion that we have described two styles of morality, whether or not we have described the morality of men and women as such. There are several questions that can be raised.

1.   Are these real gender differences, or only abstract styles that may be found more or less equally distributed among men and women? This is an empirical question that cannot be answered by speculative philosophy. The few empirical studies that have been done are, even in a generous reading, inconclusive, and probably show much less than their authors claim for them. Men–women generalities are exactly that, generalities; they should not be regarded as accurate portrayals of all or even most women and men, but might contain some interesting truth nonetheless if they described, even partly, significant numbers of either sex. Do not be afraid to test these generalities on the basis of your experience. Do the descriptions match your experience of men and women, including yourself? Evidence based on personal experience is far from conclusive, but it is not nothing either; ask your friends and observe their behavior, and see if you observe gender-based differences in their morality.

2.   If there really are such differences, the next question would be how to account for them; attempts to explain the differences have been made even before the existence of the differences has been documented. One explanation could involve biology: nature made women to be mothers, so perhaps nature has predisposed women to be nurturing and caring. Another explanation might be social: women are trained to play private roles focused on the home and family, whereas men play more public roles of work, professions, and politics: each sex has acquired moral traits suitable to its social roles. Both answers are probably partly correct, since human psychology is a complicated and little understood product of biological and genetic predispositions shaped by social conditioning. This very likely is true of intelligence and sexual preference, and might be true of whatever gender-specific differences there may be in morality.

3.   Is women's morality better than men's morality *for women?* Some feminist philosophers extol women's morality as "women's authentic voice," but they seem confused about whether the morality authentically is preferred or originates

among women, or authentically is good for women. If women's morality is not just preferred by women but also good for them, it has to be explained why adopting a morality of "caring" rather than of rules and principles is good for women, but not necessarily for men. Why should it be women for whom it is good to care and to value relationships, and men for whom it is good to follow principle? Answers based on women's biology or social role will raise red flags for many feminists.

Feminist philosophers who are excited about uncovering what they take to be an undervalued women's activity much like quilting bees or bake-offs, seem to value women's morality because it is women's, and not because it is morally better according to some nongender standard. Some even deny that there is any nongender standard of good and bad, and hold that there are different moral standards applicable to men and to women. This can be called *gender relativism*. But feminist philosophers generally do not celebrate such women's activities as watching TV soap operas, reading soft-porn romances, or shopping on the shopping channel, so they must think there is some kind of a nongender standard by which "good" women's activities can be distinguished from "bad" ones.

If, on the other hand, women's morality is not good for women, then it is not clear why women should endorse it—simply because women invented it. Why should women be given credit for inventing something that is not good for them?

4. Is women's morality preferable to men's? This is not the question whether women's morality is preferable for women, but whether it is preferable for everyone. If it is, then men should adopt it, a point made forcefully by some feminists who argue that we ought to foster nurturing and caring in everybody.

If women's morality is better for everyone, however, then it is not because the morality is women's that it is better, but because the morality is superior in itself. Women get the credit for inventing the superior morality, but what makes it superior is not that women invented it. Contrary to gender relativism, there must be some nongender standard by which the worth of competing moralities is assessed. Of course, another possibility is that neither men's nor women's morality is better for anyone; perhaps they are of equal worth and each may be rightfully chosen by anyone regardless of gender. Or perhaps what would be best for everybody might be some kind of blend of each.

If caring and nurturing are important, it does not follow that principles and strict standards are not. Many readers will probably find Emma's views about Frank Churchill more attractive than Mr. Knightly's, so it might be instructive to note that this was probably not Jane Austen's opinion, for she presents Emma as an intelligent but somewhat insubstantial young woman who is rather too taken by Frank Churchill's charm and good looks and who, in the excerpted conversation, "to her great amusement, perceived that she was taking the other side of the question from her real opinion."

5. Another question is whether it is antifeminist to admit that there might be moral differences between men and women. Classical feminism strenuously

denied any significant gender-based differences, other than the undeniable differences of gross anatomy, so it is disconcerting to some people to find "new feminists" proclaiming a "women's morality" and even vaunting the moral superiority of women over men. Some feminists fear that to hold that men and women have different morality might be to imply that there are other gender differences between the sexes, differences that feminism has long been concerned to deny. This fear may be misplaced, however, since the aim of classical feminism was to give women the freedom to do whatever they wanted; this freedom is not put in jeopardy if most or even all women want different things than men want. It is certainly true that classical feminism is often seen as denigrating certain things that many women in fact do value, such as physical attractiveness, love, motherhood, and a happy marriage to a loving and supportive man; for this reason, certain feminists are accused of being women-haters. But although no doubt some feminists can be fairly accused of trying to foist their own personal tastes and preferences on women as a group, the logic of feminism does not require an attack on such "womanly" goals, or even on "feminine" pleasures such as shopping and wearing makeup. All that is required is an attack on the notion that women have to like and want these things or else they are not "really women." Feminists who attack the idea that it is fun to shop, wear nice clothes, and even to dress to please men seem to forget that the goal of feminism is to give women the same freedom that men have, which should include the freedom to please men or not to please men according to the choice of the individual woman. Sexism can be defined as the idea that "nature is destiny": since you are female, you ought to value such and such or there is something wrong with you. By this definition, "antifeminine" feminists, who think that there is something wrong with women who value "feminine" traits and pleasures, are no less sexist than chauvinistic, role-stereotyping men.

6.   Do the alleged differences between male and female morality show something obnoxious about modern moral philosophy? Some feminists say that modern philosophy, which emphasizes principles and abstract obligations rather than sentiments and concrete human relations, reflects the male point of view and ignores the female point of view; this they take to be evidence of bias and sexism, not only in philosophy but in Western culture. Male philosophers think like men, they say, and, being chauvinists, imagine that everybody else ought to think like men too. Hence, they ignore or undervalue women's thinking.

If there is a woman's morality, it is true that standard philosophers have generally ignored it, though it is not true that no standard philosophers have incorporated elements of women's morality into their ethical systems (notably Hume, who has been called the "woman's moral philosopher" because of his emphasis on sentiments). Most male philosophers probably would not have accepted that there is such a thing as women's morality; this would be sexist if the philosophers simply overlook women and ignore what is important to them, but not if they have well-founded reasons for thinking that women and men have basically the same morality. Philosophers do not typically describe different moralities, but recommend morality: they advocate principles that they think are right and good (natural law philosophers, for example, do not say that people do follow nature; what they say is that people ought to follow nature). Is it sexist to recommend men's morality and not women's morality? It would be sexist if the philosopher ignores women and so has not even considered women's morality as something that might be recommended, or if he simply assumes that men's morality must be better than women's because it originates with men. Feminists are probably correct in suspecting that philosophers have been sexist in both of these ways.

Feminist philosophers deserve credit for calling attention to the "relationship" style of morality and pointing out its underrepresentation among standard philosophers. Their suspicion that male philosophers might have taken the "caring" style more seriously if it had originated among upper-class men is consistent with what we know about sexism in Western culture. This itself is something of an argument that there really is a women's morality, since if "caring" had not been hidden in the lives of women it might have been better represented in the books of philosophers.

Let us summarize: it is one thing to claim that there is such a thing as women's morality, that it is different from men's, that it is invented by women, and that many or most women prefer it to men's morality. All these are empirical claims that may be true but for which the evidence is at best inconclusive (some would argue that the evidence tends to indicate that women do not have any different morality than men). It is a second thing to claim that women's morality is preferable to men's morality for everybody; this is a moral position that is debated through considerations having nothing to do with gender. It is still a third thing to claim that women's morality has some special moral authority over women, and that women ought to prefer women's morality. This position looks as if it might be sexist as sexism has traditionally been defined in terms of sex-role stereotyping and gender-based roles and differences.

It is probably true that women have been ignored by Western philosophers, and for basically sexist reasons. Women's morality, if it is a good thing and invented by women, is something women can be proud of. But if feminism is supposed to liberate women from constraints that are not of their own making, feminism should not attempt to impose "women's morality" on women who may not be interested in it. No one should adopt any moral perspective for any reason other than that, after reflection, she concludes that it is morally preferable. It may well be true that some men are insufficiently caring and need to learn to be more so; by the same token, if women are too fond of caring and forgiving, they may need to learn from men to be more principled, as perhaps Jane Austen hints about Emma.

COMMUNITY AND AUTONOMY

Most people want to think for themselves. They want to make their own decisions and control their own lives, and this entails deciding for themselves how they want to live, what they want to do, and with whom they want to do it. Such people try to absorb information, reason logically, and make intelligent decisions. They look at evidence and try to keep an open mind, because they are aware that their beliefs might be mistaken. They listen to other people and take advice, but make their own evaluations about which advice is worth taking and which should be ignored. They will not accept any idea just because they are told to or because it seems easier to agree than to disagree. People who think for themselves are aware that everyone picks up ideas and values from the surrounding culture, but they reserve for themselves the right to evaluate these ideas and accept only those they think are worthwhile, since they are not willing to accept their culture's output uncritically.

We will call thinking for yourself **autonomy,** which means "self-rule." Philosophers since Socrates have regarded the conception of an autonomous person as attractive, and have considered it a significant element in a successful life. It could even be said that the message of Socrates, and of most subsequent philosophers in the Western tradition, has been: think for yourself. Do not accept any ideas just because someone else tells you to. Examine your beliefs, search for reasons and evidence, do not be afraid to change your mind when better ideas come along. In a word, be autonomous.

However, not all philosophers regard this conception of autonomy as attractive. Some philosophers think it overlooks important values. They think it places too much emphasis on the individual and not enough on the community. They also think it is based on some serious philosophical mistakes.

Philosophers who hold this are called **communitarians.** In their view, autonomy depends on a false and even unwholesome opposition between person and community. It is not possible to separate the individual from society. There is no standpoint outside of society from which the autonomous person can select values, nor is there any power of reason that enables us to examine values critically and to make morally sound choices based on logic. Values and moral standards are rooted in communities; they are created by society, not chosen freely by autonomous rational agents. We are what society makes us, with the values society instills in us; we are no more individual than society allows us to be.

Communitarians claim that communities are not based on logic but on *affective ties,* by which they mean common sentiments and a sense of sharing and belonging. For this reason, sharing values is far more important than thinking for yourself. The autonomous individual is the ultimate skeptic and subjectivist, who rejects the community's values but is unable to replace them with anything more solid or satisfying. The inevitable fruit of the quest for autonomy is something communitarians condemn as *rootlessness,* a severing of connections to family, country, history, and culture. Rootlessness leads to the moral evils of our time: uncertainty about right and wrong; collapse of the community's morality; arm's-length, legalistic contracting based on calculation of interest instead of relationships based on warmth and spontaneous affection; the dominance of the values of the self—gratification, pleasure, greed, "me first." The communitarian mistrusts the autonomous person as Caesar mistrusted Cassius: "Such men are dangerous; they think too much."

Communitarians attribute the false goal of autonomy to what they call "liberalism," sometimes "liberal individualism," which they regard as the pervasive error of our culture. Liberalism holds that individual rights and liberties are prior to society, and that society is created expressly to protect such rights and liberties. Liberalism teaches that individuals and their rights are more important than groups, and that choice of values through autonomous reflection is more important than acceptance of the community's values. Communitarians regard these ideas as pernicious philosophical errors, leading directly to an overvaluing of "individuality" at the expense of social cohesion. Since communitarians consider liberalism to be the culturally dominant philosophy, they therefore make it responsible for the bulk of society's problems. Because of liberal ideas, people become self-centered, irresponsible, and hedonistic. They throw their trash all over the landscape, discard spouses and lovers when they get bored, live beyond their means and refuse to worry about who will pay the bills, want more then they need or even than they can possibly enjoy and think they have a right to everything they want.

Communitarians make two points, which typically they do not distinguish: because values are rooted in society, autonomy is not *possible;* and because values are rooted in society, autonomy is not *desirable.*

Autonomy Is Not Possible   This sounds like social determinism, which we dismissed in Chapter Two. Contrary to social determinism, nothing really prevents you from rejecting the values of your culture and replacing them with those from some other culture or even with values you have made up yourself; evidently, large numbers of people have, to varying degrees, succeeded in doing just that. But even if social determinism were true, it would not make autonomy impossible, since autonomy might be one of the values of your culture. And, in fact, autonomy is a value of our Western culture; if it were not, the communitarian's criticism of liberalism as the source of our social ills would not make any sense.

Communitarians also argue that autonomy is not possible because values are not based on logic, but on community and affective ties. (For this reason, some feminists are also communitarians.) We have argued in this book that basic moral principles cannot be proved by logic or derived from some foundation outside of morality, so we do not disagree with the communitarian's premise. But we have also stressed the importance of critically examining your moral values and rejecting or improving those that seem wrong or illogical. It does not follow that if values are not founded in logic, they cannot be improved by logic, or that logic has no role to play in their formation. Applying logic to values is what we recommended as critical morality (see Chapter One). The autonomous person tries to be as logical as possible about values, and rejects any values that cannot measure up to logical standards; but the autonomous person recognizes that it is not logical to try to be more logical than it is possible to be.

Autonomy Is Not Desirable   Communitarians think it is a good thing to depend on your society for your values, and a bad thing to think out your values for yourself. Against this, several points can be made.

1.   Whether you should take your values from society depends on what the society's values are. Lots of societies either are or have been racist, sexist, imperialistic, brutal toward the poor and downtrodden, and morally unwholesome in many other ways, and not even communitarians think anyone ought to adopt those values. Or take a university fraternity. Maybe they party a lot, put down women, help each other cheat on tests, and are scared witless by books and ideas. These values are not good just because the guys love them. It is true that by the standards of the larger society the fraternity's values are not acceptable, but communitarians probably cannot define what they mean by a "community," and "the larger society" is not any more of a community than a fraternity, perhaps less so. In any case, communitarians do not really think that the values of "the larger society" are necessarily better than the values of some subgroup within it: communitarians, being intellectuals, are apt to prefer classical music to hard rock and art films to mall movies, and are not about to change because the larger society has the opposite preferences. Since even communitarians admit that sometimes it is better to reject community values then to adopt them, they cannot claim that adopting community values is necessarily better than rejecting community values: it all depends on the community's values.

2.   Communitarians fail to distinguish between community values and the values of community. Communitarians like fellow-feeling, friendship, trust, belonging to groups, cooperation, working on projects with other people, group success, sharing, and feeling good about everybody. We can call these **values of community.** They dislike competition, self-reliance, independence, arm's-length relationships, individual initiative, and individual success. This preference for cooperation over competition is attractive to many people, and explains why some feminists are communitarians, as are others who deplore what they see as the overcompetitiveness of our society.

Communitarians also think that it is good to endorse **community values.** But these may not be the values of community. If values of community are good values, then they are good regardless of what your community's values are. Communitarians do not endorse values of community because these values originate in their community, but because these values strike them as preferable to individualistic values. In preferring values of community to individualistic values, communitarians contradict their own premise that all values must be rooted in communities. In choosing one set of values over another, they act as the autonomous agents they pretend to oppose, choosing the values that, after reflection, they conclude are the best. Since uncritical acceptance of values is not practiced by communitarians, why should they criticize liberals for not practicing it either?

3.   Communitarians fail to distinguish between intrinsic and instrumental values. Certain classical communitarian philosophers held that the community is intrinsically good, that is, good for its own sake. The early nineteenth-century German philosopher Georg Wilhelm Friedrich Hegel, for example, held that the

state was a value in and of itself; according to Hegel, individuals exist to serve the state and not the other way around. Contemporary communitarians often flirt with the idea that it is the community that is intrinsically good: in this view, the community exists for the sake of itself, not for the sake of the individuals who comprise it. As for individuals, communitarians hint that individuals either have no value other than as members of some community or, if they do, it ought to be subordinate to the value of the community.

Making the individual subordinate to the community frightens liberals. According to them, communities have no intrinsic value. Communities are good because they serve individuals. Hence, the value of communities is entirely instrumental. The only good thing about communities is that they enable the people who live in them to lead better lives. Take that away and you take away whatever value any community might have. The doctrine that communities are intrinsically good and that individuals exist to serve communities is, according to liberals, the philosophical underpinning of statism, totalitarianism, and oppression. These are the real moral evils of our time.

4. Because liberals value the individual, liberals also value privacy, a sphere of life into which other people, especially other people organized into a government, may not intrude without the individual's permission. Into my private sphere I am free to admit anyone or no one as I please; but in public life I must deal with whomever happens to show up. Public life is governed by politics; to operate in the public life, I must bargain and compromise and follow everybody's rules. Private life is governed by whim (sometimes confused with moral principle): I am free to do anything I please, at least within certain unclear limits, and do not have to answer to anyone. Some communitarians are so enamored with communities that they want all of life's business to be conducted in public, through politics. According to this conception, no one would be able to enjoy any pleasures or engage in any activity without first getting permission from the group. Such an arrangement would destroy freedom and individuality, and make everyone the group's servant. Liberals find this prospect appalling, and are surprised that communitarians do not.

Once the confusions and bad arguments of communitarianism have been exposed, no case remains against autonomy as a central excellence of character. An autonomous person is not someone who prefers competition to cooperation, or who is afraid to trust or who does not know how to enjoy friendship and personal intimacy. Therefore, an autonomous person is not a person who rejects the values of community. But an autonomous person does not accept any values, even those of community, without thinking about them and making sure that they are the values she prefers. An autonomous person is therefore independent and self-reliant in the way that makes most sense, not by trying to stand apart from her fellows and achieving everything through her own efforts but by thinking about things and making her own decisions about what is good and what is not. Such a person is not easily bullied or pushed around, and does not panic worrying about what people think of her. She follows her own course because she thinks it is best. But she thinks this because she strives to have good reasons for her values, which she is prepared to explain. Since she knows that no one is perfect and her ideas can always be improved, she is not only willing but eager to hear what can be said on the other side. If she is convinced she is wrong, but only if she is convinced, she will change her mind. We call this strength of character.

This is what philosophers have always tried to convey, at least since Socrates.

REFERENCES AND FURTHER READING

Virtue Ethics

Aristotle's *Ethics* (called by history the *Nicomachean Ethics,* after Aristotle's father the physician Nicomacheus, to distinguish it from two lesser books on ethics that carry Aristotle's name), not really a book but lectures edited into book form centuries after Aristotle's death, is one of the great works of Western philosophy; every student should aspire to emulate its limpid prose and masterful treatment of difficult issues.

Plato's *Republic* is the earliest extant great philosophy book in the Western tradition, and is still the single most readable philosophical classic, even though on most major issues its author's views are generally regarded as extravagant.

John Cooper, *Reason and Human Good in Aristotle* (Indianapolis, IN: Hackett, 1986) is the leading recent commentary.

For those who are not put off by its historical relativism, lost-world nostalgia for cultural homogeneity, and somewhat crotchety complaints against "liberal individualism," a seminal text for both virtue ethics and communitarianism is Alasdair MacIntyre, *After Virtue,* 2nd ed. (South Bend, IN: University of Notre Dame Press, 1984).

A 1958 essay by Elizabeth Anscombe, "Modern Moral Philosophy," reprinted in vol. 3 of her *Collected Papers* (Minneapolis, MN: University of Minnesota Press, 1981), gave the initial impetus to virtue ethics.

A collection of essays by Phillipa Foot, *Virtues and Vices* (Berkeley, CA: University of California Press, 1978), is an exposition of virtue ethics by a first-rate and very influential philosopher.

Two clearly written and carefully argued books that defend the thesis that character and virtues ought to be the center of ethics are S. D. Hudson, *Human Character and Morality* (Boston: R & KP, 1986), and Joel Kupperman, *Character* (New York: Oxford University Press, 1991). Hudson is stronger on the history of the subject, especially on Aristotle and Hume, but his book is more difficult and not recommended for novices.

A collection of essays by Tom Hill, Jr., *Autonomy and Self-Respect* (New York: Cambridge University Press, 1991), contains many interesting ideas on selected aspects of moral character.

An enormous and popular anthology is Christina Summers and Fred Sommers, eds., *Vice and Virtue in Everyday Life,* 3rd ed. (Fort Worth, TX: Harcourt Brace, 1993).

More difficult material is collected in Robert B. Kruschwitz and Robert C. Roberts, eds., *The Virtues* (Belmont, CA: Wadsworth, 1987); the editors have assembled an impressive 25-page bibliography.

An interesting if idiosyncratic treatment is found in Robert Solomon, *Ethics: A Short Introduction* (Dubuque, IA: Brown & Benchmark, 1993).

Feminism

Judging by the vast quantity of books, evidently among the most important cultural subjects around. A good, short introduction to feminist ethics that navigates cautiously through the doctrinal currents is Rosemarie Tong, *Feminine and Feminist Ethics* (Belmont, CA: Wadsworth, 1993).

Eva Feder Kittay and Diana T. Meyers, eds., *Women and Moral Theory,* (Totowa, NJ: Rowman & Littlefield, 1987) is a useful anthology. Another is Marilyn Pearsall, ed., *Women and Values,* 2nd ed. (Belmont, CA: Wadsworth, 1992). This contains an important essay by Annette Baier (see below).

A collection from the "radical" point of view, especially with regard to what its contributors take to be philosophical method, is Claudia Card, ed., *Feminist Ethics* (Lawrence, KS: University Press of Kansas, 1991), which contains a thorough bibliography.

Nell Noddings, *Caring, A Feminine Approach to Ethics and Moral Education* (Berkeley, CA: University of California Press, 1984), is the leading work on its subject. Very readable is Milton Mayeroff, *On Caring* (New York: Harper & Row, 1971).

An excellent philosopher who has made contributions to virtue theory, feminism, and many other topics is Annette Baier, some of whose essays are collected in *Postures of the Mind* (Minneapolis, MN: University of Minnesota Press, 1985).

Another book with more philosophy than doctrine is by Alison M. Jaggar, *Feminist Politics and Human Nature* (Totowa, NJ: Rowman & Allenhead, 1983).

Carol Gillgan, *In a Different Voice: Psychological Theory and Women's Development* (Cambridge, MA: Harvard University Press, 1982), deserves the credit for raising the alarm that philosophical ethics (and the "moral psychology" that derives from it) ignores women and women's moral point of view.

The passage from *Emma* is cited by Elizabeth Spellman in the Card anthology; she is critical of Emma's outlook only for a class bias she somewhat tendentiously finds in it.

There is enormous popular literature, and some scholarly material, on real or (probably) imaginary gender differences. The student who is uninitiated into ideologically motivated intellectual debates should be warned to take this material with a healthy skepticism.

Supererogation

A much-reprinted essay, "Moral Saints," is by Susan Wolf (1982); a less interesting reply ("Saints," 1984) from a religious context is by Robert Adams. Both appeared originally in the *Journal of Philosophy,* vol. 79 (August 1984) and vol. 81 (July 1984), respectively.

There are two books: David Heyd, *Supererogation: Its Status in Ethical Theory* (New York: Cambridge University Press, 1982), and Gregory Mellema, *Beyond the Call of Duty: Supererogation, Obligation and Offence* (Albany, NY: State University of New York Press, 1991).

A fascinating study of people who risked their lives to rescue Jews under Hitler is Samuel P. and Pearl M. Oliner, *The Altruistic Personality: Rescuers of Jews in Nazi Europe* (New York: Free Press, 1988). They put the number of such rescuers between 50,000 and 500,000.

Communitarianism

After *After Virtue,* the student can read Michael Sandel, *Liberalism and the Limits of Justice* (New York: Cambridge University Press, 1982); more interesting, because it is broader in scope and rooted in history and literature, is Michael Walzer, *Spheres of Justice* (New York: Basic Books, 1983).

A good anthology is Noel Reynolds, Cornelius Murphey, and Robert Moffat, eds., *Liberalism and Community* (in preparation). Another is Shlomo Avineri, and Avner De-Shalit, eds., *Communitarianism and Individualism* (New York: Oxford University Press, 1992).

Chapter Eight

Utilitarianism

And behold, there was a man which had his hand withered. And they asked him, saying, Is it lawful to heal on the Sabbath days? That they might accuse him. And he said unto them, What man shall there be among you, that shall have one sheep, and if it fall into a pit on the Sabbath day, will he not lay hold on it, and lift it out? How much then is a man better than a sheep? Wherefore it is lawful to do well on the Sabbath days. Then he said to the man, Stretch forth thine hand. And he stretched it forth; and it was restored whole, like as the other.

Matthew 12:10–13

Utilitarianism is probably the single most discussed moral theory of the twentieth century. Consequently, it is the most debated, most interpreted, and most misunderstood. Some philosophers think it is clearly and obviously true; others regard it as patently false and grossly immoral. Utilitarians themselves disagree not only with their opponents, but among each other as to just what utilitarianism says and which version of utilitarianism (U) is the best. When utilitarians respond to criticism by trying to restate the theory, they are criticized anew for changing their ground or abandoning their original positions. The philosophical world is full of wolves happy to gobble down any theory that seems weak and helpless. We shall try to present U in the most plausible way we can, formulating the position so as to anticipate known criticisms, but the reader should be forewarned that it is probably safer to speak of utilitarianisms rather than utilitarianism.

We shall first try to locate utilitarianism within a broader division of moral theories. Our division follows standard practice, although the terminology we shall employ is not universally accepted. We shall classify utilitarianism as a consequentialist moral theory, so first we shall explain the difference between consequentialist and nonconsequentialist theories.

TWO KINDS OF MORAL THEORY

Consequentialism and Nonconsequentialism

Can it be morally good to do something if no good will come from doing it? When we decide what to do, should we consider anything other than the good and bad effects of our proposed actions? Consequentialists think not.

Sometimes people think they are moral, but wonder what good comes from it. "I work hard, pay my taxes, obey the law, love my family, and don't bother anyone, and what good comes of it?" they complain, perhaps thinking of some shady character who seems to be a success despite a less than admirable life. They mean no good comes to *them,* as they see it, from being moral. But suppose no good came to *anybody* from you being moral? Your hard work comes to nothing, the government wastes your tax dollars, your family does not amount to much, and nobody benefits because you deny yourself the pleasures of illegal behavior. Can it be morally good to do things that do not benefit anyone?

Suppose you are driving in the city late at night. You are alone on the streets; there is no other car in sight. But the traffic lights are working, and when you arrive at an intersection the light changes to red. You look around and see no one. Do you stop?

Chances are most people would stop; but while they are sitting at the red light, wasting time and gasoline, they might well ask themselves: "Why am I doing this? What possible good am I doing by stopping here? What harm would come if I were to hit the gas and drive on?" And they might come to the conclusion that there are no good answers to these questions, and that obeying the signals for the sake of obeying them is a stupid habit that they wish they could break.

Such a person is thinking like a consequentialist. A consequentialist is someone who does not see the point in doing something unless some good will come of doing it, or unless some harm would come of not doing it. You have probably noticed that on the highway, most people are consequentialists when it comes to the speed limit: few drivers seem to obey the speed limit just because it is the law. They do not see that anything is to be gained by driving the speed limit, and do know what is to be lost, namely, time. So they ignore the rules and drive at a speed they consider safe and reasonable for the road conditions.

Should we obey the law even if no good seems to come of it? Many people wonder about this in their business and professional lives, where they are expected to comply with regulations they regard as essentially stupid. But what about morality? Are not moral principles exactly what you should obey, whether or not good results? Consequentialists cannot see this. In the poem by Felicia Dorothea Hemans, "The Boy Stood on the Burning Deck," the young sailor remains at his post, even as the ship burns up around him. This is supposed to be an inspiring example of courageous devotion to duty, but consequentialists snicker. Noble self-sacrifice without any good coming from it for anyone does not appeal to the consequentialist. What is the point of duty if it means getting killed for nothing?

We have seen this already in the discussion of lying. Lying is wrong, but not when a lie will save someone's life. So good consequences count. But on the other hand, it does seem wrong to lie to avoid embarrassment, or to help a friend in trouble, so maybe good consequences do not justify all lies, only some of them. Many people think hard work is a moral imperative, but work for the sake of work does not seem to make much sense. Can it be good to work hard, even if nobody benefits? You might as well relax and enjoy your life.

Or consider integrity—for example, keeping your word. Who benefits? Evidently, the person to whom you have made a promise. Even though it may be inconvenient or worse for you to keep your word, you owe it to that person. But what if keeping your word does not do anyone any good, then are you obligated to keep it? Suppose you promise to take your younger brother to a movie on Saturday afternoon. You have a date that evening, and you forgot the big test first thing on Monday. As luck would have it, someone else can take your brother, but no, you have promised and he wants *you*. You ought to keep your word, but must you keep it if the same thing can be accomplished at no cost to anyone? The consequentialist does not see why.

It would seem that much of our morality is based on the good or bad effects of what we do. But doing good and avoiding doing bad is not the whole story. We acquire obligations in life, and these have to be discharged in some way. Nonconsequentialists think consequentialists overlook this side of morality. We acquire obligations in part by our voluntary action—like making promises— and in part by things happening to us or by other people doing things for or toward us. Here are examples of obligations we can acquire involuntarily. My car gets stuck in a snow bank. You come along and push it out. I did not ask you to help, but I owe you something nonetheless (sincere thanks, maybe) since you came to my aid. Or suppose you notice someone cheating. You may wish that it were not you who noticed, but it was you, and now you may feel you have an obligation to report the cheater to the professor. Why? It is your duty: cheaters should not get away with it, you reason, and if you do not report him you will be guilty of covering up. (Like the boy on the burning deck, you too believe in duty.)

Living up to your obligations is an important part of morality. If someone does you a good turn, you ought to feel grateful and want to return the favor. But you cannot discharge your obligation by doing a good turn for just anyone, but for the very person who helped you, even if you would rather help someone else instead. Or think about fairness. You enter into a living arrangement with other people. By so doing you undertake to do your fair share of the work. Why should they work harder so that you can slack off? Being fair is an important obligation that you have to learn to accept. All these obligations involve good and bad consequences, but how you acquire the obligations, how you discharge them, and how the consequences are sorted out—who gets them—are matters for morality. Or so says nonconsequentialism. These obligations can sometimes get complicated, but, says the nonconsequentialist, morality is not the simple matter of doing good and avoiding bad, as the consequentialist pretends.

Nonconsequentialism claims that considerations other than consequences must be taken into account in any theory that even hopes to explain morality. But nonconsequentialist theories differ in their views about what these other considerations are. Natural law, for example, says that to be moral we should follow nature. The divine command theory says that we should obey the Word of God. The social contract theory claims that there are certain rules we are pledged to follow, and that therefore we ought to follow them. We have met these theories already. Kant, whose theory we shall study in Chapter Nine, thinks that morality consists in being rational, in a nonconsequentialist sense of rationality that we shall try to explain.

It is time for a generalization. We shall say there are two kinds of moral theory: consequentialism and nonconsequentialism. **Consequentialism** holds that all the moral considerations noted above can be understood by attending to consequences alone. Hence, whether anything is morally good or bad depends *entirely on its consequences.* Consequentialism holds that what makes anything morally right is that it produces good consequences, and morally wrong that it produces bad ones. Nothing else makes anything good or bad. "Anything" here means not only human actions, but any human activity, product, or invention, including customs, conventions, law, religion, morality itself, and even such activities as art, literature, and philosophy. None of these can be morally good unless having or doing them produces good consequences for someone.

Nonconsequentialism denies this. Some of morality may be based on consequences, but much of morality is not. There are moral standards which may be *independent of consequences.*

The consequentialist theory that is the best candidate for an acceptable moral theory is utilitarianism. Before turning to U, let us think of some other principles that are consequentialist.

> Radical feminism: whatever is good for women is good.
>
> Business ethics, as often practiced: increase the bottom line.
>
> College athletics ethics in certain universities: winning is not the most important thing, it is the only thing.
>
> Patriotic ethics: whatever is good for my country is good.
>
> Revolutionary ethics: whatever advances the Revolution is good.
>
> The ethics of war: defeat the enemy.

These principles can be distinguished by their implicit definitions of good and bad consequences, and also by those to whom the consequences should be distributed. Business ethics, for example, says the good is profit and it should be earned for your own firm or business. Patriotism probably defines the good as national wealth, power, and prestige, which you should seek for your own country. Revolutionary ethics says the good is smashing the established order; presumably, this will benefit the oppressed masses.

These principles are consequentialist because they each hold that it is not what you do that counts, but what happens as a result of what you do. Nobody would regard any of them as a complete system of morality, but large numbers of people take each principle seriously as a guide to conduct in certain areas of life. Nonconsequentialists would not be surprised that each of the principles falls far short of stating a moral system: all the moral restraints that should limit the pursuit of the ends sought are obviously overlooked. But consequentialists would explain the failure of the principles by saying that either they exaggerate the importance of the consequences aimed at (for example, making money is not as all-important as business ethics would tell you) or want to get the consequences for too limited a set of people (for example, radical feminism thinks that men do not count). Only utilitarianism avoids these defects, at least so utilitarians think.

Five Notes on Terminology

Terminology is important. It can also be confusing. Before continuing, let us note five points.

Teleology and Deontology   If you continue to study philosophy, you will inevitably run across these words. They are not the loveliest terms you will ever meet, nor are they intuitively informative; on the contrary, they are rather misleading, but as a student of moral theory you should know them. They are alternative names for what we are calling consequentialism (**teleology**) and nonconsequentialism (**deontology**).

Both words come from Greek roots. The word "teleology" comes from the Greek, *teleos,* which means "end" in the sense of goal, aim, or purpose ("end" more commonly means terminal point, which is a different idea; thus, the terminal point of life is death since every life ends in death, but most people would not think that death is the goal, aim, or purpose of life). The word "deontology" comes from another Greek root, *deon,* which means duty. Unfortunately, the terms are not only ugly, they are misleading, for they suggest that the teleologist aims at something, whereas the deontologist acts in accordance with duty. But anyone who thinks about what he or she is doing is aiming at something; and both the teleologist and the deontologist have a conception of duty. The difference between them is what they aim at, and how they understand duty. The teleologist aims at producing good and regards this as his duty, and the deontologist aims at following moral principle, which he defines without considering consequences, and regards that as his duty.

So the issue between teleology and deontology is not between having an aim versus not having an aim, or between following duty versus not following duty. The issue is how duty is to be determined, by consequences or not by consequences. And therefore, it seems better to use our labels, consequentialism and nonconsequentialism.

Intrinsic and Instrumental (Extrinsic) Value   Some things are valuable for their own sake, others for what can be done with them. The former are said to be **intrinsically valuable,** the latter **instrumentally valuable.** Nothing can have instrumental value unless it is effective in producing something that has intrinsic value. Consequentialism holds that moral acts are valuable only for what they produce, so morality has instrumental value only. But nonconsequentialists think that morality is good for its own sake, so morality has intrinsic value. What has intrinsic value for consequentialists is the good consequences morality produces.

Right and Wrong   We have said that a consequentialist theory holds that morally right actions produce good consequences, and morally wrong actions produce bad ones. Note that this is a definition of consequentialism and not a definition of right or wrong. We have not said that right and wrong can be defined as "productive of good/bad consequences," for it is fairly clear that they cannot, at least in ordinary speech. The reason is that it is very easy to ask about anything whatever, "That produces good consequences, but is it right?" This would be an odd question if right just meant productive of good consequences. Generally, morally right means what ought to be done, and morally wrong means what ought not to be done, but, as we noted in Chapter One, such definitions tend to be circular or uninformative, since "ought to do" is no easier to define than "morally right."

We should understand consequentialism as giving a *criterion* of right and wrong. The criterion tells you what you have to look for to figure out whether something is right or wrong. Another way of thinking of the definition of consequentialism is that it states a principle of moral *justification.* You justify (defend) doing one thing rather than another by pointing to the consequences. So consequentialism is the view that in morality nothing other than consequences can justify doing one thing rather than another.

Utility and Utilitarianism   The word "utility" takes getting used to. Utility means usefulness; normally, when we think of something having utility we mean that it serves some purpose, that it is good for something (a utility infielder in baseball is useful because he plays several positions and so can fill in when the regulars are injured or resting). We often distinguish an object's utility from its aesthetic value; something may be useful, but not very pretty, like an electric generating plant (which is actually called a "utility"). People who like art often praise art precisely for its lack of utility (art for art's sake). The word "utility" does not seem to have any special moral connotation. But the idea of "useful" is exactly what the utilitarians want. Morality has no intrinsic value; it is only valuable because it is useful in producing good consequences. Morality has utility—that is, instrumental value only.

Such is terminology in philosophy that the word "utilitarianism" is often used to refer to any consequentialist or teleological theory, so that any theory that points to the consequences of doing something rather than to the act itself is called utilitarian. This terminological discrepancy results from the word "utility" being taken as a shorthand for "good consequences." But aiming at good consequences does not make one a utilitarian, since views that are not utilitarian also aim at good consequences. U aims at a very general good consequence that (presumably) everybody wants. This is happiness. This use of the term "utilitarianism" is faithful to historical precedent, since this is what Jeremy Bentham and John Stuart Mill, who first used the word "utilitarianism" as the name of a theory, meant by it. Mill calls U "the happiness theory," and says, "Actions are right in proportion as they tend to promote happiness, wrong as they tend to produce the reverse of happiness" *(Utilitarianism,* Chapter Two).

Acts and Consequences   The terminology "consequentialism" and "nonconsequentialism" is based on the difference between doing something and what happens as a result of doing it; between, that is, *acts* and *consequences.* Following common sense, we assume such a distinction can generally be made. However, it is worth noting that the lines are fairly arbitrary. Suppose I shoot you and you die. Was my act shooting you, and the consequence of my act that you died; or was my act killing you? There does not appear to be a correct answer to this question. Generally, consequences can be drawn within the description of an act just by renaming the act; for example: I strike a match, ignite the dry leaves, cause a forest fire, kill animals, and destroy habitat. We can call my act striking the match and call the fire and everything else the consequences, or we can call my act causing a fire, burning the forest, and killing animals. If we are going to distinguish between acts and consequences, we would like to be able to do so in a nonarbitrary way, but how to do this must be left to another branch of philosophy.

UTILITARIANISM

The philosophers who are considered the founders of U are Jeremy Bentham (1748–1832) and his disciple (and much greater philosopher) John Stuart Mill (1806–1873). It was Bentham who coined the phrase "principle of utility," and Mill who wrote a very important and still much-studied short book called *Utilitarianism.* But the term "utility" was in use long before Bentham and Mill, being employed notably by David Hume in the early eighteenth century; with or without the term, eighteenth-century philosophers both in Great Britain and France were particularly strong on the utilitarian idea, and it is easy to discover strands of utilitarian thinking in even earlier philosophers going back to the ancient Greeks. Since the mid-nineteenth century, U has been at or near the center of moral debate, at least among British and American philosophers, virtually every one of whom has been either a U or an opponent of U. It is Mill's theory—what he calls "the happiness theory"—that is principally followed and explained in this book.

Mill defines a "morally right" act as one that "tends to promote happiness." He says that an action is right "in proportion" as it produces happiness. And he defines a "morally wrong" action as one that "tends to produce the reverse" of happiness (presumably, unhappiness). Therefore, we define **utilitarianism** as the theory that right actions are those that tend to produce happiness, and wrong actions are those that tend to produce unhappiness.

The definition may make it seem as if every action that produces happiness is right, and every action that produces unhappiness is wrong. But some actions may produce happiness and still be wrong (a thief gets happiness from his loot), and others may produce unhappiness and still be right, for example, appropriate punishment. Our definition has to be understood as referring to a *balance* of happiness and unhappiness. Stealing is wrong because stealing produces more unhappiness than happiness, at least most of the time. And putting the thief in jail produces more happiness, not for the thief but for everybody else. (Or so U assumes. Whether these assumptions are true or not is an empirical question.)

There is a special problem with regard to wrong actions: we have to recognize that sometimes there is nothing you can do in a particular situation that prevents or avoids unhappiness. Giving somebody bad news tends to make them unhappy, but you do it anyway because they will be made more unhappy if they find out later from someone else. This shows that what is right to do with regard to unhappiness is to avoid it where possible, but to minimize it where it cannot be avoided.

We therefore distinguish between right and wrong by the balance of happiness each produces. *Right actions* are those that are likely to produce a balance of happiness, that is to say, more happiness than unhappiness on the whole. *Wrong actions,* on the contrary, are those that produce a greater balance of unhappiness than necessary in the circumstances.

Mill is careful not to say that actions are right and wrong if they *do* produce happiness and unhappiness, but only if they "tend to." This means that an action is right if it normally would produce happiness, whether or not it does in some specific situation. Suppose you buy your friend a present that she just hates. This might make her very unhappy. Was your action wrong? Not according to Mill, since giving presents to friends generally produces happiness.

It should be noted that our definition ignores the famous principle that is often associated with U and that is even taken as stating the essence of U. This is the principle of "The greatest good for the greatest number." This formula was apparently invented by the philosopher Francis Hutcheson in the eighteenth century. Unfortunately, this principle, especially when interpreted as it often is as directing us to act in such a way as to further the "general welfare," creates more than a little confusion, in that it seems to be a political rather than a moral idea, applicable to the actions of government rather than private citizens. It is true that to Mill and especially to Bentham, who was far more interested in legal and political reform than in moral theory, U was attractive in part because of its ready application to politics. Hutcheson's principle had obvious attractions for a fair-minded democrat like Bentham, who may have regarded it as a moral as well as political standard. (In Bentham's day, the principle that actually motivated government was probably something like, "Act so as to produce the greatest good for the landed aristocracy," so Hutcheson's principle if followed would have produced major political change.) Whatever the merits of the general welfare principle as a directive to government officials, as a moral principle it is clearly a non-starter, since it would direct everyone away from a personal moral life and into political action.

Maximizing and Minimizing

Few things in life are purely good or purely bad; you often have to choose the best balance of good and bad. Instead of your philosophy course, maybe you could have taken Movies 100; this is good because it is less work and more fun; it is bad because you would learn less and movies are not as important as philosophy. So you try to maximize utility by choosing the course that gives you the best balance of good over bad.

U is often considered a "maximizing and minimizing" theory, which tells you to produce the most good, or least bad, you can. Mill and Bentham call U "the greatest happiness principle," which lends support to this idea. "Maximize expected utility" is sometimes taken as a definition of U, where "expected utility" is the foreseeable balance of good over bad consequences. In U, as in consequentialism generally, there is no standard of morally good and bad other than the consequences, so it follows immediately that the more good consequences, the better, and the more bad consequences, the worse. If you have two choices, one that yields a balance of n units of good, the other a balance of $n + 1$ units of good, the second action must be better; and as between an action that yields on balance m units of bad and another that yields $m + 1$ units of bad, the second must be worse. The morally best action is thus one that results in the most favorable balance possible of good over bad consequences, that is, one that produces as much utility (happiness) as possible in the circumstances.

Therefore, it is said that according to U, what we ought to do is to maximize utility. But by our definition, U is not a maximizing and minimizing theory. We regard this common understanding of U to be mistaken. Many situations arise in which you can do something that is morally right even if it does not maximize expected utility. Suppose when you give the present to your friend, she is made happy. But you know the present is not the absolutely perfect gift, which would have made her even happier. You have not maximized expected utility, yet your action is morally right because it makes her happy. If your action is morally right, it cannot be the case that you ought to have done something else; hence, it cannot be the case that you ought to maximize utility.

However, it is fair to say that your action would have been even better if you *had* found the perfect gift and maximized utility. This is captured by Mill's saying that an action is right in proportion to how much happiness it produces. This means that the more happiness it produces, the better the action is morally. But it does not mean that only the very best action is the one that it is morally right to do.

So what we should say is that it is good to produce good, better to produce more good, and best to produce the most good, but not necessarily wrong to produce less than the most good possible.

This accords with common sense, for many people think we ought to do good and avoid bad, but few people think that we are required to do all the good we possibly can. If we were, we would never be allowed to relax from our moral obligations or enjoy any selfish pleasures. "We ought always to choose the greater good over the lesser" sounds like a fine moral principle, but in fact morality does not require that we always aim at the best, and neither does U.

If you hold that U says that we must maximize good consequences, there is a difficulty: U becomes incoherent because consequences go on forever. You might as well tell someone to maximize even numbers; you cannot, because no matter how many you produce, there is always another one. How can you produce the best consequences when the consequences are as unlimited as the even numbers? We avoid this problem by denying that U requires that we maximize good consequences.

U says that producing more happiness is better than producing less, but it does not say that we must produce the most happiness. This creates a lack of parallel between the morally right and the morally wrong that evidently confuses some philosophers. They think that since a morally wrong act is one that you morally *must not* do, a morally right act must be one that you morally *must* do. Then they assume that, according to U, what you morally must do is to produce as much good as possible; but as this is implausible, they reject U. However, to say that an action is morally right means only that it is good that you do it; it does not mean that you must do it. Some other action you might do might be better. But to say that an action is morally wrong is to say that you must not do it. Morality tells us what we ought not to do: do not lie, cheat, and steal, for example. Our definition of U does say what you must *not* do, because it says what is wrong. What is wrong is to produce a balance of unhappiness over happiness that is greater than necessary in the circumstances. But though our definition does say what is right (to produce happiness), it does not say what you *must* do. Instead, U says you *may* do any act that is right.

Actual or Expected Consequences

People sometimes deride consequentialism on the grounds that nobody can predict the future, so (they say) it is better to guide your actions by nonconsequentialist values. However, it is not true that no one can predict the future: every time you go on an airplane, you are predicting that you will arrive safely at your destination. In general, we can and do quite successfully predict the consequences of our actions. What is meant is that you cannot *foresee* the future, that is, you cannot be certain that any given event will or will not actually happen. Your predictions are generally borne out, but you cannot be certain about any given case. Since we can predict the effects of our actions, consequentialism is not endangered by the fact that we cannot be certain about what will happen. But since things do sometimes turn out differently from what we anticipated, by which consequences are our actions to be judged, the actual consequences, or the ones we expected? The answer is, by neither.

Suppose you take your elderly grandfather for a ride in the country. You intend to and expect to produce good consequences, namely, that your grandfather will have a pleasant outing. But on the road another driver runs a stop sign and hits your car, injuring your grandfather. The actual consequences of your well-intentioned jaunt are bad. So does it follow that taking your grandfather for a ride was wrong? Suppose a further complication is that your grandfather has to go to the hospital because of his injuries. While he is in the hospital, the nursing home in which he lives burns down, killing some of the residents. So now do we have to say that your action turns out to have been right after all, since it saved your grandfather's life? The answer to both these question is clearly no. You could have expected neither the collision nor the fire. Unforeseeable consequences should be irrelevant in the assessment of an action. Only the consequences you can reasonably foresee should count. We call these *rational expectations.*

Nevertheless, some consequentialists distinguish between actions being *subjectively* right and *objectively* right, saying that an action is subjectively right if the actor *thought* the consequences would be good, but objectively right if they really *are* good. Consequentialists make this distinction because they want to say what is often said by unthinking people, that an action is right if it turns out well, even if the good outcome was the result of plain dumb luck. (Unthinking people include Shakespeare: "All's well that ends well," according to him; but he was being ironical.) But this distinction is pointless. Ethics is supposed to guide us as to what to do, but since we cannot know which action is objectively right until after we do it, we can get no guidance from "objectively right" actions.

Notice that sincere beliefs and good intentions are not enough to make an action morally right. If your horoscope tells you that today is your lucky day and so you bet your tuition money on the lottery, the fact that you really believe in the power of astrology is not sufficient to make your action right because your belief is irrational. Even if against the odds you should win the lottery, your action would still have been wrong in that you should not have done it just because it was irrational, albeit done with the best of intentions. Hence, neither actual good outcomes nor sincere belief and good intention render actions morally right. Right actions, those that are morally good to do, are intelligent, that is, done on the basis of rational expectations.

This gives us a second reason why the criticism based on the infinity of consequences fails. The future goes on forever, and an action's consequences never stop, but this is a problem only if we are supposed to do the action which produces actual good consequences rather than rationally anticipated ones. The infinity of the future means that we can have little rational expectation about the remote consequences of our acts, and are therefore exempt from worry about them.

OBJECTIONS TO UTILITARIANISM, AND REPLIES

No matter how carefully you define and qualify it, U is a controversial theory. Detractors raise a whole army of difficulties against it. Let us examine some of the major objections and see how U can reply to them.

It Is Not Always Right to Aim at Happiness   U may strike you as quite a jolly theory; according to it, we should do what we can to make people happy. But every professor knows what she can do to make her students happy: give them all the grade of A. This cannot be right. A professor should try to educate her students, not make them happy. The owner of a business aims at making a profit, not making the employees happy. A coach tries to win. Even a parent, who does want his or her children to be happy, also wants them to be honest, independent, fair, brave, and so on. At best, happiness is one goal, not the goal, of action.

But the utilitarian denies that any of these other goals have value in themselves. They are valuable only because they will produce happiness in the end. A parent assumes that if a child learns to be independent, brave, and so on, that child will be happier. A coach knows the players, and the fans will be happy if the team wins. And the professor believes that knowledge is what her students need to lead a full, productive, and therefore happy life.

There is another point as well. Would it make all the students happy if they all got As? It would not, because the grades would be meaningless. There's a fallacy in this criticism. "A feather is light, therefore, a bag of feathers is light." The fallacy is in assuming that what is true of one individual is true of many individuals together: "all students" consists of each and every student; each and every student would be made happy if the professor gave him or her an A; therefore, all students would be made happy if the professor gave them all an A. This is the fallacy of composition. The way to make most students happiest is not to give them all an A, but to give each the grade he or she deserves.

Utilitarianism Overmoralizes Life   If U were a maximizing theory, that is, if it held that we should produce as much happiness as possible, it could be fairly accused of overmoralizing life. If we had to aim at maximizing happiness, we would have no lives to call our own. You would have to drop whatever you are doing (like reading this book), and go to work to help the many unfortunate people in faraway countries. It would be wrong not to donate all your spare cash to famine relief. It would be wrong, for that matter, not to donate your spare kidney to someone suffering from kidney failure. Nobody can go around trying to produce as much good as possible all the time, and the idea that we ought to do so is a kind of fanaticism that morality does not require. But we have already rejected the inference that, because U holds that more good is better than less, it also holds that we must do whatever produces the most good.

But if U does not say that we should maximize happiness, how much happiness should we produce, and for whom should we produce it? Mill does not say how much happiness to promote, or whether to promote it for everybody or just for some people; what he does say is that an action is right in proportion to the happiness it produces—that is, the more happiness an action produces, the better it is morally. If you take your family to Disneyland instead of giving the money to a worthy cause, you are producing happiness, so this is morally right, but if you were to spend the money on the needy you would be doing even more good, so that would be morally better. We should not too quickly assume that we need not be concerned with everybody; let us not panic at the fear of overmoralizing. A moral theory should hold up high moral standards that require universal concern. Even strangers and people in distant lands should be important to us; our moral concern should be extended beyond the people we know or with whom we are in some way connected and comfortable.

Bentham makes it part of his U that "each to count as one, none to count as more than one," as he put it. This goes beyond saying that everybody must count, and seems to say that everyone must count equally. This would be another kind of overmoralizing. But morality does not require such evenhandedness. Nobody should be ignored, but not everybody is entitled to as much attention as everybody else. You can't help everybody who needs you, but you have no right to pretend they don't exist either; you ought to help them, if you could do so without sacrificing other important things, and it is better that you help them than that you do not. So in morality, as in George Orwell's *Animal Farm,* all animals are equal, but some animals are more equal than others.

Bentham probably means his principle to be one of fairness rather than a principle that everybody in the entire world must count equally. What he means is that when harms and benefits are distributed, everyone is to get a fair share, neither more nor less. He probably does not mean the principle to be a way of determining what the fair share is. It is not unfair if I do more for my family than for the people next door.

But should not a moral theory say how much good we ought to produce, and for whom? Not necessarily; there may be no principled answer to these questions, and a theory would err if it provided an answer where none exists. Our only obligation to everybody is to take care not to make anybody unhappy: produce no pain, if you can avoid doing so. Should we relieve distress? Yes; if you are at the beach and someone is drowning it would be highly immoral to do nothing to save him. But your life would disappear if you tried to help everybody who needs help. How much to do is a question of judgment, not philosophical principle. We ought to help a reasonable number of people to a reasonable degree, and prevent great harms but not every harm we could prevent. This sounds like fudging, but if morality fudges, a moral theory ought to fudge as well. It is not a flaw in a moral theory to be inexact where morality is inexact.

Which people are properly of concern to us? Again, there is no principled answer; morality allows you to use your common sense or (if you prefer) moral prejudice, and U does no better. We generally consider that we have closer ties to our family and friends than to our neighbors, and closer ties to our neighbors than to the strangers across town. We all live within a set of nesting circles: your immediate family is the innermost circle, your friends and close colleagues constitute the next circle, your neighbors and fellow townspeople the next, your fellow citizens constitute a still larger but more remote circle, and so on; at the outer limits is the huge circle that contains everybody in the entire world. Morality tells us that everybody must be of some concern to us: we cannot ignore the plight of a hungry stranger just because that person is unknown to us and lives in a faraway land. But morality allows us to have closer ties and stronger moral obligations to the people in the inner circles than to those in the outer; we feed the hungry person close at home before the hungry person in the next city or country. If this is a failing, it is a failing that U and ordinary morality have in common.

A side point about proportion is this. When Mill holds that an action is right in proportion to the happiness it produces, he means that the more happiness an action produces, the better it is, so that an action that produces *2n* units of happiness is twice as good as an action that produces *n* units. But this would entail that a person who is in a position to produce lots of happiness—suppose he is the President of the United States—is going to be in a position to be much more moral than the average person, whose actions produce only a little bit of happiness because they do not affect very many people. But we do not necessarily think the President is much more moral than ordinary people, even if he does good all the time. So let us say that goodness is proportional not to how much happiness is produced absolutely, but to how much is produced relative to what is possible. Suppose there are two sets of circumstances, A and B. The most happiness possible in A is 10 units; in B, it is 100 units. If you are in A and produce 9 units, your act is morally better than if you are in B and produce 85 units.

Utilitarianism Ignores Natural Values   Certain critics conclude that U is indifferent to natural values such as family love. These critics make the following kind of argument. Suppose you are on an airplane with your slightly retarded daughter. In the next seat is the World's Best Brain Surgeon. The plane crashes, and you can save either your daughter or the surgeon, but not both. Whom do you save? It is said that U would require that you save the WBBS, because her life would do much good for many people, whereas your daughter will never be able to do much good for anyone. But, so the argument goes, you love your child and you have a complete right to save her. So U is mistaken about what you should do.

To this, certain utilitarians give this reply. Which is best for society, they ask, that parents love their children, even the retarded ones, or that they do not? The answer is surely that it is best for everyone that parents love their children. But if parents love their children, then they will naturally rescue their children when in danger, even at the expense of failing to rescue someone whose utility value is greater. That is the necessary outcome of love, so if you favor parental love on grounds of social utility, you must favor parents' rights to save their children. Hence, U does not say that parents should favor the surgeon over their own children.

This defense of U may strike you as ingenious but a little lame: is it really true that we favor parental love on grounds of social utility? Parental love is a natural value that is a good thing in itself, which is why we think that a parent who detested or abused his or her child is a pretty horrible person. Social utility is not why we value natural values. This point is correct, but the defense is not really required because the argument assumes either that U requires that we maximize good, or that we ought to consider everybody equally. But as we have seen, U says only that we ought to consider everybody, and that we do not have to maximize good. If the stranger next to you on the plane is about to die, of course you ought to be concerned about saving her if you can; but this is not to say that you must be concerned with her life equally with the life of your own daughter.

Utilitarianism Conflicts with Personal Integrity   In George Bernard Shaw's play *Major Barbara,* the Salvation Army, facing a financial crisis, receives a large donation from Lord Saxmundham. The following dialogue (from Act II) ensues between Major Barbara and the Army Commissioner, Mrs. Baines.

Barbara: Mrs. Baines, are you really going to take this money?

Mrs. Baines: Why not, dear?

Barbara: Have you forgotten that Lord Saxmundham is Bodger the whisky man? . . . Do you know that the worst thing I have had to fight here is not the devil, but Bodger, Bodger, Bodger, with his whisky, his distilleries, and his tied houses [taverns]? Are you going to make our shelter another tied house for him, and ask me to keep it?

Mrs. Baines: Dear Barbara, Lord Saxmundham has a soul to be saved like any of us. If heaven has found the way to make a good use of his money, are we to set ourselves up against the answer to our prayers? . . . Will there be less drinking or more if all these poor souls we are saving come tomorrow and find the doors of our shelters shut in their faces? . . . Do you think I am wrong to take the money?

Barbara: No God help you, you are saving the Army [She begins taking off the silver S brooch from her uniform collar].

Mrs. Baines: Barbara, what are you doing?

Barbara: I can't pray now. Perhaps I shall never pray again.

Mrs. Baines: Barbara!

Barbara: I can't bear any more. Quick march!

Mrs. Baines: You're overworked, you will be all right tomorrow. We'll never lose you. Now Jenny, step out with the old flag. Blood and Fire! [She marches out the gate with her flag].

Jenny: Glory hallelujah!

Barbara: Drunkenness and murder! My God, why hast thou forsaken me?

It is clear who is the utilitarian and who represents integrity in this (slightly abbreviated) scene. But who is right? Would you take money from someone you detest if you can do good works with it, or support yourself and your family? Suppose you need a job. You can get a very good job, but unfortunately with a company you do not admire very much, because you think they are antisocial in some way: perhaps they pollute the environment, or make products you do not like. You don't want to work for a company you regard as no more than marginally ethical. You call that integrity. What would U advise?

U points out that if you do not take the job, you will do yourself (and your family if you have one) some harm, and you will not do anyone any good because the job will go to someone else. In fact, the person who takes the job will have less integrity than you, and probably will not hesitate to help the company with its antisocial behavior. So you will possibly do a little good for society if you do take the job. As Mrs. Baines says, will there be more or less drinking if the Army refuses the money? U advises you to do what Mrs. Baines does and not think of integrity; integrity does not do anyone any good.

U is like the hangman joke: it is nasty work, but if I did not do it someone else would. This does not show integrity. We value integrity, so U is at fault here. But is it? Proponents of U typically deny that U is opposed to integrity; they point out that society would be better off if people did have integrity and did refuse to cooperate with cheaters or to participate in dirty work. We want people with integrity; it is because there is not enough integrity that unethical companies are unethical in the first place. Integrity is not antisocial, so U cannot be anti-integrity.

The integrity argument is sometimes put in terms of projects. People have a right to live their own lives, which means formulating and pursuing projects that interest them. Having projects means having commitments of some sort; a person with no commitments we regard as rather shallow, sort of drifting or following the crowd. Part of what we mean when we regard someone as having integrity is that that person has certain goals or purposes in life to which she is committed, which is why she does not follow the crowd. U would interfere with these projects by requiring us to be on call to do good all the time. We ought to be free not to do good but to pursue our own projects.

However, if having projects is what makes people happy, then U cannot be against projects. People who have no projects will not be very happy (unless making people happy becomes their project), so U cannot oppose projects. In any case, U does not say that we must do all the good that happens to come our way, but only that we must do good in reasonable amounts. This does not seem inconsistent with pursuing projects.

Morality as Instrumentally Rather Than Intrinsically Valuable   We said in Chapter One that morality should be an end-in-itself, that is, something you want not for what it brings but for its own sake. But in holding that morality has instrumental, not intrinsic, value, U regards morality as a means, not an end, something useful to produce happiness. Only happiness is desirable for its own sake.

However, U can distinguish between what is good for its own sake, and what people ought to want for its own sake. A moral person ought to want to be moral, not for the sake of something else but for the sake of being moral. But why is this good? U answers that more happiness will be produced if people value morality for its own sake, as an end, than if they value morality as a means to something else. Valuing morality for its own sake is part of good character, and U values good character, but on U grounds.

ACT AND RULE UTILITARIANISM

We can summarize our discussion of U so far by saying that U holds five principles.

1.   You should aim at producing happiness, but not necessarily the most you can.

2. The more happiness you produce, the better.

3. You must not produce unhappiness if you can avoid it.

4. You are free to decide for whom to produce the happiness.

5. You should prevent great evils if you can.

These principles avoid overmoralizing, and make U consistent with common morality on the question of production of happiness. But will they make U an acceptable moral theory? It may depend on still another point of interpretation of U.

Moral theory ought to answer two questions: What ought I to do? and What rules ought we to have in our society? How a theory answers one question may determine its answer to the other. Philosophers have drawn a distinction between two versions of U, act utilitarianism and rule utilitarianism. These offer different answers to the two questions.

Act utilitarianism (AU) holds that the basic question is, "What ought I to do?" The AU answer is to aim at promoting happiness and preventing unhappiness. But what about rules? Rules are useful only if they help you do this; they may be safely ignored if following them does not lead to greater happiness.

But this simple formula is thought by many philosophers to lead to morally questionable results. Therefore, they invented **rule utilitarianism** (RU), which is supposed to be a U improvement over AU, and which holds that rules are needed for a tolerably good society. So the basic question is, "Which rules ought we to have?" RU says, support or enact those rules that, were people to follow them, would produce happiness and prevent unhappiness. Once you have these rules in place, then what you should do is: follow the rules.

We can illustrate both AU and RU by citing "Beetle Bailey," a popular newspaper cartoon about life in the army. It is roll call at Camp Swampy. The soldiers are lined up and Sgt. Snorkel calls, "Bailey." No answer. Snorkel says, "Beetle, answer the roll." "Why?" inquires Beetle. "You can see I'm here." "RULES," thunders the good Sergeant. "The rules say you have to answer." "I refuse to answer on grounds of reasonable intelligence," Beetle replies.

The next panel consists of no picture; only the dark, large-print words, "POW! BAM! SMASH!" In the last panel, Beetle may be seen lying in his usual discombobulated heap. Lt. Fuzz asks Snorkel, "Is Private Bailey here?" Snorkel replies, "He didn't answer the roll, sir."

Now Beetle Bailey's response, "I refuse to answer on grounds of reasonable intelligence," could be the motto of the AU. If you can see that something is totally pointless and stupid, why do it? Nobody can give him a reason, except Snorkel, whose reason is his fists. Snorkel, on the other hand, believes in rules. Why he believes in rules is not clear; unlike Beetle, Snorkel is not a natural philosopher, but a lower-management bureaucrat, a worshipper of rules. But if Snorkel were an RU, he would assume that if the army made a rule, the army must have a reason for it. The rule is for the best, once the rule is in place it must be followed, and his job is to see to it that the rule is obeyed.

Here is another way of thinking about act utilitarians. They are improvisers. Take another driving problem: you are trying to make a left turn into a busy street from a parking lot. It is midday; you cannot find a break in traffic in both directions at once. So you improvise; you wait until there is a break in traffic in the near lane, then cross into the middle turning lane and use it to accelerate into the distant lanes. You know it is somewhat dangerous and also probably illegal to use the middle turning lane as an acceleration lane, but what can you do? You cannot sit there forever, and making the left turn into the acceleration lane is a lot safer than making it directly into fast-moving traffic. In other words, you have improvised a solution to your problem, choosing the method that seems to work best. You are thinking like an act utilitarian. You would not want to execute this maneuver on your driver's licensing road test, but you do not really care about rules or technically safe procedures at this point. Let other people follow "correct" procedures, and sit there for hours waiting for both lanes to clear; you want to get on with your trip.

So AU regards rules as at best useful hints, and at worst impediments to intelligent action. Rules are *rules of thumb,* that is, guidelines or helpful hints like cooking or gardening instructions ("Add a little fertilizer and work in well"). Rules may work most of the time, but creative people will no more feel bound to follow them than a creative cook would feel bound to follow every step in a recipe. If it works, do it, says creative AU. Often the reason for following rules, in the AU's opinion, is no better than Sgt. Snorkel's fists: not because it makes sense, but because society says you must and if you do not, watch out. If only people would use their native intelligence and ignore the correct ways to do things, thinks AU, we would all be better off.

Counterexamples to Act Utilitarianism

Nonconsequentialist philosophers are not so happy with this conclusion; they agree with Snorkel that following rules is important. And they claim that our morality thinks so too. They argue that because it overlooks the importance of moral rules, AU would lead us to do all sorts of actions that are morally wrong, or at least questionable. Thus, they regard AU as a seriously deficient theory. Their case is made by a series of examples.

The Zoo or the Movies   You are in charge of a child whom you have promised to take to the zoo. Through no fault of either of you, two other children are put in your care; they want to go to see a movie that is about to leave town. Your child has seen it and does not want to go again. What do you do? AU would choose the happiness of two over the happiness of one, so you would go to the movie. But what about your promise? Does that not count? Should you not tell the other two children, "Well, it's too bad, but I promised Jenny I'd take her to the zoo, so you'll have to miss your movie"? Sure they would be disappointed, but is it not important to keep your promises? The AU says no, immorally.

Kill One to Save Two?   Philosophers seem to enjoy moral dilemmas about life and death. Here is one: a mad dictator tells you that unless you kill one innocent person, he will kill two (or ten). Do you violate your moral principles and kill the innocent person, or do you refuse and watch the others die? Is it moral to take the line, "I will be moral, and if the dictator kills someone, that's on his conscience, not on mine"? Is your integrity more important than saving lives? The AU says no. Integrity is not as important as saving life. Again, this is said to be the morally wrong answer.

But maybe you think that killing one to save two is not the wrong answer. So try the next problem.

The Homeless Bum   The homeless bum is destitute, friendless, unemployed and in general no good to himself or society, but he is in great health. When he comes into the hospital to seek a night's shelter, what should the doctors do? It so happens that in the hospital are five people dying from organ failures: one has heart failure, another has lung cancer, a third needs a new liver, and two suffer from failing kidneys. To make the example more lachrymose: the five patients have loving families, solid positions in the community, are charity leaders and so on. Should the doctors sacrifice the homeless bum and harvest his five organs to save these five lives? It seems AU would say yes, but of course that is murder.

The Deathbed Promise   "Take care of my dear dog Rover when I am gone," asks your best friend Harry as his dying request. Of course you agree; you are devastated that Harry is dying, and want to make his passing as easy as possible. The day after the funeral you take Rover to the vet and have him put to sleep. Why not? You do not like dogs and Harry is dead (Rover doesn't count). The AU would countenance this, but it feels wrong, does it not, to blatantly violate a deathbed promise to a friend?

Harming the Dead   Can people be harmed after they are dead? It would be better for U if the answer were clearly negative, since presumably no one can be made unhappy after he is dead (this is sometimes termed a distinction between being "harmed" and being "hurt"), but it seems as if the answer is that they can be. One way is by treating a corpse disrespectfully; would you prefer that your corpse should be ground up and used for dog food? (If you do, you are a real U!) A second way is by destroying your reputation. Do you want nasty false stories to be spread around about you after you die? A third way is by destroying what may be called your "monument." Suppose you have invested a lot of your time and energy in building something, whether it is a house, a business, or a work of art. After you are dead, no one is interested; the house goes to rot, the work of art is put on the junk heap, and the business is allowed to go bankrupt. Your monument has been destroyed, and (arguably) you are harmed.

Since you can be harmed without being hurt or made unhappy, U would have to add a special duty saying that harming the dead is wrong. But many Us resist such an idea; why should the dead be allowed to govern the living? If no one is interested in running your business, it should be allowed to go bankrupt. It cannot matter to you: you are dead.

The Jury with a Social Conscience   Several years ago in Atlanta, there was a series of over two dozen appalling child murders. Bodies were found mutilated, floating in the river, and so on. Finally, the police made an arrest of a citizen with a previously unblemished record named Wayne Williams. His car had been seen parked near a bridge from which the body of one of the victims had been tossed. Detectives discovered a strand of fabric in the car that laboratory analysis purportedly revealed had come from a carpet in the home of one of the victims. There was not much more evidence. Williams was put on trial for two of the murders.

The most chilling fact, however, was not the evidence, but that after Williams was arrested the murders stopped. How would a jury of AUs look at this? Imagine this thought process of an AU juror: "If Williams is guilty, we ought to convict him. If we do, there will be no more murders. Unfortunately, the evidence is pretty weak. On the other hand, if he's not guilty, the fact that the murders have stopped indicates that the person who is guilty is apparently willing to let Williams take the rap. Even if Williams is innocent, there may not be any more murders if we convict him. But if we acquit him and he goes free, the killer may strike again, thinking that Williams will be blamed. So we ought to convict him whether he's guilty or not."

However, this is wrong and not justice; if the evidence is not strong enough to convict, Williams ought to be set free. We should not convict someone unless there is sufficient evidence that he is guilty, no matter what good consequences will result. So the AU is immoral. (Williams was convicted and is incarcerated in Georgia. No more such child murders have occurred in Atlanta since Williams' imprisonment.)

Who Gets It?   The U's principle is, the more happiness produced, the better. But does it not matter who gets the happiness? This is the problem of just deserts. A difficulty with U is its apparent indifference to just deserts. Suppose you are giving out "happiness units," and that Tom deserves 10 units of happiness and Mary deserves 15 units. U tells you to give each as many units as you can, but it does not seem to provide a reason why it is better to distribute the units according to desert. If the only principle is the more the better, then giving 10 units to Mary and 15 to Tom is just as good as the reverse. Bentham understood this and therefore added the principle, "Each to count as one, no one to count as more than one." This does not say that everybody must get the same amount of happiness, but that everybody is entitled to equal consideration (being counted) when punishment or reward is measured. (And that in turn presumably means that everybody is to be judged by the same standard.) But this idea seems extrautilitarian to many philosophers; they regard it as a nonconsequentialist principle that limits the application of the U principles.

These examples explain why philosophers think that AU is inadequate as a moral theory. Note how the examples point out problems with Mill's principle that the greater happiness is always preferable to the lesser: there are situations in which choosing the lesser happiness seems correct. Morality intervenes. Just deserts is a special difficulty, for we might conclude that some people do not deserve happiness at all, so that not giving them happiness is morally better than giving it to them, or giving them less is better than giving them more. In the other cases, we should at least be troubled by the choice that presents the greater good, even if we might choose it in the end.

Critics therefore think that, at the very best, U is a seriously incomplete and flawed moral theory. Even some Us are convinced that a strong case could be made against U if U were the same as AU. But they point to the other version of U—rule utilitarianism.

How Rule Utilitarianism Answers the Criticisms

RU seeks good indirectly, not by asking what acts to do but by asking what rules are needed. We ought to adopt the rules that if generally followed would produce the most good. Once rules are adopted, then what one ought to do is follow the rules. Individual choice is terminated once rules have been established, as Sgt. Snorkel explains so clearly to Beetle Bailey. That is just the point of having rules: rules are made to be followed.

Let us see how that helps the U deal with the counterexamples. What would society's rules be if rule utilitarians made the rules? Well, to begin with, there would be a rule favoring promise keeping, a rule prohibiting killing the innocent, a rule requiring juries to convict only on the evidence, a rule requiring distribution of happiness according to just deserts (it does not matter whether these are legal rules or moral rules). We would all be safer and happier with rules like these.

Consider the rule about just deserts, for example. RU would have a rule that happiness should be distributed in accordance with desert. It would have such a rule because more happiness is produced by distributing happiness according to desert than by not doing so. You earn rewards when you accomplish socially desirable goals, such as studying and learning the concepts in your philosophy class. If rewards were not proportioned to desert, a major incentive for acting in the socially responsible way would be removed. There is no U point in rewarding people for doing things that are harmful or useless. Hence, just deserts has a utilitarian justification.

So if rules are made to be followed, the people in our examples would follow the rules and reach the correct conclusions: keep your promises, do not kill the innocent, reward the deserving, and so on. They would do so even if they were utilitarians and even though following a rule in certain cases might produce less good than violating it. They would do so even though they know they will produce less happiness than they might, because they think that society needs good rules and, once good rules are adopted, they ought to be followed. According to RU, utility applies at the level of rules; at the level of actions, it is the rules that govern, and utility should be ignored.

Because RU seeks utility indirectly, it is sometimes called **indirect utilitarianism** (IU). Another form of IU focuses not on rules but on people. We can call this

character utilitarianism. This says that the way to achieve utility is to build good character into people. You do this through such things as training, moral exhortation, and religion. People who have good character value honesty, fairness, respect for rights, integrity, and so on. Such people produce good because for the most part actions that are honest, fair, and so on lead to good. But they produce the good without aiming to do so; what they aim to do is to act honestly, be fair, and respect rights, independently of any utility value. People with good character do not do bad things like killing the innocent, even if they know that sometimes there might be a net utility gain in doing so. They will not even entertain such a possibility; they think it is wrong and out of the question. A society composed of people with good character will be a better society for everybody than one composed of people who are willing to cut moral corners from time to time, according to the IU. It is far too dangerous to live among people who think that actions such as murder are open possibilities.

Now the AU is not terribly thrilled at these rescue attempts. How can U go against utility? The AU has grave doubts that there is any need for rules; the principle of utility is the only rule you need, she thinks. If it is true that following a specific rule will maximize utility most of the time, then most of the time AUs would act as the rule requires even if there were no rule. But in the cases where following the rule will go against utility, why in the world should we follow the rule, asks the skeptical AU? She calls following rules in such cases *rule worship* or *rule idolatry*. If you are not going to produce good by following the rule, then you should ignore the rule and do good. The result would be that you produce the most good overall. And the same argument holds for good character. It is fine that people have good character, says the AU, but not to the point where their character leads them to go against utility.

The RU has a reply, but it is one that makes the AU gnash her teeth. The reply is: too much thinking is not good for us. If people were allowed to think for themselves all the time, and try to figure out what to do so as to always produce utility, they would get it wrong too often and wind up making a mess of things. Even with the best utilitarian will in the world, mistakes are bound to happen, and counterutility will result. That is why rules were invented in the first place. It is just safer to follow the rules. If the rules are good ones, you will produce utility most of the time. And the same is true about having good character. Producing utility most of the time is the best a U can hope for.

Let us look at an interesting moral problem to see how RU or IU differ from AU. This is the question of noncompliance. Must you follow a good rule even if many other people are not? One view is that you ought to do what is right, even if other people are not; you cannot excuse your own misbehavior by saying everybody does it. But not everyone agrees; some people say that if you compete in an environment where dishonesty prevails, you are not prohibited from acting immorally to protect yourself. Think of athletes who take steroids, or negative attack ads in politics; if the other person does it but you do not, you may lose, even though you are the best and otherwise most honest competitor. AU seems to support this. You do not do any good by being honest, you only harm yourself, so AU would counsel the athlete to take the steroids and the politician to run the negative ads.

But RU holds that you ought to follow those rules that, if they were followed, would lead to good results; it does not say that you should follow those rules that lead to good results because they are being followed. So RU would seem to be on the side of those who think you ought to be moral even when others are not moral. And a person who has good character would feel the same way and not want to do the immoral action. If you think this is the correct answer, then on these grounds you will conclude that RU is a more moral theory than AU.

Two Questions for Rule Utilitarianism

There are many questions one could raise about RU. Here are two.

Do All Good Rules Produce Good Results?   We should distinguish between those rules that are good because they lead to good results when followed, and those rules where the good produced is the very act of following them, rather than some further result. Perhaps most of our moral rules, such as the rule against lying, are examples of the former. What is meant by the second kind of rule? An example would be one rule that is so sacred it is almost never violated by anyone in our society, namely, the rule that certain parts of the human anatomy must be covered when you are in public. The good from this rule is not in some further consequence produced—what good does it do anyone if people wear clothes or not?—but in following the rule itself. We think walking around without any clothes on is just indecent, so we prohibit it.

Although no one would be harmed if someone were to walk around nude, it is true that some people would get very angry, and would be unhappy for that reason. However, it is a mistake to think of this as a harm caused by the violation of the rule. The harm is caused by their own disapproval of the violation. It should be clear that if U counted disapproval as a kind of harm, the distinction between U and nonconsequentialism would collapse, since people always get angry when someone violates rules they think are important. Therefore, the RU will have to say that since no harm is caused, it is not morally wrong to walk around nude.

This is not necessarily a mistake. RU gives us a way of distinguishing between *moral rules* and *social conventions*. (We noted this distinction in the discussion of social contract in Chapter Six.) Moral rules are those whose violations cause harm. Social conventions are those rules where no harm is caused by a violation other than the anger some people feel at the violation itself. RU holds that it is not immoral to violate a social convention.

But maybe the line between morality and social convention is not as clear as this. It does seem wrong to violate some social conventions; if it is not morally wrong, what kind of wrong is it? Rules about rudeness and insulting people would be social conventions by the "no harm" criterion, but it is not so clear that it is not immoral to act rudely and to insult people, at least if you do so knowingly (the fact that you are expected to be embarrassed and apologize profusely if you act rudely unintentionally—for example, if you forget to thank someone for a gift—shows that the line between immoral and anticonventional behavior is not clearly drawn). Rules about treating the dead properly would be social conventions by the "no harm" criterion, but we do regard it as immoral to spread lies about the dead, or to mistreat their corpses.

So either it is morally wrong to violate some social conventions, in which case the distinction between moral rules and conventions is (oddly) not the same as the distinction between rules that it is immoral to violate and rules that it is not immoral to violate; or else the distinction between morals and conventions cannot be drawn by the "no harm" criterion. But in either case, the distinction between U and nonconsequentialism is in danger of collapsing. Some actions would be morally wrong even if they did not produce harm or unhappiness. If RU allows this, it is hard to see how RU differs from nonconsequentialism.

Is Rule Utilitarianism Schizophrenic?   A theory is schizophrenic if it wants us to believe two inconsistent things at once. Since RU regards itself as true, and since RU thinks it is good for people to believe the truth, RU wants everybody to believe in RU; yet at the same time it does not. It wants people to be nonconsequentialists. Therefore, it is schizophrenic.

This problem with RU was noted by the late-nineteenth-century philosopher Henry Sidgwick, who was himself a utilitarian. Sidgwick held that good rules are those that maximize utility, but he was the first to suspect that utility would be maximized if people followed good rules without considering utility at all. If people simply thought that certain things were right and others wrong, without considering whether these actions lead to utility, more utility would be produced than if people tried to aim at utility. But someone who thinks that certain things just are right and wrong apart from considerations of utility is not a utilitarian; that person is a nonconsequentialist. So Sidgwick came to the paradoxical conclusion that utility would be maximized if people were not utilitarians. Since U wants to maximize utility, U should want people to be nonconsequentialists.

But in that case, utilitarians will not teach utilitarianism, but nonconsequentialism. Surprisingly enough, utilitarians are in the same position in which we found the superenlightened egoist: their theory requires that they convince people that their theory is false. But the SEE is not opposed to lying and does not care if other people are well off, so this position is not inconsistent with his theory. But the U is opposed to lying and does want other people to be well off, and it seems difficult to make this consistent with lying to them and getting them to believe a false moral theory. Furthermore, the SEE does not care what happens to people in the future, but the U wants future people to be happy too, so that means someone must know the truth about morality. But if utilitarians do not teach U, who will? How will the doctrine ever be propagated, or even maintained in existence? Sidgwick's solution was what today would be regarded as totally elitist and undemocratic. There will have to be some philosophers who are Us and who teach everybody else not to be Us. They will tell everybody else that nonconsequentialism is the best, but they themselves will know better, and they will pass on this truth to their chosen disciples. (Those readers who have studied Plato will recall here Plato's philosopher-kings and the "golden lie" they tell society. Can it be true that society needs to rest on a lie?)

If this is where RU comes out, it is plainly in deep trouble. Practically, secret knowledge known only to certain philosophers is just not going to work; how are they going to keep it out of the press? And morally it seems objectionable to have an elite governing the rest of us on the basis of a lie.

HEDONISM AND ALTERNATIVES

Is the Good Pleasure?

Now we come to the question, "What is happiness?" And it can easily be thought that on this rock, U inevitably founders; for even though everyone wants happiness, people define it differently, as Aristotle noted long ago, and if we cannot agree on what happiness is, it is rather pointless to tell us that what we ought to do is to produce as much of it as possible. It is for this reason that some people hold that ethics ought to ignore unanswerable questions about happiness and focus instead on moral values and rules: "Do not lie," "Do not cheat," "Do not betray your friends," "Help those in need," "Work hard and earn your living," and so on are fine rules that can guide anyone's life, but trying to do good for people, when everybody thinks something else is good, is simply a swamp in which no one can find firm footing. This is what the arch antiutilitarian, Immanuel Kant, believed.

Bentham and Mill were perfectly aware of this difficulty, and thought they could undercut it. It is true that different people regard different things as good; but if we ask why they consider certain things good, we get a single answer after all. The answer is, pleasure. Everybody considers good precisely what brings him or her pleasure, and nothing else; and anything that does not bring pleasure, to the extent that it does not, is not good. What everybody really wants, and really considers good, is therefore pleasure. Our obligation as utilitarians is thus to promote as much pleasure for everybody as we possibly can. (We must note here, to avoid possible confusion, that under the idea of pleasure is meant also absence of pain, in which pain includes not only physical pain but mental anguish, suffering, sorrow, and so on. To say pleasure is good and should be pursued is also to say that pain, suffering, sorrow, anxiety, and so on are bad and should be avoided.)

The view that the good is pleasure is called **hedonism** (from the Greek word for pleasure, *hedone*). Since pleasure is good and pain bad, the hedonist counsels a life full of the one, and as empty of the other, as possible. Bentham in fact defines happiness this way. Though many people make a great mystery about happiness, thinking that it consists in this or that state or condition in life, to Bentham the secret of happiness is very simple: lots of pleasure and little pain. The more pleasure and the less sorrow in your life, the happier you are.

Many people find this idea extremely unappetizing. "There must be more to life than pleasure," they think. But what exactly is it? the hedonist wants to know. "How about love, how about friendship, how about art, how about wisdom, how about . . . ?" "But what good are these things if you do not enjoy them?" asks the hedonist. "The only value in all these things is the pleasure they bring; would you want them if you did not like having them? Nothing has any value but for the pleasure it brings."

"But in any case, it cannot be everyone's obligation just to produce as much pleasure as possible," the antihedonist wants to say. Remember the professor who could easily please her students by giving everybody a grade of A? Of course, it may be your obligation to do as much good for your students as you can, but you do this by educating them, not by pleasing them, since education can be quite painful at times. This reasoning misses an important point about hedonism. Sometimes it is necessary to sacrifice present pleasure for future pleasure. If education is necessary to a happy life, and if education can be painful, then some pain is necessary to a happy life. The question is, who will have more pleasure in the end, the student who will not study because it is too painful and so does not learn much, or the student who studies, learns, and then uses his or her knowledge successfully in the future? If it is the hard-working student who has the best chance of having a pleasant life, then the hedonist would argue that the professor who educates rather than amuses is actually producing more pleasure for her students in the long run.

Other people are upset over the word "hedonism." This word has come to mean something like "wine, women, and song": having a good time, partying until the wee hours, heedless of the morrow; *carpe diem,* the fun philosophy. "Producing as much pleasure as possible for everybody" conjures up images of the Roman emperors, offering chariot races and circuses to keep the people amused. But as already suggested, this is not what the word means when philosophers use it. The "fun philosophy" suggests rollicking good times, but philosophical hedonists prefer the calmer, intellectual pleasures such as listening to music or conversing with friends. The first philosophical hedonists were the Epicureans (third century B.C.), who counseled a life of serenity or calmness of spirit, which they understood as absence of pain and especially freedom from passion. They held that intense pleasures were just not worth the trouble they can cause. You can fall in love, and it is great for a while, but love also can bring great anguish, so we would do better to avoid it. The wise person shuns lovers but cultivates friends, for friendship is very pleasant and is much less likely to lead to hurt feelings. When the Epicureans advocated pleasure, they meant essentially freedom from emotional disturbances; hardly what we mean today by the word "epicureanism," which stands for refined taste in matters of food, wine, dress, and personal luxuries.

Hedonists are typically considered selfish; they want pleasure for themselves, not for others, and are thought to be so attached to pleasure they become indifferent to the fact that many people lead lives full of pain and suffering. (Seeking a life full of pleasure is sometimes condemned as nothing but a way of escaping from the fact that life for many people is full of misery. Who wants to think about the homeless and the victims of famine and civil strife? Why spoil a good day?) It is true that the Greek hedonists were interested not so much in morality as in the question that bothered the Greeks greatly: what is the best life to lead? Hence, Greek hedonism was egoistic: get pleasure for yourself. But this is not endemic to hedonism as such, and is not true of contemporary philosophical hedonists, nor of Bentham and Mill, who are interested in the principles of morality. U hedonists are altruists: their point is that the pleasure you ought to pursue is not for yourself, but for everybody. (Actually, Bentham's case is more complicated; he somewhat implausibly believes that if you maximize other people's pleasure, you automatically maximize your own.)

Quantity and Quality of Pleasure

We have said that philosophical hedonism should not be thought of as a fun philosophy; but this needs to be qualified. What pleasures does the philosophical hedonist prefer? Bentham is a great democrat: all pleasures are considered equal, as far as he is concerned. "Quantity of pleasure being equal, push-pin is as good as poetry," he writes, meaning that there can be no discrimination among pleasures simply on grounds of being pleasures. It matters not whether you get your pleasure from watching football on TV or from listening to classical music; all that counts is how much pleasure you get, the more the better. Hence, the life of your typical couch potato is just as good as the life of the greatest intellectual, provided the amount of pleasure is the same; if the couch potato enjoys his life more, his life is better.

Bentham points out that pleasures are connected with other pleasures, and that the full value of pleasure has to be measured not only by how pleasurable it is but by what other pleasures it entails. Possibly the couch potato has a boring job that he does not enjoy and misses out on all sorts of other enjoyable things as well, so that the intellectual who really loves her job as a college professor and gets to meet interesting people and read all sorts of books winds up with a lot more pleasure after all. But Bentham's point is that if the intellectual's pleasures are better, they are better because they are greater, leading to more pleasures in the end, and not because of the nature of the pleasant activity.

This democratic view scandalized a lot of people. Bentham's view was derided as a "pig philosophy," suitable not for human beings but for certain animals for whom the height of bliss is wallowing in the mud all day. Against Bentham it was pointed out that the pleasures that are the greatest are sensual pleasures, like eating and sex, and the pleasures associated with having a good time; the former are considered somewhat less than human, the latter undignified and frivolous. Is not Socrates' life better than the pig's, the critics said, even though Socrates, who spent all his life in a fruitless search for the meaning of virtue and did not indulge in sensuality or frivolity, did not enjoy the greatest kinds of pleasures?

Among the people scandalized by Bentham's view was his disciple, Mill, who was a very refined intellectual and thought that intellectual pleasures were intrinsically better than those of the common uneducated laborer. Mill wants to say that spiritual and intellectual pleasures are superior, that is, better in themselves, regardless of any connections with further pleasures. So Mill distinguishes between greater *quantity* of pleasure and what he called superior *quality* of pleasure, by which he means pleasures that are superior just because of the kind of activity (reading poetry, say) from which they are derived. This enables him to say that the pleasures of the intellectual are superior to those of the common masses, even if the intellectual pleasures are not as intense or pleasurable. Socrates may not have had as much fun in his life as the ordinary party goer, but his pleasures, those of thinking and talking about deep moral issues, were the superior ones. They were better in quality if not greater in quantity. Hence, Socrates' life was better. (Mill's view is therefore, called **qualitative hedonism,** as against Bentham's **quantitative hedonism.**)

Unfortunately, this is a contradiction; if pleasure is the only good, then the more of it the better, regardless of where it comes from. If you hold that the pleasures of talking philosophy are superior to those of watching football on TV, even if they are not necessarily greater, then you imply that what makes them superior must be something other than pleasure; this other thing is therefore an independent standard of good. Pleasures that are of higher quality must be higher for some reason other than the fact that they are pleasures.

Mill more or less admits this by the way he tries to explain what makes superior pleasures superior. He does not. Instead, he applies the "experienced person" test. If you ask the person who has experienced both kinds of pleasure, Mill says, that person will tell you that certain pleasures are better than others, even though not necessarily more pleasurable. But it is unclear why Mill thinks every experienced person will answer the same way; there must be lots of people who love football but are bored to tears watching opera (which you can see on TV occasionally). Of course, most opera lovers are probably bored to tears by football, but this begs the question. Mill tries to beg the question even more by saying in effect that the trouble with the opera-haters is that they do not really understand opera, so they are not good judges. This is true, but most likely opera fans do not understand much about football, and anyway the football fans do not understand opera precisely because they find it so boring they never bothered to study it. Mill's test assumes that there is a universal standard of taste, which is precisely what Bentham's democratic hedonism denies.

The "experienced person" test has certain unusual applications. An argument is sometimes made by certain feminists in favor of lesbian relationships as follows. Generally speaking, most heterosexual women have not tried lesbian relationships, but many lesbians have previously tried heterosexual relationships and found them unsatisfactory. Hence, women who have experienced both prefer the lesbian, which is therefore better. But this argument obviously neglects the fact that heterosexual women have not tried lesbian relationships precisely because they do not expect to like them, so nothing follows about which is really better. The argument commits Mill's "quality of pleasure" fallacy.

There is thus no way a hedonist can distinguish between pleasures other than by how much someone enjoys them. If you think certain pleasures are superior to others, that is because you think certain activities are better than others, independently of the pleasure one gets from them. You are therefore, not a hedonist, since what makes the activity better is something other than the pleasure. But this is not to say that the pleasure is not important; perhaps nothing can be good unless it produces *some* pleasure. This would make pleasure a necessary condition of good, but not a sufficient condition, and so not the definition of good or the only good. Aristotle's view is that there are certain activities that are "more human," that is, more in accord with human nature, which as we have seen in Chapter Three he regards as essentially rational. Experiencing pleasure is a byproduct of engaging in the most human activities, he thinks (overlooking the fact that among the most pleasurable activities are eating and sex, which according to Aristotle's theory should be about the least human of activities since all the animals and even insects do them). But it is doing the activities and not the pleasure we derive from them that is really good (and that constitutes happiness), he claims.

Evaluation of Hedonism

It is now time to evaluate hedonism. We do this by giving a more precise definition of hedonism, then looking at counterexamples.

Hedonism can be defined by two propositions.

1. All pleasure is good.

2. Nothing but pleasure is good.

(Strictly speaking, one would have to add comparable propositions about pain being bad, but the reader can supply these without prompting.) Both of these propositions are part of the definition, for if some pleasures are not good, then there has to be some other principle, not itself pleasure, that determines which pleasures are good and which not; and if there is something else good other than pleasure, then pleasure is not *the* good but only *a* good.

Are All Pleasures Good?   We want to say, of course not; the pleasure you get from eating junk food is not good, and neither is the pleasure some people seem to get from other people's misery. Let us take an extreme example: the sadist. The sadist gets pleasure from inflicting pain on others. There is nothing good about this pleasure. What does the hedonist say?

The hedonist says that the pleasure the sadist obtains is indeed good, insofar as it is pleasure. What is bad is the pain that he inflicts on his victim. The overall situation (the victim's pain, the sadist's pleasure) is bad because the pain is much greater than the pleasure, therefore, leaving a negative balance.

But is this correct? Compare two situations. In one, the victim suffers but the sadist does not receive pleasure. In the other, the victim suffers and the sadist does receive pleasure. Which situation is better overall? The answer is the first, not the second. Given that the victim suffers anyway, it is better that no one receive pleasure from the suffering. In fact, it would be best if the sadist received pain, not pleasure (suppose by mistake he hooked up the electric torture prod incorrectly and accidentally gave himself a strong shot of electricity. We would think this additional pain improved the situation, not worsened it). So the hedonist is wrong in saying that the addition of pleasure always makes a situation better, and the addition of pain always makes it worse.

Is Nothing Good Other Than Pleasure or Bad Other Than Pain? Here are two reasons to think not.

1.   Imagine two husbands. Each loves his wife and thinks his wife loves him, which gives him great pleasure. The first husband's wife really does love him, but the second husband's wife does not and is in fact running around with other men behind his back. Assume the second husband goes to his grave mistakenly grateful for his wife's love. The husbands' lives have equal pleasure, but do we say their lives are equally good? Ask yourself which husband you would prefer to be if you had to choose. If the first husband's life is better, then there must be something other than pleasure that makes it so. What can it be? All that distinguishes the two husbands is that the first has a true belief and the second a false one. Hence, either having true beliefs is good, or having false beliefs is bad, independently of the pleasure or pain the beliefs produce.

2.   Suppose computer science perfects a "virtual reality" pleasure machine. The scientist programs into the machine all the things you like most, hooks you up, and the computer takes over and simulates for you every great experience you have ever dreamed of. The machine is so good you cannot tell it is only a simulation. You are getting nutrition through tubes dripping nutrients into your veins, but the computer makes you think you are eating in the greatest restaurant you can imagine. You are sitting in a chair, but the computer makes you think you are exploring distant planets, or performing brain surgery, or making love to the lover of your dreams, or whatever you most want to do. (One of the beauties of the pleasure machine is that you can experience thrilling and dangerous activities like skydiving in perfect safety, yet still get the thrill of danger.) No greater pleasure is imaginable than what the pleasure machine can provide. Now, if you were given an ironclad contract that you would enter the machine and never leave, would you sign? No, you would not, but why not? Are you afraid something might go wrong? Let us assume you can be certain it works. Then would you sign? No, again. Why not, for heaven's sake? You know you will not get half as much pleasure out of real life. But what people seem to want is not only pleasure, but what we might as well call reality. People want to do things, not just imagine they are doing them. So pleasure is not the only good.

Of course, none of these arguments convince the hedonist. In the sadist and deceived husband examples, the hedonist evaluates the situation differently than does the antihedonist; for example, the hedonist denies that it matters which husband you are. Your preference for the nondeceived husband is probably due to your prejudice against pleasure, the hedonist asserts. As for the pleasure machine, the hedonist says that your objection to it is due to one simple problem: you have never actually tried one. If you were to try it, you would never want to get out. (There is evidence from psychology that when rats are allowed to give themselves pleasure via electrodes attached to the pleasure centers of their brains, they will press the bar that activates the electrodes until they drop from exhaustion.) What you suffer from is "hedonophobia," says the hedonist; you are afraid of pleasure because you do not really know how good it is. So what you actually think does not really count; what counts is what you would think once you tried the pleasure machine.

"Dolorism"

If hedonism is the theory that pleasure is the good, we will call "dolorism" the view that pleasure is bad and pain and suffering is good *(dolor* is Latin for pain). How can anyone think pleasure is bad and suffering good? The American journalist and writer H. L. Mencken offered this sardonic definition of Puritanism: "The haunting fear that someone, somewhere, might be happy." The British historian Thomas Macaulay remarked about the historical Puritans, "The Puritans opposed bearbaiting, not because it gave pain to the bear, but because it gave pleasure to the spectators." (In Elizabethan England, the popular sport of bearbaiting consisted of setting dogs on a chained bear. The spectators would bet on how many dogs the bear would kill before the dogs killed the bear. When the Puritans came to power in the seventeenth century, they banned this and many other popular amusements.)

The Puritan strand of Christianity, deriving from Martin Luther, held that man is sinful, pleasure is the work of the devil, and our vocation in life is to purge our sins and suffer. "Suffering, suffering, the Cross" said Luther, when asked if happiness were not the end of life. As Jesus suffered to atone for our sins, so each of us must suffer in our own person for penitence. Some devout Catholics mortify the flesh (monks wore hair shirts; flagellants have themselves whipped), not as an exercise of self-control but as a form of chastisement and to rise above fleshly pleasures. By suffering, we realize how unworthy and wicked we are and are moved to beg forgiveness. The true goal in life is to understand that you are a miserable sinner, beg God to forgive you, and atone for your sins by suffering.

Ideal Utilitarianism

Most readers of this book will not find dolorism terribly attractive, but may seek an alternative to hedonism. They will not find pleasure bad, yet will not think that pleasure is the only good. But then what else could be good? Pleasure and pain are states of consciousness, but it is possible to deny, as did G. E. Moore, that the only good things are states of mind. According to him, such things as a beautiful sunset or a great painting are good in themselves, whether or not anybody experienced them. Imagine two worlds, exactly alike, he said, differing only in that one contains a beautiful sunset, or the painting, and the other does not. All human experiences are the same. Which world is better?

You are supposed to answer, the world with the sunset or the painting; but suppose you do, does that prove that these things are good in themselves, apart from any experience we may have of them? No; all that is proved is that you think these things are good, not that they would be good if they did not appeal to you. So let us assume that nothing is good or bad other than what appeals to human beings. It is we who make things good or bad. (If we were intelligent dinosaurs, we might think sunsets were boring and steamy jungles wonderful. If we had a thousand eyes like the fly, we would probably detest Michelangelo and Raphael and adore certain modern artists.) This means that things are good or bad only as humans experience them. Things themselves have no value; only our experiences of things have value. But is it the pleasure in the experience or the experience itself that has the value? Hedonists say it is the pleasure: if we could experience beauty, knowledge, freedom, yet not get any pleasure from these things, they would not be good, the hedonist says.

Ideal utilitarianism (IdU) is the view that says that these and similar experiences are valuable in themselves, and ought to be produced, independent of any pleasure the experience might give you. Having knowledge about something is itself valuable, whether or not it gives you pleasure to know it. So is appreciating good art and music. So is freedom and other good things. You prove this by imagining two people identical in every way, except that one has and the other lacks the experience in question. Consider knowledge. Imagine two people identical in every way, but one person knows ten things and the other knows eleven. Which person is better off? The IdU says, the second. And why not? How can someone not be made better off if nothing happens to her other than that she learns some new item of knowledge?

You may think it is not possible to appreciate works of art and music without liking them, but that is not true. People understand why Picasso is considered a great painter, or Wagner a great composer, even if they do not like Picasso or Wagner. We can understand the standards of good art, and see how it is that these artists meet the standards. But if your taste does not run to Picasso or Wagner (you much prefer Mozart and Rembrandt), you will not get much pleasure from these works. But it is better to appreciate them than not, says the ideal U.

Since what makes these experiences good is not that they make you happy (they may, but this is not what makes them good), IdU does not say that what is morally right is to produce happiness; it says that what is morally right is to produce happiness as well as the other desirable states of mind. It is good to learn what makes Mozart or Wagner great composers, even if you do not come to like Mozart and Wagner. This is not a merely theoretical point. What is the purpose of education? Is it to teach people things that will make them happy in the long run? Or is it to instill in them an appreciation for ideal things such as art and literature? It seems that IdU would advocate spending a lot more money on ideal subjects such as art, literature, and philosophy, and quite a bit less on the more practical subjects taught in schools. The students will be better off, even if not happier.

SUMMARY

As a result of our analysis, we can now say that U consists of six propositions.

1. It is morally right to produce a balance of happiness.
2. It is morally wrong to produce a balance of unhappiness, if avoidable.
3. The greater the balance, the better (worse) your action.
4. It is wrong not to prevent great unhappiness when you can.
5. It is not wrong to produce less than the maximum of happiness possible, provided you do produce a favorable balance of happiness.
6. Nothing else is morally right or wrong.

As we have seen, these propositions may need to be supplemented with a proposition about rules.

7. Put into effect and follow those rules that, if generally followed, would produce a favorable balance of happiness.

We have explained each of these points and have shown how they strengthen U over other versions. We have also looked at certain places where U seems to fail or to be in trouble. As usual, we leave it to the reader to judge whether U as defined by these seven propositions is an adequate moral theory.

REFERENCES AND FURTHER READING

Classical utilitarians are John Stuart Mill, Jeremy Bentham, Henry Sidgwick, and G. E. Moore. Recent utilitarians include J. J. C. Smart, R. M. Hare, and Richard Brandt. Mill's short book *Utilitarianism* (1863, many editions) is one of the great works of philosophy and should be attempted by all students.

Mill's other famous work is *On Liberty* (1859, many editions). It is somewhat of a puzzle whether Mill's arguments in this short book in favor of freedom of thought and of personal privacy are founded on utilitarianism or not.

A collection of essays on Mill is by Samuel Gorovitz, ed., *Mill: Utilitarianism, Text and Critical Essays* (Indianapolis, IN: Bobbs-Merrill, 1971). Another is Jerome Schneewind, ed., *Mill* (New York: Doubleday, 1968).

The first three chapters of Bentham's *Introduction to the Principles of Morals and Legislation* (1789) contain the principles of his moral philosophy; these are found in several anthologies.

Sidgwick's *The Methods of Ethics,* first published in 1874 (7th—posthumous—edition, New York: MacMillan, 1907; reissued in 1962), is a still underappreciated classic of careful reasoning and a wonderful exploration of the logic of utilitarianism.

The book by Moore titled *Ethics* (New York: Oxford University Press, 1912) is a great classic that is now out of print but worth tracking down and reading.

A general collection is Michael Bayles, ed., *Contemporary Utilitarianism* (New York: Doubleday, 1968). Another is Amartya Sen and Bernard Williams, eds., *Utilitarianism and Beyond* (New York: Cambridge University Press, 1982).

Two books by W. D. Ross, *The Right and the Good* (New York: Oxford University Press, 1930), and *Foundations of Ethics* (New York: Oxford University Press, 1939), contain sharp criticisms.

Bernard Williams is an acute contemporary critic. See *Utilitarianism, For and Against,* two essays by Bernard Williams and J. J. C. Smart (New York: Cambridge University Press, 1973). Also see Williams' discussion in his *Ethics and the Limits of Philosophy* (London: Fontana, 1985).

Defenses and expositions are found in: Antony Quinton, *Utilitarian Ethics,* 2nd ed. (Peru, IL: Open Court, 1988); Richard Brandt, *A Theory of the Good and the Right* (New York: Oxford University Press, 1979); and Russell Hardin, *Morality Within the Limits of Reason* (Chicago: Chicago University Press, 1988).

Samuel Scheffler, *The Rejection of Consequentialism* (New York: Oxford University Press, 1982), defends a modified consequentialist position.

Classifications of ethical theories may be found in William Frankena, *Ethics,* 2nd ed. (Eaglewood Cliffs, NJ: Prentice Hall, 1973).

Chapter Nine

Kant: Evil as Irrationality

Everyone must admit that if a law is to have moral force, . . . it must carry with it absolute necessity; that, for example, the precept "Thou shalt not lie," is not valid for men alone, as if other rational beings had no need to observe it; and so with all the other moral laws properly so called; that, therefore, the basis of obligation must not be sought in the nature of man, . . . but a priori *simply in the conceptions of pure reason. . . ."*

Immanuel Kant, Preface to *The Groundwork of the Metaphysics of Morals*

Immanuel Kant (1724–1804) is one of the most important, some people would say the most important, philosophers who ever lived. His philosophy is brilliant, profound, rich, complex, and fascinating; it is also obscure, confusing, irritating, and sometimes rather incredible. No philosopher has contributed as many important ideas to the philosophical study of ethics; in fact, no philosopher comes even close, and if one considers that the same thing can be said about virtually every other branch of philosophy, one sees why Kant is generally considered to be such a towering figure in the Western philosophical tradition. Because of this, Kant's philosophy is one that all serious students of ethics must attempt to understand. It is, however, open to many interpretations on almost every important point, a fact that has given rise to a vast literature of works about his philosophy.

Although over his long life Kant set out his moral ideas in several volumes, the interpretation found here is based very largely on Kant's justly famous and indeed wondrous little book with a mouth-filling German title sometimes translated as *The Fundamental Principles of the Metaphysics of Morals,* but often called *The Groundwork.* Considered by Kant himself as an introduction to his moral philosophy, *The Groundwork,* despite its many difficulties, should be attempted at least in part by every serious student; like all Kant's writings, it more than repays serious study and will help the student develop a taste for the richness of Kant's thought and the complexities of his prose. Though only an outline of his moral system, and in need of supplement and even correction by his other works, it contains perhaps more challenging ideas per page than anything else you are likely to encounter.

KANT'S PRESUPPOSITIONS

Logic tells us that you cannot prove everything, and common sense tells us that to understand a philosopher you must distinguish what he proves, or tries to, from what he assumes. This is not easy, however, since philosophers frequently do not reveal their presuppositions. The reader is left to figure out what these are by study and analysis of the philosopher's arguments. Of course, that some idea is an assumption rather than the consequence of a proof does not mean that the idea is false; on the contrary, good method requires that we assume only what is too clearly true to require proof. Nonetheless, assumptions constitute a point of view, and those who do not share this point of view will likely find the philosopher's presuppositions mistaken and his entire theory puzzling and implausible. Kant has a point of view about what morality is, and how it might be validated or justified, which when understood enables us to understand what he is trying to accomplish in his philosophy. This point of view sets the agenda of his theory; his presuppositions determine what he has to prove and explain why he has to prove it.

Evil Is a Form of Irrationality   This is the underlying central idea in Kant. He wants to say that the evil itself—for example, deliberately deceiving someone—is irrational, so that when you do something that is wicked, your logical mind has gone to sleep, or lost control of the situation, and you are just not thinking straight. What is more, in Kant's view, the fact that it is irrational is the reason why it is wrong; it does not just happen that evil is irrational, but *irrationality is what makes evil evil.* Irrationality is thus the great sin; immorality is wrong because it is a form of irrationality.

The idea that evil is irrational has a long history, dating at least to Socrates, who thought that evil is a form of ignorance. In Socrates' view, a person who does evil things does so because there is something he does not know, some truth he has not grasped. Socrates believed that if you really knew what was truly good, you would automatically choose what is good; he was, to use earlier terminology (Chapter Five), an internal realist. Hence, he concluded that no one does evil willingly, but only through mistake.

Kant does not think that evil is a mistake in Socrates' sense: he does not think there is some knowledge (what Socrates called "wisdom") that evil people lack. Morality for Kant is not a question of knowledge but of the *logical principles that ought to guide action.* To be evil, therefore, is to be motivated by principles of action that are illogical. When you do evil, it is your logical powers that have failed, not your capacity to acquire information. A person who acts immorally is not reasoning very well; even if she draws correct inferences all the time, she fails to take into account certain principles that logic requires we employ in our thinking. In that sense, thinking that leads to immoral conclusions ("I should rob the bank") involves a logical fallacy.

So morality is based on reason. But what Kant means by reason is something very rigorous. He does not mean that ethical principles must be reasonable, or that reasonable people must agree about them, or that we should be reasonable in our judgments and moral demands. By reason, Kant means something that has the solidity of logical demonstration. Nothing less than the principle of non-contradiction is to be brought into play. A morally wrong idea (his example: "I may make a lying promise") must be shown to entail a contradiction. What Kant sets himself to do, then, is to uncover the logical principle that reveals the contradiction involved in each and every morally wrong thought. Few philosophers have set themselves as ambitious a goal.

Ethical Principles Are Universal and Necessary   This assumption motivates Kant's search to find the principles of reason that underlie ethics. If ethics were only universal but not necessary, then ethics could (possibly) be based on the common part of human nature—for example, on self-love or fellow-feeling—that just about every person possesses. Kant quite explicitly rejects this. He wants ethics to be like mathematics: *universal because necessary.* Mathematical truths must be what they are: they are true "in all possible worlds." This means they would be true no matter what else is true. Kant's very striking and out-on-a-limb position is that ethical principles appeal to all rational wills, that is to say, to everyone who acts through deliberation and intelligent decision making. Maybe you live in the "possible world" described by the TV series *Star Trek,* in which there are creatures in many regards quite different from human beings but who nonetheless think and make decisions based on their thinking. Kant says that the same principles of ethical logic apply to them as apply to us. The logic of morality is independent of all merely contingent characteristics. What language you speak, what your culture is, even—*Star Trek* again—what your outward physical form happens to be, are contingent characteristics about you: they are only the way you happen to be. Even the psychological principles that govern your alien species could be different from those that govern human beings (maybe, Spock-like, you do not experience emotions. Maybe you do experience emotions, but different ones.) But if you are capable of thinking, your logic is the same, in Kant's basic view, no matter what your contingent characteristics. Geometry would not be different for Klingons and Tribbles, and neither is morality.

Happiness Is Subordinate to Morality   Kant has a remarkably different point of view from that of the utilitarians, who think that morality consists of the rules for creating happiness. For Kant, no one has a right to happiness: happiness has to be earned by good behavior. It is not a good thing when bad people are successful and happy; hence, happiness cannot be the ultimate standard in ethics, for if it were, putting aside further consequences of the distribution, whether happiness were distributed to good or bad people would be irrelevant.

The difference between Kant and utilitarians may be put this way. Suppose you have a world, W.1, that contains exactly three equally bad people, each of whom enjoys a net of ten units of happiness. In a second world, W.2, everything is exactly the same, but the three bad people each have a net of zero units of happiness. The utilitarians would prefer W.1 to W.2, but Kant would prefer W.2 to W.1. The reason is that utilitarians hold that, further consequences aside, a situation with more happiness is better than one with less. Kant, on the other hand, holds that happiness must be proportioned to just deserts, and that things are worse, not better, when bad people, who deserve to suffer, enjoy happiness.

Another way of putting this point is to say that for Kant, *morality is an end in itself:* "Morality for morality's sake" has been said to be Kant's motto, whereas for the utilitarians, morality exists for the sake of happiness. This idea is of course very close to the popular notion that virtue is (or should be) its own reward, but that is not quite Kant's view of things. For Kant, there is really no question of reward at all; one ought to be moral just because moral is what one ought to be, and for no other extrinsic reason. One is not better off by being moral; one is just morally better. But to be morally better is precisely what one ought to be.

Kant Accepts Hume's Law   You cannot deduce moral principles from natural facts. Kant also seems to have no interest in moral realism, the theory that there are moral facts that can be known (see Chapter Five). But unlike Hume, who concludes that if morality cannot be justified by facts it cannot be justified or shown to be correct at all, Kant concludes that morality is an independent system that *must be self-validating.* Basing morality on sentiment in the Humean fashion is obviously out of the question for Kant, for two reasons. Let us grant that all people do share certain sentiments in common, for example, that people generally do not like to be murdered or deceived. Hume thinks that because of such common sentiments we might arrive at a universal morality. Kant's first objection is that the common principles could never be necessary. Sentiments are contingent because they depend on facts about human beings. Not all rational wills in every possible world will have the same sentiments. Kant's second objection is that sentiment-based moral theory has a problem with moral obligation. Why should the fact that no one likes to be murdered, including me, impose an obligation on me not to murder anyone? This is the question the Humean cannot answer; at least Kantians (and realists) think so.

Kant thinks he can evade these difficulties by regarding morality as a part of the principles of rational action. Morality is not to be regarded as strictly "true," but rather "justified" or "vindicated," as some terminology has it. We can distinguish between actions that are rational and those that are not; those that are not should not be done. But there are many kinds of irrational actions. If your friends get irritated when you argue about philosophy, it might be irrational, because it is imprudent, pointless, and self-defeating to argue with them too much. But "Do not argue philosophy" is not a moral principle. Kant's problem is to define a principle of logic the violation of which makes an action specifically immoral, as opposed to irrational in some other way. Morality is rationality of a special sort, defined in terms of special principles of the logic of ethics.

Kant, Like Hume, Is an Internalist Kant holds that to accept a moral principle is to have a reason to obey it. If moral judgments simply state facts, even moral facts, they would have no power to motivate or affect behavior. But Kant takes this in a different direction from Hume, who concludes that moral judgments are expressions of sentiment. Kant does not believe moral judgments are expressions of sentiment. For Hume, if you think that it is wrong (say) to hurt someone's feelings, then you must have a sentiment against hurting people's feelings. You have to care about this. If you did not care about it, you would not have the sentiment and you would not regard it as wrong, even if you knew that other people did regard it as wrong (they care, but you do not).

Kant thinks that this will not do as a basis of morality: the person without moral feelings would have no reason to act morally, and would be exempt from moral obligation. For Kant, reason has to be a motivation all by itself. It is not that one is reasonable because one *cares* about being reasonable; it is just that one *is* reasonable, and for this reason alone cares about being reasonable and is motivated to be reasonable. Kant holds both that unless morality is based on reason it cannot be validated, and that morality must be motivating. He therefore concludes that reason must itself be motivating, even without any sentiments to support it. To understand that hurting someone's feelings is wrong, in Kant's view, gives you a reason not to hurt the person's feelings, whatever your sentiments may be, and whether you care about it or not. This form of motivation he calls *respect for the moral law.*

The Moral Person Is One Who Acts on Principle Many people think it is important to act on principle, but Kant elevates acting on principle to the center of morality. To act on principle is to do something because you think it is right, and for no other reason. Kant points out that only rational beings have the capacity to act on the basis of conceptions about what to do and what not to do. We think: "This act is kind; kindness is morally good; therefore I shall do it"; or, "To do this would be cruel; cruelty is wrong; therefore I shall not do it." To be moral, according to Kant, is to act through such conceptions. If you are kind simply because you are a kind person, and act kindly naturally without thinking about whether it is morally right or not, you are not acting in an especially moral way, he claims. To be moral, you must set yourself the principle, "I should be kind," and act kindly because you want to act in accord with correct principles. He calls this *acting from duty.*

A person who acts on principle is a person who acts consistently. Imagine if someone said, "I make it a principle to display the flag on patriotic holidays." If it then turned out that he did not display the flag on the Fourth of July or other holidays, at some point we would conclude that he has no such principle, despite his protestations. A principle is therefore some rule that could be acted on consistently by everybody. Because of this, Kant's assumption that ethical action necessarily requires acting on principle comes to play an indispensable role in his program to derive moral truths by logic alone. For his strategy is to examine whether there are some ideas that cannot be taken as principles on which to act. If some idea cannot be taken as a principle, then acting on that idea cannot be morally correct. Thus, consider the idea, "I may make a lying promise in order to get something I want." Let us grant Kant what he thinks he can prove, that this idea cannot be taken as a principle on which to act. For Kant, this explains why that idea is morally wrong. Morality requires acting on principle, so ideas that cannot be principles on which to act cannot be morally correct.

For these doctrines, Kant is criticized by those who think he is far too rationalistic. These critics think that feelings and emotions ought to play a part in ethics, and condemn Kant's emphasis on principles, thinking, and rationality as cold and at bottom inhuman (certain feminists, for reasons explained in Chapter Seven, condemn it as antiwomen). Critics also deplore Kant's overemphasis, as they see it, on logical consistency. People who act consistently are boring, predictable, and far too rigid, they think. Such people overvalue self-control, and depreciate naturalness. This cannot be morally required. A little spontaneity or unplanned expression of the inner person should be encouraged by any good moral theory, these critics argue.

THE SUPREME PRINCIPLE OF MORALITY

One Supreme Principle?

Kant thinks that if morality is to be reduced to a science, that is, if it is to be more than a collection of unconnected and more or less arbitrary rules, there must be *one supreme principle of morality*. This principle must be such that all other moral rules and principles can be derived from it. It would be basic, because although all moral rules would derive from it, it itself would not derive from anything else. And it must be one, because if there were two or more supreme principles, it would be necessary to relate them through something else, which would then be supreme. If such a principle can be found and shown to be correct, our entire set of moral rules will have been organized into a unity and would be justified by being shown to follow from the principle. We would then have a comprehensive theory that would explain *all* our morality. Kant clearly believes such a task to be among the most important jobs for the moral philosopher.

Kant is not alone in thinking that morality can be systematized, that is, reduced to or shown to depend on one supreme principle. Utilitarians, hedonists, egoists, in fact everybody who claims that there is "one big idea" at the heart of morality, are also systematizers in search of a supreme principle, although most other philosophers do not seem to make as much of an issue about system as Kant does. But some philosophers have resisted the idea of a system, believing that there is no supreme principle of morality. They hold that morality consists of a set of independent principles that are not connected logically with each other and which cannot be derived from anything more basic. We can call this view a "no theory" theory because it holds that there just is not any one theory that can explain why we have the principles we do.

According to one of the best known "no theory" theorists, the English philosopher W. D. Ross (1877–1971), morality consists of a set of rules that are not derived from something more basic but discovered by simply thinking about each separately. Ross contends that if we all sat down and clearly thought about what rules we consider the correct ones, we would all arrive (more or less—he admits to a certain tentativeness about his list) at the following set.

1. Keep promises.
2. Make amends for previous wrongful acts.
3. Show gratitude for services or favors received.
4. Distribute rewards by merit.
5. Help other people and try to improve their condition.
6. Help yourself by improving your own condition.
7. Avoid harming others.

There is something pleasing and unpretentious about the "no theory" theory. The idea that all we need in life are a few simple rules, and no complicated philosophical theory at all, appeals to many people as workable and down to earth. For example, suppose someone should say that he or she gets along just fine by following some simple rules: work hard; do not cheat or mooch off anyone; mind your business; love your family and help your friends; obey the law and pay your taxes. The reader may think that a person may not arrive at a better set of rules after taking six courses in philosophy!

Nevertheless, it is easy to see why philosophers have rejected the "no theory" approach. Suppose we compare the list of rules stated by Ross with the homespun list set just stated. How do we know which list is better? We might well ask Ross why his list includes just the seven items it does, and no others? For example, how could Ross justify excluding from his list the following principles: always avenge insults; neither a borrower nor a lender be; always put your family and country ahead of yourself. Ross' view is that we cannot give reasons or justify any of the rules on the list; we simply intuit that they are correct. But it might seem that we need something more satisfying than intuitions; what we need is a theory that explains or justifies our intuitions. Intuitions, that is, the moral beliefs we arrive at when we think clearly, are at best data; they need to be arranged, systematized, explained, and, most importantly, vindicated. Ross can be criticized for not doing the job that philosophers are supposed to do. And because his list seems arbitrary, Ross is open to the criticism of ethnocentrism: what seems self-evident to him is likely to be the moral prejudices of his country, class, and era.

Kant's Supreme Principle

Let us return to Kant and try to understand his supreme principle of morality. Remember that for Kant morality is supposed to be derived from reason, and being rational is its own motivation: since we are rational, we already have all the motivation we need to act and think rationally. When we do not act rationally, it is because some other part of our nature, probably emotions, has caused us to ignore the reason within. Our task, one might say, is simply to respect the reason that is already there. No further reason can be given why we should be rational; to respect reason is a fundamental postulate. Hence, the supreme principle of morality in Kant's system can be said to be, "Respect the reason within you."

This may seem arbitrary: Why could someone else not take it to be a fundamental principle to ignore reason and have fun all day long? How can Kant justify his fundamental principle? He cannot. But, in Kant's defense, it must be said that the idea of trying to justify respect for reason is a bit bizarre: it does not make sense to give a reason why you should be rational. To be rational is to act and think on the basis of reasons, so it would be going round in circles to look for a reason why someone should accept reasons: if they are unwilling to accept reasons in the first place, why should they accept any reason you may give them for accepting reasons? So Kant is correct in thinking that there cannot be any real reason why we should respect reason; we simply posit that we must. And if somebody refuses to make the postulate? Kant can do no more than ask whether in fact you do not want to be rational. Of course you will want to be rational, if you only think about it, Kant obviously assumes, but even this reply is another circle, for what about the person who does not want to think about being rational? Why should such a person think about it? No reason can be given: being rational is the one thing that cannot be justified. (Another way of making the same point is this: all things that are logically valid can be shown to be so by the use of logic, except logic itself.) If you do not want to be rational, you are guilty of the error of irrationality, and if morality follows from reason (a very large condition indeed), then you are probably going to be guilty of immorality as well. But if you have already decided not to be rational, you may have a hard time understanding why you should not be irrational.

Hypothetical and Categorical Imperatives

Kant regards morality as a *set of commands,* much on the model of the Ten Commandments: Do this! Don't do that! says morality. He calls these commands imperatives. Kant distinguishes two kinds of imperatives, which he calls hypothetical imperatives and categorical imperatives; only categorical imperatives constitute morality. Both kinds of imperatives state commands, but the difference is that hypothetical imperatives contain a condition, or a hypothesis, upon which the command is based. **Categorical imperatives** state the command without any condition. So a **hypothetical imperative** has the form: on the hypothesis that p, do q. Whereas a categorical imperative says simply, do q. "If you want to be loved, you must give love in return" is a hypothetical imperative; "Love thy neighbor" is a categorical imperative.

The distinction between these two forms of imperatives can be rather subtle. Do not think that a hypothetical imperative must contain the word "if" or some other term that would mark a hypothetical statement in grammar. The grammatical form of the sentence is not necessarily a clue to the fact that the imperative is hypothetical; you must figure this out from the meaning. Let us consider some examples. Suppose you work for a company that is doing something you disapprove of strongly, say, dumping its waste material in the environment. Your problem is what to say about your company's practice when it is criticized outside the company. You ask a friend for advice and he says to you, "Well, as for me, I value loyalty in an employee above everything, so I'd never criticize my own company in public." This is a hypothetical imperative. Why? If you analyze the meaning, you understand that the advice being offered is hypothetical: if you value loyalty as I do, you will not criticize your own company in public. The hypothesis is that you do value loyalty, and the advice, not to criticize your company in public, is offered only on this condition. The friend has not said, "Do not criticize your company"; nor has he said, "Value loyalty above all." Such imperatives would be categorical.

Leaders and officers of organizations know how to use hypothetical imperatives to their advantage: "You believe we ought to have a finance committee, so you ought to be willing to serve on it." The imperative applies only on the stated condition; you are not being told that you must serve on the finance committee, but only that you must if you believe there should be one (which you do). Hypothetical imperatives do not actually say what you should do, and so cannot be the last word in moral advice. If you do not meet the condition—you do not value loyalty or do not want there to be a finance committee—the imperative does not apply to you. Only categorical imperatives can be ultimate moral principles.

The Categorical Imperative

Now the principle, "Respect the reason within you," may not seem to get us very far; something more closely related to morality is required if respect for reason is going to be translatable into moral principles. Kant seems to think that since morality consists of categorical imperatives, and since these are to be derived from something, then what they are to be derived from must be one great categorical imperative. This would be the true supreme principle of morality, which we can regard as the **Categorical Imperative** (CI). The Categorical Imperative states the supreme or overriding command, from which all lesser commands follow. We see parallels to this idea in other theories: divine command ethics, for example, has its own categorical imperative: obey the Word of God. In natural law, the categorical imperative is, "Follow nature." From these commands, all other ethical precepts derive—given, of course, that one knows what the Word of God, or nature, tells you.

So what does the CI tell you? It is at this point that Kant makes what many regard as his most important contribution to ethical theory. He introduces the idea of universalization, and makes it the central idea in ethical theory. **Universalization** holds that we must universalize our moral judgments. For Kant, the Categorical Imperative, the fundamental command of ethics, is,

"Follow the principle of universalization," or, in Kant's own words: "So act that the maxim of thy action could by thy will be a universal law" ("law of nature," he says in another passage). This is what Kant proposes as the Categorical Imperative, the supreme principle on which all of morality is supposed to depend.

UNIVERSALIZATION

Why Universalize?

Universalization says that we must apply the judgments we make to everyone. Why must we do that? Suppose we consider some moral judgment: "Henry should not steal apples." The principle of universalization holds that the moral idea in this judgment, not to steal apples, must be made universal: it should apply to everybody if it applies to anybody. Thus, if it is true that Henry should not steal apples, it is also true that no one else should steal apples, assuming, of course, that there are no relevant differences between Henry and other people. Because moral judgments are universal in this way—if they are true for anybody, they are necessarily true for everybody similarly situated—universalization is thought to be a necessary feature of morality: all moral judgments must be universal.

But why must we universalize? There are actually three answers to this question: an answer based on *logic,* a second based on *moral form,* and a third based on the *content of morality.* While drawing on all three answers, Kant overlooks the distinction among them. He wants his moral principles to be drawn from reason, for which he needs universalization based on logic; he wants morality to be based on the form of moral judgments, which are universal; and he wants universalization to produce moral content. Kant's genius in choosing universalization as the central idea in ethics is that no other principle comes close to doing all three jobs. Let us look at each of these reasons to universalize your judgments.

Universalization as a Principle of Logic   It is a simple principle of logic that *like cases must be treated alike.* Good reasoning requires that where two things are identical in suitably relevant respects, they be regarded as identical in all other relevant respects. Thus, if sick people in a medical experiment experience relief from their illness after taking a new medication, it is reasonable to suppose that other people not in the experiment will experience comparable relief from the same illness. It is illogical to assume distinctions where there are no relevant differences. Therefore, it is unreasonable, or as we say, arbitrary, to treat two things differently unless there is some relevant difference between them. If there is no relevant difference between Henry and Tom, it would be illogical, unreasonable, or arbitrary to hold that it is wrong for Henry to steal apples, without holding also that it is wrong for Tom to steal apples; and the same for Jack and Mary. Hence, reason leads us to the universal principle, "It is wrong to steal apples." As the same holds true for any other moral idea, we reach the conclusion that if any moral judgment is true at all, it is true universally.

Universalization as a Formal Principle   Whatever else morality is, it is a set of rules. *Rules,* whether moral or nonmoral, *are by definition universal* because they are stated so as to apply to everybody in a given group. For example, the rule, "All students must take a philosophy course in order to graduate," applies to all the students. If this is a rule at your university (it probably isn't), then it applies to you. The rule "Freshmen must pass composition" applies to you if you are a freshman. If you do not have to take composition if your GPA is 3.5 or better, then the rule is, "All freshmen with GPA less than 3.5 must take composition." No matter how narrowly drawn the group to which the rule applies, the rule itself is always universal.

Since moral rules are rules, they are necessarily universal; this is a formal feature of morality, in that it is true of moral rules not because of what they are about or what they say (their content) but because they are rules. Kant seems to think that any judgment that is not universal would not be based on a rule, and so would not be a moral judgment. Hence, he concludes that universalization is a defining feature of morality, and so it would be incoherent (self-contradictory) to make a moral judgment and fail to universalize it. Suppose you say to yourself, "I ought to shovel the snow off the walk of the elderly person next door." But you do not consider that anyone else similarly situated to you (that is, living next door to an elderly person, being physically fit, and so on) ought to do the same; you think, "Let others do what they think best." Your judgment is not based on the universal rule, "Let everyone in my position shovel walks," so it is not a moral judgment but a statement of your personal preference or your resolution how to act. Your rule applies only to yourself: it is a particular judgment about what you think you ought to do, and particular judgments are not rules and therefore not moral judgments. However, your companion judgment, "Let everyone do what he or she thinks best," *is* universal, so it may be a moral rule.

Universalization as a Substantive Moral Idea   Suppose Sam likes apples very much and is short of money. He would like to give himself permission to steal an apple, but does not really want to give this permission to everyone else. Sam is a philosophy student so he has heard about universalization, but unfortunately he is not impressed by what he has learned in class. He does not think being logical is that important, he does not see the point of formal considerations, and he wants to know why he must universalize his judgments. He might even be a bit sophisticated and argue that even if it is illogical not to universalize, it is not for that reason morally wrong, and he is interested in morality. After all, he argues, a person who makes a mistake in logic would not be accused of being a morally bad person!

A simple answer to Sam would be that it is morally wrong to claim a right for yourself that you would not allow to everyone else. This principle expresses the idea that there should be *no special privileges.* Morality holds that nobody should be in any way specially advantaged nor disadvantaged. To claim a special privilege—to give yourself permission to steal while not allowing others to do the same—is to be unjust, and injustice is simply wrong. This is the idea behind the importance of impartiality and our rejection of discrimination and all forms of prejudice. We do not think that such unequal treatment is illogical, though it may be, but that it is unfair to deny rights to some people while granting them to others, or to hold some people back from advancing themselves while providing plenty of opportunity to others. That the same rules, and the same conditions of competition, ought to apply to everybody seems to be simply a basic moral idea that we accept for its own intrinsic rightness.

Formalism

This last answer will not serve Kant's purposes, however, because it assumes we know that fairness or impartiality is morally good. But universalization is supposed to tell us what is morally good, so it would be blatantly circular to say that we must universalize because to universalize is morally good. Kant has to claim that universalization is mandatory for logical or formal reasons only. However, without the moral aspect of universalization, it is questionable whether Kant can solve the problem of how to get moral content from a merely logical or formal principle. That he apparently wants to do so is criticized as a major error, the mistake known as **formalism.** This is the mistake of trying to derive content from form.

Consider poetry. The difference between haiku, sonnets, and limericks is purely formal (these are even called poetic forms), consisting in the number of lines or syllables, the rhyme, and meter schemes. The content is what the poem is about. Formalism is the error of thinking that if you knew that your friend wrote sonnets, you would be able to understand what the sonnets were about. But you cannot. A sonnet might be about love, death, war, or anything the poet pleases.

The Categorical Imperative and the principle of universalization are both formal principles that do not say what to do or not to do. Form alone does not give content. There are three reasons.

1.   Any judgment can be categorical and universal. "Every good boy must be rewarded" is a universal and categorical judgment, but so is "No good deed should go unpunished." But which is morally better? You cannot answer this by knowing only that all judgments must be categorical and universal. "Hate thy neighbor!" is as categorical and universal a command as "Love thy neighbor."

2.   Universalization is actually a hypothetical idea, and so cannot be identified with categorical imperatives. Universalization says that if p is correct for anyone, then p is correct for everyone, without saying that p is correct for anyone and everyone. Thus, if it were true that Henry should steal apples, it would be true that anyone else not relevantly different from Henry should steal apples as well; if it were a good thing for Jack to rob, cheat, and steal, all universalization tells us is that it would be a good thing for everybody else like Jack to do the same. And from this, nothing follows about whether it is a good thing or not. Universalization tells you nothing about what is good and bad.

3. The claim that universalization can generate moral ideas is the reverse of the truth; in fact, universalization cannot even be applied unless you already have some moral idea. Remember that we can only universalize among people who are similarly situated or relevantly similar. This qualification is needed because universalization applies only to people in the same condition or situation. It might not be wrong for Tom to steal apples if, say, he has a starving family to support; but if he has, then he is not in the same situation as Henry. There is a relevant difference between them, and because of this relevant difference it is no longer arbitrary not to apply the rule against stealing to Tom. But as you might have suspected, this qualifier turns out to be a rathole through which all the moral content escapes. The universalization principle does not tell us which differences are relevant. So how can we know to which people any given moral idea applies? Suppose Sam, fond of apples, short of cash, but long on philosophical quibbles, wants to know why he is not relevantly different from Tom, or from Mary, who happen to have the money to buy the apples they want? Universalization alone will not tell him. Of course, we might want to distinguish between stealing to help other people and stealing to help yourself; or between stealing from need and stealing for pleasure. (Sam has his board prepaid at the university, so he is not going to go hungry.) But it is not by universalization that we can say this. Which differences are relevant and which are not is not a question of logic, but of substantive morality.

Hence, universalization tells us neither which ideas are morally correct, nor to which people the correct ideas apply.

Kant gives plenty of ammunition to those who would accuse him of formalism. He says (*Groundwork,* 23) that nothing but "simple conformity to law in general" can serve as the principle of morality. His explicit intention is to derive the moral law from the very conception of such a law. This seems to mean that from the fact that we have a concept of morality, we can deduce what the content of morality is. It is as if he said that from the fact that moral people must act on principle, we can deduce what principles they must act on. Or, from the idea of an imperative that commands categorically, we can deduce what that imperative categorically commands. Any of these alleged deductions would seem to derive content from form, and would appear to be philosophical attempts to do the impossible.

It is clear why Kant might be motivated to derive moral content from moral form. Kant thinks that moral principles have to be justified somehow; there must be some reason why it is wrong to lie and right to help people in distress. But, according to his assumptions, moral judgments cannot be based on natural fact, nor derived from God, nor reduced to sentiment or social convention. So they have to be shown to be logical. But what will show this? Perhaps their form.

One contemporary philosopher who endorses the universalization principle but cannot be accused of formalism is R. M. Hare (b. 1919). He too holds that logic requires that moral judgments be universalized, so that judgments that you do not universalize are judgments that you cannot make without logical error. If you are opposed to anyone stealing apples, you logically must oppose everyone stealing apples, including yourself; this is not a moral point but a matter of logic. Hare takes the very Kantian view that when you make a judgment, you are in effect issuing a universal imperative (Hare's term is "prescribing"): "Let no one steal apples." Nonetheless, Hare is much looser than Kant in his view of what judgments this commits us to. Unlike Kant, Hare admits that anything can be universalized as far as logic alone can tell us; but Hare holds that intelligent people simply will not want to universalize certain ideas ("Let everyone steal what they like," for example) and therefore may not consistently apply such judgments to themselves. Only a fanatic would prescribe, for example, "Let everyone kill anyone who insults them." Hare admits that the judgments that result are apt to be subjective, nonnecessary, and based not on logic but personal preference, though he insists that no bad results follow from this because intelligent people will share the same preferences on matters of importance. Where intelligent people might disagree, Hare holds, utility ought to be the test: Hare is in fact a rule utilitarian, another position that would make his theory unacceptable to Kant.

What is Kant's solution to the problem of formalism? We need another concept. Universalization alone will not serve the purpose, but perhaps in tandem with something else it might. What Kant actually says is not that you cannot universalize immoral judgments, but that you cannot do so "by thy will." Is this Hare's idea (disguised in Kantian clothing), that intelligent people will not *want* to universalize many judgments? No; Kant's idea is more rigorous logically (moral judgments must be necessary, remember). Kant claims that we cannot logically universalize some judgments, not that we would not or do not want to or would not if we were sensible Englishmen or intelligent utilitarians. He says that for the rational will, it is impossible, because illogical, to universalize morally bad ideas (what is illogical is impossible, like a square circle). To understand this, we need to explain two other Kantian ideas.

MAXIMS AND THE RATIONAL WILL

Maxims

The Categorical Imperative tells us it is morally wrong to act on a maxim that we could not will to be a universal law. Both the terms "maxim" and "will" need explanation. Let us begin with Kant's odd term "maxim," which has given some commentators much trouble. What has to be universalized is not your action itself but the maxim of your action. By **maxim,** Kant means, he tells us, the principle on which one acts. This is by no means clear, but the thought behind it is not so difficult. The central idea is what your *motive* is in acting. Kant holds that whenever anyone does anything, there is at least implicitly a principle on which he or she acts, whether or not the actor articulates that principle or even understands what it is. (Hence, it is not necessary to attribute to Kant the mistaken view that people always act with some sort of principle in mind. But he does seem to hold that people always act with a motive; this motive gives rise to the principle implicit in the action.) The principle is of a general form connecting motive with deed. Thus, if you make a lying promise to get out of a difficulty ("Lend me ten dollars and I swear I'll pay you back by Tuesday"), the maxim of your action is, "Whenever I want to escape a difficulty, I may make a lying promise." It is this that has to be universalized: can you rationally will that anybody be given the right to make lying promises to get out of trouble?

If we understand maxim this way, we see that two complaints that are made against Kant are without foundation.

1.   Universalization cannot be applied, because what is universalized depends on how the action is described, and any action can be described in many different ways. Suppose someone says, "The check is in the mail," when it is not. This could be described as a lie; but it could also be described as a lie about a check, a statement about a check, a statement about the mail, a false statement about money, a statement in English, a sentence containing six words, and so on. So how can you know under what description universalization applies? If the action is described as making a statement in English, or making a statement about a check, there seems to be no reason why it cannot be universalized.

This is not the problem it is made out to be, however, since Kant can reply that if there is any description under which the action cannot be universalized, then the action must not be done, regardless of how may descriptions there may also be under which the action can be universalized. But if we keep in mind that it is the maxim that is to be universalized, and not the action, and that the maxim includes the motive, then the problem seems to be resolved: to lie to escape a difficulty is the maxim, and this is what cannot be universalized. Although in telling the lie the liar makes a statement about the mail, a statement in English, a sentence containing six words, and so on, none of this figures in his maxim, which is to tell a lie to escape the difficulty. His motive is not to make a statement in English in order to escape the difficulty, nor talk about the mail to escape the difficulty; these are merely means by which the lie gets told.

This is not to deny that problems remain, notably with the identification of the motive, and hence of the maxim, since a person's motives may be other than how he describes them to himself: maybe the person who lies to avoid a difficulty tells himself that he is lying to save embarrassment for someone else, which might be morally more acceptable. We ought to be careful to understand the maxim to be the principle on which a person actually acts, not the principle on which the person thinks he is acting (the real as opposed to the imagined motive); though this solution raises difficulties of its own, since it means that the description of the action that the person gives to himself may not contain the actual maxim, that is, the description that guides the person's action.

2.   Kant is an absolutist who holds that we should never lie, never make false promises, and so on. The reader will recall this criticism from our discussion of lying in Chapter Six. Regarding Kant as an absolutist comes from not paying attention to the role of motive. The Categorical Imperative tells us to avoid nonuniversalizable maxims, not nonuniversalizable actions. Hence, it is not lying

that cannot be universalized, but lying to get out of a tight spot. Kant holds that lying to get out of trouble cannot be universalized. But he does not hold that lying to save a life cannot be universalized, so his theory is not inconsistent with the antiabsolutist position. Most people probably agree with Kant that we would not want to universalize lying to get out of trouble; and Kant is not prevented by his theory from agreeing with those philosophers who say we would want to universalize lying to avert murder.

Will

Let us turn to the other term Kant uses in the Categorical Imperative, "will." It is morally wrong, Kant says, to do an action that you cannot will to be a universal law (of nature). What prevents me from willing anything I please to be a universal law?

No doubt I can wish that anything be universal, but to "will" as Kant uses the term does not mean to wish or to want or to desire or to hope for. "Will" is a word logically connected with action. Anyone can amuse himself with empty wishing (for the moon, as we say), but there is no such thing as an "empty willing." The expression "to will" means something like, "to be prepared to bring something about." If you will some action to be universal, you are prepared to try to make it universal. And Kant is saying that you cannot do this about certain actions.

Consider something that is impossible: flying to the moon, say. Anybody can imagine flying to the moon, or wish that he or she could fly to the moon, or want to or even hope to be able to; one could even try to fly to the moon—for example, by jumping off a cliff wearing wings or some flying gadget. But suppose you know flying to the moon is impossible; can you still try to? This is not an empirical point about psychology (what can and cannot be attempted), but a logical point about the word "try." To try to do something is to intend to achieve it, and you cannot intend to achieve what you know cannot be achieved. What would you say about somebody who sat for hours at the drawing board with pencil, compass, and straightedge, drawing lines and circles? If you ask him what he is doing, he says he is trying to draw a round square. Your first instinct is to think that the poor fellow is just terribly confused: everybody knows that such a thing is impossible. But when you explain this to him, he immediately replies, with impatience, that he is perfectly aware that it is impossible, but he is trying to do it anyway. The poor fellow is evidently even more confused than you thought! But how? What he says seems to make little or no sense; he seems to be contradicting himself. He is very deeply confused about something, and it is not about the laws of physics or similar factual questions but about the meaning of words, either "try" or (more likely) "impossible"; if he were clear about what both these terms mean, he could not think of himself as trying to do something impossible. A person can try to do the impossible, but he cannot think that what he is trying to do is impossible. Therefore, he cannot say (unless he is joking), "I am trying to do the impossible," unless he does not understand one of the words he is using.

Now apply this to ethics, using one of Kant's examples: making a lying promise. He says no one can will that this should be a universal law. Why not? Assume that universal false promising is impossible, indeed a self-contradiction, like the round square. Knowing this, we could not will it, since it is impossible to be prepared to bring about what we know to be impossible. A person who believed he could will such a thing would be confused about something.

Rational and Reasonable Wills

But Kant says we cannot will it, not that we cannot will it if we know it is impossible. We have seen that we can will what is impossible, so long as we do not believe it is impossible. Evidently, we have to help Kant out here. When he says you cannot will the impossible, he must mean that you cannot will it unless you are not thinking very clearly, that is, unless you are confused about something. So we come to the idea of **rational will.** Kant means you cannot rationally will the impossible. If you are thinking rationally, you will not be confused about words or anything else and will recognize what is possible and what is not, and therefore could not will what is impossible. Hence, a person can will that some immorality—let us say, wanton murder—be a universal law, only if that person is not thinking very clearly. The rational person cannot will that what is immoral be universal.

The reader might be excused for thinking that Kant is making an important point but in an unnecessarily complex and cumbersome way. Many commentators have thought so. They say that Kant's important point is that there is a question that is truly central to moral thinking. Moral people will ask themselves this question when trying to decide what to do. The question does have something to do with being rational and universalizing, but has nothing to do with rational will, which is a tangent Kant takes because he want to make morality more logical and more universal than it is. The truly important question that moral people will ask themselves is this: "How would I like it if everyone did this?" A rational person admits that if she would not want everyone to be allowed to do some given act, then she should not do it either. Any right you give to yourselves you have to give to everybody, on pain of being illogical. But what rights you are willing to give to everybody is not a question of logic, but of how you see things. This is Hare's point about the fanatic: no one but a fanatic would be willing to allow everyone to be free to practice wanton murder.

Now suppose someone contemplating some action pauses to reflect, "What if everyone did this?" There seem to be at least three further questions she might ask. As we have noted, she might ask herself whether she would like it or not if everyone did this. Or, she might ask whether she could live with everyone doing this. A third question is whether life for everybody would be better or worse if everyone did it. These questions might lead to identical answers, but they might not. Let us take, for instance, untidiness. What if everyone threw his or her peanut shells on the floor? Would you like it? If you are a Felix Unger neat-freak, you most certainly would not like it. But could you live with it? Probably, provided the shells got cleaned up every week or so. Would it make life better or worse? Well, that depends; it would save a lot of getting up and down to dispose of your shells properly. And the crunch of walking on the shell-strewn floor might be rather fun. But might it attract bugs? And what would the neighbors think?

Sensible and important though these questions may be, they cannot be what Kant had in mind. Different people will answer these questions differently. How you answer depends on what you like, or think you can live with, or think would be better for everyone. Your answer might even depend on your moral convictions: you might find untidiness morally repugnant, a celibate form of living in sin, and refuse to tolerate it for that reason; and this of course undercuts the idea that your moral principles should be determined by how you answer the questions.

These questions substitute for Kant's rational will a looser idea: what do I think is *reasonable* to allow people to do? Reasonable people will be reasonable about how they answer this question, but reasonable people may at times reasonably disagree. But for Kant, there is a unique answer to moral questions, which cannot therefore depend on what anyone might reasonably be willing to allow. He needs an answer based on logic, not an answer based on what people are willing to let happen.

Our interpretation of Kant's philosophy must be as strict as he himself wanted his philosophy to be. The Categorical Imperative rules out conduct that in some way involves a contradiction. Such conduct is ruled out because it cannot be willed by a person who is thinking clearly. Any principle that rules out conduct on grounds other than strict "unwillability" is not the CI, however sensible or reasonable that principle may otherwise be. A reasonable person will regard as morally wrong whatever she would not like other people to do, but a rational person in Kantian terms will regard as wrong only that conduct that leads her into contradiction.

KANT'S FOUR EXAMPLES

How Kant Organizes the Examples

It is time to see how Kant's theory works. He illustrates the theory by giving four examples. Always the systematist, he divides moral obligations into four categories and gives one example in each category; by using his method of searching for a contradiction, he is able to deduce the correct moral duty in each category, thus "proving" that his method is correct and complete.

Kant says our moral obligations can be divided into two overlapping pairs: duties to *self* and duties to *others;* and, *perfect* and *imperfect* duties. This gives the four categories: perfect and imperfect duties to self; perfect and imperfect duties to others. Since evidently both original pairs (self/others; perfect/imperfect) are mutually exclusive and jointly comprehensive, we ought to have a complete set of duties. (Any given duty cannot be both perfect and imperfect, so the terms are exclusive; and any given duty must likewise be either perfect or imperfect, so the terms are comprehensive. This is true by definition with regard to perfect and imperfect duties. With regard to duties to self and to others, however, the applicability of the properties of exclusivity and comprehensivity is not true by definition and is not so clearly true at all: there could be some duties that are duties to both self and others, and there could be other duties—for example, to preserve the environment—that are duties neither to self nor others, at least not to other people.)

What is meant by duties to self and to others seems fairly self-evident. By perfect and imperfect duties, Kant calls attention to the fact that some duties allow us options as to their fulfillment and some do not. Kant calls the former *meritorious,* the latter *strict* duties. This difference is illustrated by the difference between donating money and paying debts. We have an obligation to help those less fortunate than we are, but we have free choice as to whom to help, when, in which circumstances, what kind and how much aid to give, and so on. It is not wrong to refuse to give money to famine relief or to aid to the homeless; what is wrong is never to give money to anybody in need at all. This obligation is said to be imperfect. On the other hand, if you owe someone money, it is not optional whether to repay that person, or when, or how much; all this is decided in advance, and your duty is to pay back according to the agreement. This duty is said to be perfect.

The four examples Kant chooses are: *suicide, lying promises,* self-improvement or *developing your talents,* and *helping people in distress.* We can see how these illustrate each of the categories. You ought never commit suicide from despair of living, so this is a perfect duty to yourself; you should never make a lying promise, so this is an example of a perfect duty to others; you owe it to yourself to develop some of your talents but not necessarily all of them, being free to choose which, so this illustrates imperfect duty to self; and you are free to choose whom to help, but must give help to someone, so this is an imperfect duty to others.

At this point Kant, always eager to arrange everything according to principles, makes another distinction between the perfect and imperfect duties. The one principle that marks off all duties is that the rational will must avoid contradiction. But in some cases, such rational willing is impossible because the maxim is itself self-contradictory. In other cases, the self-contradiction is in the universalization of the maxim. The maxim of suicide, Kant thinks, is inherently self-contradictory because, as he thinks, we kill ourselves out of self-love, which is an impulse that should lead to life. With regard to lying, we see right away that universal lying would be a contradiction; it could not even happen. It is this internal inconsistency in the maxim or in its universalization that marks off the **perfect duties.** A perfect duty is based on the impossibility of conceiving, without contradiction, something about the action.

In other cases, the imperfect duties, this is not true. There is nothing intrinsically contradictory about universal selfishness or universal idleness; as far as logic can tell us, these things could happen. Nonetheless, all duties are supposed to be based on the impossibility of rationally willing something. Must not the imperfect duties too be based on some sort of contradiction? Yes, says Kant, nimbly shifting gears, the imperfect duties also depend on a contradiction, but of another kind. Sometimes it is the will that contradicts itself. With regard to **imperfect duties,** what you will is in contradiction to something else you will. You have to give up something; you cannot (or must not; Kant is transparently murky here) give up the first thing, so you must give up whatever it was that led you into the contradiction.

So we now have a clever second way of making the four-category division. All duties are based on some sort of contradiction involving the immoral maxim, which is why the rational will avoids immoral maxims. Perfect duties involve internal contradictions in the stating of the immoral maxims; imperfect duties are those in which the immoral maxim may be stated consistently, but nonetheless the will contradicts itself. As for duties to self and others, although Kant does not explicitly make this point, only duties to others involve universalizing; duties to self involve contradiction without universalizing. And so: a perfect duty to self is one in which the contradiction inheres in the maxim; a perfect duty to others is one in which the contradiction inheres in the universalization of the maxim. An imperfect duty to self is one in which the contradiction is between the maxim and the will; an imperfect duty to others is one in which the contradiction is between the will and the universalization of the maxim. This neat, highly systematic system may be summarized as follows:

Table of Duties

	To Others	**To Self**
Perfect:	No lying promises	No suicide
Imperfect:	Charity	Talents

Organization of the Duties

	To Others	**To Self**	
	Universalize	Do not universalize	
Perfect:	Univeralized maxim is self-contradictory	Maxim itself is self-contradictory	:contradiction in maxim
Imperfect:	Universalized maxim contradicts something else willed	Maxim contradicts something else willed	:contradiction between maxim and will

We now can interpolate Kant's procedure for making moral decisions. First, consider the maxim of your action. If the maxim is internally inconsistent, it is immoral and a violation of perfect duty to self. Second, if the maxim is not internally inconsistent, try to universalize the maxim. If the maxim cannot be universalized without contradiction, it is immoral and a violation of a perfect duty to others. Third, if it can be universalized, see if the universal situation is inconsistent with some desire you cannot abandon. If it is, then your action is immoral as a violation of imperfect duty to others. Fourth, if you find no inconsistency between the maxim and something else you will, look around for some other inconsistency. If you find one, the action is immoral and a violation of imperfect duty to yourself.

Trying to understand Kant is sometimes like squeezing a pillow: just as you think you have all the feathers under your control, more pop out somewhere else. We now have reached, after considerable hard work, an understanding of the principles behind the four kinds of duty. But there is a frog at the bottom of the beer mug. Why does Kant say that his principle rests on the *universal* law (of nature)? We have seen that two—half—of his examples do not employ universalization at all. Why does Kant not make the Categorical Imperative say, "Act so that you can will without contradiction"?

It is impossible to do more than guess at an answer. Kant is trying to blend two ideas that may not be blendable. It is his way of evading the problem of formalism. His philosophical instinct tells him that universalization is a key idea in morality and that violation of universalization is a logical as well as a moral error. But perhaps he fears that universalization alone does not produce many moral principles, since far too many actions can be universalized if one is willing to accept the results ("Let everyone throw his or her peanut shells all over the floor"). So he tries to blend in his desire to make morality necessary and universal, using the only idea that can accomplish that, contradiction. This ought to mean that something is wrong if it cannot be universalized without contradiction. But he is forced to acknowledge that far too many actions can be universalized without contradiction; by the criterion of universalization, too many actions he considers immoral (such as depressive suicide) will not be ruled out. So he restricts universalization to those actions in which contradiction gives him results he wants, and searches for some other kind of contradiction to take care of the other immoral actions. Thus the odyssey of a philosopher.

Meanwhile, he has taken on a lot of debt. He has promised to show that certain immoral actions can be shown to be immoral because of the contradictions they involve us in. Can Kant possibly deliver on these promises? Can he actually show all that he has claimed he needs to show? Let us turn to the examples and see. Instead of following Kant's logical order, as explained above, we will arrange the examples from most to least successful. The best two are those that involve universalization, the lying promise and helping others. These are the duties to others, where Kant's logic makes sense. His treatment of the duties to self is far less impressive.

Kant's Examples

Lying Promises   What happens if we imagine everyone possessing the right to make lying promises to escape some difficulty? It is clear that such a situation is unimaginable, for the simple reason that after a while nobody would believe anybody and the entire exercise would be pointless. To tell a lie is to make a statement that you expect others will believe; if you do not think others will believe you, what you say, though false, is a joke or a tall tale or something of the sort, not a lie. But when everybody may lie at will, soon everybody realizes that nobody believes anybody and to lie is not only pointless but impossible: how can I even try to lie if I know you will not believe what I say? In other words, the imagined situation of universal lying-promises is inherently unstable; it inevitably breaks down after a while and there becomes no point in anyone promising anything. As soon as you recognize this, it is impossible for you to rationally will to universalize the lying promise.

This is indeed clever: the rational person cannot will a contradiction, universal lying-promising would be a contradiction, therefore the rational person cannot will universal lying-promising, therefore the rational person will not make a lying promise. The admiring reader will notice that this argument has nothing to do with the utility of not lying or with whether anyone would like it or find it tolerable if everyone told lies, but only with the purely logical points already explained having to do with what can and cannot be rationally willed. Kant here seems indeed to derive morality from pure reason, his finest moment. (Are there other moral duties that can be derived in the way Kant derives the duty not to make lying promises? The reader should examine this question as an exercise.)

Not to Help Anybody   Suppose nobody ever helped anybody. Kant admits there is no contradiction in the idea of universal indifference. He even says that a society in which nobody ever helped anybody might be a better society than one in which people talk about helping others, and sometimes do, but also cheat and betray each other. Now since we can imagine the totally indifferent society, it is not self-contradictory or impossible to will. Total indifference would surely be rather unpleasant, and likely to leave everybody badly off, but Kant refuses to rely on considerations of utility or happiness. Furthermore, a person who is sufficiently tough-skinned and independent might even adopt as a policy not to help anyone ever, even on the condition that no one would ever help him if he were in need, danger, or distress. The right kind of person might actually be proud to adopt the "no help" principle as a universal law. "Stand on your own two feet," we saw in Chapter Three, is an argument for egoism.

Nevertheless, Kant can make the argument that a rational person would not, indeed could not, will this situation of universal non-help. Why not? Because as a rational person you know that the occasion might arise when you yourself might need help, and that no matter what your previous philosophical principles might be, at that very moment you would want someone to help you. Even the biggest misanthrope, if he is rational, must be aware that if it were his car cracked up on its side in the ditch, he would want some passing motorist to stop and call an ambulance. His misanthropic principles (do not ask me for help and I will not ask you) could not prevent him from wishing that someone would come to his rescue. And, therefore, the rational person knows that he cannot truly will universal indifference. At some point, his will could very well contradict itself.

This is a perfectly plausible argument, though it is a bit of a departure from Kant's program of proving morality by reason alone since it depends on an assumption about what anybody will want. There is a more serious defect, however, even waiving the problem with such an assumption. This is that Kant does not have any real reason why the desire to be helped should be the desire we endorse, rather than the desire to adopt the rule of universal indifference. If two desires conflict, we have to abandon one, but we need some principle to decide which one to abandon. Perhaps Kant thinks that we just could not abandon the desire to be helped when we get into trouble, but can abandon the desire to be ruled by indifference. This is certainly true, and for most of us it would be an adequate answer. However, it cannot really serve Kant since it depends on a psychological fact about human nature rather than on any principle of logic.

The other two examples depart even further from Kant's program. They do not involve universalization, and, what is more serious, the internal contradiction in the will on which they rest seems arbitrarily stated and resolvable in either direction. These examples are suicide, which Kant is against, and developing your talents, which Kant believes to be a moral duty.

No Suicide   Kant thinks you should not commit suicide if you are depressed ("If adversity and hopeless sorrow have completely taken away the relish for life"). Contrary to what is often thought (and what an occasional casual remark in the text may suggest), he does not argue against suicide in general. To think that he does is a result of ignoring the maxim, which is that I may kill myself if my life is not as happy as I want it to be. So-called "rational suicide"—for example, because you are dying of painful inoperable cancer or on the verge of deteriorating mentally with Alzheimer's disease—is not at all what Kant has in mind. In these cases, the maxims would be different: "I may kill myself if I have no hope of recovering from a painful and fatal disease" is different from, "I may kill myself if my life is not going as well as I want it to."

The suicides Kant is thinking of are those that he says are based on self-love, and this is in fact their principle: out of self-love, I may take my life. What is wrong with this kind of suicide? In one passage (and in other writings), Kant says that if you kill yourself for this reason, you treat your life as merely a means to the end of your happiness; but a human person, he claims, is not a means but an end. It is sometimes necessary to make an effort and solve, or learn to live with, your troubles. Kant perhaps shares the common prejudice that suicide is the easy way out: a person feels so miserable and sorry for himself that, even though he is not fighting against insuperable odds, he gives up the struggle and kills himself rather than try to straighten out his life. "Bugging out" in face of adversity, though perhaps excusable, does not seem to be very admirable.

Perhaps, but where is the inconsistency? The question is not whether it is tragic for a person in such a condition to take his or her own life, or whether it is a pointless waste, or whether the person is to be pitied, but whether it is morally wrong. There is no question of universalizing anything here; even a person who is clinically depressed, assuming implausibly that he had the strength of mind to follow Kantian moral philosophy, might very well see nothing contradictory about a situation in which everybody sufficiently depressed had the right to take his or her own life. In fact, it would be implausible to claim that any form of suicide is excluded by the principle of universalization, and Kant does not claim it. Consider suicide from a sense of shame over having failed in your duty. The captain who goes down with the ship, or the Japanese general who commits hara-kiri after losing a battle, could both rationally will that their actions be universalized. These suicides are clearly not based on self-love but on a sense of duty. But Kant must find a contradiction somehow, for the rational will needs a contradiction if it is to reject some proposed action. Never one to be thwarted by a problem in logic, Kant cleverly finds the contradiction he needs, and indeed limits it to those suicides he opposes. When self-love leads to suicide, then it is the very urge to life which leads to death! The principle that I may kill myself from self-love amounts to saying that I may kill myself because I want to live. This principle is surely self-contradictory, so it cannot be rationally willed.

This argument may strike the reader as a bit forced. After all, depressed people kill themselves only after they become convinced that the future has no possibility of happiness for them. Ending your life because you feel that your wish for happiness is doomed to disappointment does not seem contradictory. Is it Kant's philosophy or his personal morality that says that suicide is immoral? It is important that we make this distinction. Philosophers like other people have moral opinions; these may or may not be consistent with their philosophical theories. That we sometimes disagree with their opinions does not necessarily invalidate their theories. Perhaps Kant is wrong about suicide but correct about philosophy. We have wondered if there really is any contradiction in the maxims governing suicide. But maybe suicide is not immoral. In that case, if his philosophical theory is correct, we should not be able to find any contradiction. If there is in fact no contradiction, Kant's theory tells us correctly that suicide is not immoral. That Kant himself thinks otherwise shows that even a great philosopher can have trouble applying his own principles with an unclouded mind.

Develop Your Talents   Kant thinks we have a moral duty to develop our talents. Not all of them, to be sure, which might be impossible—perhaps you cannot play piano and be a first-rate shortstop, so you have to choose—but some. What Kant is against is laziness or indifference to self-improvement. He admits that in the right situation, laziness could be universalized—for example, as he says, somewhat romantically, in the South Sea Isles, where (suppose) food grows on trees, the weather is benign, and no one has to work for a living. But even in such a paradise, there is a moral duty toward self-improvement.

Many people think there is such a moral duty. They think life would be rather pointless if a person were to bum around and do nothing all day, day after day; what is the point of being a human being if you are going to live like a clam (even a clam works for a living!)? But such reflections are neither here nor there; where is the contradiction? Kant writes: "He asks whether his maxim of neglect of his natural gifts . . . agrees with what is called duty. He sees that a system of nature could indeed subsist with such a universal law, although men (like the South Sea islanders) should let their talents rust and resolve to devote themselves merely to idleness . . . but he cannot possibly *will* that this should be a universal law of nature. . . . For, as a rational being, he necessarily wills that his faculties be developed, since they serve him, and have been given him, for all sorts of purposes" (*Groundwork*, 49).

This is pretty feeble. For one thing, he seems to have forgotten that he is supposed to show a contradiction between two different states of the will. What is it that the lazy person wills that contradicts his will to be lazy? Since Kant cannot answer, he talks about laziness contradicting some vague "purposes"; later, he says laziness contradicts "the end which nature has in view" for us. But is not this reliance on nature's purposes a non-Kantian, even anti-Kantian, argument? Kant assumes a natural law premise that talents exist for a reason and ought to be used for that reason; he has forgotten that his philosophy is founded on the assumption that you cannot base morality on facts about nature.

But even if we grant that we have talents for a purpose, what follows? Just because you have something for a purpose does not mean you have to use it for that purpose; Kant sounds like the scolding mother: "Don't eat with your hands, your fork is there for a purpose." Maybe to eat with your fork is her purpose, but it is not necessarily her child's purpose, and why should it be? The point in question is, why is it irrational to use your talents for nonstandard purposes, or not to use them at all? (Kant, to argue *ad hominem* and unfairly, fathered no children. Evidently, he did not think he had a moral duty to use his reproductive capacity for the purpose for which it had been given.)

Again, we seem to see the philosopher's moral opinion taking control of his moral theory. But in this example, we cut a bit closer to the theory itself, for many people would share Kant's opinion against laziness, and thus conclude that if the theory does not find some way to rule it out, it is the theory that is defective. If you would be at fault even under the South Seas condition of unlimited abundance for allowing your talents to rust, then either there's a Kantian-type reason, or not. A Kantian reason would be that something is contradictory somewhere; what could that be? If no contradiction can be found and laziness is wrong anyway, Kant's theory stands convicted of, at least, incompleteness. The Categorical Imperative is not the one supreme principle, however important it may be. (On the other hand, if you find the idea of universal laziness rather attractive, and would be happy to volunteer for such an arrangement if it were possible, then for you Kant's theory is not damaged by the failure of this example.)

What is the upshot of this examination of Kant's examples? The two examples based on universalization work fairly well; the other two do not. Maybe Kant's initial instinct was right after all. If there is a single key idea in ethics, it is universalization. Let us abandon contradiction as a dead end imposed by an ultrarationalist who wants morality to be more logically rigorous than it can be. Let us return to universalization and see how far we can get with the principle that you may not do anything unless you are willing to allow everybody to do it as well.

THE PRINCIPLE OF UNIVERSALIZATION ONCE AGAIN

The Test of Sufficient and Necessary Condition

Let us backtrack a bit and recall that universalization is supposed to give us the criterion for moral obligation. Whether or not something is a moral obligation is to be determined by whether or not it can be universalized.

But we have both negative and positive obligations: obligations not to do things, such as killing people or telling lies (these things are morally wrong, or prohibited), and obligations to do things, such as taking care of your sick child (these things are morally required or obligatory). We must decide whether universalization provides the criterion for both negative and positive obligations, or for one only, and if for one, then for which? But universalization itself can be negative or positive: either you can, or you cannot, universalize any given action. We must clarify whether it is because an action can be universalized, or because it cannot be universalized, that it is a (negative or positive) obligation.

Once we decide what we are trying to discover, we can examine the problem by employing the test of necessary and sufficient conditions. If universalization gives the test for obligation, universalization must be either a necessary or a sufficient condition, preferably both, for obligation. This means that if you are going to know whether an action is or is not a moral obligation (positive or negative) by employing the criterion of universalization, then the criterion must be good enough to tell you (sufficient condition) and you must need to use it if you are to find out (necessary condition); if it is neither, the criterion is irrelevant; if it is not sufficient, it needs to be supplemented; if it is not necessary, then something else could be used instead.

Let us explore further the difference between sufficient and necessary condition. To do this, we need a short lesson in basic logic.

Consider two conditions, and call them X and Y. For illustration:

> Let X = The day being cold.
>
> Let Y = Snow falling.

We know that being cold is a necessary condition of snow, but not a sufficient condition: it cannot snow unless it is cold, but that it is cold is not enough to guarantee that it will snow. Put schematically, we can say:

X is a sufficient condition for Y: never X without Y. This is false in the example, as we know. In fact, a day can be cold without snow falling.

X is a necessary condition for Y: never Y without X. And this is true in the example. You cannot have snow falling unless the day is cold.

So in this example, if you wanted to discover whether X is a necessary and sufficient condition for Y, you would have to search for a day in which (a) X was true but Y was not; and (b) Y was true but X was not. You would find lots of examples of (a) but none of (b), so you would conclude that X is a necessary but not a sufficient condition for Y. Note that even a single example of either (a) or (b) would be enough to refute the condition. If it can happen once that there is cold without snow, then cold is not sufficient for snow. If it can happen once that there is snow without cold, then cold is not necessary for snow.

Let us apply this to universalization. Let us consider an action, call it A. And now let us set out the six conditions that enter into the question of universalizing.

1. A can be universalized.

2. A cannot be universalized.

3. A is morally wrong.

4. A is not morally wrong.

5. A is morally obligatory.

6. A is not morally obligatory.

Now we have eight possible combinations to deal with: 1 and 2 combined with 3 and 4, to give four possibilities; and again, 1 and 2 combined with 5 and 6 to give four more. The first set would give us: (1, 3), (1, 4), (2, 3), (2, 4). The second set gives: (1, 5), (1, 6), (2, 5), (2, 6). What is this all about? Take the first combination, (1, 3). This means that A can be universalized and A is morally wrong. Or take the fifth combination: (1, 5). This means A can be universalized and A is morally obligatory. And so on. We have to examine each of these combinations.

Happily, only two of the combinations present the theses of universalization: these are (2, 3) and (1, 5). The most obvious thing to think is that negative universalization applies to negative obligations: if something cannot be universalized, then it is morally wrong. This is surely what Kant thought. The key point is what cannot be universalized: if some action cannot be universalized, the action is wrong, so nonuniversalizability is sufficient to make something wrong. But are we also saying that everything morally wrong cannot be universalized—in other words, if something can be universalized, then it is not morally wrong? This would be the necessary condition. Perhaps Kant held this; we must consider it. Together, this pair of conditions is stated by (2, 3). If 2 and 3 always go together, then negative universalization is both necessary and sufficient for negative obligation. We will call (2, 3) the **negative universalization thesis** (NUT).

Kant might also have thought that universalization means (1, 5); if you can universalize, your action is a positive obligation; and, unless you can universalize, it is not a positive obligation. Again, both sufficient and necessary conditions for positive obligation are given by (1, 5). We call (1, 5) the **positive universalization thesis** (PUT). But as all sorts of trivia can be universalized, only the necessary condition part of PUT is truly plausible. This holds that unless you can universalize, your action cannot be a positive obligation.

Now we are going to test NUT and PUT by the test of sufficient and necessary conditions. To do so, we must notice which other combinations would have to be true for the theses to be false. These we call the counter combinations. Be aware that NUT and PUT really have two parts, since they each hold that universalization is both a sufficient and a necessary condition. This means that there will have to be four counter combinations, one each for necessary and sufficient conditions of NUT and PUT. If we can find only one instance in the counter combination, then the relevant thesis–part is refuted.

This is by no means as complicated as it seems. In fact, it is rather neat. Let us set everything out schematically once again, and the reader will grasp what has just been said. We will use NO and PO to indicate negative and positive obligation.

> NUT: negative universalization is necessary and sufficient for NO. This says that (2, 3) is always true.

> NUT counterthesis (–S): negative universalization is not a sufficient condition for NO. This says that (2, 4) could be true.

> NUT counterthesis (–N): negative universalization is not a necessary condition for NO. This says that (1, 3) could be true.

The reader should consider the countertheses and verify that they state correctly what would be the case if negative universalization were either not a sufficient or not a necessary condition for negative obligation. If it were not sufficient, then this would be because there could be a case in which A cannot be universalized but is not morally wrong, which is (2, 4); if it were not necessary, then this would be because A is morally wrong even though it can be universalized, which is (1, 3).

Now let us turn to positive universalization.

> PUT: Positive universalization is necessary and sufficient for PO. This says that (1, 5) is always true.

> PUT counterthesis (–S): positive universalization is not a sufficient condition for PO. This says that (1, 6) could be true.

> PUT counterthesis (–N): positive universalization is not a necessary condition for PO. This says that (2, 5) could be true.

This is complicated at first, but it is nothing but an exercise in basic logic. Having mastered the logic fully, the student will be delighted to apply it to our problem of universalization. All we have to do is look for examples illustrating each of the four countertheses. Only one example proves the counterthesis and refutes part of the universalization thesis.

Here is a list of plausible counterexamples.

(2, 4). Action A cannot be universalized but A is not morally wrong. NU is not sufficient for NO. Example: You go to Yellowstone National Park on the Fourth of July. If everyone did this, the park would have to close by 8 A.M. Second example: you escape the troubles of civilization by going to live in the woods. If everybody did this, there would be no woods left to escape into. Third example: you are a celebrated German philosopher who is too busy thinking to bother raising children. If everyone did this, the human race would become extinct. In fact, fourth example, if everybody became a professor of philosophy, the human race would be in sorry shape.

(1, 3). A can be universalized, but A is morally wrong. NU is not necessary for NO. First example: you abort your seven-month fetus because you have been invited to go skiing in Colorado. Second example: you tell nasty stories about your friends behind their backs. Third example: you alter your driver's license to give yourself a birthdate twenty-one years ago.

(1, 6). A can be universalized, but A is not morally obligatory. PU is not sufficient for PO. Example: When you get out of bed, you put your left foot on the floor before your right foot.

(2, 5). A cannot be universalized, but A is morally obligatory. PU is not necessary for PO. First example: you feel you have an obligation to defend your country, so you volunteer for the army. Second example: you feel compelled to protect wildlife, so you move to Alaska to study bears. [But we shall leave further discussion of (2, 5) for later, when we talk about the "Cyrano problem."]

Have we left anything out? Yes. No doubt the reader has been scarcely able to contain his or her curiosity wondering what has happened to the two remaining combinations, (1, 4) and (2, 6). Are these to be abandoned, ruining the beautiful Kant-like methodicalness of the presentation? Not at all. These two combinations give us the necessary and sufficient condition for the absence of obligations.

(1, 4) says that A can be universalized and is not morally prohibited. This means that an action that can be universalized may be done, and an action may not be done unless it can be universalized. So here, universalization gives the sufficient and necessary condition for permissions.

(2, 6) says that A cannot be universalized and is not morally obligatory. This means that an action that cannot be universalized is not obligatory (negative universalization is a sufficient condition for absence of obligation), and only actions that cannot be universalized are not obligatory (negative universalization is a necessary condition for absence of positive obligation). So here, universalization give the necessary and sufficient conditions for nonobligatoriness.

This gives us two more theses, concerning the absence of negative or positive obligation. We shall call these:

PUnoNOT: Positive universalization is a sufficient and necessary condition for the absence of NO. This is what (1, 4) says.

NUnoPOT: Negative universalization is a sufficient and necessary condition for the absence of PO. This is what (2, 6) says.

One could set out the combinations that would provide the counterexamples to these two theses. But it is not necessary, for the reader will have noticed the close relation of (1, 4) and (2, 6) to (2, 3) and (1 , 5). In fact, (1, 4) and (2, 3) say precisely the same thing. And (2, 6) and (1, 5) also say precisely the same thing.

This will not surprise you if you have studied logic. Think of it this way. If p is the necessary and sufficient condition for q, then the denial of p is the necessary and sufficient condition for the denial of q. Now 2 is supposed to be the necessary and sufficient condition of 3, so the denial of 2, which is 1, must be the necessary and sufficient condition for the denial of 3, which is 4. Or look at it this way. Suppose 2 and 3 always go together, which is what NUT states. In that case, take away 2 and 3 and what do you have? Their negations, 1 and 4, which therefore must also always go together. So if 2 and 3 go together, 1 and 4 must as well. And the same for the other two pairs. Therefore, if NUT can be refuted, that is, if NU is not the necessary and sufficient condition for NO, then PUnoNOT also is automatically refuted. And the same for PUT and NUnoPOT.

What Good Is Universalization?

Nonetheless, there are lots of examples of (2, 3). These are all the cases in which we take seriously the idea, What if everybody (or nobody) did that? What if nobody paid their taxes? What if nobody ever voted? What if everybody disconnected their automobile emission controls? What if everybody walked all over the newly planted grass? What if everybody cheated on their final exams? What if everybody mooched off their parents and never earned any money? What if everybody threw their garbage out the window? What if nobody recycled? What if everybody . . . ?

Most of these are cases in which no particular bad thing would come about if only one, or a few, people did the action; the evil results when lots of people do it. In situations like this, a person who accepts the benefits of other people's restraint but does not practice similar restraint himself is simply a freeloader or a parasite, the vile creature we met earlier in our discussion of egoism. After this long discussion, two tentative conclusions about such free-loading may seem in order. First, there is no reason why freeloading is wrong other than its fundamental unfairness. Why should others work so you may eat? Taking more than your fair share is unfair. Second, there does not seem to be any principled way to determine which actions are those about which the principle of universalization states the reason why they are wrong. We think there are certain things people have a right to do, even if no one would want them universalized, such as studying philosophy or not having children. We think this for reasons that are difficult to specify, but have nothing to do with universalization: we seem to have some very vague idea of basic human rights that can be evoked here, according to which people have rights, based on some theory of what rights are, which are not overridden by universalizing considerations. Perhaps not much more can be said about it.

The Cyrano Problem

You will recall that Cyrano de Bergerac had a basic principle in his moral code: "Always revenge insults to the nose." It is perfectly clear that he took this to be a very important, indeed the most important, obligation. Does he thereby have to universalize, under pain of logical or moral error? Let us assume Cyrano does not think that anyone else has such an obligation; it is purely personal. But why? One reason might be that no one has such an obligation because no one has such a nose. But in that case, would Cyrano be required to universalize to all people who might be in the same condition as he is, that is, endowed with a nose prominent enough to be ridiculed? Suppose he thinks not; his idea is that whether you take insult at ridicule is a matter of your own personal honor, which might differ from person to person. Furthermore, he is aware that not everybody is as adept with the sword as he is, so not everybody is in a position to challenge all nose-insultors to mortal combat. Let us pretend that Cyrano has a brother, Milquetoast de Bergerac, who sports an equally enormous nose but actually thinks that his nose is funny and jokes about it himself. Cyrano, we will imagine, is not only fond of his brother, but actually envies him; he wishes that he, Cyrano, could regard his own affliction (as he sees it) as lightly as Milquetoast does his. Since Cyrano actually thinks his brother is better off just because Milquetoast does not feel any nose-obligation, it is clear that Cyrano will not universalize what he takes to be his own moral obligation. He does not think that everybody is under the same obligation he is under. Nonetheless, he thinks he himself cannot let nose-insults pass.

Obligations that you feel you are under but which you neither think are universal nor even want to be universal, we regard as components of a *personal moral code*. Most everybody holds some principles of that kind. Some people feel an obligation to help the downtrodden, others to work with battered wives, others an obligation to study, learn, and get ahead in life. Characters in fiction are often defined by their dominant personal moral obligation (Hamlet feels an obligation to avenge his father's murder; Bruce Wayne, an obligation to clean the crooks out of Gotham City). We accept these as moral obligations even though we do not universalize them. (Must Hamlet think that every son of a murdered father has an obligation to avenge his father's murder? Not at all. It is his burden, imposed by his conscience—and his father's ghost.) These personal obligations are in addition to all the universal ones. They add an important touch of individuality to our morality. They in part constitute our moral character, and help distinguish each of us from everybody else.

Universal obligations ("Pay your debts," "Be kind to animals," "Do not cheat at cards") are not voluntary; we expect everybody to live up to them, whether they want to or not. But personal obligations are voluntary: a personal moral code is something that a person is free to adopt or not as he or she chooses. But though a personal code is voluntary, it does not seem voluntary to its possessor. Cyrano probably thinks he has no choice but to avenge nose-insults; it is not that he likes or even wants to challenge strangers to duels, he is driven to it by his sensitivity, pride, and sense of honor. Even though he finds it onerous, not to mention dangerous, to fight duels all the time, to him not to avenge an insult would be as disgraceful as to tell a lie or fail to pay his debts.

We need to explain personal moral codes. Are they justified, and, if so, how? How to explain the somewhat odd features that they are both voluntary and not voluntary? Are there limits to what principles they should contain? Suppose Milquctoast said to Cyrano, "You only think you have an obligation to avenge nose-insults. But you do not really. It is not like paying your debts or other points of honor; everybody has those obligations. In the next century, there will come along a philosopher who will say, if you cannot or will not universalize, there can be no obligation. I agree with this." What would Cyrano reply? How would such a discussion continue? One thing that seems clear is that it is not going to be Kant's theory that provides the material for a sympathetic analysis of personal codes. In fact, the right we have to adopt personal codes may be taken as an indication of a rather large gap in Kant's theory. It is difficult to see how Kant can admit that anything might be morally obligatory yet not universalizable. Universalization is certainly important, but misplaced emphasis on universalization will lead you to ignore something that may be equally important.

Conclusion: Is Morality Based on Logic?

After this long exploration, what is our conclusion? Is it more logical to be moral than immoral? Some points seem clear.

1. Kant has not given a method that arrives at "correct" moral conclusions in each of his four categories of duty.

2. Universalization is neither a necessary nor sufficient condition of obligation, positive or negative, so it cannot be universalization that makes right acts right and wrong act wrong.

3. There seems to be no principle by which we can decide where universalization should be applied and where it should not.

4. You cannot arrive at moral duties by looking for contradiction alone, so contradiction or its absence cannot be the principle distinguishing right from wrong.

5. People who are reasonable will generally arrive at good moral principles, but being reasonable will not lead to unique answers to moral questions.

6. Nonetheless, thinking logically is an important part of being moral, and the principle of universalization, if not the last word about morality, is part of thinking logically and an important moral consideration. A person who refuses to universalize at the least comes under suspicion of being selfish and unjust.

OTHER ASPECTS OF KANT'S MORAL PHILOSOPHY

Was Kant aware of all this? Kant's thought is very rich, and it is also very suggestive, which contributes to the difficulty in interpreting Kant, and makes inevitable disagreements about which ideas are really central to his thinking. In this section, we shall briefly touch on several important ideas that have been influential in contemporary ethical thought. Though we have presented Kant without drawing on these ideas, it would be misleading to ignore them. They constitute an important Kantian complement to the central claim that morality is based on logic. Our presentation tries to interpret Kant rather than follow him faithfully. We shall try to present these ideas in a way that in itself constitutes a fairly attractive ethical picture.

Autonomy

Kant says a moral person is autonomous. He explains this, in his terminology, by saying that a moral will gives laws unto itself. The property of giving laws unto itself Kant takes to be a defining property of a moral will. What does this mean? Autonomy means self-rule, as opposed to rule from outside. For Kant, a person rules himself when he lives by rules (laws) of his own making. But how can living by rules of your own making characterize a person who is moral? Does not a moral person live by the rules of morality, which most typically are not of his own making? Would we not suspect that a person who lives by his own rules, who is as we say "a law unto himself," is something of an outlaw, or an extreme individualist, or at least an eccentric? None of these descriptions seem to characterize the moral person.

We have to distinguish among three different conceptions of autonomy: *identity, logic,* and *responsibility.* All begin with the idea of self-rule, which is itself understood as thinking for yourself.

Identity Autonomy   To think for yourself means to act so as to express your individual identity. The autonomous person values self-discovery, individuality, having a unique identity and knowing who you are. What is important is to know your own self and act as your self decrees. You deny the authority of other people to tell you what to do, and are not afraid of being different, shocking, or unconventional. You rule yourself in the sense that you have your own personality that is present in your actions.

Kant does not understand autonomy this way. Wanting to be unique or different or unconventional or even wanting to be just yourself is not self-rule based on thinking, as Kant understands thinking. Thinking involves using logic to arrive at conclusions. Kant would not consider identity autonomy as a kind of autonomy at all, since it would appear to be ungoverned by any laws other than "Be yourself."

Logic Autonomy   This is Kant's conception. A person who is "logic-autonomous" thinks for herself by trying to be as logical as possible. She also rejects convention, but she tries to rise above her own personal point of view to see everything from the standpoint of what is most reasonable.

Given what we already know about Kant's view regarding the rationality of morality, we can understand how Kant can say that the laws that an autonomous person gives to herself are moral laws, that is, such laws as accord with the Categorical Imperative. To be reasonable for Kant *is* to live by the CI, and so if the autonomous person is reasonable, then the laws that such a person gives to herself will be exactly those laws prescribed by morality. The autonomous person, the person who is her own ruler precisely because she thinks for herself and makes her own decisions, is the person whose decisions will be good moral decisions, those dictated by the CI.

Kant's idea of giving laws to yourself is more interesting than his idea that the laws you give to yourself are those sanctioned by the CI. His point here is that a person who is moral thinks things out and makes decisions based on her thinking. What this means is that unless you think things out for yourself, your decisions have little moral worth, even if they are morally correct. Morality requires that you think for yourself and make up your own mind. Just "getting it right" because your mind is stocked with conventional moral ideas is not enough to make you a morally good person.

There is an important reason for this. If you act morally on the basis of something other than your own thinking—for example, because of convention, or even because of your good upbringing—then you do not really understand why what you do is the best thing to do. You do it because other people say so, or because you have been trained that way. In an important sense, it is not you who is doing it at all; you are out of the picture, and it is the people who put the ideas into your mind who are controlling your thinking. If you act from convention or from any motivation other than your own thinking, you are not autonomous because you are not ruled by your self, but by others. But if it is not you who is acting, then it is not you who is acting morally; it is the people who stocked your mind with moral ideas who acted morally, not you.

Kant's conception is both important and extreme. It is important first because a conception of autonomy in which autonomy is thought of as involving the use of reason is an attractive conception of autonomy. But more interesting, the idea that a person is not really moral if she only imitates the morality of others is an attractive conception of morality. But Kant's conception can be criticized because of his identification of the self with the logical mind. For him, autonomy and morality do not *involve* the use of reason, but are made to be *identical* with the use of reason. This is Kant's rationalistic extremism.

Responsibility Autonomy   What is needed is a third conception. The responsibly autonomous person thinks for herself to take responsibility for her life. She does not want to follow the crowd and be guided by fashion or convention, or to allow other people to influence her decisions too much, nor does she want her thinking to be clouded by emotions or prejudice. So she subjects her opinions to criticism, recognizes her own fallibility, and seeks the advice of others. She uses logic to help her develop her opinions, without assuming that logic alone will enable her to reach stable views about right and wrong. She has confidence in her ability to think well, and so is confident of her moral opinions. Because she tries to make herself responsible for her moral views, we can say that she rules herself. Her principles are those she has reached after intelligent consideration. She gives laws unto herself.

Autonomy so understood should most properly be regarded as a necessary rather than a sufficient condition of being moral; if you do not think about your values, then you are not moral even if you happen to have the correct values, but you will not necessarily arrive at the correct values just by being autonomous and thinking about them. (It is typical of Kant's excessive reliance on logic that he seems to think that autonomy is sufficient as well as necessary for morality: if you think about values logically, in his view, you will arrive at those dictated by the CI.)

Responsibility autonomy is essentially the conception of autonomy noted in Chapter Seven. It is closer to Aristotle's view than to Kant's, for though Aristotle holds that a morally good person has developed good character through training and habit, and whose moral responses have become integrated into her personality so that she acts morally by second nature, he also holds that we are responsible for our own character (*Nicomachean Ethics,* III, 5). Character can always be improved, and you need to examine yourself to maintain your confidence that you are as good as you can be. Moral complacence is not a virtue; training needs to be improved by reflection. Autonomy is an important aspect of moral character in Aristotle's view, but it is autonomy in the "responsibility" sense.

What would Kant say about the person who is moral because she is well brought up? In his view, if you are basically honest because that is the way you have been brought up, but have not really thought about it very much, then "Be honest" is not a moral law you have given to yourself; it is not really you but those who brought you up who are honest, and the fact that you are honest does not make you a moral person.

This seems awfully harsh on the many people who have a good upbringing. Kant seems to suggest that such people have an obligation to remake their character, replacing personality traits with logical thinking. Clearly, the problem here is Kant's reduction of the self to the rational mind. Such a reduction is to be avoided, for the self contains elements that, though not beyond the control of reason, are not themselves rational. A theory that took due account of these elements would accept the responsibility conception of autonomy.

So Aristotle and Kant agree that autonomy is an important aspect of moral action. To try to formulate good moral opinions and to adopt only those that we can endorse after reflection is morally important, and one way by which we distinguish morally good people from morally indifferent people. The person who has been brought up right without arriving at an understanding of reasons, who never tries to figure out these reasons, who never wonders whether the character he has acquired is really as good as it ought to be, and whether the actions he does by second nature are always the best to do, is hardly an admirable creature. He is, as Aristotle says, somewhat less than fully human.

Dignity and Respect

Kant tells us that every human being has dignity in virtue of the fact that he or she is a rational agent. Dignity is a characteristic that is universal, and not therefore part of a person's individual character, but dignity can be acknowledged or violated, both in your own person and in others. Dignity and respect thus have two faces, one looking inward toward your own dignity, the other outward toward the dignity of others. A person can respect himself and behave with dignity, and can respect other people and treat them with dignity. Someone who does not act with dignity and respect toward his own person, Kant suggests, is unlikely to act with dignity or respect toward other people: if you do not respect yourself, it is unlikely that you will respect others.

To act with dignity toward yourself is to know your own worth and to demand that others treat you accordingly. Dignity is therefore founded on a sense of self-worth, the recognition of which one claims as a right. It is not dignified to be too eager that people appreciate you, even less to beg them to do it; you must show that you are worthy of respect and let them respect you of their own free will. The opposite of dignity is humiliation (not humility). You violate your own dignity by foolish or self-abasing conduct. Kant says (in his *Lectures on Ethics*) that a person who is servile, or plays the buffoon, or loses control of his temper, or gets drunk, or complains about his bad luck "offends against the dignity of his manhood." A person humiliates himself also if he wants too much to be liked or loved, and fails to earn love by merit.

A person is humiliated by others if he is shamed, degraded, or disgraced, as when his faults are held up to public dissection; or if he is patronized or belittled, which means to be treated as less than fully rational; or if his choices and values are not taken seriously, or are regarded as trivial and ridiculous. Ridicule is a great vehicle of humiliation. So is mass processing: we feel humiliated when our individuality is not recognized and we are treated impersonally, like a number or a mere member of the crowd. Therefore, humiliation readily occurs in the course of doing good, as happens in large institutions such as hospitals and universities. Indignities can be inflicted unintentionally by people acting with the best of motives.

An important point about dignity is that it can maintain and indeed strengthen itself in the face of adversity. Strength is a great source of dignity, so poverty or hard luck or poor health can actually bring out the inner dignity in the victim, by calling into play a strength of character that may not be brought out under more fortunate circumstances.

What is the connection between dignity and rationality? Kant is wrong in thinking that dignity is intrinsically connected with rationality, as shown by the fact that dignity is not confined to human beings: cats, for example, have dignity. What is true is that rationality makes us capable of both wanting and losing dignity, and then suffering its loss. So being rational is not what endows you with dignity, but it does endow you with the capacity to value dignity—hence to want it and hence to suffer its absence.

It is therefore better to think of dignity, not as an inherent condition of rational agents but as a somewhat fragile state of mind essential to our well-being. This explains a puzzle about dignity, which is why it rankles so much to be humiliated. The actual occasion of humiliation can be small: someone treats you rudely, or calls you a bad name, or ridicules a minor personal eccentricity. Our indignation at such trivial affronts—we call them slights—indicates the importance to us of our dignity. Resentment is the name of the feeling we have when our dignity has been attacked: that small affronts can lead to large resentment shows the importance we attach to being treated with dignity. Since dignity is both important and subject to abuse, the sense of dignity has to be cultivated and nourished. We ought to treat each other with dignity; but as Kant says, first we must treat ourselves with dignity, by not humiliating, shaming, or embarrassing ourselves. By respecting your own dignity, you respect the dignity of others.

Respect goes rather deeper than dignity and is more fundamental still. Kant says that everybody is entitled to basic respect, that is, to be treated as a person of inherent worth. (To have basic worth is intrinsic to being a person, as opposed to being a mere thing or object, in Kant's view.) Respect is thus a universal right, and is not founded on some personal characteristic. Respect in this sense is a foundation of morality *(the* foundation, Kant sometimes hints).

In more ordinary terms, we respect a person because of her intelligence, or her courage, or her coolness under pressure, or her ambition, or because of many other personal characteristics that we find admirable. Respect is the homage we pay to merit. It follows that respect should be measured by what is done to deserve it; you respect a person by treating her as she deserves, neither better or worse. Thus, it does not show respect to pretend that a person is good when she is really bad, or out of misplaced goodwill to ignore her failings.

The opposite of respect is contempt; regarding yourself or others with contempt is a serious source of moral deficiency. To be contemptuous of someone is to regard that person of little or no worth. When you act contemptuously, you make someone "feel small," as if they did not really exist or as if their existence is a thing of little importance. Degrading and demeaning talk or conduct shows contempt because it assigns a place to the person addressed. It is a way of asserting the superiority of the speaker and the inferiority of the person addressed. So is superficial chumminess. All contempt is wrong, and deep contemptuousness is a foundation for immorality, since if you are contemptuous of someone the internal controls that normally prevent you from acting badly are eroded. We necessarily dislike people for whom we have contempt, and if you dislike someone it is easy to wrong him.

To lack respect for yourself is to regard yourself in the same way: as a person of little worth. A person who lacks self-respect is not only pitiful, but also dangerous; he very probably dislikes others as much or more as he dislikes himself. Is it possible to respect yourself even if, possibly on very good evidence, you regard yourself as weak, a failure, and in general as not much use to yourself or anyone else? Yes, if you follow Kant, because whatever else you think of yourself you do know that you have a rational mind and are capable of living by the moral law. A person who lives by the moral law is worthy of respect and has within himself the foundation of a sense of self-worth, no matter what other personal failings he may suffer from. Thus, respect for the moral law is the basis of respect for one's self as well as for others.

Ends and Means

Another point Kant emphasizes is the distinction between ends and means. Human beings are ends-in-themselves, he says, not mere means or things. If nothing were an end-in-itself, then nothing could have any value, Kant rightly points out, and only human beings qualify as being ends-in-themselves. Kant's argument here is a use of the infinite regress: since a thing has value either for its own sake or for its usefulness in obtaining something else, and if nothing had value for its own sake, then everything would have value only for the purpose of obtaining something else; but this leads to a regress in which nothing has any value. Kant thinks the idea of people being ends-in-themselves is so important that he makes it one of the formulations of the Categorical Imperative: "So act as to treat human beings always as ends and never as means only" (*Groundwork,* 57).

In general, it is clear what Kant has in mind by treating people as means: using them, manipulating them, or treating them as if they existed for your personal convenience. That is to treat a person as an object, as Kant puts it. To so act is to regard the other person as having no worth other than the worth he has for you, so we can see that treating people as mere means is equivalent to treating them with contempt. This explains why nobody likes to feel used or manipulated.

It is true that we cannot avoid treating people as means, since most of our encounters with other people occur in impersonal contexts in which we are trying to accomplish something. At the supermarket checkout line, I want the cashier to check me out correctly and quickly; I am not interested in her moral character or her rational mind or her personal well-being or much else about her other than her work efficiency. We break this impersonality, however, by making a few remarks such as "How are you today?" to acknowledge our common humanity. The test of whether I regard her as a mere means to my own convenience would come if something untoward should happen. If she should suddenly take sick and my main reaction is irritation at the time I am wasting, then I do regard her as a means and am acting immorally, according to Kant.

It is a little less clear what we have to do to treat people as ends. Since Kant's official view is that only morality has real worth, it might seem that we treat people as ends when we act in such a way that they are aided to become moral. But this is far too narrow. One view would be to say that since people have, or rather in Kant's theory are, rational wills, we treat them as ends when we appeal to them on the level of rational decision making. Manipulation—for example, by lying or bullying—is wrong because it is an appeal to confusion, mistake, or fear rather than to reason. We treat people as ends when we respect their capacity to make choices and the choices they freely make.

Another complementary but somewhat broader view would be that we must recognize that people have goals, projects, and lives of their own, which they have a right to lead as much as the next person. Provided that these projects are morally acceptable, I treat people as ends when I recognize their projects as equally valid as are my own, and therefore do not try to put my own goals ahead of theirs, nor try to deflect them from their projects to make them assist me in mine.

SUMMARY

Books on Kant will never end, but this chapter must, so let us summarize Kant's teaching: remember that you are a rational creature and try to respect the reason within you; think for yourself and do not follow the crowd; treat yourself and others with dignity and respect; remember that other people have goals and projects that are just as worthy as your own; take due care not to do what you are not willing for everyone else to do.

Putting these ideas together gives a rather admirable and engaging moral theory, or at least the basis for one. If you are looking for a morality, you could do worse than follow Kant.

REFERENCES AND FURTHER READING

Although Kant is probably the most difficult philosopher a student will be asked to read, if you measure value by cost–benefit ratio (what you learn for the time and effort you put in) rather than by sheer work, there is no philosopher more worth reading.

The Groundwork [Fundamental Principles] of the Metaphysics of Morals (1785) is actually a preliminary version of Kant's great work on ethics, the *Critique of Practical Reason* (1788). There are three English translations, by T. K. Abbot, H. J. Paton, and L. W. Beck; excerpts are widely reprinted. Beck is also a translator of the *Critique* and an excellent commentator on all aspects of Kant's philosophy.

The text (Beck's translation) with essays is edited by Robert Paul Wolf, *Kant: Foundations, Text and Critical Essays* (Indianapolis, IN: Bobbs-Merrill, 1969).

Wolf has also written a commentary, *The Autonomy of Reason: A Commentary on Kant's "Groundwork"* (New York: Harper & Row, 1973).

There are other minor writings by Kant on ethics, notably his *Lectures on Ethics,* trans. by Louis Infield, and reprinted recently in a facsimile edition (New York: Harper & Row, 1969), and the elaborately organized *Metaphysics of Morals.*

H. B. Acton, *Kant's Moral Philosophy* (London: Macmillan, 1970), and W. D. Ross, *Kant's Ethical Theory* (New York: Oxford University Press, 1954) are standard introductions. So is H. J. Paton, *The Categorical Imperative* (Chicago: Chicago University Press, 1948). An excellent commentary is Mary Gregor, *Laws of Freedom* (New York: Barnes & Noble, 1963). Helpful also is Bruce Aune, *Kant's Theory of Morals* (Princeton, NJ: Princeton University Press, 1979).

T. E. Hill, *Dignity and Practical Reason in Kant's Moral Theory* (Ithaca, NY: Cornell University Press, 1992) has many insightful suggestions.

Trenchant criticism of Kant's excessive rationalism is found in Richard Taylor, *Good and Evil* (Buffalo, NY: Prometheus, 1984).

The books by R. M. Hare are *The Language of Morals* (1952; rev. 1961), *Freedom and Reason* (1965), and *Moral Thinking* (1981) (all Oxford University Press), and all are difficult.

Chapter Ten

The Meaning
of Life

More than any other time in history, mankind faces a crossroads. One path leads to despair and utter hopelessness. The other, to total extinction. Let us pray that we have the wisdom to choose correctly.

Woody Allen, "My Speech to the Graduates"

HOW THE QUESTION OF THE
MEANING OF LIFE ARISES

How could anyone question whether life has meaning? Let us see.

1. Sometimes when people are depressed or unhappy they say things like, "My life has no meaning," or, "All the meaning has gone out of my life." This is a way of saying that they see no point in living or that it does not matter to them whether they are alive or dead. Sometimes people think that life has lost its meaning because of some misfortune that has happened to them, such as an unhappy love affair or a career setback. Other times people feel this way after reflecting on some of life's unpleasant features: people get sick, grow old, and die; they suffer from hunger, disasters, and distress; they are misunderstood and their good qualities unrecognized or taken to be something other than they are. In the end, everyone is going to die anyway; when you reflect that your real value as a person is unappreciated in your life and that you are inevitably going to be forgotten after you are dead, you may wonder what the point of anything really is. Why live if you will end up dead and forgotten?

2. Another way of questioning the meaning of life is by reflecting on values. Suppose it is true, as some philosophers think (recall Chapters Two and Five), that values are not real, that they are not objective or "out there," independent of

300

our thinking. In that case, there is no objective truth by which a person ought to live, which justifies one's choices and decisions. Since there is no real reason to do one thing rather than anything else, it might be thought that it does not really matter what happens or what you do. You are more or less at sea, left to your own devices for creating whatever meaning or value your life is to have. The nonexistence of objective values places each of us in a rather difficult situation, at least in the opinion of some philosophers, for we are forced, whether we like it or not, simply to decide what our values will be: each of us must create his or her own fundamental truths, without any hope that the choices made will be the correct ones. But how can choices be made if there is no real guidance, no real reason why you should choose one value over any other, nothing even remotely resembling proof that your decisions will be good, or wise, or moral? You cannot even hope that you might be better off if you choose one set of values as opposed to some other; for it is entirely up to you to decide for yourself what you want to count as being better off. Whatever we choose, it is all meaningless in the sense that it makes no difference, for no choices make any more sense (objectively) than any others. No wonder that existentialists see our condition as characterized by what they call anguish, a special sort of agony of the soul brought on by the encounter with meaninglessness.

The situation thus described can be quite poignant. Suppose you interest yourself in some project or in some cause—for example, raising money to send food to hungry people, or working to eliminate some form of tyranny or oppression somewhere. You then study philosophy and come to the conclusion that there are no objective values, that it makes no difference whatever to the universe whether the people in famine-afflicted countries starve or live, or whether the people living without freedom are oppressed or liberated. Objectively speaking, the goal for which you are striving is no more valid than its opposite, or than any other. If you are at all thoughtful, this philosophical conclusion is very likely going to give you pause: if it really does not matter what happens, why am I trying to accomplish one thing rather than another? Well, no doubt it matters to you, but this answer is not going to be adequate; you will soon ask, why should it matter to me, if it really does not matter objectively? Why should I care what I do, if what I do does not make any real difference? And this kind of questioning is destructive not only of all action, but of all concern as well. If there are no objectively correct values, then in the ultimate sense nothing matters, nothing has any meaning, and nothing is worth being concerned about.

3.   But the meaning of life can be questioned through reflections that may not at all be connected with depression or with philosophical anxiety. People who are thoughtful often wonder whether there is any reason for their lives. Why are we here? What does it all mean? Does life add up to something in the end? Might there be some purpose to life that makes sense of what we are and what we do? Or do we have to conclude that life has no special significance, that it just goes on, leading nowhere and achieving nothing other than its own perpetuation?

These questions ask for what we may call an ultimate justification. We want to know the point or purpose of life, not from our own personal point of view, or even from the point of view (if there is such a point of view) of people in general; we want to know the purpose of life from the point of view of the universe itself. What difference do our lives make in the ultimate scheme of things, the scheme in which sooner or later everything perishes and is forgotten? We all pass through life but once; what we want is some affirmation that somehow it is better that we have lived than not, that something has been gained or accomplished by our brief journey. We do not wish to have lived in vain. We want to find the sense that can be made from our having been alive.

Philosophy and religion are expected to answer all these questions; perhaps it is more correct to say that philosophy and religion began as answers to these questions. Perhaps one difference between philosophy and religion is that religion still claims to answer them, while much philosophy today at most thinks it can investigate or examine such questions without answering them. The enduring popularity of religion, which is always being killed off by philosophers and other skeptical intellectuals only to rise again from its own intellectual ashes, can possibly be explained by the simple fact that people (by which is meant deep thinkers as well as ordinary nonintellectual people) are not satisfied to hear that life has no meaning, or that if it does have meaning, then no one knows what that meaning is. People want life to have meaning, and are willing to accept some point of view that claims to tell them what the meaning of life is. This is why religion seems to be more powerful than skeptical arguments, and why even sophisticated, educated people continue to entertain religious ideas that philosophers have long since exposed to scathing logical critique.

IS THE MEANING OF LIFE A KIND OF KNOWLEDGE?

But suppose you wanted to know what the meaning of life is, what would you want to know? What are people looking for when they look for the meaning of life (MoL), or when they hope that life has a meaning? When we ask a question, we hope to receive an answer, presumably an answer that can be stated in some form of intelligible words, that is, a proposition. So let us begin by asking whether the MoL is something that can be stated in a proposition. This would make the MoL similar to a certain kind of knowledge, that is, to information that can be acquired and passed on to others. According to this view, people who do not know what the MoL is, or wonder about it, lack some piece of information that others possibly possess.

This may seem to make sense, because people want to know what the MoL is, and requests for knowledge seem to be requests for some kind of information. Nevertheless, there are certain difficulties with holding that the MoL is a kind of knowledge. What kind of knowledge would it be? Presumably, whatever this knowledge is, it is valuable; indeed, highly valuable, or perhaps the most valuable knowledge one can learn. Knowledge can be valuable for two reasons: either it is interesting, or it is useful. Thus, astronomy and history are valuable because they are interesting; there is really not a lot of use to which one can put the knowledge that the universe is perhaps 12 billion years old, or that Julius Caesar was murdered by Brutus in the Roman Forum in 44 B.C. On the other hand, cookery and auto mechanics are valuable because they are useful (they may be interesting as well, but perhaps few people would learn cookery if they did not want to cook, or auto mechanics if they did not intend to fix cars). But the MoL cannot be merely interesting because of its evident importance; we expect that knowing the MoL will do something for us, even transform our lives, and not merely satisfy our intellectual curiosity or enlarge our understanding. No one's life is going to be transformed just by learning some new facts about something.

But how can this knowledge be useful? Suppose you discovered the piece of knowledge that constitutes the MoL (suppose someone who knows told it to you). What would you do with this knowledge? What good would it do you to have it? What use would you put it to? Well, one way this knowledge is not useful is in a practical or commercial sense. And that brings us to one of the many bad jokes told about the MoL. It seems that a man went in search of the MoL. He had heard of a wise old sage who lived in a cave high in the Himalayan mountains, and who was reputed to know the secret of the MoL. After months of travel and after overcoming all the usual obstacles, our seeker after knowledge arrived at the sage's cave, inquired what the MoL was, and (in what is an unusual twist for this kind of joke) received an answer. Now he knew the MoL. And so what did he do? He went back to Beverly Hills, wrote a hit song called "The Meaning of Life," and became rich and famous overnight.

Why is this story farcical? The story is correct in supposing that the MoL is something useful to know, but it is wrong in what the usefulness of the knowledge is. It is not knowledge that is commercially valuable; we do not want to know the MoL to sell this knowledge to other people. Knowing the MoL is supposed to be valuable to you in a personal way; the knowledge enhances your life, but not by giving you the chance to get rich. And for the same reason, the knowledge is not valuable in a merely practical sense either. Practical knowledge is valuable because it enables you to achieve your ends; if you do not happen to have those ends, the knowledge is useless to you. Knowing auto mechanics is valuable only if you want to fix cars; it would not be very valuable to people living in a society without automobiles (how valuable is it to you to know how to shoe a horse, or to fix a wagon wheel?). But the knowledge we are talking about is supposed to be valuable no matter what your ends happen to be, since it enables you to see your life in a different way, and to understand what life is all about and why it is worth living.

There certainly can be knowledge that enables you to see your life differently, and that makes your life seem more worth living. Suppose you suffered from the worry that nobody really liked you; or perhaps you are worried and unhappy because you think you are not understanding your philosophy class very well and are probably going to fail. But then you learn something. You find out that you do have some good friends after all; or you take a philosophy test and get a good grade. This knowledge removes a source of anxiety in your life and makes you feel a lot better about everything. You might even think that some meaning has been restored to your life.

But for knowledge to work this way, it has to be fairly clear just what in your life is the source of the anxiety. What do you want that seems to you to be missing? In our examples, it was friends and grades. If the absence of these things makes you feel bad, it is natural that when you learn that the desired things are present, you feel much better. We can specify what knowledge (if you can get it) would remove the anxiety. But suppose you are worried about whether life has any meaning. What is it that you might come to know that would remove that anxiety? Of course, you might come to know all sorts of new information; but which of these facts would count as knowledge of the MoL? How could some fact count as being the MoL? Suppose you discover something truly wonderful, let us say the kind of thing people are often told by religions—for example, that God is love, or that Jesus is your personal savior. Now the question here is not how you might come to know such facts; we will just assume that somehow you really find that they are true. The question is how such knowledge can be the MoL. Of course, if you are looking for a personal savior, then knowing that you have one will make you happy and relieve whatever anxieties you may have felt worrying that perhaps you do not have a personal savior. But even if your worries are relieved on that point, it is not evident why the existence of a personal savior should be the MoL. And we might say the same about any piece of knowledge we acquired: why should *that* fact be the MoL?

This explains why, in those bad MoL jokes in which the sage tells the traveller what the MoL is, he always says something that seems idiotic, such as "Life is a fountain." The point is that no new information could count as the MoL, whether the information is profound or utterly trivial. There is really nothing for the sage to say, not because life has no meaning, but because the MoL is not the kind of thing that can be stated in a proposition or which can be explained from one person to the next. (And so, as the jokes often continue, the traveller is disappointed with the wisdom he has received from the sage: "You mean I've come all the way from Beverly Hills just so you can tell me life is a fountain?" And the sage retorts defensively, "Well, so maybe life isn't a fountain." Or perhaps, more aggressively, "Listen, what do you expect? If I knew the meaning of life, do you think I'd be sitting up here in a cave in the mountains?")

There is another possibility. Perhaps the MoL consists in the kind of knowledge that cannot be explained, stated, or validated. Perhaps the MoL is a kind of knowledge, but the kind you know without being able to say *what* you know. But is there such knowledge? Something like it is perhaps what some people mean by "wisdom," something that the Greek philosophers regarded as the true end of philosophy (a word that means, after all, "love of wisdom"). But what is wisdom? Well, it is something like knowing how to live, not in the biological sense of surviving or staying alive, but in a moral or spiritual sense of knowing what choices to make, of knowing what is important and what is not important in life. Wisdom, as Plato forcefully pointed out, is difficult to attain, partly because there are so many counterfeits offered to us, things that seem attractive, and really are pleasurable and fun, but are really not all that valuable in the end. (As we noted in Chapter Four, Plato likes to draw an analogy with healthy food, which really is good for you but may not be all that pleasant to eat, and pastry and other sweets, which may be pleasant but are not really very good for you. Plato counsels that we avoid the blandishments of pastry chefs and listen to dieticians who know what is healthy to eat; his point is that we have to be equally careful in picking our spiritual advisors.) To be wise, Plato argues, consists in knowing what is truly valuable and what only seems to be valuable, so that we can pursue the good and avoid the counterfeit.

This is probably unobjectionable as far as it goes, but our question is, what kind of knowledge is this wisdom? Plato may or may not have thought that wisdom can be explained or stated: certainly he shows Socrates searching for wisdom by asking people questions, getting them to tell him what they think about important things in life, and then subjecting their ideas to logical analysis; as if, in the end, the most important ideas will have to be validated by logic. So Plato does seem to think that wisdom is something that can be defined in a coherent form of words. And in one of his dialogues, he makes Socrates say that a person who knows something can explain why it is that what he knows is true. Surely dieticians, to make use of Plato's own analogy, know not only what is good, but why it is good, and they can explain this to anyone who inquires. On the other hand, Plato in some of the most famous of his dialogues (the *Republic,* the *Symposium*) also seems to endorse a more mystical view of wisdom, the highest knowledge, suggesting that it consists in an intellectual grasp of some thought that is not capable of being further explained. And he also seems to take the line that once a person attains this knowledge, the knowledge imbeds itself into the soul, so that you automatically come to love it. Thus, this nonpropositional knowledge makes you wise, not only in the intellectual sense of causing you to understand some thought, but in the emotive, motivational sense of causing you to see your life in a different, more meaningful way.

Whatever Plato's own views on the status of the most important kind of knowledge, philosophers ever since Plato have debated whether there can be such a thing as nonpropositional knowledge, knowledge that is simply grasped by the mind even though it cannot be demonstrated, explained, or even stated. This problem takes us far afield from our subject; but we should note here that, even if there is such knowledge, and some people have it, one might wonder how anyone could know they have it: how can a person distinguish between actually having the knowledge, and just thinking (mistakenly) they have it? (This is not to say that there are no methods for attaining such knowledge, but these methods are likely to be non- or extrarational: they are alleged to consist in such techniques as engaging in trance-like meditation, or contemplating inscrutable Zen riddles, or perhaps taking chemical stimulants.) Typically, those who claim there is such knowledge also claim that once you get it, you just know you have it, so the question how you know does not arise; but since there is no question of checking or confirming what you know, it is not easy to see how the possibility of error can be avoided. If there is such knowledge, of course, it is rather pointless to write books about it: if you think you have it and want other people to share it, all you can do is give them some hints about how to go about attaining it. And it is an interesting question how someone who does not yet have the knowledge is going to be able to recognize the people who already do have it: are not all pseudo-gurus, cult leaders, false prophets, messiahs, and other disreputable tricksters, fakers who claim to possess mystical knowledge that they in fact lack (as their gullible followers—who would have profited by reading Plato—often discover too late)?

So it is unlikely that the MoL consists in some piece of knowledge. If the MoL could be stated in a proposition, it is difficult to see how knowing some fact might constitute having meaning in one's life; if the MoL consists in some non-propositional knowledge such as wisdom or knowing how to live, then it is difficult to see how one could know what this is, or how to find it, or whether or not one had actually attained it.

We must return to our bad joke, which turns out to have a certain wisdom after all. For if the MoL really is some fact you can know, then it is indeed hard to see what you can do with this information, other than package it and sell it (or give it away of course, which is what the sage does in the story). Simply knowing that the MoL is X (whatever X may be) will not by itself make your life more meaningful. You may need to know facts to have a meaningful life (a life of ignorance perhaps cannot be very meaningful), but your life does not become meaningful simply because you have picked up a new piece of information. The knowledge has to fit into your life in some way. If the person in our story had been told by the sage that the MoL is to love thy neighbor, the joke would have lost its point, for there would then be something he could do with the knowledge he acquired. But "Love thy neighbor" is neither a fact nor a piece of propositional knowledge. It is an injunction to feel a certain sentiment.

But in that case, what is meant by wisdom? Is there such a thing as knowing how to live and what is important in life? The answer is yes, these are real things and they can be known. But they are not facts that can be stated in propositions. We shall come back to this at the end of the chapter.

IS THE MEANING OF LIFE HAPPINESS?

Let us turn to the question of what someone might lack if he or she felt (or thought) that his or her life lacked meaning. What is missing such that if they had it, they would no longer feel this way? We indicated above that there is a close connection between having no meaning in life and being unhappy. Perhaps these are the same thing? Could it be that someone who thinks that life has no meaning is merely thinking that he or she is unhappy, albeit expressing this in a rather odd way?

It might very well be said that for a person to be happy, his or her life must be meaningful. A person who leads a trivial, meaningless, pointless existence perhaps is not really happy. We should be careful here, however, just because the ingredients of happiness vary so much from one person to another; what may seem a boring and trivial existence to one person may not seem so to another.

Perhaps what we should say is that if a person thinks his or her existence is meaningless and trivial, then that person cannot be happy. But perhaps this is not really saying very much, because thinking that your life is boring and pointless is an expression of dissatisfaction; and of course if you are dissatisfied with your life you cannot be happy, since happiness is, in part, being satisfied with your life. But in any case, even if having meaning is necessary for happiness, it would not be identical with happiness unless it was also enough for happiness, that is, sufficient for happiness.

So is having meaning in your life enough to make you happy? Suppose a person lacks everything else of value in life (whatever that may be). Would that person be happy nonetheless, if only there were meaning in his or her life? Many people might be inclined to answer yes to this. They might think of people who, although their lives seem to lack most of the normal ingredients of happiness, nevertheless have led meaningful lives and are happy. For example, perhaps these people lack romance, adventure, wealth, security, a good job, a loving family, a nice place to live, and yet, at the same time, they have an occupation, perhaps working for some charity or public interest organization, or even doing something personal such as research and study on a subject that interests them (such as the history of baseball or the Kennedy assassination). This occupation seems enough to give their lives meaning, and so to make them happy.

If this were all true, then we could conclude that meaning is both the necessary and sufficient condition for happiness: all happy people have meaningful lives, and all people with meaningful lives are happy. This would show that meaning and happiness always occur together: whenever you have meaning you have happiness, and whenever you have happiness you have meaning. But even so we might not want to say that meaning is the same thing as happiness; they might be two different things that always go together (we would have to explain why this is so; it could not be merely a coincidence). In that case, we would have discovered in a certain sense how to obtain meaning in life: just be happy, and meaning will automatically follow. But we would not have found out what meaning is, which was our original question.

To this point, we have some reason to think that having meaning in one's life is not just another way of saying that one is happy. This conclusion is reinforced when we consider that there are many ways to be unhappy; being unhappy because your life has no meaning, or has lost what meaning it had, is perhaps only one way of being unhappy. Meaninglessness is unhappiness of a special kind, and not unhappiness itself. But in that case, meaning is not sufficient for happiness, though it is perhaps necessary. So perhaps the most we can say is that a person who has meaning in his or her life is not necessarily rendered happy by that fact, but is protected against a special kind of unhappiness, the unhappiness that comes from the feeling that life has lost its meaning. And it is pretty evident that one can be unhappy for many other reasons.

But now we must turn to the question, what actually is lost when life loses its meaning? To be clear what we are trying to identify by this question, let us distinguish between the cause of life's losing its meaning, and the philosophical idea that one comes to hold when one reaches the conclusion that life has lost its meaning. We are interested in the idea, and not in the cause or the reason why one comes to hold this idea. What we want to do is to define or explain the idea that life has no meaning. What is it that life does not have? And a good way to understand this idea is to consider what is said by someone who has actually experienced the loss of meaning, and written about it, as have a number of authors. Perhaps the best and most famous of these is Count Leo Tolstoy (1828–1910), the famous Russian novelist.

Tolstoy's spiritual crisis, or loss of meaning, which he reports in his autobiographical *Confession,* occurred when he was in his mid-fifties, and at the height of his fame and powers. *War and Peace* and *Anna Karenina* had established him as the leading European novelist of his day; he could confidently say to himself that his name was known throughout the world and that his reputation would endure as long as people read books. He was rich; he was blessed with physical strength and health; his mental powers were inexhaustible; and, furthermore, he enjoyed a loving family to whom he was devoted. And in the midst of all this extraordinary good fortune, gradually the meaning went out of his life, and he began to feel as if all of this was as nothing to him, and that all he had accomplished, all that he was yet to accomplish, were of no value to him whatever.

Why? Because he began to reflect on death. He imagined that a man is like a traveller lost in a vast desert. The traveller falls into a deep pit, at the bottom of which is a monster waiting to devour him. He clutches at a little twig growing on the side of the pit, and so momentarily saves himself from the monster. But then he notices that two mice, one black and one white, are gnawing at the twig to which he clutches. So do we precariously cling to life, but time, represented by the two mice of night and day, inevitably draws us to our end. Soon, Tolstoy reflects, all his friends will be gone; one day his children too will die; and he himself must come to an end, leaving nothing but "stench and worms."

In the face of the inevitability of death, says Tolstoy, there are only four possible responses. The first is to ignore the problem, living in a condition of blissful ignorance reminiscent of Adam and Eve before the Fall. (Animals are enviable in that they seem to be unaware of the fact that they will die.) This is not, however, really possible for any intelligent human. The second is to admit the problem but simply go through the motions of life, acting as if what you did will make some difference, even though you know it will not. Perhaps most people live their lives trying to pretend that their life really matters, even though they know it does not. There is a certain nobility to this but on the whole it is a pretty desperate solution. A third possibility is to devote yourself to pleasure; if you are going to die anyway, you might as well have as good a time as possible while you are still around. This was the solution Tolstoy saw in his intellectual friends, who passed their time in witty and intelligent conversation that Tolstoy saw as the equivalent of idle amusements; it is not a solution so much as a running away from the problem. The fourth possibility is suicide; since there is no point to living, one very logical solution is to bring life to an end. Most people, however, are too afraid of death to take this seriously as a possible option.

None of these responses is really acceptable. So what is a person to do? What is the correct response to the inevitability of death? Tolstoy finds the answer in faith. What is needed is to reestablish meaning in life, and this cannot be done by intellect; there is no intellectual or philosophical answer that can restore meaning. Therefore, it is necessary to achieve religious faith—but not, Tolstoy believes, the complicated overintellectualized faith of theologians, who think that doctrinal answers can be given to the problem of meaning, but what Tolstoy regards as the simple, unspoiled faith of unlettered peasants, who simply know that God's love makes everything all right in the end. Without this faith, however (and Tolstoy's intellectual friends did not have it), then one might as well either adopt a life devoted to pleasure, or kill oneself. There is really no other possibility.

What should we think of this? Tolstoy's analysis of the situation, given the hypothesis that the fact of death makes life lose its meaning, is quite acute. What can you do once your life has lost its meaning, other than kill yourself, or pretend not to notice, or try to escape your unhappiness in constant pleasure? Because of this, as the French existential philosopher Albert Camus (1913–1960) once said, the problem of suicide is the central problem of philosophy; either philosophy proves that there really is meaning in life, or suicide appears to be the only logical answer. (Camus, who did not think faith was possible for thinking people, held that philosophy could not find an answer; but, as we will see, he thought there was nonetheless an alternative to suicide.) Religious people, as already noted, would agree with Tolstoy that the answer lies in faith, although Tolstoy does not explain how such faith is to be achieved, or why it should not be regarded as simply one more form of escapism. But the main question Tolstoy's crisis raises is whether he was correct in concluding that the knowledge of death does take the meaning out of life. And a very simple argument shows that he was not correct. We call this "the death argument."

THE DEATH ARGUMENT

Death is a scary subject. Most people do not look forward to death, and wish to postpone it as long as possible; thinking about death, whether their own or the death of others close to them, is a depressing exercise for normal people. At the same time, sensible people might feel that Tolstoy's view of death is obsessive, morbid, and entirely unnecessary. Their response to him might be that, of course, everyone is going to die; so what else is new? But this is not entirely fair, for Tolstoy's claim is that the person who avoids thinking about death or goes on with normal life knowing that he or she will surely die, is practicing a form of escapism that Tolstoy finds unappealing. What is needed to answer Tolstoy is an argument that shows that death is not destructive of meaning, that one can rationally acknowledge death and still have a meaningful life. Fortunately, such an argument exists.

Tolstoy's basic claim is that the fact of death makes all of life meaningless. To make out this assertion, he must hold that apart from death, life would be good; but the badness of death overcomes or cancels the goodness of life.

But the **death argument** shows that this is a very bad point. This argument is simplicity itself. It begins with an understanding of death: death is nothing but the annihilation of life. But if that is the case, it follows immediately that if death is bad, it must be the case that life is good. And therefore, it cannot be true that the badness of death takes away from the goodness of life and renders life bad as well. Hence, Tolstoy (and he is not alone in making this argument) is simply mistaken in arguing that the fact that you will die makes life not worth living.

The reader will see that the death argument depends on the claim that death is nothing but the termination of life. Death is not a reality in itself; it is a mere nothingness, as darkness may be said to be the absence of light (or as evil is sometimes, by certain metaphysicians, said to be the absence of good). If death were a positive reality in itself, the death argument would not work, because it might be the case that a bad positive reality might remove or cancel the goodness in a different, good, positive reality (as a fire that is "bad" can destroy a house that is "good"). But as death is nothing in itself, its badness must consist only in the termination of something else; this termination could not be bad unless the thing terminated (life) were good. Therefore, the badness of death can never be used to prove that life also is bad. On the contrary, the badness of death proves that life is good.

And this conclusion is in accord with common sense. Why do we fear death? True, some people fear death because they understand death other than as a mere absence or termination of life; they see death as a destination, or a journey, or a kind of new life, which has special horrors of its own. But apart from these philosophical-religious views, we dislike death precisely because we do not want life to end. We do not fear death as something bad in itself. People do not want to die; but this is not because death is something they do not want to have, but because life is something they do not want to lose.

So far, we have agreed with Tolstoy that death is bad. But even this point can be challenged. Classically, Epicurus (died 270 B.C.) argued against the fear of death as follows. Do not fear death, he taught: for when you are, death is not; and when death is, you are not. Therefore, death cannot harm you.

Epicurus' argument is clever, but not convincing; he seems to waver between regarding death as nothing but the absence of life, and regarding death as something positive in itself. His premises seem to assume that death is nothing but the absence of life (when death is, you are not). But his conclusion (death cannot harm you) seems to regard death as a positive thing that might be harmful. He overlooks that what is "harmful" about death is what he has stated in his second premise: when death is, you are not. It is the absence of you—your total annihilation—that you regard as a harm, or more properly as the worst possible form of harm. So although Epicurus is correct in holding that death cannot cause you harm, he is wrong in concluding that there is nothing harmful about death. Death itself is harmful, in that what death is, a person's total nonexistence, is itself harmful. (But even this way of putting it is a bit odd, since calling something harmful implies that there is someone present who is harmed by the thing. In the case of death, the harm consists precisely in the person being no longer present.)

But there are other grounds for considering that death is not the evil it is made out to be. For consider the alternative. If there were no death, we would all live forever. Eternal life is usually regarded as something good, indeed wonderful. Religions attract multitudes by promising them eternal life, as if it were just obvious that such a thing is what we all want. But would eternal life be so wonderful? "Eternal" means infinite; to say we shall live eternally or forever is to say that we shall have an infinite amount of time at our disposal in the future. What are we going to do to fill that time? If you assume that the number of different things any person can do is finite, it follows that sooner or later we shall have done everything that can possibly be done. (Think of this concretely. Suppose you wanted to read every book ever written. The number of books, however large, is necessarily finite; there cannot be an infinite number of real books. So sooner or later you will have read them all. What do you read next?) Once we have done everything possible, we will still have infinite time ahead of us, which we shall have to fill somehow. There will be nothing to do other than to repeat what we have already done; and once we have repeated everything, we shall have to repeat it again, and so on, without end. This does not sound like such a wonderful thing; actually, eternal life seems rather boring, the same things endlessly repeated. (As an alternative, one might just sit there doing nothing for all eternity. This seems even more boring.)

People fail to notice this because they think that living in eternity is different from living here on earth. In eternity, it is held, you will sit at the right hand of God, enjoying eternal blessedness (assuming no different fate is in store for you). And eternal blessedness could not be boring. No doubt this is true, but it is true only by definition; eternal blessedness is not boring simply because we define eternal blessedness as a nonboring condition. But in fact we have no conception whatever of a permanent nonboring condition; in our experience, everything gets boring sooner or later if we have too much of it. In life as we know it, we require variety to maintain our interest in things. It is true that, for all anybody knows, eternity might be completely different from life as we know it; but life as we know it is the only standard we have by which to judge anything. And by this standard, eternity is not terribly attractive. To hold that eternal life is attractive, therefore, is simply to assert, without really comprehending, that eternity is completely different from anything we ever experience on earth. This is a pure question of faith; eternity as we can understand it is apt to be boring, but if someone wants to hope for an incomprehensible eternity that is not boring, logic alone cannot rule this out.

There is another point about death. If we really did have all eternity before us, we might never actually do anything. This is because as we actually are, we require the pressure of time to help us accomplish things. If we really could put everything off until tomorrow, we probably would; but as life is short, we know that what does not get done today may not get done at all. However, in eternity life is not short, and there is no reason not to put things off until tomorrow, so we might well pass all eternity postponing things we really feel like eventually doing.

Hence, we have a dilemma. We like life, so we do not want to die. At the same time, we do not want to live forever (or we would not if the above arguments were convincing), and the only way to avoid this is to die. The dilemma is that both alternatives are undesirable; dying is bad because life is good, and not dying is bad because living forever is not good. So, finally, perhaps the best thing to say is this: life is good, but living forever is not good, so death is necessary sooner or later; but the best thing would be later rather than sooner.

All of the above assumes our definition of death as the complete absence of life, that is, of biological and conscious processes. Death is a negation, not a positive entity in itself. This point is, however, not so clear to many people who think death is a positive reality. An expression of that idea was put by Shakespeare into the mouth of Claudio, a character in *Measure for Measure* (III, i, 118):

> "... *to die, and go we know not where,*
> . . . .
> *To bathe in fiery floods, or to reside*
> *In thrilling region of thick-ribbèd ice—*
> *To be imprison'd in the viewless winds,*
> *And blown with restless violence round about*
> *The pendent world, or to be worse than worst*
> *Of those that lawless and incertain thought*
> *Imagine howling— 'tis too horrible!*
> *The weariest and most loathèd worldly life*
> *That age, ache, penury, and imprisonment*
> *Can lay on nature is a paradise*
> *To what we fear of death.*

To which Isabella replies: "Alas, alas!"

Though Isabella might better grieve over Claudio's bad philosophy, he is not alone: that death is not merely the extinction of life is such a strong thought that it has even been asserted by certain philosophers who seem to want to make out that death is something, a kind of positive reality in its own right. The best known of these philosophers is the German crypto-Nazi, Martin Heidegger (1889–1976). Heidegger argues, although in the most obscure and confused way imaginable, that all of life is a progress toward death. Death is the reality that each of us must face; therefore, we must understand its nature. The attempt to understand death is the great problem of life; unfortunately, however, the only way to understand death is to die, at which time it is too late. So life is necessarily tragic, infected, so to speak, with the need to understand something that by its nature is incomprehensible to us.

This is a problem, however, only if death is thought of as a mysterious, incomprehensible reality. If death is the mere negation of life, then there is nothing incomprehensible about it: when we are dead, we simply will no longer be alive. Even if Heidegger is right in asserting that it is very important to understand this, he is wrong in claiming that there is some deep mystery about it. Further, if there is a tragedy about death, Heidegger has misunderstood what that tragedy is. The fact about death is that we do not want to die—yet death is inevitable. So sooner or later something will happen to us that we very much prefer to avoid. If there is a tragedy in this, it is quite the opposite of what Heidegger thinks. The tragedy is not that we want to understand what death is, but cannot; the tragedy is that we understand only too well what death is—the permanent extinction of each of us—and do not like it at all.

On this subject then, perhaps the last words should be granted to David Hume, who, lucid as ever on his deathbed, said that he was no more unhappy to think that he would not exist after his life was over than he was to think that he had not existed before it began. Or as a contemporary philosopher, A. J. Ayer, puts it, "Why should it worry me more, if at all, that I shall not be alive in the year 2050 than that I was not alive in the year 1850? The way things are going, the latter . . . might well prove the better time to have lived. In the very long . . . history of the universe, there is a relatively minute period that contains my life. . . . [W]hy should it matter to me at what points . . . this minute stretch begins and ceases?"

REPETITIVE POINTLESSNESS, ULTIMATE INSIGNIFICANCE, AND ABSURDITY

Given the above observations, the claim that death renders life tragic or meaningless seems much exaggerated. What other reflections might lead someone to conclude that life is meaningless? We shall note three that are quite commonly made: repetitive pointlessness, ultimate insignificance, and absurdity.

Repetitive Pointlessness   That life is, in the end, nothing but pointless repetition, is illustrated in a famous essay by Camus, who draws on the Greek myth of Sisyphus. This ancient hero sinned against the gods by stealing their secrets (in one version, Sisyphus learned how to escape death). For this the gods condemned him to spend all eternity pushing a large boulder to the top of a hill. After Sisyphus pushed the boulder to the top, it would roll down again, and so on without cease. It is the pointless repetitiveness of Sisyphus' task that Camus takes to be illustrative of the condition of human life: we are all condemned to pass our lives in endless repetitive labor that leads nowhere and accomplishes nothing. Sisyphus is supposed to exemplify the human condition, a kind of mythical prototype of the middle-level manager type, forever caught in the rat race: freeway, office, freeway, dinner, bed, and then the same process the following day. Or we might say the same about the factory worker, or the store clerk, or for that matter even the college student!

There are two aspects to Sisyphus' ordeal: *repetitiveness* and *pointlessness*. In some moods, anyone can think of his or her life as Sisyphus-like in both these aspects: there is plenty of repetitiveness in anyone's life, and many people can truly ask themselves, where does it all lead and what will it get me? "After years of going to the office day after day, you retire and die and so what?" one might easily ask when reflecting on the meaning of life. It has perhaps been fairly said that "Life isn't one damn thing after another; it's the same damn thing over and over again." Yet at the same time, perhaps few people's lives are absent of all variation and interest; we have already noted that variety is an important ingredient in a happy life, and most people are able to arrange things so that at least some variation in the dull routine manages to creep in from time to time. As for pointlessness, it all depends on what one counts as giving a point to life; most people do have goals at which they aim, such as attaining an education, developing a career, raising a family, and so on; and achieving these goals, or even striving toward them, gives their lives some point. So there are two problems with the story of Sisyphus. First, it is not really an accurate description of the lives of many people, and hence cannot be taken as an encapsulation of the human condition, or of human life as such. It is true, perhaps, that some people's lives resemble the life of Sisyphus, and no doubt these people are unhappy because their lives lack meaning, but all this shows is something to be avoided. And indeed, "Do not live like Sisyphus if you can avoid it!" is a fairly obvious sort of injunction.

The second problem is that the story does not specify what would count as *not* leading a life of repetitive pointlessness. This is an important failure in philosophical attempts to characterize human life as generally unhappy, meaningless, and disappointing. If, like Camus and many other philosophers, you are going to hold that human life is essentially characterized by some undesirable quality such as pointlessness, you must specify what would count as life's having a point, and then explain why no one's life can attain this. Camus, as other philosophers, fails even to consider this. Take Camus' own life. He wrote novels and essays, became famous, won the Nobel Prize, and died in a car crash at the age of 47. His books are still read today, translated into almost all languages. So did Camus consider his own life Sisyphus-like by being pointless? Well, maybe he did; but then, what would he count as life having a point? For most people, a life like Camus', apart from the tragic early death, would seem quite satisfactory. If it did not satisfy Camus, what would have satisfied him? The point is not to argue about how much success is enough, but to note that either Camus can specify what would count as life having a point, or he cannot. If he can, then he cannot really prove that no life can attain whatever it takes to give life a point. Set the standards too high, and few people will be able to attain them; but if you set the standards so high that nobody can attain them, it might be asked whether such high standards are not arbitrary and too personal. Why should everybody be bound by your high standards?

On the other hand, if you simply refuse or fail to specify what would count as a life having a point, simply saying that nothing can possibly give life a point, no matter what achievement or success, then you are guilty of proving your case by asserting it. For if there is nothing that can give life a point, then of course life will not have a point; but that is a tautology. The "if" proposition has to be proved. What you have to show is why there is nothing that can give life a point; why what most people ordinarily regard as giving life a point (for example, achieving certain goals or a reasonable level of happiness) really is not a point after all. In other words, you have to show that every life, no matter what, is really no different from that of Sisyphus. Or even stronger: that no life would be any different from that of Sisyphus, no matter what that life contained.

The problem we have been noticing can be illustrated by reference to the German philosopher, Arthur Schopenhauer (1788–1860), who attempted to establish pessimism as a philosophy. All human life, he thought, swings between desire and satisfaction. When we desire something, we are unhappy because we do not have it; when we get it, we are bored because our desire has been satisfied and there is nothing to do but wait for the next desire to come along. Hence, human life is miserable. Schopenhauer therefore counsels nirvana, or the extinction of all desire, which comes very close to the extinction of life itself.

The problem with this analysis of human misery is this. Of course it may be true that some desires, when you have satisfied them, leave you feeling bored. This is the case of those desires that are, in a sense, false: the person did not really want the thing he thought he wanted, or did not want it as much as he thought he did, so when he achieves it, he is not satisfied. But what is Schopenhauer's proof that all desires are like this? Why cannot there be a desire such that, when you get what you desire, you are content, and not bored? Schopenhauer seems simply to define a desire as that which, when satisfied, leaves you bored; which is another case of proving the proposition by assertion and not by evidence. His view is that nothing can count as real satisfaction. But he has not explained what real satisfaction would be, so as to then show why nothing can attain it.

Now in fairness to Camus, it should be noted that his intention is not necessarily to claim that the Sisyphus story is the model or type of all human existence (he is not very clear on whether he holds this or not). Rather, his main interest is in recommending what would count as an acceptable (to him, and presumably, to the reader as well) response to anyone who was in the Sisyphusean situation. What is this? It is *defiance*. Sisyphus is doomed, but as Camus sees it, he need not reconcile himself to this doom. Bloodied but unbowed, Sisyphus performs his endless task, refusing to accept with his will what he must accept in his outward behavior.

Camus' idea, crudely put, is that what gives meaning to life is not what kind of life one leads—for any kind of life amounts to the same pointless repetitiveness—but the spirit in which the life is led. The meaning of life comes not from the life that is lived, but from the frame of mind in which it is lived. But not any old frame of mind will give life meaning, it appears. Fate, Camus seems to think, is cruel; this is the overwhelming fact that cannot be escaped. The question then becomes, not what you will do about it, but what attitude you will take toward it. A person who meekly or humbly accepts his or her fate, a person whose attitude is one of resignation and compliance before the inevitable (the will of Allah, as Muslims say), Camus strongly suggests, has a life which, for that very reason, is deprived of meaning, that is to say, is deprived of all the meaning a human life can have. Meaning comes from defiance of fate.

The reader will recognize here the underlying view of the Romantic hero: never give up, fight on against the odds, and never admit defeat. Camus would have made a great football coach, except that the coach expects to win the game and Camus begins by acknowledging that the game cannot be won. The question here is not whether the attitude of defiance Camus recommends is an attractive one—this you can decide for yourself—but whether such an attitude is sufficient to make an otherwise pointless life in some way meaningful. If by meaningful we mean, roughly, worth living, then perhaps you may wonder whether any life as dreary as Sisyphus' can be made worth living, no matter what attitude one takes toward it. But perhaps Camus is saying no more than that this is the best we humans can do.

Ultimate Insignificance   The notion that, from the objective point of view, life is pretty bleak, but that some modicum of salvation can be found if one adopts the correct attitude—this is in a way the essence of Romantic heroics— seems to be less appealing now than it once was. There are, of course, many variations on the same basic theme. The English philosopher Bertrand Russell (1876–1972), for example, one of the most important philosophers and social thinkers of the twentieth century and one of the most intelligent people who ever lived (judging by his incredible store of knowledge and his vast output of books and articles), at one point in his life expressed his own version of Romantic heroics from a standpoint quite different from that of Camus. Russell points out that science, and in particular astronomy, makes clear that *human life is of total insignificance.* In the context of the vast scale of the universe, humans, who came into existence as the accidental result of forces beyond our control, may be seen as little specks of protoplasm scurrying around on the surface of a very minor planet in a very minor solar system in one of the billions and billions of galaxies that form the universe. The chance configuration of forces that allowed this bit of life to come into existence will soon enough, on the astronomical time scale, destroy it, and all that it has created, leaving no trace behind. Russell, in his own bit of imagery, regards human life as a kind of joke God and the devil have created for their own amusement; soon they will get tired of watching the human comedy and will eradicate it, turning to other amusements. This idea that life is a bad joke played by God—or somebody—on us who are its victims, is a powerful expression of a certain mood brought about by reflecting on the ultimate insignificance of everything we humans value and would wish to preserve.

Like Camus, Russell holds that what is important is what you do with this basic insight. But Russell's argument is actually much deeper and more sophisticated than Camus'. There are certain ideals that humans have created and which we value above all: truth, love, and art, for example. The important thing in the face of insignificance is to cherish and preserve these ideals as best we can. To abandon oneself to despair or dismay is the real defeat, just as a shallow optimism, a naive faith that things really do matter somehow in the end, is simply a way of pretending the problem does not exist. In particular in mathematics, which Russell throughout his long life seems to have regarded as ultimate truth and beauty combined, we are able to apprehend in a way something truly eternal, and thus to a certain (limited and metaphorical) extent escape total destruction. We can at least glimpse the imperishable, though we cannot avoid perishing.

Readers will recognize in all this what the French call a *cri de coeur,* a certain plaintive cry: we are so insignificant! And so we are. In the great scheme of things, humans just do not count for very much. Look up at the sky on a clear, star-filled night. It is vast, and we are tiny. Or stand on the shore of the ocean and experience the same effect. But, one might ask in a crude sort of way, so what? Why should any of this make any difference? Well, think of an insect. There is nothing more insignificant. If that particular insect had never lived—if you end its life prematurely by squishing it—absolutely no difference would be made to anyone or anything; even the other insects will not notice. The thought that a person's life—any person's—is no more significant than an insect's, is worrisome to some people.

But why should it be? The question is, what do people want who have this worry? What would make them think that our lives were not insignificant? If the problem is the sheer size of the universe, then consider this thought experiment. Suppose the rest of the universe simply did not exist. Everything else would be the same, including all of human life (although a few astrophysicists would need to find other employment). Then the earth and its inhabitants would not be an insignificant part of a vast universe; we would *be* the universe. Would this make anyone feel better?

Why should it? How would the absence of the universe add meaning to our lives? And if it cannot, then why should the presence of the universe take the meaning away?

Of course, there is another sense in which someone might worry about being insignificant. A person might worry that he himself, personally, is insignificant. He might wish that he were famous, or very important (the President of the United States, or Albert Einstein, or somebody like that), and feel bad that he is not and probably will never be. Obviously, in a sense such a worry is foolish, since by definition very few—amazingly few—people can ever become important or famous. (If there were 10,000 important Americans, they would constitute approximately 0.003 percent of the entire U.S. population. Anybody's chance of becoming one of them would be 1/30,000.) So to have such an ambition and to make the meaning of your life depend on its fulfillment is a very risky gamble. But in any case, this is a different point about meaning than the point we have been examining. Wanting to become famous or important is an ambition some-one might have, and we have already noted that meaning—in the sense of happi-ness, or feeling that your life is or has been worthwhile—depends in part on set-ting and achieving goals. Whether being famous is a wise goal to set can be left for a later discussion.

Absurdity The third idea that is said to take the meaning from life is that *life is absurd.* The absurdity of life, or of existence, has been a favorite theme of exis-tential philosophy as well as various kinds of absurdist literature and art. Absurdity means that life is irrational or makes no sense. There are two different reactions to this basic insight. Existentialist philosophers emphasize the tragic side of absurdity: the basic meaningless of life produces anxiety, a sense of the abyss, of being adrift without guidance, of disconnectedness, of the basic horror in everything. Some, such as Jean-Paul Sartre (1905–1980), hold that because there are no values, no meaning, even no truth, people have absolute freedom, and are therefore, faced with the almost intolerable burden of creating values and making choices without guidance or support. Any attempt to look outside the individual for guidance—to history, to religion, to culture, to philosophy, even to your friends or spiritual counselor—Sartre regards as an escape from the basic freedom of choice each individual faces. There is, as some philosophers put it, no appeal from the choices one makes: no confirmation or validation that one has done the right thing. We are left helplessly groping in the dark. This lonely groping in the dark fills existentialists with dread.

The other sense of absurdity is that life is basically ridiculous, not a tragedy but a farce. It is as if one lived in a Woody Allen movie, playing the Woody Allen character. Nothing ever goes right, nothing means what you think it means, your best efforts turn into preposterous near misses, just when you think you have everything figured out and under control some trivial event sends you spinning. It would be funny if it were not happening to you; and even you can see how ridiculous it all is. A famous artist, Marcel Duchamps, once exhibited a toilet bowl in an art show. "I am ridiculous," he was saying, "but I am not any more ridiculous than you are, with your pretensions to great art and deep meaning. All of life—all of art, all of philosophy—is absurd, and we only pretend that there are deep truths revealed to us by art, literature and the rest of high culture. Like a group of people trying to run in a field of mud, we are all ridiculous. Self-mockery is the only honest response to life."

To summarize: we see that there are many possible responses to the presumed meaningless of life: suicide, pleasure, or going through the motions, as Tolstoy said, but also defiance, upholding our ideals, honest acceptance, sheer terror, self-mockery, and perhaps others as well. But is it really necessary to accept that life has no meaning? What would we have to think to conclude that maybe life does have meaning after all?

"BIG PICTURE" MEANING AND FAITH

The previous discussion leads us to the following point. One way in which life is said to attain meaning is by being part of some larger scheme of things. We call this "big picture" meaning. Those who think life has no meaning think that there is no big picture of which our lives are a part. To the question, "What does it all mean, and what is the purpose of it all?" they respond that it all means nothing whatever; and, there is no purpose to it all ("it" being human life, life in general, the entire universe, or whatever you please). There is no meaning to life, because there is no purpose, no larger picture, no ultimate reason, of which our lives are a part and which would give them some point. So, the basic idea here seems to be that if there were a big picture or some basic scheme of things, life would have meaning after all; but, unfortunately, there is not. Or is there?

Let us see how the big picture might give life meaning. Take some familiar examples: team sports, for instance. Were you to observe a player on a team, let us say the shortstop on a baseball team, if you did not know baseball you would probably think his actions were totally screwy and meaningless. He runs this way and that, tries to catch the ball, sometimes throws the ball and sometimes does not, runs to the base and takes a throw from another player . . . all perfectly unintelligible, unless you know that what you are watching is a baseball game, and that the shortstop is playing his position according to the rules of the game. When you understand what the game is all about, then everything the shortstop does makes sense. You understand his role in the game, and how what he does contributes to his team's success. In other words, once you grasp the big picture, that is, the purpose of the game and the player's role in the game, you understand the meaning of the player's actions.

Another example might be the army. No soldier ever knows what is going on, and no soldier has very much significance all alone. Any individual soldier is entirely replaceable since there are millions of others exactly the same. Yet each has a role, however small, to play in the military scheme of things. If you eliminated any given soldier, not much would be different, and the army would go on as before. But if you eliminate enough individual soldiers, the army cannot function and will be defeated. So while each soldier may seem insignificant, when you add up all the tiny units you wind up with a very important total. So both the importance and the meaning of each individual can be understood by reference to some big picture of which each is a part. The big picture tells us the purpose of what they are doing, the reason for it, and the end it serves. It makes their actions intelligible. And the same could be true for any kind of organized enterprise in which people engage, whether it be a business, a political party, a public interest organization, and so on. Each person's actions make sense only in the context of the large scheme of things.

Someone who does not see the big picture might very well think that the individual's actions are pointless. And so they would be, taken out of context. Often, as in the army, the individuals themselves do not see the big picture, and so do not understand why they are doing what they are told to do. They may well think that what they are doing is meaningless and stupid. But, at least if the army is well run, in actual fact there is a big picture to which they are contributing.

Let us look at this more closely. What do we want a big picture theory of meaning to do for us? The following:

1. It must explain the purpose of human life.

2. It must enable anyone to explain the major events in his or her life by reference to this purpose.

3. It must justify suffering (including death), that is, show how or why suffering contributes to the purpose and is necessary in the larger scheme of things.

4. It must explain the purpose of life in a way that seems good; that is, it must reconcile us to the end of life.

Any big picture theory is going to proceed by telling some kind of a story, but not any story will satisfy all four criteria. For example, suppose the story is this:

there is a race of Superbeings who are making a journey through the universe. By wise preordination, the gods have provided the Super-race with resting points where they can refresh themselves and restore their provisions. One such resting place is earth. As the gods must work through the laws of nature, all of evolution has been allowed to happen so that when the Super-race arrives, there will be ample food so they may continue on their journey. The food will be the top of the natural food chain, namely, us. We are here to provide food for the Super-race on the next stage of their journey. Our duty is to wait, reproduce, and maintain ourselves in sufficient numbers so that there will be ample food. For hundreds and thousands of (earth) years, the human race did not multiply fast enough. So the gods enabled us to develop science, technology, and industrial civilization so that there would be enough of us when the time comes. We have become so adept at multiplying that we now double our numbers every twenty years or so. As the earth cannot sustain such increases indefinitely, the gods have arranged things so that when the carrying capacity of the earth reaches its limit, the Super-race will arrive. We do not know when this will be (we do not know how many human beings the earth can sustain; all previous predictions have turned out to be wild underestimations), although many local strains on the earth's capacity have begun to appear. But it cannot be too far distant; perhaps a hundred years, perhaps a thousand.

Is this far-fetched? Suppose you are a wise old tuna fish, trying to explain the purpose of tuna life. Might not you tell such a tale, with human beings taking the place of the Super-race? (Human beings would be the Super-race from the standpoint of tuna fish.)

This story satisfies the first criterion, and with a little imaginative elaboration, could be improved to satisfy the second and third criteria as well. But it does not satisfy the fourth criterion, since it is not a story that human beings like. It does not provide us with a meaning to which we can be reconciled; to be food for a Super-race is not what we have in mind when we demand to know why we are here. This is not very good for us. We do not come out ahead in the end; we have nothing to gain, however glorious it may be to make a contribution to the progress of superior beings.

The reason that a big picture must satisfy the fourth criterion has been suggested earlier in this chapter. There we saw that the desire that life have meaning was in part a desire that life have some sort of ultimate justification. But now we see that it is not enough that your mere existence be justified, but that your values, hopes, and fondest ambitions be justified as well. This means that what you want from the big picture is that your values be proved to be acceptable in the larger scheme of things. The fourth criterion in effect guarantees that the big picture will do this. And since most people do not value the destruction of the human race, or that the human race be used for the benefit of some other sort of being, the story we told will not be appealing as a big picture giving the meaning of life.

One story that does satisfy the fourth criterion, as well as the other three, is religion, and notably orthodox Judeo-Christian religion. This tells a story in which human beings come out very well, defeating Satan and enjoying eternal blessedness at the right hand of God. We could not possibly ask for a better ending. Almost by definition of good ending, in fact, the religious story promises the best possible ending there could be: the righteous enjoy eternal bliss, and the wicked are doomed to their just reward. Nothing could better satisfy our deepest wishes.

Any big picture depends on faith, for there is evidently no way of proving by reason that the story told by the big picture is true. So the next question is, how much of the picture does one have to believe in order to believe enough to think that life has a meaning? And the answer is, not very much; in fact, one need not believe any of the details of the big picture at all, so long as one believes that there is a big picture. To understand this, imagine you have a ticket to a play: you have no idea what this play is about, but you have heard that it is excellent and you know the author is a famous playwright. Unfortunately, by bad luck you are late and do not arrive at the theater until the first act is well under way, with the result that you cannot understand what is happening. Who are these people and what are they doing, you keep thinking as the action unfolds. Even worse luck, your pager goes off just before the last act comes to an end, and you have to leave the theater before the dénouement. Consequently, you never come close to figuring out what the play was all about. But do you assume it had no meaning? On the contrary, you might well assume there must be a meaning. You have great confidence that the author would not write a meaningless, totally stupid play; and you also suspect that the author is a lot smarter than you are, so perhaps the meaning is disguised and difficult to understand. You might even think that there might be more than one meaning to the play; perhaps the author meant the play to have several meanings, so that different viewers could understand the play in different ways depending on their own points of view, and all of these interpretations might be correct. Since you have not seen enough of the play, you cannot prove that the play has any meaning at all; it might be just a jumble, a terribly constructed piece of work that the other members of the audience pretend to like because they are bedazzled by the reputation of the author. But you have great faith that this is not the case.

And perhaps life is like that. Clearly, we cannot prove it is; but can anyone really prove it is not? Perhaps there is a big picture that simply is beyond our grasp: life has meaning, all right, but no one can really figure out what that meaning is. And this is another reason why the wise gurus in the MoL jokes never give an intelligible answer. The gurus know the deepest truth anyone can know, which is that the deepest truth that exists is not a truth anyone can know. When the oracle tells Socrates he is the wisest person in Greece, Socrates, who thinks he knows nothing worth knowing, understands the oracle to mean that at least he, Socrates, knows that he knows nothing; whereas most of the other Greeks imagined, falsely, they knew something important. Like the gurus in the stories, Socrates was wise because he knew that he did not know, which is all the wisdom it is possible to have.

It is for this reason that many people believe that faith is necessary if life is to have meaning. Since they also hold that without meaning, life is not worth living, they conclude that it is faith that makes life worth living. Without faith, life is barely tolerable, everything becomes valueless, and activities lose their point. To avoid this unhappy conclusion, thinkers such as Tolstoy argue that we must believe in some meaning, even if we cannot understand what that meaning is. This argument is perhaps the most persuasive argument possible for religion; for though religions postulate entities and principles that many people find impossible to accept in today's logical and scientific world, the importance of religion is that it gives people something to believe in, namely, that life makes sense and that there is some ultimate justification after all.

The analogy with a play may seem to support the faith argument—how can you enjoy the play unless you have faith that it means something?— but only up to a point, for our confidence in the playwright is not based on faith alone but on the experience of other playgoers who are familiar with the author's work, including the play in question. They know that the work makes sense, from experience. But by the definition of our problem, no one has any experience that the author's work makes sense or has any meaning whatever; we are all basing our confidence in the author on faith. But many people will not find it intelligible to believe in something while at the same time admitting there is not the slightest reason to believe in it. Such a faith can be justified only by practical necessity—the choice between faith or the abyss—but such practical necessity, however compelling, some people do not regard as possible grounds for belief. You cannot believe something just because it is better for you to believe it; you also need evidence that it is true, which is lacking in the present case.

Another difficulty with the faith solution is that it may seem that having faith in an unknowable meaning to life is utterly pointless: what good does it do you to believe that life has a meaning if you must remain totally ignorant of what that meaning is? Indeed, some skeptic might wonder, how does such a belief differ from no belief at all? Both believing that life has a meaning and believing that life has no meaning would seem to come to the same thing, if you have no idea what the meaning might be. Believing that some unknowable meaning exists cannot possibly make a difference in what you do, or in what you expect to get out of life: if the meaning is unknowable, you cannot know what it tells you to do or what will happen to you or for you if you do one thing or some other thing. Your actions are exactly the same as if you did not hold the belief; the belief makes no difference to your life, and so there is no difference between you and the person who does not hold the belief in the first place. Your faith is totally pointless.

IS THE QUESTION OF MEANING MEANINGFUL?

But this reflection suggests a new approach. Do we even know what we are trying to find out when we ask for the meaning of life? Perhaps the question itself does not even mean anything. That would certainly explain why it is so difficult to answer; how can you answer a question that is meaningless? Consider the child's question, how high is up? You cannot answer, not because you do not know the answer, but because there cannot be an answer: the question does not make sense. Maybe the question, what is the meaning of life? does not make sense either.

But can such an apparently deep and important question actually make no sense? The profundity of the question is no bar to its being meaningless; there is indeed one quite important school of philosophical thought, called *logical positivism,* that claims that almost all of the apparently deep philosophical questions actually do not mean anything; this is indeed precisely why they strike us as profound. For example, does the world really exist, or is all my experience an illusion? Do I have a mind or a soul, or am I a machine? Is the world a unity or an irreducible plurality of different things? Is there some reality behind or beneath the appearances I experience? All these questions, traditionally regarded as both the deepest and most perplexing questions that philosophers address, are resolved by logical positivists in one swift stroke. They are all meaningless. That is why they seem so perplexing, that is why in turn they seem profound, and that is why no one has ever succeeded in answering them.

But what makes an apparently significant question meaningless? One answer sometimes given is that a question is meaningless if it consists in an unintelligible combination of words. Taken separately, each word has a meaning, but put together, the result has none. Let us see how this operates with respect to the question about the meaning of life. To discover what this question means, let us ask what it might be for something to have a meaning. Begin by noticing what kinds of things do have meaning. Clearly words, sentences, books, and so on have meaning: the meaning of the word "dog" is, simply, the animal dog. (The word "dog" is not an animal, and the animal dog is not a word. The animal has no meaning; the word means the animal.) Similarly, the meaning of the sentence "It rained yesterday" is that it rained yesterday. (That it rained yesterday is also the meaning of the—French—sentence, *"Il pleuvait hier."* This shows that sentences are in languages, but meanings are not.) What else other than words has meaning? Actions have meaning: if I send you flowers, for example, it may mean I love you (or it may mean something else; if you get flowers from me, you might ask, what does it mean, that he sent me these flowers?) And finally, certain natural occurrences have meaning—for example, smoke means fire, or dark clouds mean it will rain. These examples enable us to see what meaning is: meaning is a connection from one thing to some other thing. Very roughly put, a thing (word, action, occurrence) has meaning if it is connected with another thing in such a way that a person who is presented with the first thing is thereby led to think of the second thing. Sometimes this connection is founded on natural facts such as cause (clouds) and effect (rain); sometimes on human psychology; and sometimes on certain social conventions, notably those of language (sending flowers is also a social convention, though a nonlinguistic one). So, because of your knowledge of facts and conventions, when you are presented with the word "dog," you think of the animal; when the flowers arrive, you think of the sender's possible love; when you see the clouds, you think of rain. The meaning of the thing that is presented is the other thing with which it is connected.

But if that is an explanation of meaning, it is perfectly clear that it makes little sense to attribute meaning to life, for life is not connected with some other thing in such a way that, when you think of life, you are thereby led to think of this other thing that is its meaning. Life, that is to say, does not signify anything other than itself; it simply is. And therefore, life is not the kind of thing that could have a meaning, for only that can have a meaning which is connected with something else so as to draw a person's thought from itself to that other thing. So while it may make sense to ask, "What is the meaning of these clouds?" or, "What is the meaning of these flowers my friend just sent me?", it cannot make sense to ask, "What is the meaning of life?" Despite its apparent importance, and despite the fact that it has the grammatical form of a question, the question is actually meaningless.

Logical positivists often make a somewhat different argument about meaning, but one that leads to the same conclusion. They ask, what is a question? Or better, what is it to understand a question? The answer to this question gives us a theory about what makes questions meaningful. According to this view, we understand a question by understanding what kind of an answer would be correct. This is not to say that we have to know what the answer is, but we do have to know what might count as an answer, what would be an answer. For example, you do not know (no one knows) what is the correct answer to this question: how many galaxies are there in the universe? But if you understand the question, you right away know that the answer is going to be some number, and a very large number at that. If someone wondered whether, perhaps, the answer to the question might be $E = mc^2$, or every prime number between 100 and 10,000, such a person would show that he or she simply had not understood what the question means. Or suppose you asked someone, what is their favorite music, or favorite musician, and they replied by naming a movie, or something else even more irrelevant; this would again show that they failed to understand the question. And the reason for this is very simple: a question is a request for a certain kind of information. What the question means, then, is given by the range of information in which the answer might be found. "Who is your favorite musician?" asks for information about musicians, and so its meaning is given by names of musicians: in effect, the question asks you to pick from among this list. Any question, according to this view, asks you to pick from among a certain list of possible answers. Since the meaning of the question is the range of its possible answers, until such a range of answers has been specified, no meaning has been given to the question.

But if we apply this simple point to the question about the meaning of life, we see that no one who asks this question has any idea what would count as an answer. There is no range of possible answers, one of which is the correct answer. Since no one knows what might give life meaning, no one can specify what the range of answers should be. And, therefore, no one understands the question being asked; but this is not because the question is so terribly profound that it is too deep for us to comprehend. No one understands the question because the question has not been given a meaning.

IF LIFE HAS NO MEANING, WHAT THEN?

This conclusion is not going to satisfy people who are searching for meaning. They argue that it is important to try to answer questions even if we do not understand them very well. This is Socrates' idea too: "Good question; no answer." But is this the best answer we can give? To this point, we have been suggesting that either life has no meaning, or, if it does, the meaning is beyond our capacity to understand. But is there another possibility? Let us call *big picture optimists* those who, like Tolstoy, believe it is possible to find some meaning to life, either through faith or possibly even through philosophy. We distinguish them from *skeptical pessimists,* who deny that there is any meaning to be found in life, and therefore, opt for despair. These thinkers regard the tenets of faith as irrational, and conclude that religious believers are practicing an acute form of self-delusion. (Like Camus and Russell, they are apt to opt for some kind of "heroic attitude" solution.) Both optimists and pessimists agree that unless life has meaning, then life is deprived of much or all of its spark or savor, and there is no real point in going on. What they disagree about is whether it is possible to find the meaning that is needed to make life worthwhile. Optimists think that you can, and so say that human life is worth living after all, while pessimists say you cannot, and so conclude either that life is not worth living, or that it must be lived under the cloud of failure and despair.

But the premise that meaning is needed to make life worthwhile can be challenged. Must it follow that if life has no meaning, then nothing is worthwhile? To explain this point, let us distinguish between life in general and the life of any particular human person. When it is said that life has no meaning, what is meant is that there is nothing that life is about, no reason (other than biological and accidental) why we are here, no purpose our lives serve. As far as the universe is concerned, we might as well not exist at all; there is no ultimate justification for our lives. But now it has to be asked, why should this matter to us? Might not our individual lives still have meaning, even if life as such has none?

Perhaps it is not so difficult to see how this might be. What does give meaning to the life of an individual person? Such things as engaging in worthwhile activities, having interesting goals and projects, enjoying the company of friends and loved ones, having a sense of self-worth—in short, being of use to yourself and to other people, acting in such a way that you make a difference in the world, however small it may be. Your life has meaning, we might say, if, at the end of it, somebody can truly say that the world is a better place than it would have been had you never lived. Now, this is something that cannot be done for you, either by the universe or by other people; giving meaning to your life is something you must do for yourself. And you must do it, as the existentialists quite correctly point out, without any sure proof that what you are doing is correct; for it is not the universe that is going to be glad you existed, but people with whom you interacted in your life. There is thus no ultimate justification, no proof that your life, your ideals, and your projects really matter. In this sense, meaning is not a kind of knowledge at all—we cannot know that our life has meaning—but at bottom a feeling, a sense of well-being from having made a difference.

But will just any kind of activity suffice? The reader will recall from Chapters Four and Seven that Aristotle claims that some activities are more excellent than others, and that only those activities that manifest a high degree of human excellence can really make life worthwhile. However, it is not clear that it is possible to describe a truly objective set of the most excellent activities. Is studying philosophy truly more excellent than playing sports (as Aristotle holds), or only more excellent for a person like Aristotle? Perhaps for the nonintellectual, playing sports or fooling with cars is more excellent than thinking deep thoughts. One of Aristotle's points is that whatever you do, you should try to do it as well as you can; being good at fixing cars might be far better for some people than being bad at playing the piano. Perhaps what we should say, at least as a working hypothesis, is that everybody is probably good at something, and that what is most likely to give any person's life real meaning is finding what he or she is good at and then developing the skill to do it well. This is what is likely to make your life of most use to yourself, and to other people as well: ineptness is as frustrating to its possessor as it is irritating to others who may depend on you to accomplish something. In other words, being indolent, achieving nothing, living a life in which nothing very worthwhile is ever accomplished, is likely in the end to be dull, tedious, of little worth, and without much meaning (which may be the truth underlying Kant's claim that we have a duty to ourselves to develop our talents).

But will just any activities fit this picture? Cannot it be objected that nasty people—Mafia hit men, child molesters, neo-Nazi racists—also have projects that engage their attention and have talents that they develop, but we would not want to say their lives have meaning? If there is no ultimate justification, then is not any meaningful life as good as any other? Aristotle's reply presumably would be that killing people is not a form of human excellence, but here Aristotle fails to distinguish between being moral and having a fulfilling life. Not every kind of immorality takes meaning from your life, and some kinds may add meaning; for example, many people think hunting animals and even eating meat are immoral, but there is no doubt that these activities are the source of much meaning for many hunters and gourmets. To have meaning means that your life is elevated in a certain way, raised above the ordinary humdrum and given a purpose or a point; and there is no guarantee that this can be achieved through moral actions alone. So even the life of a Mafia chief can be meaningful, because the Mafia chief, as much as (even more than) more honest or conventional people, engages in challenging activities that engage his fullest talents and give his life a purpose (to take over the drug trade in a city is a purpose, however ignoble). If a life is a success because it is interesting and fulfilling, then it is worth living and meaningful. We can thus answer the question posed earlier about wisdom. Wisdom is what the Greeks said it is: knowing how to live. But this knowledge is not what Plato seemed to think, an intellectual grasp of some proposition or thought. It is knowing how to arrange your life so that your life has meaning, in the way best described by Aristotle: making best use of your inner strengths and capacities so as to make your life worthwhile to yourself and to others.

MEANING AND MORALITY

But does not a meaningful life require some morality? If the Mafia chief dies, rich and surrounded by his loving family and loyal associates, we can say he has had a meaningful life and that it has not been without moral qualities: love, friendship, loyalty, and respect are moral qualities that can enter even the life of a criminal. Without any of these, it is doubtful that anyone would regard his or her own life as successful. But we have also said that for one's life to be meaningful one must make a contribution, or give someone some reason to be glad that you have lived. This is the role of morality; Mafia chiefs no doubt give most people a reason to be sorry that they have lived (which is why society puts them in jail if it can). On balance, such a life ought not to have been lived. So perhaps what we should say is that no life can be meaningful in the sense of personally satisfying if it lacks all moral qualities, and no life can be meaningful in the sense of its final net worth if its overall contribution to society is negative: a truly valuable life is one of which more people than not have reason to be glad that the life was lived.

We have talked about the ultimate justification of our lives. There are two distinct things that are wanted from ultimate justification. One is to justify morality, the other to justify the lives we lead. If our argument is correct, there is no ultimate justification for our lives, just because there is nothing that makes life as such meaningful: each life has to be justified or made meaningful by the person whose life it is. We have also indicated that if there are no moral facts (and even if there are moral facts, since it is unclear how they can be known), then morality depends on certain sentiments and attitudes for which there is also no validation. But we now see that there is more to it than that. To have meaning in your life requires that you create a meaningful life for yourself through interesting activities; but this is evidently not enough. Unless some morality also enters your life—love, friendship, loyalty, trust, contribution—your life will be less than fully meaningful and perhaps not very meaningful in the end. This justification is not ultimate (the universe does not really care whether you have a meaningful life or whether your life contains morality), but perhaps it is the most ultimate justification for morality we can attain.

REFERENCES AND FURTHER READING

There are two anthologies with the same title: *The Meaning of Life,* edited by E. D. Klemke (New York: Oxford University Press, 1981), containing many standard essays, somewhat arbitrarily classified as theistic or nontheistic; and *The Meaning of Life,* edited by Steven Sanders and David Cheney (Englewood Cliffs, NJ: Prentice Hall, 1980).

Christina Sommers and Fred Sommers, eds., *Vice and Virtue in Everyday Life,* 3rd ed. (Fort Worth: Harcourt Brace, 1993), has a section that also contains much standard material.

The Super-race illustration is borrowed from a wonderful and very long essay by Robert Nozick, "Philosophy and the Meaning of Life," the last chapter in his *Philosophical Explanations* (Cambridge, MA: Harvard University Press, 1981).

The quote from A. J. Ayer is from his collection of essays, *The Meaning of Life* (New York: Scribners, 1990), an amusing title (and an amusing essay) by an author who is generally considered the quintessential logical positivist.

The Myth of Sisyphus by Albert Camus (New York: Random House, 1942; English trans. by Justin O'Brien, 1955) contains his reflections on absurdity, suicide, and other existentialist topics.

Bertrand Russell's famous essay is called "A [originally "The"] Free Man's Worship." It was written in 1903, became enormously popular, and has often been reprinted, for example in the anthologies by Klemke and the Sommerses.

Tolstoy's "My Confession" may also be found in both the Klemke anthology and that by Sommers and Sommers. The massive biography by Henri Troyat, *Tolstoy* (New York: Doubleday, 1967), describes Tolstoy's loss of meaning in Part V ("Conflict"), Ch. 3 ("Art and Faith"), pp. 372ff.

Glossary

Absolute moral truth: a moral principle that must always be followed, without exception.

Absolutism: the view that there are absolute moral truths.

Act utilitarianism (AU): whenever you act, your aim should be to promote happiness and prevent unhappiness.

Autonomy: thinking for oneself, being independent and self-reliant, making one's own decisions about what is good and what is not.

Belief-desire theory: actions result from desires, which make one want to do something, and beliefs, which give one the information needed to carry out those desires.

Categorical imperative: any unconditional command. *See* Hypothetical imperative.

Categorical Imperative, The (CI): follow the principle of universalization, "So act that the maxim of thy action could be a universal law (of nature)" (Kant).

Challenge (to ethics) as such: to require explanation, defense, or justification (of ethics).

Challenge (to ethics) from above: to provoke (ethical ideas) to become better.

Challenge (to ethics) from below: to unmask or expose (ethics) as less grand or noble than it is thought to be.

Character utilitarianism: the way to achieve utility is to build good character into people.

Communitarianism: values and moral standards are rooted in communities and based on affective ties, not logic, hence autonomy is either desirable or impossible.

Community values: the values held by some community. *See* Values of community.

Consequentialism: whether anything is morally good or bad depends entirely on its consequences; something is morally right if it produces good consequences, and morally wrong if it produces bad consequences.

Cultural chauvinism: the belief that my culture is superior to other peoples'.

Cultural imperialism: the belief that we have the right, even the moral duty, to suppress the inferior morality of other peoples and impose our own.

329

Cultural relativism (CR): morality necessarily depends on culture.

Death argument: since death is nothing but the annihilation of life, if death is bad, life must be good; hence, the fact of death cannot destroy the value of life.

Definitional fallacy: one cannot define values in natural laws (e.g., "Good means pleasure").

Deontology: *See* Nonconsequentialism.

Determinism: people do not have free will.

Divine command theory: we ought to obey God's commands because God tells us to; something is an ethical truth because God says it is.

"Dolorism": pleasure is bad, pain and suffering good.

Duty all things considered: a duty one has after considering everything that needs to be considered. *See Prima facie* duty.

Duty ethics (DE): the study of obligations, duty, and moral rules.

Egoism: you have duties only to yourself.

Emotivism: *See* Sophisticated subjectivism.

Enlightened egoism (EnE): it is beneficial to support morality even when it is not in one's direct interest to do so.

Error theory (ET): we are mistaken when we believe our moral opinions are either true or false.

Ethical egoism (EE): the only morally good thing is to pursue one's own interests. *See* Psychological egoism.

Evolutionary ethics (EvE): moral value can be determined scientifically by the principles of Darwinian evolution.

Externalism: moral beliefs do not necessarily motivate moral action.

Fact-value fallacy: one cannot argue from facts to values.

Flourishing view (FV): the virtues are desirable because they are linked to flourishing, a condition of the soul that would be chosen by any rational person who is in a condition to choose.

Formalism: trying to derive moral content from form of moral judgments; a criticism made of Kant's Categorical Imperative.

Foundationalism: ethical ideas can be justified by being derived from something that is not itself an ethical idea.

Golden Mean: all virtues are at a midpoint between two extremes, an excess and a deficiency (Aristotle).

Hedonism: the good is pleasure; all pleasure is good, and nothing but pleasure is good.

Heroic duties: acts that are morally commendable and required; doing them earns one special praise but failing to perform them earns one rebuke. *See* Ordinary duties.

Heroic saints: people whose lives are dedicated to something, either moral perfection or a heroic goal. *See* Ordinary saints.

Hume's Law: *See* Fact-value fallacy.

Hypothetical imperative: states a command that contains a condition upon which the command is based. *See* Categorical imperative.

Ideal utilitarianism (IdU): some experiences are valuable in themselves and ought to be produced, independent of any pleasure the experience might give one.

Immoralism: it is permissible to harm others when it is in one's interest to do so.

Imperfect duty: a duty that allows options as to its fulfillment (e.g., "Help the poor") (Kant). *See* Perfect duty.

Indirect utilitarianism (IU): one should seek utility indirectly, by establishing good rules or promoting good character, rather than by aiming to do good directly.

Instrumental (extrinsic) value: having value for what can be done with it. *See* Intrinsic value.

Intelligent egoism (IE): developing a plan of action to attain as much good for oneself as possible over a period of time; recognizing that you have to give something to get something.

Internalism: to hold a moral belief is to be motivated to act on it.

Intrinsic value: having value for its own sake. *See* Instrumental (extrinsic) value.

Is-ought fallacy: *See* Fact-value fallacy.

Main virtues: the four main virtues of the ancient Greeks were justice, temperance, courage, and wisdom; the medievals valued four natural virtues—justice, temperance, prudence, and fortitude—and three theological virtues—faith, hope, and love.

Master virtue: a superior virtue that holds all the other virtues together (justice, according to Plato).

Maxim: the principle on which one acts (Kant).

Minimal ethics: what the law does not require need not be done.

Moral facts: like natural facts, part of the world, independent of what people think or believe.

Moral isolationism: we can't understand other cultures, especially distant ones, so we are in no position to judge them.

Moral realism (MR): there are moral facts.

Motivating virtues: traits that make us want to do things.

Natural law: nature has purposes that humans ought to follow.

Naturalism: ethics is based on nature.

Naturalistic fallacy: values cannot be derived from facts about nature.

Negative universalization thesis (NUT): an action that cannot be universalized is morally wrong.

Nonaltruism: it is not morally required to help anyone if it is not in your interest to do so.

Nonconsequentialism: Morality may in part be based on consequences, but much of it is not; some acts are right (or wrong) independently of the consequences of doing them.

Ordinary duties: acts that are expected of everybody. *See* Heroic duties.

Ordinary saints: people who have the standard virtues to a large degree; they attain high levels of morality not by extraordinary or heroic deeds but by living their normal lives decently. *See* Heroic saints.

Perfect duty: a duty that does not allow options as to its fulfillment (e.g., "Pay your debts") (Kant). *See* Imperfect duty.

Positive universalization thesis (PUT): an action that can be universalized is morally required.

Pragmatism: ideas are instruments for action, and are true (or good) if they help you attain your ends.

***Prima facie* duty**: an act that would be one's duty unless overridden by something more important morally. *See* Duty all things considered.

Priority of the virtues: obligations can be explained through the virtues; or, obligations are morally important because virtue is morally important.

Projectivism: things are not good or bad in themselves; the belief that they are is part of our tendency to project our ideas onto the external world.

Psychological egoism (PE): human motivation is essentially selfish. *See* Ethical egoism.

Qualitative hedonism: the value of a pleasure is measured by the kind of activity that produces the pleasure.

Quantitative hedonism: the value of a pleasure is measured by how great the pleasure is.

Quasirealism: moral opinions can be true or false even though there are no moral facts that make them true or false.

Rational will: what one can call will when one is thinking rationally, that is, not confused about what is and what is not possible (Kant).

Realist externalism (RE): there are moral facts, yet one can have a moral belief and not be motivated to act morally; REs can accept the belief-desire theory.

Realist internalism (RI): there are moral facts, and one's belief that something is right motivates one to do it; RIs must reject the belief-desire theory.

Relativism: there are no universal moral truths; all morality is relative either to individuals or cultures.

Rigorism: we are always required to do our moral best.

Rule utilitarianism (RU): one should support and follow those rules that, if people were to follow them, would produce happiness and prevent unhappiness.

Seven deadly sins: pride, envy, lust, gluttony, anger, covetousness, and sloth (medieval theology).

Simple subjectivism (SimpS): ethics is only a matter of opinion. *See* Sophisticated subjectivism.

Slippery slope-ophobia: the fear that even a single transgression puts one in danger of sliding down a slippery slope; an argument for absolutism.

Social account: there are social reasons to explain our belief that our moral opinions are true and false.

Social contract: the set of rules that everyone in society has implicitly agreed to follow.

Social determinism: no one can think beyond the limits of his or her culture.

Sociobiology: right and wrong are based on basic behaviors that are part of our nature.

Sophisticated subjectivism (SophS): an ethical utterance is only an expression of the attitude of the speaker. *See* Simple subjectivism.

Strict moralism (SM): some transgressions (such as lying) are so evil that no moral good can outweigh them, hence they should never be done; a form of absolutism.

Strong ethical egoism: it is wrong not to do what is in your own interest.

Strong immoralism (SIm): it is wrong not to harm someone when it is in one's interest to do so.

Strong nonaltruism (SNa): it is wrong to help anyone unless it is in one's interest to do so.

Stupid egoism (SE): refusing to help someone when it is not immediately advantageous to you to do so.

Subjectivism: morality is relative to individuals.

Subjectivist internalism (SI): moral opinions motivate, and are neither knowledge nor beliefs but attitudes and sentiments; SIs accept the belief-desire theory.

Superenlightened egoism (SEE): act morally only if necessary to avoid getting caught, or to prevent others from following your example and abandoning morality.

Supererogatory acts: acts that are morally commendable and not morally required; doing them earns one praise, but failing to perform them earns one no rebuke.

Supervenience: relationship of dependence between two things such that to say B supervenes on A is to say that B depends on A or is based on A (B because of A).

Teleology: *See* Consequentialism.

Unity of the virtues: all the virtues are the same thing (wisdom, according to Plato).

Universal moral truth (UMT): a moral principle that is true for (applies to) everyone, regardless of epoch, culture, religion, stage of civilization, personal creed, and so on.

Universal value: a value that is held by every culture.

Universalization: we must universalize our moral judgments.

Utilitarianism (U): right actions are those that tend to produce happiness, and wrong actions are those that tend to promote unhappiness.

Values of community: the values of belonging to a community, such as friendship, trust, cooperation, sharing, and feeling good about everybody. *See* Community values.

Virtue ethics (VE): the study of the virtues; virtue ethics makes good character, or the virtues, a central part of ethical theory.

Virtues of self-control: cool, calculating virtues that look beyond the present moment to the broader picture and to long-range consequences.

Weak ethical egoism: it is not required to be altruistic.

Weak immoralism (WIm): it is not wrong to harm someone when it is in one's interest to do so.

Weak nonaltruism (WNa): it is not required to help anyone unless it is in one's interest to do so.

List of Abbreviations

AU: Act utilitarianism

CI: Categorical Imperative

CR: Cultural relativism

DE: Duty ethics

EE: Ethical egoism

EnE: Enlightened egoism

ET: Error theory

EvE: Evolutionary ethics

FV: Flourishing view

IdU: Ideal utilitarianism

IE: Intelligent egoism

IU: Indirect utilitarianism

MoL: Meaning of life

MR: Moral relativism

NUT: Negative universalization thesis

PE: Psychological egoism

PUT: Positive universalization thesis

RE: Realist externalism

RI: Realist internalism

RU: Rule utilitarianism

SE: Stupid egoism

SEE: Superenlightened egoism

SI: Subjectivist internalism

SIm: Strong immoralism

SimpS: Simple subjectivism

SM: Strict moralism

SNa: Strong nonaltruism

SophS: Sophisticated subjectivism

SS-ophobe: Slippery slope-ophobe

U: Utilitarianism

UMT: Universal moral truth

VE: Virtue ethics

WIm: Weak immoralism

WNa: Weal nonaltruism

Index

Abortion, 22, 40

Absolute idealism, 109–112

Absolutism, 164–170

  in Kant, 274–275

Act and rule utilitarianism. *See* Utilitarianism

Activity, in pragmatism, 101–102

Allen, Woody, 300, 318

Altruism, 24, 48–59, 62, 67–68

Aquinas, St. Thomas, 77, 90

  on natural law, 93, 95–97

Aristotle, 11, 85, 97, 189, 191–193, 197, 250, 254, 326

  on autonomy, 294–295

  on ends and means, 91

  on ethics and nature, 85

  on God, 80

  the Golden Mean, 204–205

  on happiness and flourishing, 190–195

  and human function, 94–95

  on natural ends, 194

  and natural law, 90, 93–95

  on perception, 187–188

  on virtue, 95, 187–188, 198–200, 201, 203–205

Athanasius, Saint, 171–172, 178–179

Attitudes and attitude theory, 27, 29–35, 93, 144, 149, 153–155

Austen, Jane, 212, 215, 217

Autonomy

  in Aristotle, 294–295

  and community, 217–222

  in Kant, 292–295

  theories of, 292–295

Ayer, A. J., 29, 32, 313

Aymé, Marcel, 158

Bay of Pigs, 166

"Beetle Bailey," 242, 246

Belief-desire theory, 129, 132–133

Bentham, Jeremy, 77, 232–234, 238, 250, 252–253

Bible, 21–23, 75, 80, 83, 91, 96, 190, 194, 198, 226

Blackburn, Simon. 134, 137–139. *See also* Quasirealism

Blanshard, Brand, 109

Bradley, F. H., 109, 111

Butler, Joseph, 50

Camus, Albert, 309, 313–316, 325

Caring, 184, 213–215

  as basis of morality, 139–140

Categorical Imperative, 268–269, 271, 273, 275, 277, 280, 297

  and contradictions, 277

  examples of, 278, 281–285

Character, 184–185, 189, 193, 196, 201–202, 211, 247

Christianity, 132

Communitarianism, 218–222

Community, in Royce, 111–112

Concepts, thick, 104

Configurations, logical, 137–139

Consequence morality. *See* Morality

Consequences, 226–228, 233–236
 and lying, 173, 177–178, 181

Conventions, social, 174, 181, 248–249

Courage, 201–204, 210–211

Cultural chauvinism and
imperialism, 37, 42, 43

Cultural relativism, 26, 35
 arguments for, 37
 problems of, 37–41

Cyrano de Bergerac, 288, 290–291

Darwin, Charles, 97

Death argument, 309–313

Deception
 and common morality, 171–172
 connection with lying, 178–179
 intentional, 160–162, 181
 and lying, 171–173

De Gaulle, Charles, 161–162

Deontology, 230

Descartes, René, 75, 136

Determinism, 68–73
 social, 36, 37, 219

Dewey, John, 100–103, 106

Dickens, Charles, 194

Dignity, in Kant, 295–297

Disagreement, moral, 146–149

Divine command theory, 80, 82, 84, 268

"Dolorism," 256

Duchamps, Marcel, 318

Duties
 heroic and ordinary, 209–211
 perfect and imperfect, 277–281
 prima facie, 167–168, 171, 174, 176, 181
 to self and to others, 277–281
 table of, in Kant, 279

Duty ethics, 184–186, 188–189

Education, moral, 10–13

Edwards, Paul, 29

Egoism, 18, 24, 48–68, 265
 arguments against, 60–65
 arguments for, 55–57, 66–68
 assessed, 65–68
 and conventional morality, 52
 enlightened, 58–60, 62–64
 ethical, 48, 51–68
 in Hobbes, 57–60, 62
 immoralism and nonaltrusim, 53–54, 66
 intelligent and stupid, 54, 58–60
 psychological, 48–51, 58–59, 68
 superenlightened, 63–64, 66, 150, 249
 versions of, 52–54

Ekman, Paul, 160

Elizabeth I, 119, 122

Emerson, Ralph Waldo, 112, 149

Emotions, moral, 12, 13

Emotivism, 32, 33

Ends and means
 in Aristotle, 91
 in Dewey, 100–102
 in Kant, 297–298

Engels, Friedrich, 22

Epicurus and epicureans, 251, 310

Error theory, 134–136, 141, 143

Ethics, 3
 business, 229
 challenges to, 18–24
 evolutionary, 93, 97–100, 106
 minimal, 20

Evil, as irrationality, 261–262

Existentialism, 77, 309, 317

Externalism, 132–133

Facts
 domain of, 116–118, 120, 141–142
 moral, 115, 118–127, 139–141, 143, 145,
 153

Faith, and meaning of life, 331–332, 325

Feminism, 23, 214–217, 219, 229–230, 265

Flourishing view. *See* Virtues

Formalism, 271–273

Foundationalism, in ethics, 76

Franklin, Benjamin, 199, 206, 209

Free-rider problem, 66

Freud, Sigmund, 87, 108, 112

Gandhi, Mahatma, 207

Geach, P. T., 137

Gestures, 30

God, 7, 19, 22–23, 76, 80–84, 90, 94–97, 132–133, 136, 144, 147, 189, 192, 194, 206, 207, 256, 268, 311, 321

Golden Mean, 204–205

Green, T. H., 109

Happiness
  in Aristotle, 190-195, 250
  in Kant, 262
  and pleasure, 250
  and utilitarianism, 232, 235–239, 241–242
  and virtue, 190–195

Hare, R. M., 139–140, 272–273

Harm, to the dead, 244

Hebrews, ancient, 190, 192, 194

Hedonism, 250–256, 265
  evaluation of, 254–256
  quantitative and qualitative, 252–254

Hegel, G. W. F., 220–221

Heidegger, Martin, 312

Henry VIII, 116–117, 120, 122

Heroes, 184, 207

Hitler, Adolf, 112, 123

Hobbes, Thomas, 49, 51, 52, 57–60, 64, 77

Homer, 197

Humans, function of, in Aristotle, 94–95

Hume, David, 77, 104, 115, 127–130, 134, 216, 232, 263–264
  on death, 313
  and moral realism, 127
  on morality and human nature, 144–146
  and projectivism, 115, 135–136, 143–146
  on reasons to be moral, 151–155
  on sentiments, 129–131, 134
  on virtue, 185, 188, 200, 202

Hume's Law, 104–105, 127, 263

Hutcheson, Francis, 233

Hypotheses
  ad hoc, 121–122, 126
  inert, 123

Imperatives, hypothetical and categorical, 267–269

Inclination, in Aquinas, 95–97

Insignificance, ultimate, 316–317

Integrity, 239–241

Internalism, 128–129, 131–133
  in Kant, 264

Intuitionism, 77, 121–122

Jesus, 19, 20, 23, 198–199, 207

Jews, 210–211

Just deserts, and utilitarianism, 245–246

Justification
  in ethics, 76–77
  ultimate, 302, 320, 327

Kant, Immanuel, 77, 250, 260–298, 326
  as absolutist, 274–275
  on autonomy, 292–295
  and Categorical Imperative, 268–269
  on deception, 171, 172
  on dignity, 295–297
  on ends and means, 297–298
  as formalist, 270–273
  on happiness, 262–263
  on lying, 160, 165
  on maxims, 273–275
  morality and logic, 261–262, 266–267

and personal moral codes, 290–291
presuppositions of, 261–265
and projectivism, 143
on reason and motivation, 264–265, 267
relations to Hume, 263–264
on respect, 175, 177, 264, 295–297
social contract argument of, 174
and supreme principle of morality, 266–267
and utilitarianism, 262–263
Kennedy, John F., 166, 307
King, Martin Luther, Jr., 207
Koran, 80

Landers, Ann, 2
Law, and ethics, 20–23
Lies
harmless, 164, 179
kinds of, 163–164, 170, 179–180
self-serving, 164, 179–180
Life
and "big picture," 318–322
eternal, 311
and faith, 318–322
and happiness, 306–309
and knowledge, 302–306
meaning of, 300–327
meaningfulness of, 322–325
and morality, 327
Lincoln, Abraham, 207, 209
Locke, John, 77
Logical positivism, 323–324
Luther, Martin, 256
Lying, 158–182
and deception, 178–179
defined, 159–164
ease of, 179–181
promises, in Kant, 278, 280, 281
theories of, 173–178

MacCauley, Thomas, 256
MacIntyre, Alasdair, 200
Mackie, John L., 134–137
Mafia, 112, 326–327

Marx, Karl, 22, 87
Maximizing and minimizing, 234–235
Maxims
and duties, 277–280
in Kant, 273–275
Mead, Margaret, 175, 177
Men, moral character of, 212–217
Mencken, H. L., 256
Merimée, Prosper, 38
Michelangelo, 257
Mill, John Stuart, 77, 86, 232–234, 237–238, 245, 250, 252–253
Milton, John, 132–133
Moore, G. E., 77, 104–106, 256
Moral, reasons to be, 149–155
Moral isolationism, 45
Moral philosophy, and women, 216–217
Moral realism, 115–119, 120, 124, 125, 127, 129, 131, 133, 134, 139, 140, 146, 148, 149, 152, 153, 154
Moral rules, 8, 248–249
Moral theory, 3
and moral education, 10–13
and science, 7–10
Moral truths, universal, 23, 24–27, 36, 43–46, 115, 262
absolute, 26
Moralist, strict, 167–170
Morality, 3, 4
and caring, 140
characteristics of, 5–7
consequentialist, 226, 227–236
and knowledge, 10–12
and motivation, 127–134
nonconsequentialist, 226–230, 232, 235, 243
supreme principle of, in Kant, 266–267
Motivation
in Hume, 127–130
in Kant, 264–265, 267
and moral facts, 127, 130
and realism, 128
and reason, 128–129

Mozart, Wolfgang, 88, 257

Natural law, 89, 93–99
Naturalism
  problems of, 90–92
  theories of, 92–93
Naturalistic fallacy, 103–106
Nature, senses of, 86–90
Nazis, 210–211, 326
Nietzsche, Friedrich, 76

Obligation
  negative and positive, 285–289
  personal, 290–291
Opinion, 9, 27–29, 129
  conventional and reflective, 10
Optimism, "big picture," 325
Orwell, George, 123, 238

Perception, moral, 12
Persuasive definitions, 32
Pessimism, 325
Picasso, Pablo, 257
Plato, 1–3, 11, 77, 83–85, 89, 110, 189,
  196, 197, 199, 203, 304–306, 326
  and egoism, 53, 55, 57, 66
  on ethics and nature, 85
  and foundations of ethics, 77
  and God, 83, 84
  on the healthy soul, 106–109, 150–151
  and moral realism, 127
  on vice, 193, 196
  on virtue, 196, 197, 203–204
Pleasure machine, 255–256
Pleasure. *See* Hedonism
Pointlessness, 313–316
Pragmatism, 100–103
Pride, 205–206
Principle, acting on, 264–265
Privacy, 221
Projectivism, 115, 135–136, 144–155
Puritans, 208–209, 256

Quasirealism, 115, 136, 140–144, 145,
  149
Questions, open and closed, 116–118

Rand, Ayn, 53, 56
Raphael, 257
Realism, moral. *See* Moral realism
Relativism, 19, 24. *See also*
  Subjectivism; Cultural relativism
  gender, 215
Religion, 7, 8
  and ethics, 18, 20–23, 78–85
Respect
  and cultural relativism, 37, 41–44
  in Kant, 264, 295–297
  and lying, 173, 175–177, 181
Right and wrong, utilitarian
  criterion of, 231, 233
Ross, W. D., 266
Royce, Josiah, 109, 111, 112
Russell, Bertrand, 134, 151, 206, 316,
  325

Saints, 184, 204, 207–209
Samurai, 45
Sartre, Jean Paul, 317–318
Satan, 132–133, 320
Schopenhauer, Arthur, 315
Science, and morality, 7–10
Self, in ethics, 106
Self-control, virtues of, 202–203
Self-realization, 106, 109–112
Selfishness. *See* Egoism
Sensible knave, in Hume, 152-153
Sensitivity, moral, 12, 13
Sentiments, in Hume, 129–131, 134
Shakespeare, William, 18, 48, 108, 115,
  116–118, 158, 179, 184, 193, 196, 202, 312
Shaw, George Bernard, 239
Sidgwick, Henry, 77, 249
Singer, Peter, 20
Sins, seven deadly, 202, 205–206

Sisyphus, myth of, 313–316

Slippery-slope arguments, 165, 167–170

Social account, 135–136

Social contract, 55–56, 57–60, 66
  and lying, 173–175, 181

Sociobiology, 93, 97–100

Socrates, 1, 2, 4, 10–11, 13, 14, 19, 66, 127, 133, 198–199, 207, 218, 222, 261, 305, 321, 325
  and internalism, 133
  and moral education, 10, 11

Sophists, 1

Soul, healthy, in Plato, 106–109, 150–151

Spencer, Herbert, 97

Spinoza, Baruch, 189

Star Trek, 262

Stevenson, Adlai, 166

Stevenson, C. L. 29, 32

Stoics, 85–86, 189

Subjectivism, 26–35, 93, 130, 133–134, 137, 139–141
  simple, 26, 27–29
  sophisticated, 26, 27, 29–35, 115

Suicide, 278, 282–283

Summum bonum, 189

Supererogation, 209–212

Supervenience, 123–127

Teleology, 230–231

Ten Commandments, 80, 82, 83, 267

Thoreau, Henry David, 88, 112

Tolstoy, Leo, 308–310, 318, 322, 325

Truth, and quasirealism, 141–143

Universal moral truths. *See* Moral truths, universal

Universalization, 268–273, 285–290, 291

Utilitarianism, 226, 229, 230, 231, 232–250, 265
  act and rule, 241–243, 245–250

act, counterexamples to, 243–246
  and good character, 247
  ideal, 256–258
  indirect, 246–247
  and Kant, 262–263
  as maximizing theory, 234–235
  objections and replies, 236–241
  and pleasure, 252
  principal theses of, 241–243
  summary of, 242–243, 258

Values
  community, 218–222
  intrinsic and instrumental (extrinsic), 220–221, 230–231, 241
  natural, 239
  universal, 36

Vices, 184, 193–196, 201, 205–207

Virtue, 1, 2, 11, 14
  as knowledge, 10–11

Virtue ethics, 184–190, 195, 207–208

Virtues, 184–209
  in Aristotle, 95, 194–195, 197–199, 200–201
  Christian, 198
  and flourishing, 190–196
  Greek view of, 197–199
  Hebrew view of, 190, 192, 194
  intellectual, 201
  medieval, 194, 197
  moral and nonmoral, 201-202
  motivating, 201–203
  and practices, 201
  principle of, 200–201
  priority of, 186–190

Wagner, Richard, 257

Will, rational and reasonable, 275–277

Williams, Bernard, 45

Williams, Ted, 81

Williams, Wayne, 245

Women, moral character of, 212–217

Zen, 305